ADULT DEPARTMENT

1. Fine Schedule
   1 - 5 days overdue ...... grace period, no fine
   6 -10 days overdue .... 25¢ per item
   11-19 days overdue .... 75¢ per item
   20th day overdue .... $2.00 per item
2. Injury to books beyond reasonable wear and all
   losses shall be paid for.
3. Each borrower is held responsible for all books
   drawn on his card and for all fines accruing on
   the same.

FOND DU LAC PUBLIC LIBRARY
FOND DU LAC, WISCONSIN

DEMCO

THE NEW NEGRO ON CAMPUS

RAYMOND WOLTERS

The New Negro on Campus

Black College Rebellions of the 1920s

PRINCETON UNIVERSITY PRESS

Copyright © 1975 by Princeton University Press

PUBLISHED BY PRINCETON UNIVERSITY PRESS, PRINCETON AND LONDON

ALL RIGHTS RESERVED

Library of Congress Cataloging in Publication Data will
be found on the last printed page of this book

Publication of this book has been aided by
The Andrew W. Mellon Foundation

This book has been composed in Linotype Janson

Printed in the United States of America
by Princeton University Press, Princeton, New Jersey

CONTENTS

PREFACE

IN THIS study I have characterized the black college rebellions of the 1920s through a series of detailed observations from, as it were, different points on the compass. In the Introduction and Conclusion I have portrayed the rebellions of the 1920s against the general sweep of black college history. And in the substantive chapters that make up most of this book I have described the particular conditions that contributed to the emergence of protest on several campuses. This approach seemed especially appropriate for a historical monograph; it allowed me to mine a rich vein of previously neglected source materials and also encouraged attention to the multitude of details that make historical events complex and unique rather than parts of a predictable pattern.

The focus of this book is on the issues involved in protests that in the 1920s led to the forced resignations of several presidents of black colleges and to unrest among black students and alumni throughout the United States. There were then some seventy-nine black colleges in the land, and this book contains case studies of all the major types of black colleges. Fisk was the leading liberal arts college for Negroes, and Howard was the only black multiversity. Tuskegee and Hampton were the nation's most prominent industrial institutes. Florida A. & M. and Lincoln (Mo.) were state-supported, land-grant colleges. Wilberforce was managed by a Negro church, and Lincoln (Pa.) was controlled by a white church board. Students were in the vanguard of some black college rebellions, but alumni and administrators took the lead on other occasions.

This book deals with academic politics and the aspirations of black intellectuals as well as with student rebellions. It is concerned most of all with the growing conviction that blacks should have more control over the institutions that shaped their lives. Half a century of education and progress had produced college-bred Negroes who were imbued with great racial pride and aspirations, who were convinced that their race had developed educators who were qualified to man and manage their own institutions, and who were in full spiritual rebellion against the paternalistic assumption that blacks were not able to govern themselves.

I want to thank the National Endowment for the Humanities, the American Council of Learned Societies, and the University of Delaware for generous grants that enabled me to make several trips collecting materials for this book and freed me from classroom teaching in 1971–1972. I am also grateful to Pete Daniel, Richard E. Ellis, James M. McPherson, Ronald T. Takaki, and Mary Wolters for perceptive critical readings and valuable suggestions. Where I took their advice, the manuscript has undoubtedly been improved. Yet I should confess that I have clung rather obstinately to the traditional form of historical exposition, in which narration, evocation, and explanation are joined within a descriptive chronology. Rather than employ the methods currently in vogue among behaviorally oriented social scientists, I have tried to combine two very traditional methods of analysis—that of the "scientific" historian who bases his work on neglected primary sources, and that of the "narrator" who is trying above all to tell an interesting story.

THE NEW NEGRO ON CAMPUS

CHAPTER I

Introduction

AMERICANS of the generation after the Civil War [1861 to 1865] generally recognized the necessity of educating the recently emancipated slaves. They knew that the four million black freedmen, if neglected and left in ignorance, would "fall an easy prey to wicked and designing men, and become a terrible scourge to the nation."[1] Yet among whites there were substantial differences of opinion concerning the proper education of the freedmen. Many descendants of the antebellum abolitionists believed that Negro ignorance was not innate but the product of slavery and oppression, and they insisted that blacks should be exposed to the same curriculum that was thought to be effective in educating and civilizing white people. Many others, especially in the southern states, believed that Negroes should be given only the rudimentary vocational training that was especially suited to the menial roles accorded blacks in the South and throughout the nation. Thus Negro education became a subject of intense controversy, with the vocationally oriented accommodationists becoming more influential in the years between 1880 and the First World War, and the egalitarians struggling during the 1920s to regain the ascendancy they had enjoyed during the era of Reconstruction.

I

Before the guns of the Civil War had been stilled, northern benevolent societies and denominational bodies, the

---

[1] Methodist Episcopal Church, *Annual Report of the Freedmen's Aid Society, 1872*, p. 40, quoted in Dwight O. W. Holmes, *The Evolution of the Negro College* (College Park, Md.: McGrath Publishing Co., 1934), p. 69n.

Negro church, and the Freedmen's Bureau had begun the heroic task of educating the freedmen. "Behind the mists of ruin and rapine waved the calico dresses of women who dared, and after the hoarse mouthings of the field guns rang the rhythm of the alphabet," W. E. B. Du Bois recalled. "Bereaved now of a father, now of a brother, now of more than these," the Yankee teachers came "seeking a life work in planting the New England schoolhouses among the white and black of the South." Booker T. Washington later acknowledged that "the part that the Yankee teachers played in the education of the Negroes immediately after the war will make one of the most thrilling parts of the history of this country." Du Bois saluted this "crusade of the sixties, that finest thing in American history," when teachers came South "not to keep Negroes in their place, but to raise them out of the defilement of the places where slavery had wallowed them."[2]

These missionaries of the sixties rejected southern demands that they begin with industrial and manual training that would prepare blacks for skilled work, and later add the sequence of elementary and secondary schools, and, still later, colleges. They believed they would be throwing their money to the winds if they established elementary or vocational schools without providing also for the higher education of master teachers. Hence they founded colleges—Fisk, Howard, Hampton, Talladega, Atlanta, and others—which by 1900, according to Du Bois, "trained in Greek and Latin and mathematics, two thousand men; and these men trained full fifty thousand others in morals and manners, and they in turn taught thrift and the alphabet to nine mil-

[2] W. E. B. Du Bois, *The Souls of Black Folk* (Greenwich, Conn.: Crest Reprints, 1961), p. 31; Booker T. Washington, *Up From Slavery* (New York: Bantam Pathfinders Edition, 1963), pp. 42–43; Du Bois, "Of the Training of Black Men," *Atlantic Monthly* 90 (September 1902): 294.

lions of men. . . . It was a miracle—the most wonderful peace-battle of the nineteenth century."³

Yet most white southerners feared that any education of blacks beyond the elementary level would lead to increased dissatisfaction with the inferior status accorded Negroes in the South. The editor of the *New Orleans Times-Democrat* warned that "The higher education of the Negro unfits him for the work that it is intended that he shall do, and cultivates ambitions that can never be realized." Throughout the South planters feared that education would undermine black willingness to work in the fields and would make Negroes less deferential, submissive, and dependent. Southerners intuitively recognized that no aristocracy—whether of caste or class—could maintain its privileges in the face of an egalitarian educational system. Many heartily endorsed Sen. James K. Vardaman's contention that "What the North is sending South is not money but dynamite; this education is ruining our Negroes. They're demanding equality."⁴

In addition to believing that higher education of the Negro was mischievous and tended to disturb good relations between the races, many white southerners considered the missionaries' crusade a mad experiment. They claimed that the Yankees, bemused by their dream of racial equality, had ignored the limited aptitude and capabilities of the Negro and had mistakenly stressed a curriculum designed for people in the highest degree of civilization. At a time when Social Darwinism was in vogue, many people—blacks

---

³ W. E. B. Du Bois, "The Talented Tenth," in Booker T. Washington, et al., *The Negro Problem* (New York: James Pott & Co., 1903), p. 47. The best account of black education during and after Reconstruction is James M. McPherson's forthcoming book, *The Antislavery Legacy.*

⁴ *New Orleans Times-Democrat,* quoted in "A Blow at Negro Education," *Current Literature* 36 (January–June 1904): 491–492; James K. Vardaman, quoted in Ray Stannard Baker, *Following the Color Line* (New York: Harper Torchbook Edition, 1964), p. 247.

as well as whites—believed that the races were at different stages of cultural evolution and that it was necessary to adjust the level of the educational curriculum accordingly. "The educational requirements of the people who are only a few hundred years out of the jungle are not the same as those of people who have had thousands of years of civilization," the black president of Georgia Normal College explained. "The great mass of our people need to be trained in agriculture, the mechanical arts, the trades and industries, and in the art of homemaking."[5]

Making a similar point, a black professor at the West Virginia Collegiate Institute suggested that the solution to the problem posed by races "at unequal stages in cultural evolution" lay in "a system of unequal education. Thus for the vanguard of civilization there must be provided an education commensurate with its cultural status; for the rearguard an education likewise commensurate with its status." Booker T. Washington lamented that "in the past in missionary and educational work . . . men have tried to use, with these simple people just freed from slavery and with no past, no inherited traditions of learning, the same methods of education which they have used in New England, with all its inherited traditions and desires."[6]

The prevailing view of the post-Reconstruction era held that if blacks were not innately inferior they were, at the very least, at a relatively primitive stage of cultural evolution and thus incapable of mastering the standard liberal arts. "The silently growing assumption of the age," Du Bois observed, "is that the period of probation of races is past, and that the backward races of today are of proved ineffi-

---

[5] Joseph Winthrop Holley, *You Can't Build a Chimney from the Top* (New York: William-Frederick Press, 1948), p. 82.

[6] F. C. Sumner, "Philosophy of Negro Education," *Educational Review* 71 (January 1926): 42–45; Booker T. Washington, *The Future of the American Negro* (Boston: Small, Maynard and Co., 1899), pp. 25–26.

ciency."[7] Thus it was inevitable that the white South, when it returned to power after Reconstruction, would limit Negro college education to the preparation of the few professionals needed to insure a hermetic caste system while the remaining masses of blacks would be reeducated for service. In this way vocational training became a corollary of white supremacy, with black men and women expected to learn the elementary lessons of carpentry, gardening, and homemaking that would make them useful helots.

Under the circumstances, the surprise was not that the collegiate training of Negroes was restricted but that the white South did not renounce all Negro education. That this possibility was avoided was doubtless due in no small part to the influence of Samuel Chapman Armstrong, a brevet brigadier general in the United States army who skillfully directed Hampton Institute away from the egalitarian ideals of its missionary incorporators and toward the path of agricultural and vocational training. Armstrong's approach was developed by Booker T. Washington, a Hampton graduate who founded Tuskegee Institute and became the apostle of industrial education for Negroes. Armstrong and Washington believed that the power realities in the South made it necessary for blacks to renounce agitation, postpone demands for equality and full citizenship rights, and develop the skills and traditional middle-class virtues that would enable Negroes to earn a living and win the respect of neighbors. Their emphasis on traditional morality and vocational training was perfectly attuned to the temper of the post-Reconstruction South and may well have saved Negro education from total destruction. Only a program that promised not to raise the Negro out of his "place" but to make him a more efficient servant and laborer could have reconciled many whites to the idea of Negro education.

This program of vocational training could not have been

[7] Du Bois, *Souls of Black Folk*, p. 189.

developed without crucial support from northern capital, and Armstrong and Washington made special efforts to establish an alliance with the well-to-do. Many wealthy capitalists knew that the egalitarian programs of the Reconstruction era could not be continued after the restoration of white supremacy. The previous alliance of black and white egalitarians had to be modified, and black collaboration with the dominant whites along the lines pioneered at Hampton and Tuskegee was an alternative strategy that responded with the new power realities. Yet it allowed northern men of wealth—many of whom had been influenced by the abolitionist tradition as well as by Social Darwinism—to continue their benefactions on behalf of the Negro.

At the close of the nineteenth century an organization that came to be known as the Conference for Education in the South began to meet annually to organize the flow of charitable funds for Negro education, and in the twentieth century the Slater, Jeanes, Phelps-Stokes, and Rosenwald foundations, the Southern Education Board, and the Rockefeller General Education Board continued the tradition of philanthropic assistance to black schools. This is not to deny the continuing importance of the Protestant church boards. The Congregationalist American Missionary Association, the Freedmen's Aid Society of the Methodist Episcopal Church, the American Baptist Home Mission Society, and the Presbyterian Board of Missions for the Freedmen all remained active and continued to emphasize academic higher education. Yet the church boards were on the defensive, and the missionary colleges found it increasingly difficult to raise additional funds.

The secular philanthropists believed it was necessary to work within the framework and traditions of the white South. Hence they sought to accomplish what could be done rather than follow the example of the Yankee missionaries who tried to do what should be done. The philanthro-

8

pists also believed that extreme caution was essential in promoting any educational program and knew that their own resources were so limited that they would be doing a real disservice to the cause of Negro education if their gifts were used by Southerners as an excuse for not providing public education for blacks. For this reason they "proceeded tentatively, making annual grants to selected schools, but taking care to do nothing which might become an obstacle to the development of a sound system of public education supported by taxation." The General Education Board "kept steadily in view the obvious fact that in the education of the Negro as of the whites the public school must be the main reliance . . . [and] therefore resolved that, while certain privately managed institutions must be aided, its main purpose required that it cooperate with progressive Southern sentiment in creating publicly supported educational systems."[8]

Thus the foundations took care to avoid alienating the white South. The Slater Foundation decided as early as 1882 to confine its assistance to schools that offered vocational training, while the Jeanes Fund appointed teachers to supervise industrial work, and the Rosenwald Foundation financed the construction of elementary schools. The activities of the General Education Board were more varied, but the emphasis prior to the First World War was clearly on elementary and vocational training. The board cooperated with the Jeanes Fund in supplying teachers to supervise industrial work, joined with the Slater Foundation in financing "county training schools," and sponsored 4-H and

[8] General Education Board, *Annual Report*, 1919–1920, p. 87; General Education Board, *The General Education Board: An Account of Its Activities, 1902–1914* (New York, privately published, 1915), pp. 192–193. The most thorough study of organized philanthropy is Henry S. Enck's "The Burden Bourne: Northern White Philanthropy and Southern Black Industrial Education, 1900–1915" (unpublished Ph.D. dissertation, University of Cincinnati, 1970).

9

homemakers' clubs. The board also employed state agents who worked as liaison men encouraging public sentiment on behalf of public education, "not by foisting upon the South a program from outside, but by cooperating with Southern leaders in sympathetically working out a program framed by them on the basis of local conditions and local considerations."[9]

Acting independently but in response to the same general forces, the federal government also used its influence on behalf of vocational training for blacks. Noting that the Morrill Act of 1862 made no special provision for Negro colleges and that only three southern states had designated Negro schools as recipients of federal funds under the land-grant program, the Congress in 1890 enacted a second Morrill Act that forbade discrimination and required that land-grant monies be distributed among blacks as well as whites. Yet egalitarians warned that this legislation had unfortunate racial implications—a prophecy that was fulfilled when state governments used the federal land-grant money to transform academically oriented black colleges into institutes that fostered vocational training as especially suited to a predetermined, subordinate role for the Negro in American society.

The trend in this direction was heightened when Congress, through the Smith-Lever and Smith-Hughes acts of 1914 and 1917, rounded out the program of vocational and agricultural training and established a county-agent bureaucracy. The county agents then assumed responsibility for seeing that the land-grant colleges, and especially black institutions, did not stray from the gospel of vocationalism. Together this combination of secular philanthropy and federal largesse altered the course of the black colleges and initiated a second, vocational phase in the history of Negro higher education.[10]

[9] General Education Board, *Account of Its Activities*, p. 14.

[10] There was an "industrial education vogue" in the late nineteenth and early twentieth centuries, and many job-training programs were

The new vocationalism was dictated by considerations of expediency—by the belief that the white South would not permit Negro education unless it was disguised in the garb of "job training." But the philanthropists' insistence that "our work is education, not agitation" left many blacks with the suspicion that appeals to feasibility camouflaged a belief that Negroes were particularly suited for training in simple skills. These suspicions were reinforced when influential philanthropist William H. Baldwin, the first chairman of the General Education Board, announced his opposition "to the so-called higher education of Negroes" and conceded that the black man "should not be educated out of his environment." Baldwin's colleague Wallace Buttrick similarly disarmed southern suspicions with assurances that "we have no thought of colonizing teachers from the North, nor of transplanting northern ideas. On the contrary, we believe that the teachers of the South should be the product of the soil of the South, and that your schools should be organized by yourselves in harmony with your traditions and institutions."[11]

Du Bois no doubt expressed the sentiment of many blacks when he stated that behind the facade of vocational training there lay a "design of rich and intelligent people, and particularly . . . those who masquerade as the Negroes'

---

established for whites who were not going to college. Most whites welcomed this training as a spur to social mobility, an opportunity for some to rise from the ranks of unskilled labor. Many blacks, on the other hand, suspected that the introduction of trade training into the Negro *colleges* was a device to put a ceiling on the educational ambitions of the race, a new way of "keeping the Negro in his place." They noted that the black institutes of college grade were not training their students for positions comparable to those held by graduates of the leading white colleges of engineering.

[11] Raymond B. Fosdick, *Adventure in Giving: The Story of the General Education Board* (New York: Harper and Row, 1962), p. 183; William H. Baldwin, quoted in ibid., p. 11; Wallace Buttrick, quoted in ibid., p. 23.

'friends' . . . to educate a race of scullions and then complain of their lack of proven ability."[12]

In addition to stressing the importance of vocational training, the philanthropists insisted that moral discipline should be an integral part of Negro education. On this point, at least, they found themselves in substantial agreement with the Yankee missionaries. Thus black students at both vocational institutes and missionary colleges were required to attend daily chapel exercises. Social life was closely supervised. Women were not allowed to receive male callers, preceptresses were authorized to inspect incoming mail, and machinelike schedules prescribed the student's activities for virtually every hour of the day, from compulsory inspection at about 6 a.m. to lights out at 10 p.m.

Teachers in the Negro schools believed that most students could not learn unless they broke away from the black folk culture and assimilated the values of the white middle class. It was "with heavy hearts" that teachers watched "some of our scholars returning to their homes in the evening, for we know that there everything tends to overthrow the religious and moral teaching received during the day." The teachers spared no adjectives in describing the wretched condition of the youths' home environment—filthy one-room cabins with no books or intellectual stimulation and with illiterate parents who did not understand the meaning of sobriety or chastity. President William W. Patton of Howard University explained that this home life would keep youths at the same level as their parents. There was no hope unless the black student entered the new environment of schools where "in addition to having access to books he goes where the entire conception and standard of living is different and elevated; where religion is intelligent; where morals are pure; where manners are refined; where language is grammatical; where clothing is whole and neat." The black schools stressed the importance of discipline, obedience,

---

[12] W. E. B. Du Bois, "Education," *Crisis* 10 (July 1915): 132; Du Bois, "The Year in Colored Colleges," *Crisis* 4 (July 1912): 136.

and a precise daily routine. Such a regimen, it was hoped, would transform the students' character and serve as a healthy contrast to the lax child-rearing practices of many black families.[13]

Some black adults criticized these paternalistic efforts to impose middle-class values on lower-class youths. But many others endorsed the missionaries' effort to prove the Negro equal to the Caucasian by making him just like a white man. The distinguished black sociologist Charles S. Johnson praised the discipline of the black colleges, "No less stern rectitude and concern could have broken the grip of habits adjusted to a now outmoded life of irresponsibility, and re-shaped them to a new and more serious purpose." Du Bois acknowledged that "it will not do in the South to leave moral training to individual homes, since their homes are just recovering from the debauchery of slavery."[14]

Black students naturally objected to regimentation on the campus, but the discipline was tolerable in the late nineteenth century when it was thought to be prompted by Christian piety and was applied to white students as well as blacks. Yet the tradition of piety remained in force at the black schools long after the leading white colleges had de-emphasized their concern for moral uplift and had begun to stress secular scholarship. Thus many blacks suspected that the extraordinarily strict regulations still in force in their schools during the 1920s were prompted by a racist belief that Negroes were particularly sensuous beings who could not discipline themselves and were not prepared to exercise free will. Back of this view, they believed, lay the fear that if Negroes were allowed the exercise of liberty they would become too dangerous to live in the white community.

Beyond trade training and moral discipline, the secular

[13] This paragraph is based on information in McPherson, *Antislavery Legacy*, chaps. 9, 14.

[14] Charles S. Johnson, *The Negro College Graduate* (Chapel Hill: University of North Carolina Press, 1937), pp. 280, 286–287; W. E. B. Du Bois, quoted in McPherson, *Antislavery Legacy*, chap. 9.

philanthropists emphasized the need for establishing better schools for southern whites. They feared that exclusive concern for black schools would alienate the white South, and so they promoted universal public education—for whites and blacks—and consoled themselves with the belief that the education of white youths was the shortest road to the education of the Negro. According to this reasoning, ignorance was the basic cause of white racism and the education "of one untaught white man to the point that knowledge and not prejudice will guide his conduct . . . is worth more to the black man himself than the education of ten Negroes." The secular philanthropists hoped that white education would dispel suspicion and destroy the economic basis of racial discrimination, and they eventually devoted more of their time and money to the campaign to upgrade white schools than to work on behalf of blacks. But this strategy was sadly mistaken, for the development of white public schools within the context of racism only increased the temptation to appropriate the Negro's fair share of the funds. Consequently, as Louis Harlan has demonstrated, the gap between expenditures for black and white education grew progressively wider during the first three decades of the twentieth century.[15]

Cut off from the aid of secular philanthropy and the federal government, the black missionary colleges were starved for funds. Yet except for exposing schools that were collecting money on the basis of false claims, the philanthropists showed little interest in Negro higher education. Instead, their allegedly definitive 724-page survey of Negro education, published in 1916 under the joint auspices of the United States Bureau of Education and the Phelps-Stokes Fund, advanced a tripartite thesis that neatly summarized the views then prevailing in the white South: that collegiate

[15] Louis R. Harlan, *Separate and Unequal: Public School Campaigns and Racism in the Southern Seaboard States, 1901–1915* (Chapel Hil': University of North Carolina Press, 1958), pp. 92–93, 259, and *passim*.

14

education among blacks should be curtailed and more emphasis placed on vocational training; that Negro education could not succeed without the cooperation of the white South; and that there should be greater unity of purpose among educators working in black schools.[16]

Black and white egalitarians naturally rejected these proposals. They insisted that it was absolutely essential that Negroes develop liberally educated leaders who could hold their own with the best products of the white educational system. They noted that cooperation with the white South was difficult because most white Southerners opposed full-manhood education for Negroes and would tolerate only a second-class, demeaning education that trained blacks for subordinate roles in society. And they feared that a greater degree of philanthropic unity would lead to the domination of the remaining missionary boards by secular foundations that had surrendered to the white South and adopted the extraordinary thesis that the education of whites must be attended to before any significant progress could be made in the training of blacks.[17]

Yet these egalitarians enjoyed little popularity in an age that saw no need for the higher education of a supposedly backward race. Instead, a definite ideology of special education became increasingly popular. Blacks were to be given a special vocational curriculum to prepare them for their special responsibilities. The schools, initially conceived by the missionaries as institutions that would promote cultural assimilation and teach the skills needed for upward social mobility, were to serve instead as the formal channels for socializing youth in the etiquette of American race relations.

---

[16] Thomas Jesse Jones, ed., *Negro Education: A Study of the Private and Higher Schools for Colored People in the United States*, prepared in cooperation with the Phelps-Stokes Fund (U.S. Department of Interior, Bureau of Education Bulletin 38, 1916).

[17] For examples of this criticism see W. E. B. Du Bois, "Negro Education," *Crisis* 15 (February 1918): 173–178; and Du Bois, "Thomas Jesse Jones," *Crisis* 22 (October 1921): 252–256.

Blacks were to be taught to think of themselves as inferior menials while whites would be instilled with the conviction that they were members of a master caste. Special education became a way of life to which blacks were exposed for the purpose of perpetuating their subordinate status. An entire race was to be educated not for participation in the mainstream of American life, but for humble service in the backwaters.

And yet, as Henry Allen Bullock has noted, "Despite all the planning that had been put into the Negro education movement, it was quite evident, even at the start, that some of its by-products would contradict its aims and rise to threaten the social system it was engineered to preserve."[18] Segregation, after all, required that blacks provide their own leaders, and this meant that a critical minority of blacks had to be trained in medicine, law, journalism, theology, and other professions. And by an irony of fate, the reorganization of southern agriculture and organized labor's opposition to the employment of skilled black workers left teaching as the most reliable source of employment for black college graduates. Under the circumstances, even the land-grant A. & M. colleges, while offering a veneer of vocational courses, enrolled most of their students in teacher-training programs that resembled the liberal and classical studies then in vogue at the best white colleges. The black students were segregated, of course, and generally received inferior training, but the ideal of aspiration was preserved. Thus many Negroes were not prepared to adjust to a subordinate status, but instead demanded the right to participate fully in the promise of American life.

The challenge to racism on the campus broke forth with unprecedented force during the 1920s, when blacks returned from the "war to make the world safe for democracy" with a fierce determination to "marshal every ounce

[18] Henry Allen Bullock, *A History of Negro Education in the South* (Cambridge: Harvard University Press, 1967), p. 160.

of our brain and brawn to fight a sterner, longer, more un-
bending battle against the forces of hell in our own land."[19]
The rising tide of Negro protest was manifested in many
ways—in the warfare of the Red Summer, 1919; in Marcus
Garvey's black nationalist movement; in the resurgence of
black pride celebrated by the authors of the Harlem literary
renaissance; in the development of Negro-controlled busi-
nesses and institutions; in the growth of the NAACP, the
Urban League, and the black press; in the substantial black
migration from the rural South to the urban North—in so
many ways that whites came to recognize that new Negroes
who had rejected compromise and accommodation were
now ascendant in the black community and determined to
enjoy all the rights and privileges of American citizens.

The wave of rebellion that engulfed most of the leading
black colleges of the 1920s was one of the most significant
aspects of the New Negro protest movement. As Negroes
massed together in black cities within the city, they discovered larger social and economic opportunities and a greater
need for higher education and professional training. The
number of students enrolled in the black colleges of the day
increased six times over—from 2,132 in 1917 to 13,580 in
1927[20]—and the black community demanded a higher type
of education that would enable its youth to take advantage
of new opportunities. Far from being grateful for the financial aid that the government and secular philanthropy had
showered on the vocational schools, the black students, professors, and alumni of the 1920s were bitter with resentment
and feared that the higher aspirations of the race had been
sacrificed in order to obtain money from the powers that
ruled.

College-bred Negroes had long thought of themselves as
a black vanguard leading the struggle for racial emancipation. They were convinced that the higher education of

[19] W. E. B. Du Bois, "Returning Soldiers," *Crisis* 18 (May 1919): 14.
[20] "Enrollment in Negro Universities and Colleges," *School and
Society* 28 (29 September 1928): 401–402.

black leaders was essential for the progress of the race, and they were determined to regain control of their colleges. The details of their struggle varied according to the circumstances and personalities at the different campuses, but throughout the black college rebellions of the 1920s there was a rejection of the condescending belief that whites unerringly knew the best methods of Negro education and an insistence that black youths must be trained according to principles endorsed by the black community. "We propose to speak for ourselves and to be represented by spokesmen whom we elect," Du Bois proclaimed. "And whenever in any case this policy is contravened we are going to fight that decision in every civilized way, and to the last ditch."[21]

II

The spirit of W. E. B. Du Bois hovered over the black college rebellions of the 1920s. The editor of the *Crisis* instigated the confrontation at Fisk University and publicized and celebrated collegiate protest throughout the land. Indeed, Du Bois's role in the protest movement looms so large that it is not possible to comprehend the phenomenon without understanding his educational thought.

As the foremost advocate of college training for talented black youths, Du Bois wrestled with the problem of appropriate training throughout his long life. He shifted emphases on several occasions, but divergent statements often focused on different aspects of complex truth and Du Bois's educational thought was really more kaleidoscopic than paradoxical. The essential ideological ingredients were present at the turn of the twentieth century, but the configuration of elements changed as Du Bois adjusted to shifting external circumstances.

In one of his early essays on education, the young Du Bois wrote, "The Negro race, like all others, is going to be saved

[21] Du Bois, "Thomas Jesse Jones," p. 256.

by its exceptional men." He believed that "the problem of education" focused on training a "Talented Tenth" to become "leaders of thought and missionaries of culture among their people." To Du Bois it was rank heresy to suggest that liberal education was the privilege of whites and a dangerous delusion for blacks; and he contended that the Negro school system should differ "in no essential particular" from educational systems throughout the world. Black students should be trained "by long and rigorous courses of study similar to those which the world over have been designed to strengthen the intellectual powers [and] fortify character."[22]

This concern with broad liberal training remained with Du Bois to the end of his life. His 1910 Atlanta University report on *The College-Bred Negro American* emphasized that the course of study in Negro colleges did "not call for any peculiar modification, but should, on the whole, conform to the general type of curriculum designed for the preparation of broadly educated men to take their places in modern civilization." In 1918 he asserted that educators who ignored "the great heritage of human thought" while emphasizing vocational training were "pitifully wrong and, if the comparison must be made, more wrong than the man who would sacrifice modern technique to the heritage of ancient thought." Throughout the first quarter of the twentieth century, when many critics were ridiculing the blacks' desire to study the classics, Du Bois insisted that the traditional curriculum was essential to developing "thoroughly educated men according to modern standards." In 1927 he rejoiced that "that 'silly' desire for 'Greek and Latin' . . . has saved the Negro race." As late as 1958–1959—his ninetieth year—he reiterated that "the riddle of existence" was revealed by the curriculum of the pharoahs and Greeks, "the

[22] Du Bois, "Talented Tenth," pp. 33, 75; Du Bois, "The Training of Negroes for Social Power," *Outlook* 75 (17 October 1903): 410–411.

trivium and *quadrivium* [that] is today laid before the freedmen's sons by Atlanta University."[23]

Du Bois placed greatest emphasis on liberal education during the first years of the twentieth century, when the controversy with Booker T. Washington was at its height. Washington disparaged what he called "mere book learning," said that the Negro schools and colleges should stress manual training, and suggested that the classical curriculum was a major cause of the Negro's failure to improve his economic position more rapidly. Du Bois, on the other hand, was adamantly opposed to the movement to create a special vocational curriculum for the race, the black studies of an earlier generation, which taught Negroes to cook, sew, and make bricks at a time when college-bound youth were learning to read, write, and cipher.

Du Bois was convinced that no system of education could succeed without qualified teachers who had received higher training in the liberal arts. Fortunately, the Yankees who went to the Negro South after the Civil War recognized this and established colleges which in the first generation after Emancipation gave liberal educations to a few thousand Negroes who then trained teachers who taught the alphabet to the black masses. Of course the Yankee missionaries had their faults, but they recognized, as Washington and many philanthropists did not, that "progress in human affairs is more often a pull than a push, a surging forward of the exceptional man, and the lifting of his duller brethren slowly and painfully to his vantage ground." They focused on teacher training, knowing that it would be a waste of time and money to establish common schools without first providing for the higher training of exceptional teachers. In-

[23] W. E. B. Du Bois and Augustus Granville Dill, eds., *The College-Bred Negro American* (Atlanta University Publications, No. 15, 1910), p. 7; Du Bois, "Negro Education," p. 175; Du Bois, "Higher Education," *Crisis* 34 (September 1927): 239; Du Bois, *Autobiography* (New York: International Publishers, 1968), p. 212.

deed, according to Du Bois the success enjoyed by Tuskegee and other industrial schools was "due primarily to the white colleges of the North and the black colleges of the South, which trained the teachers who today conduct these institutions." Du Bois was particularly irritated because "one of the effects of Mr. Washington's propaganda has been to throw doubt upon the expediency of such training for Negroes."[24]

Even in the midst of the contention with Washington, however, Du Bois recognized that in addition to transmitting universal culture the black college should be "a center of sociological research" in what is now called black studies. From 1897 to 1910 he presided over annual research conferences at Atlanta University, issuing regular scholarly reports on matters such as the health, religion, education, criminal and business activities of Negroes, and he returned to this work in the late 1930s and early 1940s. Du Bois was a pioneer in researching and teaching the history and sociology of blacks; he considered this scholarship his "real life work," and he always insisted that black colleges had a special duty to see that "the unique and marvelous life and experience of the black race in America" was neither distorted, neglected, nor consigned entirely to white scholars.[25]

Du Bois also knew that many blacks found it difficult to identify positively with their race, and he stressed the importance of instruction that would build race pride and self-esteem. The Negro college had great responsibilities: In addition to offering a general education in the liberal arts, it should be "a center of applied knowledge and guide of action," training students to apply their higher learning "to the solutions of the Negro problem." Scarcely less im-

[24] Du Bois, *Souls of Black Folk*, p. 78; Du Bois, "Talented Tenth," pp. 60, 74.
[25] Du Bois, *Autobiography*, pp. 201, 213, 339, 313-314, 323.

portant, the black college should make its students aware of their heritage and potential and thereby destroy the "inner paralysis and lack of self-confidence" that rendered blacks "helpless before the white world."[26]

Thus Du Bois qualified his earlier contention that the college curriculum knew no racial boundaries. Yet he never forgot that special education had been misused in the past to train blacks as menials and dependents, and of course he had nothing like this in mind. While the emphasis on black studies involved some change of thought and modification of method, it was not irreconcilable with Du Bois's insistence on broad training. He continued to stress the importance of the liberal arts, adding only that "this knowledge of the world should focus at least in part on the black world in which most colored students live."[27]

Although Du Bois was explicitly committed to the struggle for full acceptance in American society, his concern for black studies and a parallel belief that Negroes had yet to make their full contribution to world civilization led him to stress group solidarity until the distinct black "message" was fully delivered. Along with many other intellectuals of his age, Du Bois believed that races, as well as individuals, contributed to culture, with the English justly renowned for individualism, the Germans for philosophy, the Romance nations for literature and art, and the other races striving "each in its own way, to develop for civilization its particular message." He was also convinced that members of one race could not always be trusted to guide another to realization of its highest cultural possibilities. Thus, "if among the gaily colored banners that deck the broad ramparts of civilization is to hang one uncompromising[ly] black," it was essential that black colleges develop proud, self-con-

[26] W. E. B. Du Bois, "The Negro College," *Crisis* 40 (August 1933): 175–177; Du Bois, "Does the Negro Need Separate Schools?" *Journal of Negro Education* 4 (July 1935): 333.

[27] W. E. B. Du Bois, "The Future and Function of the Private Negro College," *Crisis* 53 (August 1946): 254.

fident leaders who would develop the full potential of the Negro race.[28]

This emphasis on blackness was especially notable during the 1880s and 1890s when Du Bois was a student at Fisk and Harvard universities. At black Fisk Du Bois had discovered "not a lost group, but . . . a microcosm of a world and a civilization in potentiality." At Harvard he voluntarily withdrew from white society and mixed with the off-campus blacks who "were getting to have a common culture pattern which made them an interlocking mass." By 1897 he was writing that the Negro had begun to have "a dim feeling that, to attain his place in the world, he must be himself, and not another," and he confessed that he ever felt his "two-ness—an American, a Negro; two souls, two thoughts, two unreconciled strivings; two warring ideals in one dark body." He repeatedly praised liberally educated Negroes who could "assimilate the culture and common sense of modern civilization . . . and can take hold of Negro communities and raise and train them by force of precept and example." But he also maintained that the Negro destiny was not merely to imitate and assimilate Anglo-Saxon culture but to develop "a stalwart originality which shall unswervingly follow Negro ideals."[29]

Liberal training, black studies, and ethnic mystique— these incongruous concepts came together in an unusual symbiosis that has perplexed commentators who focus on one aspect of Du Bois's thought to the neglect of others. Yet

[28] W. E. B. Du Bois, "The Conservation of Races," American Negro Academy, *Occasional Papers, No. 2* (Washington, D. C., 1897): 9–10; Du Bois, *Dusk of Dawn: An Essay Toward an Autobiography of a Race Concept* (New York: Harcourt, Brace & World, 1940), p. 70.
[29] Du Bois, *Autobiography*, pp. 108, 137; Du Bois, "Strivings of the Negro People," *Atlantic Monthly* 80 (August 1897): 194–196; Du Bois, "The Relation of the Negroes to the Whites in the South," *Annals of the American Academy of Political and Social Science* 18 (July-December 1901): 128; Du Bois, "Conservation of Races," p. 10.

Du Bois's basic ideas were by no means irreconcilable. He always felt a certain dichotomy: Even as a student he wondered "how far can love for my oppressed race accord with love for the oppressing country?" And toward the end of his eighth decade he still believed that "American Negroes are not simply Americans, or simply Negroes," but a distinct minority group with a unique culture and history "which they cannot escape because it is in the marrow of their bones." This duality inevitably led to a reluctance to come to grips with the basic questions of identity: "Am I an American or am I a Negro? Can I be both?" But eventually Du Bois had to decide, and he chose what we today call cultural pluralism. As he saw it, blacks wished neither to Africanize America nor to bleach their Negro blood, but simply "to make it possible for a man to be both a Negro and an American. . . ." "We want to be Americans, full-fledged Americans, with all the rights of other American citizens," he insisted. But that was not all. Negroes must fight for equal opportunity and also proudly develop their unique talents. Thus Du Bois was a fastidious black Brahmin—a connoisseur of the best in Western culture, a devoted chronicler of African contributions to civilization, and also an exhorter urging Negro Americans to make their own special gift to the world. To focus on any one aspect of this complex thought to the neglect of others is to miss the central thrust which insisted that Negroes should be both black and American.[30]

Du Bois believed that the early years of the twentieth century formed one of the most critical periods in American Negro history, for this was the time when northern and southern whites reconciled their differences and came together in support of a new Trinity: white supremacy, black subordination, and industrial progress. On the other hand,

---

[30] Du Bois, *Autobiography*, p. 169; Du Bois, "Private Negro College," p. 235; Du Bois, "Conservation of Races," p. 11; Du Bois, "Strivings of the Negro People," pp. 194–195; Du Bois, "Criteria of Negro Art," *Crisis* 32 (October 1926): 290.

as Du Bois saw it, the black colleges were graduating men and women who demanded all the rights and privileges of first-class citizens. The leaders of the nation's business and philanthropy realized that this opposition to racism—"the silly idealism of Negroes, half-trained in missionary 'colleges' "—threatened to destroy the sectional and racial compromises that were prerequisites for economic growth. Hence they decided to squelch any Negro who held unconventional views on the proper training of blacks or the general state of race relations. Yet suppressing outspoken blacks was not an easy task, and the effort might never have achieved a measure of success without the support of Booker T. Washington who, according to Du Bois, said "on the whole, the things that the white community wanted him to say," and in return found his own prestige and power reinforced by the wealth of northern philanthropy.[31]

Du Bois insisted that beyond the differing emphasis on vocational and liberal education, the controversy with Washington had centered around the manner in which patronage was dispensed at Tuskegee Institute. The leaders of business and philanthropy conferred with Washington before giving appointments or promotions to Negroes, with the tacit understanding that the Tuskegeean's approval would be withheld from any black who threatened the status quo. The process involved much cruelty and disappointment for unconventional thinkers, as Du Bois himself learned when financial support for his Atlanta University conferences was sharply restricted after his first public disagreement with Washington. In this way "the Negro intelligentsia was . . . suppressed and hammered into conformity," while Tuskegee was exalted as the capital of black America. By ostracizing blacks who protested against racial injustice while rewarding those who obligingly adapted to the harsh reality of white supremacy, Washington and the philanthropists taught Negroes to accept what the whites

[31] Du Bois, *Autobiography*, p. 240; Du Bois, "Thomas Jesse Jones," p. 253.

were willing to offer, taught them to be a "humble, patient, hardworking group of laborers, whose ultimate destiny would be determined by their white employers."[32]

Throughout the first three decades of the twentieth century Du Bois wrote editorials and articles against this accommodationism that became known as the Tuskegee Compromise, emphasizing that the suppression of black protest "was not solely the idea and activity of black folk at Tuskegee . . . [but] was largely encouraged and given financial aid through certain white groups and individuals in the North." The philanthropists had "surrendered entirely to the white South on the matter of Negro education," and had undertaken especially "to restrain and starve Negro higher education and to concentrate upon what they regarded as the Hampton-Tuskegee industrial plan." They "sneered at 'Latin' and 'Greek,' " told Negroes "that the higher training of youth is unnecessary and wasteful," and so ostracized the leading black colleges that Du Bois at one time feared that "ten years will see the annihilation of higher negro training in the South."[33]

By the 1920s the financial condition of the black colleges had improved a bit, but far from being satisfied Du Bois believed that the black colleges had been forced to compromise their principles in return for money. Thus Hampton, which in the 1920s accepted the dictates of white Virginia and provided a segregated Jim Crow residence and dining room for white visitors, was "the pet of philanthropy" with an endowment that exceeded the combined total of the leading Negro colleges. Atlanta University, by way of contrast, insisted on integrating its faculty and dining room and was told it would not receive philanthropic support unless

[32] Du Bois, *Autobiography*, pp. 229–231, 239–241; Du Bois, *Dusk of Dawn*, pp. 69–77.

[33] Du Bois, *Autobiography*, p. 239; Du Bois, "The General Education Board," *Crisis* 37 (July 1930): 229–230; Du Bois, "Training of Negroes," p. 414.

26

it surrendered some of its "radicalism" and accepted conventional notions of what a Negro institution should be.[34]

Du Bois believed that a "corrupt bargain" had been consummated. At the Capon Springs conferences promoting universal education for the South, in the much publicized fund-raising campaigns on behalf of Hampton and Tuskegee, in the organization of the Southern Education Board, and the operation of the General Education Board, educators had come together and endorsed the proposition that no Negro school could survive if it antagonized the white South. And then to cement this arrangement, secular philanthropy agreed to reward the Negro who came "with his hat in hand and flatters and cajoles the philanthropist . . . [while] the Negro who shows the slightest independence of thought or character is apt to be read out of all possible influence not only by the white South but by the philanthropic North."[35]

"It is a shame," Du Bois wrote in 1925, "that our dependence on the rich for donations to absolutely necessary causes makes intelligent, free and self-respecting manhood and frank and honest criticism increasingly difficult among us. If someone starts to tell the truth, or discloses incompetency, or rebels at injustice, [he will be greeted by] a chorus of 'Sh!' You're opposing the General Education Board! 'Hush!' You're making enemies in the Rockefeller Foundation! 'Keep still!' or the Phelps-Stokes Fund will get you." Du Bois acknowledged that this fear might be exaggerated in some cases, but the fear existed and it was "sapping the manhood of the race. It is breeding cowards and sycophants. It is lifting fools and flatterers to place and power and crucifying honest men."[36]

[34] W. E. B. Du Bois, "The Dilemma of the Negro," *American Mercury* 3 (October 1924): 183; Du Bois, "Negroes in College," *Nation* 122 (3 March 1926): 228–230.
[35] Du Bois, "Negro Education," p. 15.
[36] W. E. B. Du Bois, "Gifts and Education," *Crisis* 29 (February 1925): 151–152.

The final battle against the Tuskegee Compromise could not be waged until after the death of Washington in 1915, for a word from the Tuskegeean would have cut off black leaders and educators from badly needed philanthropic support. Indeed, since the First World War diverted Negro attention in the years immediately following Washington's death, it was really not until the 1920s that the critics of Tuskegee could mount the full force of their assault. Then, as the New Negro movement burst upon the scene with its insistence that blacks should enjoy all the rights of citizenship, a swelling number of blacks demanded that Negroes themselves must have a voice in the management of the major institutions that shaped their lives. For Du Bois the college protest movement of the 1920s involved nothing less than "the tremendous question as to whether Negro youth shall be trained as Negro parents wish or as Southern whites and Northern copperheads demand."[37]

[37] W. E. B. Du Bois, "Fisk," *Crisis* 29 (April 1925): 247.

CHAPTER II

W. E. B. Du Bois and the Rebellion at Fisk University

I

Established shortly after the Civil War in abandoned Union army barracks, Fisk University in Nashville, Tennessee, was generally recognized as the nation's preeminent liberal arts college for Negroes. Named in honor of Gen. Clinton B. Fisk, an assistant commissioner of the Freedmen's Bureau, and supported initially by contributions from the Congregationalist American Missionary Association, Fisk was led during its crucial first quarter-century by paragons of the Yankee missionary genre. Graduates of the university were prominent in every field, and many blacks thought that Fisk offered the best undergraduate education available to Negroes. Parents ambitious for the success of their children were known to scrimp, save, and sacrifice to send their offspring to this elite institution whose diploma conferred automatic status upon its alumni.[1]

Most outward signs indicated that Fisk was enjoying unprecedented success in the years after the First World War. Originally, Fisk was a secondary school with a few college courses; by the 1920s approximately half of Fisk's six hundred students were enrolled in the college division. The well-landscaped forty-acre campus was studded with twenty buildings—the most famous of which, Jubilee Hall, had been financed by students with the proceeds from the European and American concerts of the famed Jubilee Singers.

[1] The best history of Fisk University is by Joe M. Richardson of Florida State University. I am indebted to Prof. Richardson for permitting me to read the relevant portions of his manuscript.

And the young white president of Fisk, Fayette Avery Mc-
Kenzie, a sociologist at Ohio State University before becoming Fisk's fourth chief executive in 1915, was highly regarded in all sections of the country and had worked
assiduously, and with unprecedented success, to persuade
organized philanthropy to use some of its funds to support
the higher education of Negroes.

The year before Fayette McKenzie assumed his duties at
Fisk a special committee of the General Education Board
had suggested that perhaps organized philanthropy should
"take hold of the most promising Negro college—Fisk University" and develop it as a model for black higher education. McKenzie seized on this theme and noted that although
"the scattered results of the last half-century have demonstrated the capacity of the race to take the higher education" there was not a single first-class black university anywhere in the world. McKenzie believed that clearly "the
hour has struck for a big thing," and he insisted that Fisk
was "eager to do a greater work." Yet he knew that Fisk
could not become a model institution without a sizable endowment, and sufficient money could be raised only by convincing men of wealth that Fisk's quest for funds was not
just "a casual appeal which wins the approval of everybody,
as the appeal of one worthy cause among a thousand worthy
causes, . . . [but] the appeal that compels because it is the
appeal of an institution unique in its philosophy and service." McKenzie's motto was, "Let us dare to be a university,"
and his goal was to make Fisk a distinguished center of
learning, with academic standards set "as high for the colored youth as they are set for the white youth." Fisk would
not fulfill its mission until the world acknowledged "first,
that a Negro as such, in his native mentality, is capable of
the highest scholarship, and second that a Negro college,
with a student body of hundreds if not thousands of only
colored students, can measure up at every point with the
standard colleges of the land."[2]

[2] Raymond B. Fosdick, *Adventure in Giving: The Story of the General Education Board* (New York: Harper and Row, 1962), p.

McKenzie also believed that Fisk should continue its traditional efforts to instill exemplary personal habits and traits of character. He had "the old-fashioned notion that instead of the college adapting itself to the life of the streets and adopting codes of conduct because they were the 'mode,' ... the streets should lift themselves to the college level." McKenzie deeply regretted "the laxity in so many of the higher institutions, which had so surrendered supervision and wise control of student life as to undermine the foundations of high character." Fisk should continue to exercise "wise guidance in the field of daily life and of social convention." As he saw it, habit was the basis of character, and one of the important goals of the university was "to teach through the daily processes of life itself the lessons of regularity, promptness, reliability, continuity and thoroughness." Hence the Fisk Code of Discipline was a detailed set of rules that prescribed "not only by line upon line, and precept upon precept, but by regularity upon regularity, even requirement upon requirement."[3]

At Fisk the hours are set for meals, sleep, recitation and study. Attendance is required upon religious services; the social relationships of the two sexes are carefully supervised; the young women are carefully chaperoned; dancing between the sexes is not countenanced; smoking is forbidden; dishonesty in any form is considered a reasonable bar to attendance upon the university.

The fact that some of our institutions feel no sense of responsibility along some of these lines is no necessary argument against the Fisk policy. That policy is desired by most parents, is tolerable to most students, and admirable in its product in the eyes of the general public. . . .[4]

190; Fayette McKenzie, *President's Report 1919–1923* (pamphlets), Fisk Archives; Isaac Fisher, "An Appraisal of the Work Done by President Fayette Avery McKenzie at Fisk University" (typescript), Papers of Fayette Avery McKenzie, Tennessee State Archives (hereafter cited as McKenzie Papers).
[3] Fayette McKenzie, *President's Report, 1919–1920.*
[4] Ibid.

31

The emphasis on scholarship and discipline soon paid handsome dividends. By the mid-1920s many leading universities recognized the quality of Fisk's academic work and accepted its students as transfers and candidates for graduate degrees. And then, after McKenzie established Fisk's academic reputation, the trustees launched a campaign to raise a satisfactory endowment. Basing their appeal on "the quality of the work already done," the trustees managed to raise a $1,000,000 endowment—with the largest contributions from the Rockefeller General Education Board ($500,000) and the Carnegie Corporation ($250,000). Other sizable gifts came from the John F. Slater Fund, the J. C. Penney Foundation, prominent individuals in New York, Boston, Philadelphia, Chicago, and Cleveland, and the white citizens of Nashville who, in a notable departure from traditional southern opposition to higher education for Negroes, themselves contributed $50,000. This million-dollar endowment was an unprecedented fund for a Negro college and, as the trustees acknowledged, the new money put Fisk University "beyond the possibility of cavil in a class by itself, as the leading institution of its kind in the world."[5]

With the successful completion of the endowment campaign, praise was naturally showered on the university and its young president. *Opportunity*, the journal of the National Urban League, recalled, "There was a time not far back when only those schools which promised . . . to turn out *manual* workers could hope for any liberal support." The *New York Times* hailed the endowment as an indication of

[5] Fisk trustees to Fayette McKenzie, *Fisk News*, October 1924; Isaac Fisher, "How the Million-Dollar Endowment for Fisk?" *Fisk News*, October 1924; Paul Cravath, quoted in Fayette McKenzie to alumni, 7 January 1925 (copy), Papers of W. E. B. Du Bois, University of Massachusetts (hereafter cited as WEBD Papers); Fisk trustees to Carnegie Foundation, 1916, McKenzie Papers; *New York Times*, 20 July 1924; *Nashville Banner*, 20 July 1924; *Nashville Tennessean*, 4 June 1924.

"an awakening realization of the need of thoroughly
equipped professional men and women to serve and to
guide the massed groups who have left their old rural environment in the cabins of the South and who find themselves in industrial centers . . . with new spiritual, social and
material problems at their doors." The trustees of the university gave special recognition to President McKenzie's
achievement in demonstrating "the need of college education for colored people and giving proof that Fisk University was worthy to be the first administrator of this first million-dollar endowment for college education for colored
people."[6]
Yet within a year of the announcement of this great financial triumph Fayette McKenzie was forced out of the presidency of Fisk by dissident black students and alumni who
were convinced that in striving for money Fisk had sacrificed integrity and accepted white demands that it insult
and humiliate blacks to make them know their place. Among
the many friends of the university who believed that the
school had lost its soul, none was more influential in sound-
ing the alarm and organizing the opposition than its most
distinguished alumnus, W. E. B. Du Bois.

II

Fayette McKenzie knew that the church boards were
hard pressed for funds in the 1920s and that the money
needed for Fisk's endowment could be raised only from the
secular foundations and educational boards that were closely attuned to the thinking of the white South. Under these
circumstances a certain amount of compromise was inevitable. McKenzie had to convince the men of wealth that Fisk
had not departed too far from the Tuskegee ideal, that its

6 "Fisk's Million Dollar Endowment Fund," *Opportunity* 8 (August
1924): 227–228; "A Million for Fisk," *New York Times*, 20 July
1924; Fisk trustees to Fayette McKenzie, *Fisk News*, October
1924; Isaac Fisher, "How the Million-Dollar Endowment?"

students were not radical egalitarians but young men and women who had learned to make peace with the reality of the caste system. To this end, the student government association was disbanded and dissent forbidden. The *Fisk Herald*, the oldest student publication among Negro colleges, was suspended; and the alumni journal, the *Fisk News*, became, according to Du Bois, "one of the most abject and whining of the organs which seek to placate the forces dominant today in the South." A request for university recognition for a campus chapter of the NAACP was denied, and the librarian was instructed to inspect NAACP literature and excise articles deemed too radical. A Draconian code of student discipline was rigorously enforced and justified with repeated statements that black adolescents were particularly sensuous beings who would abandon themselves to indulgence if they were not subjected to firm control.[7]

Special Jim Crow entertainments were arranged for benefactors of the university, one of many ways in which Fisk seemed to endorse the inevitability, if not the propriety, of segregation. The president of the board of trustees endorsed "complete separation" as "the only solution to the Negro problem" and urged contributions to Fisk and other colleges that were educating blacks to build and lead "a separate Negro society."[8]

All of this naturally outraged many alumni, who felt that Fisk had gone beyond the necessities of the situation and was giving all its thought and attention to the white South while forgetting the black community to which the university primarily belonged. These alumni kept Du Bois posted,

[7] W. E. B. Du Bois, "Fisk University" (1924 typescript), WEBD Papers; Du Bois, "Diuturni Silenti" (1924 typescript), WEBD Papers; George Streator and Charles Lewis, "A Brief History of the Fisk Trouble" (mimeographed pamphlet), Papers of Julius Rosenwald, University of Chicago (hereafter cited as Rosenwald Papers).

[8] *New Student*, 14 February 1925; Paul D. Cravath, quoted in *Cleveland Times*, 2 June 1923.

as did his daughter Yolande, a student at Fisk from 1920 to 1924, and in his inner heart the editor came to agree with those who gibed, "Yesterday Fisk had a president; tomorrow she will have a million dollars." Still, Du Bois hesitated and kept an uneasy silence because "Fisk was in the throes of gathering a desperately needed endowment and it seemed unfair and unwise to raise a disturbing voice at so critical a time." Yet he acknowledged that the cost of this silence was tremendous, and as soon as the success of Fisk's million-dollar endowment was assured Du Bois came forward "to utter a protest, a plea, and a warning."[9]

Du Bois issued his challenge on the Fisk campus, which he visited in June of 1924 to witness his daughter's graduation and to address the alumni in conjunction with the commencement exercises. He participated in the traditional baccalaureate procession and then, without giving any warning of his intentions and in the presence of President McKenzie and several of the trustees, Du Bois announced that he had "never known an institution whose alumni on the whole are more bitter and disgusted . . . than the alumni of Fisk University today." Du Bois confessed that, since he had "neither money nor monied friends" and since his thoughts were "distasteful to those from whom Fisk . . . was expecting financial aid," he had for some time "taken refuge in silence even when I sensed wrong." Yet he knew that "it would never do for purposes of expediency to lie to the world as Galileo once lied when he knew that his heart held the truth." So, he said, he came to Fisk "to criticize and to say openly and before your face what so many of your graduates are saying secretly and behind your back."[10]

Du Bois insisted that "of all the essentials that make an institution of learning, money is the least." Indeed, it was secured at too great a cost if, to command secular philan-

9 W. E. B. Du Bois, "Dilemma of the Negro," *American Mercury* 3 (October 1924): 183; Du Bois, "Fisk University"; Du Bois, "Fisk," *Crisis* 28 (October 1924): 251–252.
10 Du Bois, "Diuturni Silenti."

thropy, Fisk had to win the sympathy of southern whites by humiliating and repressing its students. Du Bois had taught for fifteen years in black boarding schools, and he knew the need for proper discipline, especially during the first generation after slavery. Yet he believed that the black students of the 1920s had come of age. They should no longer tolerate the sort of petty dictation that seemed natural when Fisk began and when the Negro was obviously in tutelage; the students of the 1920s were free men, not freedmen. "No one stands for proper discipline of youth stronger than I," he declared. But that "discipline does not mean the abolition of all rights to student meetings and organizations except under personal faculty supervision; . . . discipline does not demand the suppression of the student periodical, of the student athletic association and of practically every student activity. And, above all, discipline includes Freedom. Black folk want their children reared under all necessary restraints but they demand for them at the same time that equally necessary freedom and self-respect without which manhood and womanhood is impossible. Fisk University today denies this and denies it openly and frankly and bases its denial on 'race,' so far as it explains it at all."[11]

From the outset Du Bois recognized that his speech was "only the first gun of a long campaign" and that he would have to gather irrefutable evidence to support his contentions. Thus he wrote to faculty members, students, and graduates of Fisk, asking for statements that could be used to expose the McKenzie administration. Several of these correspondents replied, and the picture that emerged was one of kowtowing to the white South, repressing student initiative, and enforcing disciplinary rules that undermined self-respect and taught black students to regard themselves as inferiors who should uncomplainingly accept racial discrimination.[12]

[11] Ibid.; Du Bois, "Fisk," *Crisis* 29 (April 1925): 247–251.
[12] W. E. B. Du Bois to John Wesley Work, 26 June 1924, WEBD Papers.

A. D. Philippse reported, "The rules of Fisk are many and by far not all printed in the catalogue. It is forbidden for two students of opposite sex to meet each other without the presence and permission of the dean of women or of a teacher. A girl and boy could be sent home for walking together in broad daylight. . . . The honor system has not been installed at Fisk, because the consensus of opinion of the ruling classes is that the students *will* cheat."[13]

Abigail Jackson, a matron at Fisk and a niece of the university's first president, Erastus Milo Cravath, reported that the students were in "rebellion against petty authority in an aggravated form." She had been told more than once, she said, that she was "not a sufficiently strict chaperone" and that "young Negroes were much more susceptible to sex differences than white folks."[14]

Several coeds complained about the dress code which (at a time when the white girls across town at Peabody College were wearing flapper skirts and stockings made of the new synthetics) forbade dresses made of silk or satin and required high necks, long sleeves, black hats, and cotton stockings. One girl observed, "The girl part of the student body might have been able to get along with the orders forbidding them to talk with the boys on the campus or in college buildings. They might even have been peaceful, but not satisfied, with the order which forbade them dancing with boys, but when they are to keep on wearing cotton stockings and gingham dresses it was too much."[15]

Other correspondents objected to the glee clubs singing old-time spirituals—not because they objected to the music itself but because many whites and some blacks considered the spirituals "darkey songs" that symbolized dependent, hat-in-hand accommodation rather than manly self-asser-

[13] A. D. Philippse, quoted in *Fisk Herald* 33, no. 2 (1925).
[14] Abigail Jackson to W. E. B. Du Bois, 20 January 1925, WEBD Papers.
[15] Coeds to W. E. B. Du Bois, quoted in *Chicago Defender*, 28 February 1925.

tion. There were also specific complaints that President Mc-Kenzie on one occasion took the girls' glee club up a back alley and through the kitchen entrance into a Nashville rathskeller where they sang in a smoke-filled room for the white shriners of Al Menah Temple. And when the male glee club departed for England the university arranged a Jim Crow concert in Nashville. Bishop Isaiah Scott of the A. M. E. Church was insulted and refused service when he innocently tried to purchase a ticket at the white box office.[16]

Du Bois's correspondents characterized President Mc-Kenzie as an overbearing patriarch who suppressed critics, rewarded sycophants, and destroyed the confidence of black youth. One graduate recalled an incident where McKenzie "with his unspeakable egotism and czaristic spirit" expelled two students who criticized university policies and then tried to prevent their transferring to Howard University. One of McKenzie's secretaries reported that the president "had a horror of the honest, outspoken, fearless person. . . . He had no use for the criticism or the people who offered suggestions, and he could swallow more flattery than any man I ever knew." One student wrote that English majors were required to prepare five-thousand-word essays on "Reasons Why Dr. McKenzie Should Be Retained at Fisk University" and were promised that the best essays would be published in the *Fisk News*.[17]

Other students claimed that McKenzie had come to look upon his black charges with something of the disdain the world has long felt for charity scholars. The students were thought to have no right to complain, since they did not pay

[16] There is considerable correspondence on these matters in the WEBD Papers, and Du Bois discussed the subject in "Dilemma of the Negro," p. 184.

[17] G. M. McClellan to W. E. B. Du Bois, 10 March 1925, WEBD Papers; unidentified secretary, quoted in *Fisk Herald* 33, no. 2 (1925); Du Bois to N. B. Brascher, 17 November 1924, WEBD Papers.

their own way. It was said that the president's favorite expression was, "If you don't like Fisk University, get out!" James W. Ford, an alumnus and army veteran who later became prominent in radical politics, recalled that on one occasion he addressed a group of students on "the contributions of black men from all parts of the world to the [First World] War." Upon the completion of Ford's speech, President McKenzie told the students "that there was nothing to feel 'chesty' about; that we had contributed no more than anybody else."[18]

Testimony such as this reinforced Du Bois's belief that students were being "humiliated and insulted in order to attract the sympathy of Southern whites." He feared that the McKenzie administration was undermining initiative and self-respect and subtly persuading the elite of black youth to forsake egalitarian principles and adjust to the times. Thus Du Bois assiduously collected depositions and then proceeded to bring this information to the attention of the trustees, the alumni, and the larger public. He was convinced that the controversy at Fisk would serve as a model for all Negro colleges—"an example either for the Powers that furnish the Cash or for the awakening youth and their supporters"—and thus he concluded that "there has not been a fight for academic freedom in a long time that approaches this in importance." Of course it would be a "long, hard fight," but Du Bois assured his friends that "this fight is going on until McKenzie leaves Fisk." "We are not going to let up a single minute."[19]

Du Bois arranged several conferences at which various

[18] [Illegible] to A. D. Philippse, January 1925, WEBD Papers; James W. Ford to W. E. B. Du Bois, 20 February 1925, WEBD Papers.
[19] Du Bois, "Fisk," Crisis 28: 251–252; J. Covington Coleman to Du Bois, Crisis 30 (August 1925): 189; Du Bois to Freda Kirchway, 20 February 1925, WEBD Papers; Du Bois to J. D. Fowler, 22 October 1924, WEBD Papers; Du Bois to George W. Streator, 15 September 1924, WEBD Papers; Du Bois to J. T. Phillips, 4 March 1925, WEBD Papers.

professors and students informed members of the board of trustees of their objections to the McKenzie administration. Then in the fall of 1924 Du Bois went on a lecture tour and made a point of speaking to Fisk alumni clubs where, as one newspaper put it, he produced "documentary evidence to support his contention that Fayette Avery McKenzie . . . should be removed from his position." In January 1925 Du Bois invited about 150 alumni to a special conference in New York. There they established a new alumni association and resurrected the *Fisk Herald* to publish evidence that incriminated or embarrassed McKenzie. Du Bois served as editor of this *Herald* and he promised, "Unless McKenzie is removed from Fisk, I intend to publish every word of evidence I hold to prove he is unfit and a detriment to the cause of higher education for our race." The first issue reprinted the fighting words of Du Bois's baccalaureate address, and the second contained a generous sample of the testimony Du Bois had collected and an editorial proclaiming, "Fisk University has fallen on evil days; it has gotten money and lost the Spirit. . . . This great institution must be rescued or it will die."[20]

The controversy at Fisk reveals a good deal about the nature of Du Bois's leadership. It was the dynamic force of his words—in this case editorials for the *Crisis* and the *Fisk Herald*, articles for the *American Mercury* and *Nation*, speeches to the alumni, and a voluminous correspondence— that catapulted Du Bois to the fore as the leader of a popular movement. Certainly he is almost unique among scholars, a man who became a leader by impressing his personal-

[20] W. E. B. Du Bois to W. N. DeBerry, 23 June 1924, WEBD Papers; Du Bois to Hollingsworth Wood, 24 July, 15 November 1924, WEBD Papers; Du Bois to Paul Cravath, 18 September 1924, WEBD Papers; Du Bois to Hollingsworth Wood and William Baldwin, 13 November 1924, WEBD Papers; *Chicago Defender*, 24 January 1925; Du Bois to F. A. Steward, 17 December 1924, WEBD Papers; Du Bois to Alumni, 27 January 1925, WEBD Papers; *Fisk Herald* 33, no. 1 (1925).

ity upon others by means of the written word. But although it is this blending of literary gifts with a strenuous will that is the hallmark of Du Bois's genius, the devoted attention to detail which he demonstrated in the campaign to oust McKenzie calls into question the generally accepted view that he lacked the temperament and administrative ability to execute plans but was merely a "propagandist who stirred up controversies . . . and formulated theoretical blueprints which other men were to bring into actuality."[21]

At Fisk, Du Bois was at once provocateur and administrator, but his strategy focused on journalistic exposure. Specific examples of injustice were publicized in the hope that this would arouse decent men to reform. "Our general plans include simply publicity," he confided, "facts and statements to lay before the Trustees; facts and statements to lay before the alumni and before the public. I think publicity and publicity alone will in the end win."[22]

This publicity did not act in a vacuum, and it was effective largely because it so enraged McKenzie that the president of Fisk was unable to compromise. McKenzie was a stickler for discipline, a martinet who was never inclined to make concessions. The criticism from Du Bois—a certified outside agitator—steeled the president's always strong will and reinforced his self-righteousness to the point that he became, in effect, immobilized. McKenzie claimed that Du Bois's baccalaureate address was characterized by "sarcasm and sneering," that Fisk was "under attack from bolshevistic, if not anarchistic elements of society." He was particularly upset by Du Bois's decision to do battle in public "instead of going like a man to the president and stating his case." One member of the faculty wrote confidentially that after Du Bois's speech there was "a very apparent stiffening

[21] Elliott M. Rudwick, *W. E. B. Du Bois: Propagandist of the Negro Protest* (Philadelphia: University of Pennsylvania Press, 1960), p. 165.

[22] W. E. B. Du Bois to Abigail Jackson, 22 October 1924, WEBD Papers.

41

of his [McKenzie's] attitude." This was also true of trustees such as Robert McMurdy, who felt that "the whole matter might have been argued out and diplomatized originally, but the virulence of Du Bois . . . [has] rendered it absolutely impossible to deal with conditions in that way."[23]

McKenzie soon convinced himself that there was an unspoken, hidden issue far more important than the objections to his disciplinary policies and fund-raising tactics. He believed that behind the grave charges "that we are selling our principles for money and thereby meeting the desires of capitalism to control Negro education" lurked the desire "to get rid of white participation in Negro education, not [only] at Fisk but in all similar institutions." "Nothing is so popular with colored audiences as denunciation of whites and nothing so unpopular as its absence," he claimed. To one of the trustees McKenzie confided that "it is quite obvious that every type of critic of white people . . . are combined at the moment in an attempt to get their several ends by downing me."[24]

The real objection of the critics, according to McKenzie, was not to his policies but to the principle of interracial cooperation on which Fisk had been founded. This was a precious principle, and one that had to be maintained if black colleges were to enjoy the financial support that was essential for the survival of Negro education. Thus McKenzie concluded, "My personality and my defects are altogether negligible now in the great issues that have been forced to the front." Although staying at Fisk had become

[23] Fayette McKenzie to Paul Cravath, 1924, McKenzie Papers; Fayette McKenzie to Everett O. Fisk, 11 May 1925, McKenzie Papers; Mrs. Fayette McKenzie to Thomas Jesse Jones, 19 October 1924, McKenzie Papers; [Illegible] to A. D. Philippse (n. d.), WEBD Papers; Robert McMurdy to Paul Cravath, 16 April 1925, McKenzie Papers.

[24] Fayette McKenzie, quoted in *Nashville Banner*, 5 February, 8 February 1925; McKenzie to Cravath, 1924; McKenzie to Jones, 19 February 1925, McKenzie Papers.

a "very difficult thing for me and my family," he believed that "remaining here longer [is] the only solution to the very critical problem now facing Fisk University and perhaps facing all college education for Negroes."[25] Although Du Bois definitely wanted to establish Negro control over colleges for Negroes, and even developed a plan whereby Fisk's black alumni eventually would elect a majority of the trustees, he never suggested that whites should have no voice at Fisk. He did believe that "the time has come when the claims of colored men for the presidency of our Negro schools should be considered and considered on the same terms as the claims of white men." He insisted, however, that "there are a number of white men . . . who would make excellent presidents." Moreover, the faculty should remain racially mixed: "Colored teachers alone will intensify racial cleavage; white teachers alone would be drawing the color line in a fatal and all too obvious place."[26]

Of course faculty members should have faith in their black students and be able to work sympathetically *with* as well as *for* Negroes. The evolution of southern race relations had made such cooperation increasingly difficult, but Du Bois never doubted that some whites could overcome the difficulties of ordinary social intercourse and meet with blacks as men. He insisted that it was false to assert, as one trustee did, that the protest at Fisk aimed at "the elimination of white people from colored schools." "I do not care whether the next president of Fisk University is black, white, or green," Du Bois wrote. "I have absolutely no interest in his race or color. I believe that President McKenzie

[25] Fayette McKenzie to W. W. Boyd, 13 May 1925, McKenzie Papers; McKenzie to Jones, 19 February 1925.
[26] W. E. B. Du Bois, Memorandum on representation of Fisk Alumni on the Board of Trustees, 10 August 1925, WEBD Papers; Du Bois, "Fisk," *Crisis* 29: 247–251; Du Bois, "Fisk," *Crisis* 28: 251–252.

43

is not the proper man for the place not because he is white but because he is a bad president."[27]

There were some people at Fisk who placed more emphasis on color than Du Bois, and the question of race assumed considerable importance in some of the other black college rebellions of the 1920s, especially at Howard University. It seems in retrospect, however, that McKenzie exaggerated the racialist factor in the hope that this would prompt an unqualified endorsement from the board of trustees. His strict discipline had been under attack for some time, and for more than two years he had asked the trustees to endorse again the Fisk Code of Discipline and to give him their full support in its enforcement. Such an endorsement was prepared, but one black member of the executive committee, W. N. DeBerry, refused to sign it, and others had reservations. Finally an unsigned copy of the statement was sent to the president, but, as Mrs. McKenzie confided, "such delayed endorsement meant very little."[28]

In the meantime McKenzie learned that some trustees were conferring with Du Bois and that at least two, Hollingsworth Wood and William Baldwin, had expressed reservations about McKenzie's policies. This was particularly disturbing, for McKenzie knew that "so long as alumni and students and faithless employees suspected and hoped for trustee support as against me, they would maintain and develop their campaign." Under the circumstances, he may have welcomed a polarizing confrontation that would force the trustees to take an unequivocal position. As Mrs. McKenzie explained to a sympathetic trustee: "Now to my point: . . . at the end of this . . . year either we will leave Fisk or Mr. McKenzie will have the unqualified unanimous endorsement at all times of the board of trust."[29]

[27] Thomas Jesse Jones to Fayette McKenzie, 1 May 1925, McKenzie Papers; Du Bois to G. Victor Cools, 28 April 1925, WEBD Papers.

[28] Mrs. Fayette McKenzie to Thomas Jesse Jones, 19 October 1924, McKenzie Papers.

[29] McKenzie to Jones, 19 February 1925.

III

When the trustees traveled to Nashville for their annual meeting in November 1924, they witnessed what was then an unusual sight: a demonstration by about one hundred students chanting "Away with the czar!" and "Down with the tyrant!" Lists of grievances were posted on doors and bulletin boards, protesting against the suppression of the student newspaper and council, the close faculty supervision of dramatics, debating, and the literary clubs, the discontinuance of intercollegiate baseball and track, and the decline of football to the point where Fisk had recently fallen to Tuskegee by a score of sixty-seven to zero. Seven students met with the trustees and asked for "greater freedom" and specifically for a student council and newspaper, the reorganization of athletics, the substitution of an honor system for the Fisk Code of Discipline, and the establishment of fraternities and sororities. The demands were far from radical, for, the *New York Age* observed, "Most of the privileges asked for are now allowed in the leading colleges of the country." This, indeed, was the bone of contention, for the students at Fisk were demanding the same freedom and opportunity that was offered whites across town at Vanderbilt where, the student *Hustler* noted, "We have these things, even though we may misuse them sometimes. We don't have to fight for student council, publications, honor system, athletics, fraternities."[30]

Paul Cravath, the president of the board of trustees, said he was "deeply impressed and pleased with the fair and manly way in which the students conducted their case." He

[30] *East Tennessee News*, 20 November 1924; *Chicago Whip*, 29 November 1924; *Philadelphia Tribune*, 6 December 1924; Streator and Lewis, "Brief History"; Albon Holsey, Memorandum to Mr. Graves, 7 April 1925, Rosenwald Papers; Minutes of the Meeting of the Fisk Board of Trustees, 17 November 1924 (copy), Papers of Robert Russa Moton, Tuskegee Institute (hereafter cited as Moton Papers); *New York Age*, 28 February 1925; handwritten statement, dated 26 February 1925, WEBD Papers.

characterized their complaints and proposals as "constructive criticisms." The students were promised that there would be no reprisals against those who spoke to the trustees, and there was general agreement that further trouble could be avoided by modifying some of the unpopular policies. To this end the trustees suggested that a faculty-student committee be established to negotiate differences.[31]

President McKenzie was willing to consider the possibility of a student council and an athletic association and did authorize slight changes in the girls' dress code (allowing them to wear any shape hat as long as it was black). But he was altogether opposed to fraternities and to permitting students to administer a more relaxed code of discipline. He insisted on the prohibition of smoking and dancing, refused to allow male and female students to walk together except at specific hours and then only with chaperones present, and demanded that the basic regimen of Fisk be maintained —from compulsory attendance at 6:30 a.m. breakfast to lights out at 10 p.m.[32]

Fisk had always insisted on its "right to be of its own special type," with "supervision and restraints approaching the puritanic," and McKenzie refused to modify this policy "regardless of outside views and outside practices" and certainly not at a time when Du Bois had issued a challenge to school authority. The central question, as McKenzie saw it, was, "Can the university maintain its integrity and its authority, or must it function under the direction or by the consent of a group of students working under pressure from outside?" When he traveled to New York to meet with the trustees in January 1925, McKenzie was not inclined toward

[31] Minutes of Fisk Board of Trustees, 17 November 1924; George Streator to A. D. Philippse (n.d.), WEBD Papers; statement of Charles Lewis, quoted in *Nashville Banner*, 10 February 1925; Du Bois, "Fisk," *Crisis* 29: 247–251.

[32] Dean of women to parents of female students, 26 December 1924, WEBD Papers.

compromise. The fact that other colleges did not set hours for meals, sleep, recitation, and study, and did not closely supervise social relationships was, he insisted, "no necessary argument against the Fisk policy." Upon returning to Nashville from his meeting with the trustees, McKenzie complacently stated that "a complete ignoring of the charges made against the administration will be the policy of the Board of Trustees of Fisk University." To make certain that everyone understood the situation the president of Fisk then announced a new regulation forbidding conversations between male and female students. McKenzie prided himself on being, in his words, "as reactionary as the Ten Commandments."[33]

Thus the faculty-student committee reached stalemate, and the students became impatient. Twice during the first week of December 1924 impromptu after-curfew demonstrations were held, with students pounding on garbage cans and cheering for Du Bois. One undergraduate wrote to the president that student dissatisfaction was widespread since Fisk was, he pointed out, the only school that held strictly to the ideals of an earlier generation. Another student complained that "the McKenzie administration will do nothing more than it has already. The few changes made were for no other purpose than to quiet the students. There hasn't been any change in the spirit of the place. The atmosphere is the same. The only modifications don't amount to a hill of beans when you come to think about it."[34]

The controversy suddenly came to a head when the students rose in wrath on February 4, 1925. More than one hundred men of Livingstone Hall ignored the 10 p.m. cur-

[33] Fayette McKenzie, quoted in *Nashville Banner*, 5 February, 8 February, 9 February 1925; McKenzie, *President's Report, 1919–1920;* McKenzie, quoted in *East Tennessee News*, 26 March 1925; McKenzie, quoted in W. E. B. Du Bois, "Fisk," *Crisis* 29: 247–251.

[34] *Philadelphia Tribune*, 6 December 1924; Otis H. Boatright to Fayette McKenzie, 23 June 1924, McKenzie Papers; George Streator to A. D. Philippse, 20 December 1924, WEBD Papers.

few and instead sang, yelled, smashed windows, and told the faculty that it would not be safe for any authorities to come out and that they were "going to keep up this sort of thing until the President's hair was white." According to the dean of women, "The disorderly students overturned chapel seats, broke windows, . . . all the while keeping up a steady shouting of 'Du Bois!' 'Du Bois!' and 'Before I'll be a slave, I'll be buried in my grave.' " At midnight, after President McKenzie called on the civil authorities to quell the disturbance, fifty Nashville policemen were dispatched to the campus. Fortunately there was little violence, probably because the demonstrators had disbanded and retired to their dormitory rooms before the police arrived. McKenzie then gave the officer in charge the names of seven students who were to be arrested and charged with inciting to riot. The police escorted the rest of the students to the president's office, where they were required either to sign a document denouncing the protest or to withdraw from the university and leave the campus.[35]

President McKenzie no doubt hoped that his firm action would silence critics and force the trustees to rally unequivocally to his support, but neither expectation was realized. Instead, the decision to call white police to a black campus infuriated most Negroes. Two graduates of the university, Charles W. Wesley and J. Alston Atkins, complained that calling the police "was as froth with danger as striking a match near a barrel of powder." A. L. Jackson of the Chicago Urban League dismissed the resort to police power as a "stupid move." "No man, white or black, who knows anything about the South and southern attitudes could help but know that such a move would bring . . . trouble and lots of it," Jackson observed. "Better to have a few

[35] There was extensive coverage of the disturbance in the major Negro weeklies and in the *Nashville Banner* and the *Nashville Tennessean*. The quotation is from the dean of women, Dora Scriber, to Alumni, 14 February 1925, WEBD Papers.

broken window glasses than broken heads at the hands of bullying police officials."[36] The *Chicago Defender* condemned the president of Fisk in a sardonic editorial entitled, "McKenzie, You're Through." "You turned loose the Nashville police . . . You called the Black Mariah—the whistle blew and the clang of the bell was heard in the city streets! Mac, you went crazy!"[37] NAACP Field Secretary William Pickens noted, "When [McKenzie] called in those cops he could not have done better to alienate the regard of colored people, even if he had first held a three-day conference on the subject to find the best ways and means to make himself disliked."[38]

The black community of Nashville was particularly alarmed by the possibility of white violence. During the year 1924 a local black minister had been killed by a police officer, a black businessman was shot in his place of business by a white saloonkeeper who went unpunished, two black women were assaulted on streetcars by unchallenged white men, and a Negro youth was taken from the county hospital by a band of white men and lynched. Local blacks were understandably aroused by McKenzie's resort to the police. On the day following the disturbance at Fisk more than 2,500 black citizens of Nashville gathered at St. John's A. M. E. Church and condemned McKenzie's inability "to cope with the situation and not resort to civil authority"; they formally declared that his "usefulness as president of Fisk is at an end."[39]

[36] Charles W. Wesley and J. Alston Atkins to Paul Cravath, 16 April 1925, WEBD Papers; A. L. Jackson, "The Onlooker," *Chicago Defender*, 21 February 1925.

[37] *Chicago Defender*, 14 February 1925.

[38] William Pickens, quoted in *East Tennessee News*, 26 March 1925.

[39] Lester C. Lamon, "The Black Community in Nashville and the Fisk University Student Strike of 1924–1925," *Journal of Southern History*, 40 (May 1974): 236; *Nashville Tennessean*, 6 February 1925; *Nashville Banner*, 10 February 1925.

The opposition to McKenzie increased further when, under cross-examination at the trial of the arrested students, the president admitted that he "had no actual proof that they were in the disturbance," but simply suspected "that they might be behind this or anything of its nature." The seven students identified by McKenzie were the same seven who had met with the trustees in November, but two had been away from the campus on the night of the disturbance. McKenzie quickly realized his mistake and asked that the incitement charges be dismissed. The boys were still found guilty of disorderly conduct and given suspended $50 fines, but when the defense counsel moved for an appeal and threatened to sue McKenzie for malicious prosecution, a special notarized agreement was made whereby the court annulled the convictions for disorderly conduct and the university agreed to grant the students honorable dismissals and to raise no objections to their transferring to other colleges."[40]

[40] The relevant portion of the court transcript was published in the *New York Age*, 7 March 1925. Notarized statements signed by Luetta McMurtry (Notary Public), Fayette McKenzie, and seven Fisk students, 9 February, 10 February 1925, WEBD Papers. It should be noted that President McKenzie did not live up to the spirit of his notarized promise not to place "any objection or impediment in the way of the matriculation [of suspended students] in any other educational institution." While the students were given credit for their academic work at Fisk, their transcripts did not indicate whether or not they had been honorably dismissed; instead each transcript forwarded to Howard University contained a statement to the effect that the student "withdrew during student walk-out." It was the standard policy at Howard and most other universities to accept only those transfer students who had been honorably dismissed from their previous college. McKenzie would grant honorable dismissals only to students who stated that they were not in sympathy with the strike, even though they withdrew from Fisk at that time. The result was that very few of the student rebels were able to transfer to other universities. W. E. B. Du Bois viewed this as another example of the lengths to which McKenzie would go to make black students subservient. He charged that "the authorities

The prosecution of a few student leaders aroused the Fisk student body. On the day after the disturbance, the students met in the chapel, protested against singling out a few leaders for punishment, declared that all students were in the controversy together, and voted to go on strike until all were given the same punishment. The boycott of classes remained in force for ten weeks and was remarkably effective. Many students left Nashville, and a large number of seniors applied *en masse* for transfer admission to Howard University.[41]

The support given by members of the local black community undoubtedly contributed to the effectiveness of the student strike. In a significant display of solidarity across generational lines, the Negro Board of Trade, composed of Nashville's leading black businessmen, established a conciliation committee that tried to persuade McKenzie to grant the students' demands. When this effort failed several black businessmen rallied to the support of the rebellious students. Two former presidents of the Fisk Alumni Association, T. Clay Moore and Dr. J. T. Phillips, coordinated a program to house the striking students in black Nashville and provided small loans for those who were destitute. When McKenzie asked local merchants not to cash money orders sent by parents to cover the travel expenses of students who wished to leave Nashville, Meredith G. Ferguson, a bookkeeper at the black-owned Citizen Savings Bank and Trust Company, used his own savings and cashed the

---

of Fisk University have not only deliberately perjured themselves, but are seeking to ruin the careers of every student who dares to leave the institution." There are many documents on this topic in the WEBD Papers. McKenzie's rejoinder, a typescript entitled "Reply to Unfortunate Mis-Statements," is available in the Rosenwald Papers.

[41] *Nashville Banner*, 6 February, 9 February 1925; *Nashville Tennessean*, 7 February, 10 February 1925; Streator and Lewis, "Brief History"; *Additional Letters from Parents of Fisk Students* (1925 pamphlet), Moton Papers.

students' checks. The Negro Board of Trade sponsored an open meeting which, after hearing statements from student leaders, local businessmen, and prominent alumni, condemned McKenzie for turning a deaf ear to the students' "reasonable and practicable" requests.[42]

The students were no doubt encouraged by additional support from Fisk alumni and friends throughout the country. A delegation of representatives from the Chicago Fisk Club traveled to Nashville and complained that Fisk's disciplinary policies indicated that the McKenzie administration was out of sympathy with the aspirations of the race and was trying to persuade Negroes "to adjust . . . to the times rather than to the principles of life." The Louisville Fisk Club chastised President McKenzie for "stubbornly and persistently . . . refusing to counsel with alumni and friends of the institution," and the New York Fisk Club formally called for McKenzie's resignation. Other alumni groups, such as the Hampton Alumni Club of New York, also endorsed the cause of the Fisk students who, it was claimed, had been "penalized for nothing less than trying to be men and women holding the same ideals and measured by civilization's best standards." The Student Council at Howard University sent a particularly gratifying message of sympathy to the brothers and sisters at Fisk.[43]

While the black community generally supported the students, the great majority of white Nashvillians rallied to the support of President McKenzie. The chamber of commerce formally noted that "Dr. McKenzie has done much to cement the good feeling between the white and colored races in Nashville and the South. He has understood the needs of both . . . and at no time in the history of Nashville

[42] *Nashville Tennessean*, 6 February, 7 February, 10 February, 11 February 1925; *Nashville Banner*, 9 February, 10 February 1925; Lamon, "The Black Community in Nashville," p. 241.

[43] Resolutions and statemenst of the Chicago Fisk Club, 13 February, 17 February 1925, WEBD Papers; *New York Age*, 14 February, 14 March 1925; *Baltimore Afro-American*, 7 February 1925.

has a better feeling existed than during the presidency of Dr. McKenzie at Fisk."[44]

Nashville's major white newspapers endorsed the "swift and effective measures that [McKenzie] took to restore order," and warned blacks that "if such demonstrations are repeated and such agitators as Du Bois are encouraged, then it may be safely predicted that the benefactors of the institution will question the wisdom of continuing that support which has made expansion possible." Claiming that the student strike was a "mutiny and a disgrace," the *Nashville Banner* praised McKenzie because "he is not radical in his teachings or . . . to the point of giving the youth under his direction false instructions as to their demanded *equality of rights* in all respects or to directing their steps along dangerous paths to a goal they can never attain."[45]

Elated by this praise, President McKenzie confided to one trustee that he had never before known such universal acclaim: "Everywhere I receive very strong commendation. At the Kiwanis Club, they gave me practically an ovation when I went there for the usual Friday dinner. The Exchange Club asked me to be their guest the following Tuesday and I declined because of the danger of too much applause. The following week they renewed the invitation and said it was to be a very quiet suggestion of their appreciation of me and that I would not be asked to speak. But when I was introduced from the far corner of the table, everybody in the room rose to his feet and a great many yelled as well as a great many cheered with their hands clapping. Somehow I feel that never before in the United States has a white man in our work had such a hold upon a city as I now have on Nashville."[46]

Yet it was generally understood that this influence did not

[44] Resolution of the Nashville Chamber of Commerce, 12 June 1925, McKenzie Papers.

[45] *Nashville Tennessean*, 6 February 1925; *Nashville Banner*, 7 February 1925.

[46] McKenzie to Jones, 19 February 1925.

extend beyond white Nashville; the members of the Hawaiian Club took the precaution of asking their black waiters to leave the dining room during McKenzie's address.[47] While basking in the praise of white Nashville, McKenzie worked diligently to discredit his critics. Rumors were circulated to the effect that dissident students were responsible for a small fire on the Fisk campus, although the private correspondence of student leaders makes it clear that they knew nothing of the origin of the blaze. It was also reported in the press, again without foundation, that protesting students had assaulted Dr. W. F. Waters, an outspoken supporter of the administration. Other more accurate reports noted that some students were boycotting classes not in protest against McKenzie's policies but to avoid the intimidation and ostracism of their fellows. McKenzie insisted that the rebellious students had no legitimate grievances but had been duped by "outside influences" with ulterior purposes, especially Du Bois who, it was insinuated, desired the presidency of Fisk.[48]

This attribution of the controversy to the untoward influence Du Bois exercised over impressionable youth became the refrain of the university's official explanations. Thus dean of women Dora Scriber explained that while "the general setting of the situation here is the condition of

[47] *Chicago Defender*, 14 February 1925.
[48] George Streator to Dr. Boutte, 7 March 1925, WEBD Papers; Streator to W. E. B. Du Bois, 31 March 1925, WEBD Papers; *Pittsburgh Courier*, 14 March 1925; *Baltimore Afro-American*, 28 March 1925; *Nashville Tennessean*, 8 February 1925; *Nashville Banner*, 9 February 1925; *Nashville Globe*, 13 February 1925; statements of Fayette McKenzie, quoted in *Nashville Banner*, 5 February, 6 February 1925. In a private communication McKenzie wrote, "The *Crisis* Editor in his speech in June made himself liable to the law of incitement to riot. . . . Trouble can be secured almost anywhere in the world, particularly young people can be stirred with considerable ease by those willing to preach rebellion, especially when they can link rebellion up with large prejudicial forces." McKenzie, "Comments on April Editorial in *Crisis*" (typescript), Rosenwald Papers.

54

the world since the beginning of the World War and the spirit of present-day youth, impatient of all guidance, . . . the more immediate setting is Dr. Du Bois's address to the alumni at commencement last June, and his agitation all this school year which inflamed a small group of students to try to weld the whole body of students into united opposition to the administration." J. C. Napier, a black attorney and a member of Fisk's board of trustees, believed Du Bois had "a personal grievance . . . [and] a selfish axe to grind." Mrs. Arch Trawick, a white trustee, added, "It was easy for [Du Bois] to inflame young, impressionable students, to make them feel sorry for themselves, and to rouse them to a course of violence and lawlessness."[49]

McKenzie also took special pains to see that the students' parents received newspaper clippings slanted toward the administration's version of the controversy. During February and March several members of the faculty devoted part of their time to this publicity campaign, and it is clear that these efforts had considerable influence. More than a hundred parents, including those of two of the arrested students, wrote letters endorsing the administration and stressing the importance of authority, discipline, and democratic simplicity. One father contended that "no student has got any business to make any demonstration against the president." Another condemned the "irresponsible and youthful subordinates [who rose] up against authority, however much merit may seem to be in their contentions."[50]

Several parents endorsed Fisk's "puritanical and straightlaced notions." Dr. and Mrs. A. W. Davis assured McKenzie

[49] Scriber to Alumni, 14 February 1925; statement of J. C. Napier, quoted in *Nashville Banner*, 5 February 1925; Mrs. Arch Trawick to W. C. Graves, 12 March 1925, Rosenwald Papers.

[50] The letters in this and the next two paragraphs were collected by ~~ident~~ McKenzie and published as two pamphlets, *Letters and ~~ams~~ from Parents* and *Additional Letters from Parents of Fisk ~~. A~~ copy of the first is available in the Fisk Archives and a ~~e~~ second is available in the Moton Papers.

55

that "the rules and regulations at Fisk are entirely satisfactory to us, and we think to all parents who are striving to bring their daughters up as pure Christian young women." Mr. and Mrs. Ernest W. Roberts allowed their daughter to attend Fisk only because the disciplinary code assured them that they "were sending her away from our home and fireside into another Christian home where she would be as safe and secure as here." Similarly, Dr. W. W. Sumlin of Nashville, who visited the campus during the strike and was scandalized to see coeds wearing flapper skirts "split almost to their waists exposing their nakedness," promised his support for the president "as long as you and Fisk University stand against smoking, gaming, and debauchery of the young men and against spectacular and suggestive dress and actions in the young ladies."

Several parents supported the administration's prohibition of Greek letter fraternities because, as S. W. Jefferson put it, "We do not need any more snobbishness and caste systems among us." Others endorsed the requirement that the girls wear uniforms, since "hundreds of parents are striving to educate their girls and if they (the girls) are allowed to be extravagant and irresponsible, many parents cannot keep them there. The few who are able to dress in the latest and most expensive styles will simply break down the fundamental principles for which the school has always stood."

To counteract the administration's propaganda, the students organized an effective publicity campaign of their own, emphasizing that the protest was nonviolent and aimed at the redress of specific grievances: "There was no riot," but only "a demonstration against what we believe to be the tyrannical rules of the present administration"; and they deplored "the fact that the little demonstration . . . was mistaken for riot and insurrection." Their goals were not "to smoke, dance, or to keep late hours," as the administration suggested, but to have a student government association, the reorganization of athletics, the establishment of fraternities and sororities, and a revision of minor rules and regulations.[51]

While emphasizing their specific grievances and demands, the students emphatically rejected contentions that their protest was prompted by outside agitation. The claim that Du Bois was responsible for the controversy was particularly annoying, for the students were convinced that it was they who, "after much persuasion, had enlisted [Du Bois] on our side." They naturally resented the implication that they were immature, excitable children. It was not outside agitation but objective conditions at the university that prompted the rebellion, one student declared. Another pointed out that "blaming the whole thing on the New York Fisk Club is creating among southern whites a renewed hatred of any type of Negro except the hat-in-hand type."[52]

Du Bois admitted both publicly and privately that he knew nothing of the student uprising until he saw the press dispatches. He confessed, "If I had been asked I should have advised against the 'riot' because I doubted the stamina of the students to carry it through." George Streator and Charles Lewis, the most vocal student leaders, confided that they had begun to organize the opposition to McKenzie as early as 1922. But even Streator was away from the campus on the night of the disturbance at Livingstone Hall, a very strong indication that the uprising was spontaneous.[53]

Above all, the students denied charges that their primary goal was to force whites out of Negro education. The per-

[51] Statement of George Streator, Ernest Crossley, and F. J. Anderson, Jr., quoted in *Nashville Banner*, 5 February 1925; "Fisk Students to Citizens of Nashville," *Nashville Banner*, 7 February 1925; Albon Holsey, Memorandum for Mr. Graves (n.d.), Rosenwald Papers.

[52] Statement of unidentified Fisk students, *Nashville Banner*, 10 February 1925; Miriam Garrott Hall to Fayette McKenzie, 3 March 1925, WEBD Papers; George Streator to Mr. and Mrs. Herbert Miller, 9 March 1925, WEBD Papers.

[53] W. E. B. Du Bois to Streator, 13 March 1925, WEBD Papers; Du Bois, "Fisk," *Crisis* 29: 247–251; Streator to Boutte, 7 March 1925.

centage of blacks on the Fisk faculty had increased from 3 percent in the 1890s to 37 percent in the mid-1920s, but Streator insisted that the students wanted neither "a Negro president nor a white president, but a President." To combat what they called "exaggerated rumors of what [we] are asking and standing for," the striking students in mass meeting formally declared "that this is not a race issue. We are not asking for a colored faculty, but believe that the present arrangement is wisest for the best interests of the institution."[54]

Similarly, when the trustees distributed a questionnaire to the alumni they learned that most graduates believed that Fisk should "continue its tradition of a white President and a mixed Negro and white faculty." Du Bois contended that the race issue was a "red herring" and part of an "extraordinary effort . . . to divert attention from the main issue." The students' pamphlet, "A Brief History of the Fisk Trouble," suggested that "the race issue was injected by Dr. McKenzie and by men and women more or less intimately connected with the Administration." The Fisk controversy did elicit elements of race pride and confidence that there were a number of Negroes who were capable of presiding over the institution, but the evidence will not support the judgment that "every undergraduate on the campus" knew that race was the central issue in the dispute.[55]

[54] James M. McPherson, "White Liberals and Black Power in Negro Education, 1865–1915," *American Historical Review* 75 (June 1970): 1380; Arthur J. Klein, *Survey of Negro Colleges and Universities* (U. S. Department of Interior, Bureau of Education Bulletin 7, 1928), pp. 739–742; George Streator, quoted in *Nashville Banner*, 10 February 1925; "Fisk Students to Citizens of Nashville," *Nashville Banner*, 7 February 1925.

[55] Paul Cravath, letter to the editor of the *New York Times*, 25 February 1926; W. E. B. Du Bois, "The Fight at Fisk" (typescript), WEBD Papers; Du Bois to Marguerite J. Tillar, 24 February 1925, WEBD Papers; Streator and Lewis, "Brief History"; Robert H. Brisbane, *The Black Vanguard* (Valley Forge, Pa.: Judson Press, 1970), p. 105.

In addition to clarifying their position on the specific issues, the students cultivated personal contacts that could help them in the struggle against McKenzie. Immediately after the February demonstration, they sent telegrams to the trustees, requesting "a fair and impartial investigation." Their strike was not "disloyalty to the institution, but a protest against the autocratic methods of President McKenzie," and especially his "action in summarily arousing innocent students from sleep and rushing them off to jail and holding them there until the hour of trial." Charles Lewis and E. N. Anderson were very active in presenting the students' case to various organizations in Nashville, and Streator spent six weeks without a job (though he was receiving a subsistence stipend from Du Bois) "working on pro-McKenzie, anti-Du Bois alumni who come here to investigate." He had spoken to "fully four thousand people," had written 376 letters and 40 telegrams, and in this way had "tried to counteract . . . McKenzie's pamphlets, letters and lies." Du Bois was doing the same thing at the national level, coordinating the protests of various alumni clubs, providing inside information for newspapers and magazines, and writing for the April *Crisis* an editorial on "Fisk" that was a masterpiece of polemical literature.[56]

Although effective public relations was a big help, the protest movement succeeded primarily because the students themselves maintained extraordinary solidarity and dedication to the boycott of classes. Estimates of the number of striking students are not altogether reliable, since the administration exaggerated the number attending class while student leaders stressed the number who had walked out. Yet even the administration acknowledged that half of

[56] E. N. Anderson, A. W. Hoursey, W. H. Stepp, and C. Warner Lawson telegram to Paul Cravath, quoted in *Nashville Banner*, 7 February 1925; *New York Age*, 7 March 1925; W. E. B. Du Bois telegram to F. A. Steward, 17 February 1925, WEBD Papers; George Streator to Du Bois, 17 March 1925, WEBD Papers; Du Bois, "Fisk," *Crisis* 29: 247–251.

the three hundred college students were still boycotting classes in mid-March, five weeks after the strike began. Student leader Streator boasted in a confidential letter, "We don't need to do anything except tell the students: 'Boycott this, or boycott that,' and believe me they do it to a finish!"[57]

Some students were attending classes, but according to Streator most of these were "showing their hostility to McKenzie by a very thorough program of noncooperation with faculty and President. The campus is lifeless. If this spirit pervades the group as it shows signs of doing, it will be as effective as another walkout."[58]

President McKenzie had promised that Fisk would continue with "classes as usual, even if the number of students at Fisk University gets as low as ten." He suggested, indeed, that perhaps the strike was "the best thing that ever happened to Fisk," since "a small body of loyal students will be far happier, and they will secure a much finer education than could be secured by a larger body of disaffected students."[59]

Yet most trustees knew it would be impossible to operate a college without students. To be sure, the trustees released a formal statement declaring that they were "squarely and unanimously behind Dr. F. A. McKenzie in the present crisis at Fisk." But Hollingsworth Wood, the white vice-president of the board who was sent to Nashville, believed that most of the students' demands were reasonable and that McKenzie's reliance on the police betrayed an autocratic personality and, more significantly, a lack of sympathy for the students. After meeting with Wood, McKenzie confided to a close friend, "We gave very different interpretations, inasmuch as he [Wood] felt that the situation might

[57] *Additional Letters from Parents of Fisk Students.* Streator to Philippse (n.d.).

[58] Streator to Boutte, 7 March 1925.

[59] Fayette McKenzie, quoted in *Nashville Banner*, 6 February, 9 February 1925; McKenzie, quoted in *Baltimore Afro-American*, 14 February 1925.

have been saved if I had moved more rapidly in granting concessions to the students and I argued that the situation was one which could not have been saved in any such way, that the fundamental error had been on the part of the trustees that they had not in some way compelled the students and the alumni to know that they would not tolerate the methods and machinations of outsiders and of students against the discipline and authority of the institution."[60]

There were trustees who agreed with McKenzie on this point, but evidently the majority sided with Wood, for they established a Greater Fisk Committee to inquire into the whole controversy and suggest possible remedies. McKenzie thoroughly opposed this move, since he knew that the disaffected students and alumni would continue their opposition if the trustees did anything other than "to declare all the criticism brought against the administration false or trivial and say that there is just one thing to do at this time . . . maintain the integrity and the authority of the university without question and without purchase in the form of concession of any kind whatsoever."[61]

Knowing that he had lost the support of several trustees, McKenzie submitted his resignation on April 16, 1925. The trustees, moving with unusual speed, accepted the resignation four days later. Paul Cravath probably expressed the feelings of most trustees when he observed that the trouble had "been dealt with as smoothly as we could have hoped." Nevertheless, Thomas Jesse Jones, one of McKenzie's staunchest supporters on the board, was so angry and certain that the whole controversy indicated that Caucasians were being forced out of Negro education that he proposed "a complete colored faculty from President down."[62]

[60] Statement of the Fisk Board of Trustees, quoted in *Nashville Banner*, 12 February 1925.

[61] McKenzie to Jones, 19 February 1925.

[62] Fayette McKenzie to Paul Cravath, 16 April 1925, McKenzie Papers; Minutes of the Meeting of the Fisk Board of Trustees, 20 April 1925, Moton Papers; Cravath to Robert Russa Moton, 24 April 1925, Moton Papers; Jones to McKenzie, 1 May 1925.

The trustees summarily rejected Jones's proposal, and instead properly acknowledged McKenzie's major contributions to the development of Fisk University:

You became president at a time when it was of the first importance that the educational standards of the institution should be revised and strengthened so that it would receive the support of the friends of higher education of the Negro whose cooperation was deemed essential. That you have succeeded in doing. Fisk is now recognized by other institutions as a standard American college. It is because of this success that the trustees were able to secure the support of the general education fund of the Carnegie Corporation and others in raising the fund of $1,000,000 which was completed a few months ago. You are entitled to your full share of the credit for raising that fund.[63]

The student strike at Fisk University was an extraordinary event. In the midst of the "roaring twenties" the elite of black youth, enrolled in a prestige college whose diploma was eagerly sought as a passport to social and professional success in black America, startled the educational world, and perhaps themselves, with the militancy of their inspired action. Du Bois provided some of the inspiration for the revolt, and of course he was elated by the success of the strike. He thanked God that the Fisk students had "the guts to yell and fight when their noses are rubbed in the mud." Here was the Talented Tenth in action, and he hailed the student "who hits power in high places, white power, power backed by unlimited wealth; hits it openly and between the eyes; talks face to face and not down 'at the big gate.' God speed the breed! Suppose we do lose Fisk; suppose we lose every cent that the entrenched millionaires have set aside to buy our freedom and stifle our complaints. They have the power, they have the wealth, but glory to God we still own our own souls and led by young men like these at Fisk, let

[63] Minutes of Fisk Board of Trustees, 20 April 1925.

us neither flinch nor falter but fight and fight and fight again. Let us never forget that the arch enemy of the Negro race is the false philanthropist who kicks us in the mouth when we cry out in honest and justifiable protest."[64] For Du Bois the protest was essentially against the organized philanthropy that had endorsed and promulgated white supremacy as a prerequisite for the sectional reconciliation that was an antecedent condition for American economic growth in the late nineteenth and early twentieth centuries. Thus, as he saw it, the fight against white philanthropy was "more than opposition to a program of education. It was opposition to a system and that system was part of the economic development of the United States at that time."[65] Some of the other participants in the Fisk controversy no doubt agreed with Du Bois's analysis of the situation, and all must have been influenced by his thought. Yet most of the Fisk students of 1924–1925 did not dwell on the larger ramifications of their protest; their focus was on disciplinary rules that were far more stringent than those at most white colleges of the day, and on the basic assumption that Negroes were not prepared to exercise free will.

IV

Fayette McKenzie departed from Nashville immediately after the acceptance of his resignation, and the trustees appointed a temporary administrative committee to direct the university's affairs until a new president could be inaugurated. Herbert A. Miller, an Ohio State University sociologist and the son-in-law of Fisk's first president, Erastus Milo Cravath, agreed to serve as chairman of this committee and made weekly trips to Nashville to confer with four faculty members who assumed responsibility for day-to-day administration. This committee immediately permitted the

[64] Du Bois, "Fisk," *Crisis* 29: 247–251.
[65] W. E. B. Du Bois, *Autobiography* (New York: International Pubishers, 1968), p. 241.

establishment of a student newspaper and recommended that alumni be named to the board of trustees. Over the course of several months the committee acceded to most of the students' specific proposals. The suspended student leaders were readmitted to the university; the process of revising the Fisk Code of Discipline was begun and an elected Student Council was given responsibility for enforcing the new regulations; fraternities and sororities were organized on the campus; and the new football coach, H. W. "Tubby" Johnson, reorganized athletics so effectively that the Fisk "Bulldogs" soon dominated the black gridiron and became known as "The Fastest Team in Colored America."[66]

Naturally the dissident students and alumni were elated by the inauguration of so many changes. The leaders of the student strike urged a return to classes and cooperation with the new authorities, and the members of the senior class took out a $25,000 endowment insurance policy, with the university named as the irrevocable beneficiary. For his part, Du Bois ceased all criticism of Fisk, confessing that it was best "to stop fighting when we have won." He urged blacks to recognize that "Negro higher education is going to be supported by Negroes themselves . . . or it is going to cease to function." He appealed to his fellow alumni to rally in support of their school with contributions and donations: "Here is the time for every Fiskite and every forward looking black to give 'till it hurts.' " Overwhelmed by their own success, Streator and the other student leaders could find little to protest against and used their column in the new

[66] *Baltimore Afro-American*, 2 May, 9 May 1925; *New York Age*, 30 May 1925; *Philadelphia Tribune*, 6 June 1925; Herbert A. Miller, "Report to the Alumni Association of Fisk University," *Fisk News*, May 1925; "Memorandum of Findings of the Greater Fisk Committee," 20 April 1925, Moton Papers; Marcia Lynn Johnson, "Student Protest at Fisk University in the 1920s," *Negro History Bulletin* 33 (October 1970): 137–140; W. E. B. Du Bois, "Athletics in Negro Colleges," *Crisis* 37 (June 1930): 209–210.

student newspaper to warn of the dangers of apathy now that victory had been achieved.[67] Of course there were some complaints from members of the old guard. Prof. Addie F. Sweet criticized the administrative committee for lavishing praise on the students and ignoring "several serious discipline cases." Dr. S. N. Vass noted the legalization of dancing and smoking on the campus and concluded that Fisk was abandoning some of the basic discipline of Christian education. And Dr. W. W. Sumlin complained that the new university was inhabited by wanton youths who were converting "the noble Fisk into a place of jazz."[68]

The trustees endorsed the changes that brought Fisk into closer conformity with what they called the "world trend toward a larger liberty," and also sought a new president who would foster and consolidate the new freedom. At the same time, however, the trustees believed that to avoid a sharp break with Fisk's academic and religious traditions and to ensure continued financial support from organized white philanthropy it was essential that a white clergyman be named as the successor to McKenzie. Finally, after searching for more than six months, they found a white missionary who possessed the necessary combination of Christian zeal, fund-raising skill, academic competence, and tolerant egalitarianism.[69]

When first approached by the trustees late in 1925, thirty-five-year-old Thomas Elsa Jones was a Ph.D. candidate at Columbia University. A Quaker-pacifist founder of the

[67] *Chicago Defender*, 17 April 1926; *New York Age*, 17 April 1926; W. E. B. Du Bois to Dr. and Mrs. E. L. Dunnings, 13 May 1925, WEBD Papers; Du Bois, "Lincoln, Howard, Fisk," *Crisis* 34 (March 1927): 33; Du Bois, "The New Fisk," *Crisis* 30 (June 1925): 60–61; George Streator, "Free Lance," *Fisk Herald*, February 1926.

[68] Addie F. Sweet to Mrs. Fayette McKenzie, 17 January 1926, McKenzie Papers; S. N. Vass, quoted in *Fisk Herald*, March 1927; W. E. Sumlin, quoted in *New York Age*, 21 February 1925.

[69] Minutes of the Meeting of the Fisk Board of Trustees, 13 July 1926, Moton Papers.

American Friends Service Committee, Jones had dedicated his life to nonmilitary alternative service and had spent seven years working with the Friends' Mission in Japan. While serving in Japan, Jones discovered that most successful missionaries immersed themselves in the native culture and then, after establishing intimate personal relations, subtly fostered the Japanese interest in the language, music, culture, and religion of the West. The opportunity to perform a similar service at Fisk, interpreting the black world to the white and the white to the black, thus had an enormous appeal to Jones and his wife, who recognized immediately that the presidency of Fisk would be "more of a 'missionary job' in the old sense than returning to Tokyo."[70]

Jones realized at the outset that no work of racial reconciliation could succeed if blacks were opposed to having a white president of Fisk. He immediately set out to determine the thinking of blacks on this matter and his first experience was far from encouraging. Striking up a conversation with a fellow Columbia graduate student, a black man who had taken his bachelor's degree at Fisk, Jones inquired about the recent turmoil on the campus and asked the student if any white man could serve effectively as Fisk's president. The black replied, "No, it's time for a black to take over." When Jones then told the student that he had been offered the presidency the student was visibly embarrassed, began to stutter, and cautiously observed that "it really depends on what kind of a white person you are."[71]

Thus Jones was aware at the outset that blacks had ambivalent feelings, and he himself initially believed that "the Negroes [should] run their own schools, staff them and finance them." But after talking with a large number of Negroes, Jones revised his view and concluded that most blacks were more interested in personal character than skin

[70] Mrs. Thomas Elsa Jones to Friends of the F.F.M.C., 7 February 1926, copy in possession of Dr. Jones; interview with Thomas Elsa Jones, 7 January 1971.
[71] Interview with Jones, 7 January 1971.

pigmentation and did not want the complete separation that an all-black institution would involve. "They want to find White people with whom they can live, forgetting color and racial lines. They do not wish to be 'spoon fed.' They wish to be respected as men and they want institutions that will be equal to the best in the country in scholarship and at the same time motivated by a spirit of Christian reconciliation and natural association that will make everyone feel that he is as good as the best American and that there is no position or ambition for which he need not strive."[72]

The editors of the Fisk student newspaper assured the new president-elect of their hearty cooperation if he adhered to "the principles of student government and student expression." In turn, Jones left little doubt that he sympathized with the basic ideals of the students. In his private correspondence he characterized McKenzie as "militarily possessed with all the faults and stupidity of that philosophy," and in his inaugural address on the Fisk campus he noted that black students had properly rejected "mid-Victorianism," and he welcomed the demise of "the simple-minded Uncle Tom type of Negro." He promptly approved the revised regulations and, indeed, proposed some further changes—allowing male and female students to walk together on campus and to date on weekends, permitting a few chaperoned dances, authorizing a special smoking room in the Chocolate Shop, and giving the Student Council legislative authority as well as the power to enforce discipline. More significantly perhaps, Jones also worked enthusiastically with those who were promoting the study of Negro life and history. He added courses in black history and literature to the curriculum at Fisk; sponsored an annual conference for the most prominent scholars of black America; and secured an impressive collection of Negro art and artifacts. He encouraged the development of a social science department which, under the direction of Charles

[72] Thomas Elsa Jones to Gilbert Bowles, 6 February 1926, copy in possession of Dr. Jones.

S. Johnson in the 1930s, became one of the nation's foremost centers of research on race relations. Anticipating some of the action-oriented black studies programs of our own day, Jones offered university credit to students who worked in the planning and operation of a slum clearance-redevelopment project adjacent to the Fisk campus or on a university-owned cotton cooperative near Memphis.[73]

Jones agreed with much of Du Bois's analysis of the controversy over black higher education, and this must also have ingratiated the new president with the erstwhile rebels. During his first year as president Jones noted that the enrollment in such basic trades as wheelwrighting, blacksmithing, and shoemaking was lagging at Hampton and Tuskegee, and he gloated that the addition of college courses at these industrial schools was a tacit admission that in the past the race had overemphasized trade training at the expense of college education.[74]

These comments naturally infuriated philanthropists such as George Foster Peabody who feared that Jones had been "more influenced by Du Bois than it is comfortable to think." Robert Russa Moton of Tuskegee reminded Fisk's new president that almost all of Fisk's million-dollar endowment had come from friends of industrial education for Negroes and that in the past "several other colleges" had failed to enlist support "because of the attacks they have made upon the work of Hampton and Tuskegee." Jones recognized the error of his rhetoric, apologized to the philanthropists, and thereafter was careful to avoid provocative statements.[75]

[73] *Fisk Herald*, March 1926; Jones to Bowles, 6 February 1926; Jones, quoted in the *Tuskegee Messenger* 30 (October 1926); Jones, quoted in *New York Times*, 8 December 1926; Jones, "Report to the Board of Trustees," 6 December 1926, Moton Papers; Jones, "Progress at Fisk University" (1930 pamphlet), Fisk Archives; interview with Jones, 7 January 1971.

[74] Thomas Elsa Jones, preface to *Fisk and the Future of the Race* (1927 pamphlet), Rosenwald Papers.

[75] George Foster Peabody to Robert Russa Moton, 13 June 1927, Moton Papers; Peabody to James E. Gregg, 17 June 1927, Papers of

Yet the incident undoubtedly established a further bond with Du Bois, Streator, and other Negroes. One enthusiast called the new president "the blackest white man I have ever known." Jones established exceptionally good rapport during his first year in office, and he was soon assuring his friends that "the period of unsettlement is largely forgotten." "The spirit of cooperative goodwill now found in the faculty and the students and alumni is a great encouragement and leads us to believe that we can go forward without fear that the ground will crumble under our feet."[76]

Jones encountered many problems and difficulties during his twenty-one years as president of Fisk, but on the whole his tenure was remarkably successful. The foundation for this success was established at the outset, when Jones devised policies that would appeal to blacks who proposed to think for themselves and to be represented by spokesmen of their own choosing.

George Foster Peabody, Library of Congress (hereafter cited as Peabody Papers); Peabody to Francis Greenwood Peabody, 1 December 1927, Moton Papers; Moton to Jones, 3 June 1927, Rosenwald Papers; Jones to Moton, 9 June, 14 June 1927, Rosenwald Papers.

[76] John R. Scotford, "The New Negro Education," *Christian Century*, 12 January 1928, p. 48, Thomas Elsa Jones to Julius Rosenwald, 22 June 1927, 25 August, 12 April 1929, Rosenwald Papers.

CHAPTER III

James Stanley Durkee and the Rising Tide of Color at Howard University

I

If Fisk was the nation's most prominent liberal arts college for blacks, Howard was the leading Negro university. Established in 1867 on a hilltop in Washington, D. C., and named in honor of Gen. Oliver O. Howard, the commissioner of the Freedmen's Bureau and a founder and third president of the university, Howard in 1925 enrolled approximately two thousand students, almost one-sixth of the total number of American Negroes then in college. Howard was the only black multiversity of the 1920s—with more than 150 professors. It had graduate schools in theology, law, medicine, dentistry, and pharmacy, and undergraduate programs in engineering, architecture, education, home economics, and commerce, as well as in the traditional arts and sciences. Howard's students and alumni generally thought of their school as "the capstone of Negro education," and even as proud a son of Fisk as W. E. B. Du Bois conceded that Howard was "our greatest university."[1]

Although members of the American Missionary Associa-

[1] Arthur J. Klein, *Survey of Negro Colleges and Universities* (U. S. Department of Interior, Bureau of Education Bulletin 7, 1928), pp. 194, 946–947; W. E. B. Du Bois, "Howard and Lincoln," *Crisis* 32 (May 1926): 7–8. There are two good histories of Howard University: Walter Dyson, *Howard University: The Capstone of Negro Education* (Washington, D. C.: Graduate School of Howard University, 1941), and Rayford Logan, *Howard University: The First Hundred Years* (New York: New York University Press, 1969).

tion played decisive roles in founding and fostering Howard and are memorialized today by a striking Congregational spire atop the Founders Library, the university itself was nondenominational. Howard was initially supported by grants from various church boards and the Freedmen's Bureau. But the United States Congress began making annual appropriations for the university in 1879, and by the 1920s this federal assistance had become the mainstay of Howard's finances. Prior to 1928 there was no specific authorization for this government aid, however, and officials of the university lived in constant fear that the congressional appropriation would be terminated. Yet Congress never stopped its assistance, and as a result Howard, of all the private Negro universities and colleges, was the least dependent on white philanthropy.[2]

This financial independence from church boards and organized philanthropy freed Howard's black students from the tutelary discipline that prevailed at Fisk and opened the way to extracurricular activities similar to those enjoyed by most white students. Those interested in journalism gravitated toward one of two student publications, the *Hilltop* and the *Journal*, while embryonic politicians tried out for the Kappa Sigma Debating Club and campaigned for seats on the Student Council. Students with a flair for literature or the fine arts competed for positions in *Stylus*, the literary magazine, the Howard Players, a widely acclaimed dramatic company, or one of the several musical groups on campus. The university fielded athletic teams in most intercollegiate sports, and the annual Thanksgiving Day football game between the "Bisons" of Howard and the "Lions" of Lincoln University (Pa.) was the most popular event in black sports and the high point of a very active social season.[3]

As the only black university located in the midst of

[2] Dyson, *Howard University*, pp. 301–314.

[3] Logan, *Howard University*, pp. 214–220; *Howard University Catalogue, 1923–1924*, pp. 51–54.

a large concentration of Negroes, Howard attracted many poor students who could not afford the cost of room and board at sequestered residential colleges. Nevertheless, a good number of Howard's students came from the relatively well-to-do black middle class and could afford some of the expensive diversions of the jazz age. The seven Greek-letter fraternities and sororities on campus sponsored many social events, and one young critic of the affluent bourgeoisie complained that many students were neglecting their studies and focusing "on theatre-going, card parties, dances, all-night sprees, gambling and anything to get a thrill out of life." Another presented itemized bills showing that it was possible to get by with $30 worth of textbooks but that "unless she wants to appear like a guest at a wedding feast without wedding garments, no girl will think of coming to Howard without a wardrobe costing $455 at a minimum." After visiting the hilltop, one correspondent for a nationally circulated student journal perceptively noted that although "the economic position of the colored people is for the most part a straitened one, and in consequence many a student at Howard has to 'work his way through,' nevertheless the social and athletic life of the university is a full one; and it is nowhere better realized than at Howard that the real spirit of a university education is not to be sought in lectures and reading alone."[4]

While social life on the hilltop was spirited, the leaders of the university were not prepared to forsake all responsibility for the moral and spiritual care of their students. The *Howard Catalogue* proclaimed that the university was "distinctly Christian in spirit and work," and the campus branches of the YMCA and YWCA were charged with re-

[4] Charles H. Thompson, "The Socio-Economic Status of Negro College Students," *Journal of Negro Education* 2 (January 1923): 26; Mac Arlene Johnson, "The Typical College Youth at Howard," *Howard Hilltop*, 10 April 1925; J. Wycliffe Keller, quoted in the *Baltimore Afro-American*, 25 May 1923; William A. Robson, "A Visit to a Negro University," *New Student* 2 (10 February 1923): 2.

sponsibility for "providing a wholesome recreational and social life as a substitute for undesirable resorts in the city." The *University Rules and Regulations* contained none of the detailed Victorian provisions for dress, study, and deportment found at other black colleges. It assumed, however, that every student would refrain from "indulgence in intoxicating drinks, visiting saloons or places of corrupting influence," and would "conform to the recognized standards of morality, good order, and becoming conduct."[5]

James Stanley Durkee, a Congregationalist pastor who in 1918 had become the eleventh in an almost unbroken line of Howard's white clergymen-presidents, was no less concerned with inculcating Christian morality than his predecessors. In his view, the university was responsible for maintaining "the early religious training and spontaneous impulses of the student while we guide him into the realm where intellect shall be pilot and emotion the engine." He repeatedly insisted that character was even more important than scholarship; and since man was "infinitely greater than mere intellect," Durkee believed that Howard must be "more than an 'educational factory.'" As president of the university, Durkee encouraged members of the faculty to take a personal interest in the moral welfare of the students, and devotional exercises were held in the university chapel in order to stimulate "life surrender to Christ."[6]

Yet those who have enjoyed a measure of freedom are as likely to protest against restrictions as those who have been shackled with prohibitions. There were relatively few restraints at Howard, but the students became impatient with the remaining curbs and regulations. In 1922 several students in the School of Applied Science were suspended for

[5] *Howard University Catalogue, 1923–1924*, p. 52; *Howard University Catalogue, 1925–1926*, p. 54; *Howard University Rules and Regulations* (pamphlet), Howard Archives.

[6] J. Stanley Durkee, "President's Annual Report, 1924," pp. 7, 11 (typescript), Howard Archives; Durkee, "Address to Students," *Howard University Record* 16 (November 1921): 9–14.

73

having more than eight unexcused absences from the required noon chapel service. Realizing that many additional students would have been suspended if the rules had been applied uniformly, the students placarded the campus with demands that "Compulsory Chapel Must Go." More than seventy engineering and architecture students wrote that they would withdraw from the university if regulations continued to be enforced selectively. The trustees initially rejected this appeal for voluntary chapel attendance, but the faculty was more sympathetic, perhaps because the professors themselves were required to attend chapel and the deans resented having to "twist their necks throughout services to check on absentees."[7]

President Durkee and the trustees eventually rescinded the unpopular regulation requiring attendance at noon chapel. But this occurred only after the faculty voted in favor of voluntary services and exchanged a "red-hot correspondence" threatening to jeopardize the university's congressional appropriation by claiming that compulsory chapel violated constitutional provisions relating to the separation of church and state. The students hailed this rescission as "a victory and an opportunity." They had insisted throughout the controversy that "religion is a matter of spontaneity . . . [and] cannot be forced, and any movement which has as its purpose the compulsory spread of religion defeats its own end."[8]

Of course President Durkee was deeply troubled by "the restlessness [that] reveals itself in a desire to avoid all religious instruction, even of daily chapel attendance." He

[7] "How We Got Voluntary Chapel," *Howard University Journal*, 24 March 1922; Z. Alexander Looby to editor of *Howard University Journal*, 14 April 1922; *Baltimore Afro-American*, 3 March 1922; *Kansas City Call*, 11 March 1922; J. Stanley Durkee, "President's Annual Report, 1922," p. 22 (typescript), Howard Archives; Alumnus, "Durkeeism at Howard University," *Baltimore Afro-American*, 9 May 1925.

[8] Alumnus, "Durkeeism," 9 May 1925; "A Victory and an Opportunity," *Howard University Journal*, 24 March 1922.

tried to make the voluntary services attractive by arranging for short addresses by visiting congressmen, scholars, clergymen, and race leaders (including Marcus Garvey, on one occasion), but he lamented, "The three or four score students who now attend are a small force among so many hundreds of students."[9]

Perhaps the president was mollified by the enthusiastic attendance at Sunday evening vespers. Miss Lulu Vere Childers's choir ranked second only to football in popularity of extracurricular events and inspired one columnist for the *Howard University Record* to exclaim, "It would do any music lover good to hear 'sweet jordan roll' from over five hundred student voices." Yet even choral music could become a source of controversy, for many students complained that singing spirituals for white visitors partook more of *puttin' on ole massa* in the plantation tradition than of the manly self-assertion associated with the postwar New Negro. But here again President Durkee and the trustees reluctantly yielded to student pressure. They allowed the choir to choose its own repertoire and thereby demonstrated an ability to adjust to changing times and a general flexibility in dealing with students that was notably absent among the leaders at Fisk and also, as we shall see, at Hampton Institute.[10]

Similarly, when the Student Council hinted it might authorize a strike if it were not given coequal authority with the administration in disciplinary cases, President Durkee allowed the council to proceed with an ambitious plan to

[9] J. Stanley Durkee, "President's Annual Report, 1921," p. 11 (typescript), Howard Archives; Barbara McCall, "A New Day: A History of the Student and Alumni Protest that 'Emancipated' Howard University" (seminar paper, University of Delaware, 1969); *Howard Hilltop*, 22 January 1924; Durkee, "Annual Report, 1922," p. 22.

[10] *Howard University Record*, February 1919, quoted in Logan, *Howard University*, p. 220; Alumnus, "Durkeeism," 28 November 1925; Zora Neale Hurston, "The Hue and Cry About Howard University," *Messenger* 7 (September 1925): 315–317, 319, 338.

revise its charter and reorganize student government. The student newspaper hailed the new charter as an omen of "a new day" when students on the hilltop would be emancipated from "a constitution of fine rhetoric but no power" and would be "free at last . . . to be governed by themselves." The charter provided that the council would have primary responsibility for supervising extracurricular activities, that it would act "jointly with the administrative officers" in disciplinary affairs, and that it could make recommendations on all matters that affected the student body.[11]

Thus despite his own personal belief that "if ever student bodies needed direction . . . , that time is now," President Durkee often compromised with students who demanded autonomy outside the classroom. He must have had reservations about the extreme devotion to extracurricular affairs that led some students to prize membership in leading college fraternities more than scholarship and gave rise to the maxim that one should not let studies interfere with a college education. Nevertheless, Durkee recognized that recreation and social life were important and, if properly developed, would complement and encourage scholarship and religion. By employing a responsive (or cooptive) strategy Durkee satisfactorily resolved several minor protests during his first six years in office and managed to make an uneasy peace with students at Howard. Unlike President McKenzie of Fisk, Durkee realized that the black youth of the 1920s had come of age and would no longer tolerate the discipline that had been imposed on earlier generations of students.[12]

Yet, as many executives have discovered to their sorrow, it is not always possible to reconcile groups with fundamentally different interests and aspirations. Durkee soon learned that he could not accede to certain student demands without alienating other essential components of the

[11] *Howard Hilltop*, 22 January, 29 February 1924, 13 March 1925; *Baltimore Afro-American*, 23 February 1923.

[12] J. Stanley Durkee, "Annual Report, 1922," p. 22.

Howard community. Compromise was possible as long as the students were concerned with extracurricular organization and discipline, but student demands for "a larger measure of participation in college control" inevitably led to difficult confrontations with the faculty and trustees. Shortly after the release of the charter of the new student government association, one student group began to make plans for evaluating instructors, and in March of 1924 the new Student Council submitted two "epoch-making recommendations." In the first, the council declared its opposition to "compulsory military training and . . . war on any conditions." It recommended the abolition of the requirement that all male students must have at least two years of military training.[13]

Even more controversial were the council's recommendations that a black man "who can freely mingle with the . . . male students and really know their yearnings and aspirations" be appointed as dean of men and that "six [white] faculty members . . . be requested to submit their resignations." According to the students, these white professors were "too 'old-fogey' and out of date . . . [and] were merely drawing salaries." Beyond this, the white professors held "pivot positions" through which it was alleged that the faculty was "controlled by members of the other race."[14]

Durkee was able to deal effectively with matters of discipline and social activity, but these new demands created enormous problems for the president. Abolition of compulsory ROTC might endanger the university's annual congressional appropriation, and the exclusion of whites simply because of their color ran counter to the university's historic opposition to racial discrimination. A new mood had begun to permeate the campus, however, and many students had come to emphasize group solidarity and self-determination. This rising tide of racial consciousness was also shared by

[13] "Why a Student Strike?" *Baltimore Afro-American*, 28 February 1925; *Howard Hilltop*, 29 March, 10 April 1925.
[14] *Howard Hilltop*, 29 March 1925.

many professors and graduates and created a situation that would have taxed the ability of any white president and one that James Stanley Durkee was singularly ill-prepared to handle.

II

Racial tension did not begin at Howard in the 1920s, and to appreciate the dimensions of the problem it is necessary to pause and consider earlier instances when the impulse toward self-help and racial pride culminated in black demands for a larger role in the management of the university. One of the most bitter racial controversies of the Reconstruction period occurred in 1874–1875 when, upon the resignation of General Howard, many blacks supported the presidential candidacy of John Mercer Langston, the dean of the law school and vice-president of the university. Twenty law students expressed the hope that "Langston's color will not operate as an invidious bar to his election," and Frederick Douglass declared that it was the desire of the colored members of the board of trustees that the position should be given to a colored man. But the white Congregationalists who controlled the board doubted Langston's talent for fund raising and believed that the vice-president, who had pointedly refused to join any church, "was not the man to hold the institution to the religious and moral ideas on which it was founded." The trustees offered the presidency to a succession of white ministers, and Langston resigned from the university with an angry charge that the trustees were thwarting the development of the race.[15]

Intermittent Negro criticism of Howard's white presi-

[15] John Mercer Langston, *From the Virginia Plantation to the National Capitol* (New York: Arno Press, 1969), pp. 297–298, 310–317; Dyson, *Howard University*, pp. 56–60; Logan, Howard University, pp. 73–81; James M. McPherson, "White Liberals and Black Power in Negro Education, 1865-1915," *American Historical Review* 75 (June 1970): 1364–1365; *New York Evening Post*, 15 July 1875.

dents persisted, but many blacks were mollified by the knowledge that the Negro deans had established semiautonomous spheres of power within their colleges—a condition that led Howard historian Walter Dyson to conclude that the power of most of the white presidents was circumscribed so severely that the black deans were actually "in control."[16]

Hence John Gordon, a white Presbyterian who was named president in 1903, touched off an acrimonious struggle when he moved to restrict the independence of the deans by establishing one-year terms of office. This controversy, while not solely racial in origin, inevitably assumed racial overtones as it became essentially a confrontation between a white president and two black deans, George William Cook and Lewis B. Moore. Many Negroes rallied behind the deans, and when one group of black students hissed the president and marched out of chapel to hold an "indignation meeting" the deans flatly refused the president's demand that the students be suspended.[17]

Although President Gordon was not without black supporters, most Negroes rallied behind a campaign to force his resignation. Archibald H. Grimke, a black attorney who organized the movement to oust Gordon, stated that during the era of Reconstruction the white South had ostracized whites who came to teach Negroes. Thus, he said, the teachers were forced into close, daily contact with their black students—a condition that was largely responsible for the considerable success of the early black colleges. With the passage of time and the development of the Jim Crow system, white teachers were presented with a dilemma. They could not retain the necessary good relations with the white community if they became the constant companions of blacks, and they could not hold their black students if they

[16] McPherson, "White Liberals and Black Power," pp. 1365–1366; Dyson, *Howard University*, p. 63.

[17] Logan, *Howard University*, p. 146; *New York Age*, 11 May, 21 December 1905.

accepted the color line and lived in white neighborhoods, joined white clubs, and sent their children to white schools. The duties of the president of a Negro college were thus seriously complicated, and Grimke charged that Gordon had foundered on these complications. Gordon, it was alleged, refused "to give up everything and . . . identify himself in all respects with the race," but rather, "in order to get himself and his family into the social swim of the capital . . . accepted the color line . . . which forbids on pain of ostracism any social contact of white people with colored." He sent his children to white schools in Washington, thereby breaking the custom of previous presidents who had enrolled their children at Howard; he was accused of holding himself aloof from black students and professors. It was also noted that he found various ways to avoid inviting black dignitaries to dine at the president's mansion (as, for example, when he entertained Samuel Coleridge Taylor, the distinguished black composer, at a dinner in the "laboratory" of the home economics department).[18]

Incidents such as these persuaded many Negroes that there were "good grounds for their suspicion . . . that the only interest such white teachers have in them and their education is in the money which attaches to those positions." Grimke insisted that Gordon must decide either "to be president of Howard University, with all that the position implies of social abnegation for himself and his family, of complete identification of himself in all respects with the interests of the people with whom he has cast his lot, or to be a white man in the narrow sense, hankering after the fleshpots of the society of his own race in this colorphobia-ridden city."[19]

Nor was Grimke alone in censuring Gordon. A large

[18] Archibald H. Grimke discussed these points in columns appearing regularly in the New York Age; see especially the issues of 18 May, 25 May, 1 June 1905.
[19] New York Age, 18 May, 1 June, 8 June 1905.

number of Washington alumni turned out when William Sinclair, the financial agent of the university from 1888 to 1903, called a public meeting to consider the controversy. Though insisting that there was "no objection to white teachers or officers as such, but only to those who betray their trust and abuse their positions by displaying race prejudice," these alumni called for Gordon's resignation. They claimed that "as a consequence of his inability to understand the colored people, he has deeply wounded . . . the sensibilities of the students and of the colored men connected with the teaching force . . . [and] has offended again and again the *amour propre*, the race pride, of these men."[20]

Amid cries that there should be "a colored president for a colored school," the exasperated Gordon resigned in 1906. With different factions in the black community lining up behind competing black candidates, a battle for the succession seemed to be in the offing. The trustees, however, selected another white president, Wilbur P. Thirkield, a Methodist who had served for seventeen years as president of the black Gammon Theological Seminary and one of those unusual men who could overcome the difficulties of interracial relations. Thirkield's appointment met with general approval in the black community, but another "unholy scramble" for the presidency occurred in 1912 when Thirkield resigned to become a bishop in the Methodist Episcopal Church. Deans Lewis B. Moore, George William Cook, and Kelly Miller all vied for the presidency. "If any two of the three deans had withdrawn from the contest in favor of the third, a black man would have been elected president of Howard." None of the deans would retire from the struggle, however, and the trustees then chose Stephen M. Newman, a white Congregationalist who was willing to keep

[20] William A. Sinclair to Archibald H. Grimke, May 1905, Papers of Archibald H. Grimke, Howard University (hereafter cited as Grimke Papers).

peace on the campus by deferring to "The Triumverate" of black deans.[21] Thus although the presidency was in white hands, effective power resided with the deans, especially during the years of Newman's administration, 1912 to 1918. With blacks also occupying two-thirds of the faculty positions, it was clear that white influence was waning at Howard and blacks were coming to play a larger role in the direction of the institution. This trend toward greater black participation raised expectations and increased the longing for the day when a Negro would be named as president of the university.[22]

III

Given this history, all white presidents had reason to anticipate extraordinary problems, and the situation was aggravated by the wave of racial pride and self-consciousness that swept the nation in the 1920s. Of course the mood of the "New Negro" was most pronounced among black intellectuals in Harlem, but it also affected the predominantly middle-class campuses. This was especially true of Howard where several blacks reflected and created a frame of mind that must have mystified President Durkee even as it intensified his difficulties.

Central to the new mood was the conviction that the Negro colleges had outgrown the idealism of the missionary impulse. In the nineteenth century all American colleges emphasized piety. By the turn of the twentieth century, however, the better white colleges stressed secular

[21] *Washington Bee*, 30 December 1905, 27 January 1906, 1 June 1912; Dyson, *Howard University*, pp. 368–375, 391–396; *New York Age*, 10 May 1906; Wilbur Thirkield to Archibald H. Grimke, 27 June 1906, Grimke Papers; McPherson, "White Liberals and Black Power," p. 1367.
[22] McPherson, "White Liberals and Black Power," p. 1385.

scholarship, and many blacks suspected that the continuation of religious education in the Negro colleges was a means of limiting the opportunities of the race. E. Franklin Frazier, who took his baccalaureate degree at Howard in 1916 and later returned to become one of the university's most distinguished scholars, asserted that whites wanted Negro education to "unlock the mysteries of heaven," but had grave reservations when black teachers "unfolded the mysteries of this world." Making a similar point, Prof. G. David Houston of Howard's English department urged black colleges to forsake "the mildewed objective of making professing Christians and developing prospective preachers." Endorsing Frazier's contention that there was "too much inspiration and too little information" in black education, Houston believed that Negroes needed "less preaching and more teaching." Both men were aware that the better white colleges had dropped their nineteenth-century emphasis on piety and had ceased appointing clerical leaders. So, too, the black college should also abandon "the delusion that its president must be a Minister of the Gospel."[23]

Yet this break with the missionary tradition was not prompted solely by the insistence that black collegians should have the same educational opportunities as whites. Beyond this was the belief that, as Frazier put it, "the Negro must avoid the danger of unconsciously assimilating values which . . . have no meaning for him." Expanding on this theme, Dean Kelly Miller asserted that the "awful moral severity" of the Protestant ethos did not comport with the Negro's "joyous African temperament," and hence the black student was "probably less responsive to the religious appeal than the white student." Historian Carter G. Woodson called on blacks to develop a stalwart and indigenous spiritual ethos. He complained that in religion the Ne-

[23] E. Franklin Frazier, "A Note on Negro Education," *Opportunity* 2 (March 1924): 75; G. David Houston, "Weaknesses of the Negro College," *Crisis* 20 (July 1920): 122.

gro merely "borrowed the ideas of his traducers instead of delving into things and working out some thought of his own."[24]

These Howard professors were middle-class men who admired family stability and the work ethic and opposed many "Negro" characteristics as the unworthy products of an oppressive environment. But they also rejected what Frazier called "the servile way in which Negroes imitated the white man's ideals and values and his fear of being different." They insisted that certain aspects of the black subculture should be legitimized and embellished. Thus Miller complained that by dwelling on "a picture in which all worthwhile deeds are ascribed to white men and none to blacks," the standard history courses and textbooks undermined black pride and caused many students to be "ashamed even to study about themselves."[25]

With the founding of the Association for the Study of Negro Life and History in 1915, Carter G. Woodson launched a veritable crusade to bolster racial pride by presenting authentic Negro history in the schools. He was convinced that textbooks emphasizing the primitive quality of the African background and the servile character of the Afro-American experience left blacks with the conviction that they were "inferior and should be content with an underprivileged status." Having studied the classics while a student at Berea and Harvard, Woodson was not intrinsically opposed to the standard curriculum. Yet he knew that if Negroes spent all their time admiring the achievements of Caucasians they would inevitably come "to despise themselves and all other races which are now subject to exploitation." In his view, then, it was necessary for black colleges

[24] Frazier, "Negro Education," p. 77; Kelly Miller, "The Higher Education of the Negro Is at the Crossroads," *Educational Review* 72 (December 1926): 276; Carter G. Woodson, *The Mis-Education of the Negro* (Washington: Associated Publishers, 1933), p. 61.

[25] Frazier, "Negro Education," pp. 76–77; Kelly Miller, "Negro History," *Opportunity* 4 (March 1926): 85–86.

to offer courses specifically designed to rehabilitate the Negro psychologically.[26]

Philosophy professor Alain Locke also recognized that self-esteem was a necessary prerequisite for unembarrassed interracial contacts. In scores of articles and especially in a remarkable 1925 anthology that gave its name, *The New Negro*, to the black arts movement of the decade, Locke celebrated Negro poetry, fiction, drama, scholarship, music, and art as the necessary foundation for building a self-confident race that could face whites with equanimity. He agreed with Frazier that the black American had for too long been "a spectator of civilization incapable of participation." Each new artistic work was evidence for Locke that the Negro had become "a conscious contributor [who] lays aside the status of beneficiary and ward for that of collaborator and participant." He believed with James Weldon Johnson, a fellow anthologist and celebrant of Negro art, that "nothing can go farther to destroy race prejudice than the recognition of the Negro as a creator and contributor to American civilization." Great Negro artists who could catch the imagination of the world, Locke said, would do much to "educate the American public out of its worst and most unfair provincialisms. . . ."[27]

The cultural renaissance was a valuable antidote to the view that blacks were inherently inferior, but professors at Howard were frustrated when they tried to supplement the university's curriculum with courses that would legitimize the sense of group identification. As early as 1901 the board of trustees refused to support Miller's proposal that the uni-

[26] Carter G. Woodson, *The Negro in Our History* (Washington: Associated Publishers, 1931), p. 573.

[27] Alain Locke, ed., *The New Negro* (New York: Albert & Charles Boni, 1925); Frazier, "Negro Education," pp. 75–76; Locke, quoted in Nathan I. Huggins, *Harlem Renaissance* (New York: Oxford University Press, 1971), p. 59; James Weldon Johnson, quoted in Gilbert Osofsky, *Harlem: The Making of a Ghetto* (New York: Harper & Row, 1966), p. 182; Locke, "Roland Hayes," *Opportunity* 1 (December 1923): 356.

versity subsidize the scholarly publications of the American Negro Academy. And in 1915–1916 the board rejected Locke's request for a course in "interracial relations," as well as a general faculty appeal for a course on "Negro problems." Even Woodson, who was named dean of the college in 1919, failed to receive permission to develop a course in Afro-American history, and this doubtless contributed to his angry decision to leave Howard and devote full time to his association and its *Journal of Negro History*.[28]

A course in American Negro history was finally organized at Howard in 1920, and with the advent of Prof. William Leo Hansberry in 1922 the university also began to offer courses on the African past. Yet throughout the 1920s the university found it difficult to recognize the academic legitimacy of black studies and its commitment to the field was slim. The courses in African history were considered expendable, and despite an outstanding record as a teacher and scholar Hansberry was kept for years without being given tenure and finally retired after decades of service as an associate professor.[29]

Only in drama did the artistic renaissance manifest itself on the hilltop. Here the Howard Players, under the direction of Prof. Montgomery Gregory, won wide critical acclaim for their ambitious productions of original Negro plays. Leonard Hall of the *Washington Daily News* hailed the attempt "to build a structure of native Negro drama, to be interpreted by people of the race," and Du Bois celebrated this work "as one of the significant achievements of

[28] Logan, *Howard University*, pp. 115–116, 171, 208; "Carter G. Woodson, 1875–1950," *Journal of the National Medical Association* 62 (September 1970): 389–390.

[29] "A New Course in History at Howard University," *Howard University Record* 17 (March 1923): 237–239; John Hope Franklin, "Courses Concerning the Negro in Negro Colleges," *Quarterly Review of Higher Education Among Negroes* 8 (July 1940): 138–144; Richard A. Long, paper read to the 55th annual meeting of the Association for the Study of Negro Life and History, 23 October 1970.

the race." Yet the university itself was less appreciative, and
after fourteen years on the faculty Gregory severed his connection with the university in 1924. In a plaintive letter of
resignation he explained that "the financial strain of trying
to properly rear a family of four growing children on my
present compensation, plus the added burden of having to
teach night school and summer school, to say nothing of re-
sorting to outside work, has grown more difficult and embarrassing." Thus Gregory accepted a job in the public
schools of Atlantic City, New Jersey, "at practically twice
the amount of my Howard salary."[30]

For Locke, who ardently believed that the leading black
colleges should become "radiant centers of Negro culture,"
Howard's official indifference to the black renaissance was
particularly exasperating. Negro colleges, in his view,
should not be mere reflections of the Anglo-Saxon model,
separate only because the white colleges they emulated
would not admit their students. Instead, they should recognize their responsibility to see that in the formative years
of "a sensitive personal and racial adolescence" black students were exposed to "the positive rather than to the nega-
tive aspects of race." Locke did not want an education that
made black students worship another race. He insisted that
"Negro education, to the extent that it is separate, ought to
be free to develop its own racial interests and special aims
for both positive and compensatory reasons." But Negro
education, as it was then organized, constantly reminded
the black student "of the unpleasant side of the race problem," and Locke feared that youth trained in such an atmosphere of "spirit-dampening condescension" would come to

[30] Leonard Hall, quoted in *Howard University Record* 17 (January
1923): 114; W. E. B. Du Bois, quoted in Dyson, *Howard University*,
p. 149; Montgomery Gregory to J. Stanley Durkee, 14 August 1924,
in Carter G. Woodson, ed., *The Works of Francis J. Grimke* (Washington: Associated Publishers, 1942), IV: 399–400. The Howard
Players presented the works of many white playwrights, but they
specialized in the production of works by blacks.

despise their race and would leave the campus as a talented tenth committed not to group service but to bourgeois individualism.[31]

Among other members of the faculty, Kelly Miller also insisted that "our colleges and universities must find some way to relate their motive to the awakening in the Negro of his dormant artistic powers." Trained as a mathematician at Howard and Johns Hopkins, Miller had turned to the infant fields of sociology and race relations and during the first four decades of the twentieth century he wrote perceptively and prolifically on the Negro's history and social problems. As one of the leading experts in black studies, Miller noted wistfully in 1926 that "the cultural life of the race is not now focusing at Fisk nor Atlanta, or Howard or Wilberforce, but in New York," and he urged the black colleges to exercise some independence and supplement "the older types of art and taste" with "a new cultural motive in the direction of the Negro renaissance."[32]

Locke insisted that the chief aim of black education was to train "a racially inspired and devoted professional class with group service as their ideal." Like him, Miller believed that the Negro college must inspire its youth with an "enthusiasm for racial service and uplift." As Miller observed the collegiate scene of the 1920s, however, he lamented that the black schools were "failing to arouse the aspiration and quicken the enthusiasm as they were wont to do in the more primitive and privative days." At the turn of the century and before, the black graduate "offered himself as a missionary to redeem his people." In the 1920s, however, "the mercenary motive ha[d] all but supplanted missionary zeal as the aim and objective of the higher education of the Negro." The black colleges had become "factories to grind out stabilized workers in the professions, and . . . the most help-

[31] Alain Locke, "Negro Education Bids for Par," *Survey* 54 (September 1925): 570, 593.

[32] "Kelly Miller Says," *Baltimore Afro-American*, 20 February 1926.

88

ful indication of the younger college men is seen in the organization of fraternities."[33]

Miller claimed that these were "not words of criticism" but merely "admonitory questions that inevitably arise in the mind of one who for fully a generation has watched the drift and tendency . . . toward things concrete and material." The black college students, in his view, had been swept away by a tide of selfish materialism that dampened altruistic service to the race. He repeatedly appealed to blacks "to return to the spirit of consecration and race devotion which dominated the college world fifty years ago." The race would not progress unless its educated leaders recognized their "racial responsibility and duty" and assumed the "rightful place in race leadership which their culture calls for and which the situation demands." He yearned "for the return of that social spirit which actuated the youth a generation ago. Then every student was preparing to reclaim and uplift his race; now the burden of his ambition is to achieve a distinguished career. Then the objective of his ambition was social, now it is selfish."[34]

Nor was Miller alone in holding these views. Locke also noted that the race was losing its "finest social products" as able black students succumbed to the "prevalent materialistic individualism of middle-class American life." He concluded that "if there is anything . . . particularly needed in Negro education it is the motive and ideal of group service." Similarly, Frazier observed that many black students were "adopting a narrow and selfish individualism . . . [and] are preparing themselves for the professions as a means to wealth and enjoyment, and not as a means for deeper and more responsible participation in our civilization."[35]

[33] Locke, "Negro Education Bids," p. 570; "Kelly Miller Says," 13 April, 16 November 1923, 27 December 1924, 20 February 1926.

[34] "Kelly Miller Says," 8 June, 16 November, 13 April, 12 October 1923, 27 October 1924.

[35] Locke, "Negro Education Bids," p. 570; Frazier, "Negro Education," p. 76.

Woodson insisted that the absence of compensatory black studies left the educated Negro professional man unprepared to lead the black masses which had "been belittled by his teachers to the extent that he can hardly find delight in undertaking what his education has led him to think impossible." The same educational process that inspired the Caucasian "with the thought that he is everything and has accomplished everything worthwhile, depresses and crushes at the same time the spark of genius in the Negro by making him feel that his race does not amount to much and will never measure up to the standards of other people." Under the circumstances, Woodson concluded, it was hardly surprising to discover that instead of preparing themselves "for the uplift of a downtrodden people," black students were simply memorizing "certain facts to pass examinations for jobs. After they obtain these positions they pay little attention to humanity."[36]

During the 1920s, then, several prominent professors at Howard came to believe that the curriculum had to be modified if the university were to achieve its goal of training capable and dedicated black leaders. Yet the trustees, although resigned to the necessity of permitting some courses in black studies, rejected several proposals for courses in this area. Under the circumstances it was inevitable that many professors would conclude that the board— 60 percent of whose members were white—lacked a sense of urgency about the need for black studies. Some of these professors believed that white paternalism, especially the missionary variety, prevented the black colleges from developing an emancipated, autonomous spirituality. Locke, for example, believed that "missionarism and self-leadership are incompatible." For him, "the Negro college of the present day requires and demands, if not group exclusiveness, at least group management and . . . self-determination." And for Houston, "religious domination" had made

[36] Woodson, *Mis-Education of the Negro*, pp. 6, xxxiii, 55-56.

the Negro college "deaf to the newer demands of the age,
. . . more of a medieval monastery than a modern and pro-
gressive institution."[37] Miller was more favorably disposed toward organized religion, which he believed had succeeded in instilling a sense
of social commitment in earlier generations of black students. But for a variety of reasons apart from his own personal ambitions Miller nevertheless endorsed the growing
demand for black leadership. He knew that the Negro race
had developed "a number of men who are qualified by
every test of efficiency and experience to man and manage
their own institutions." He also recognized that the choice
of white presidents inevitably implied that blacks were not
qualified for such responsibilities. Moreover, having organized the important Sanhedren Conference of 1924—where
the delegates had demanded that blacks direct their own
education in this "era of self-help and self-direction"—Miller saw an "inevitable drift" toward black autonomy. He
doubtless wanted to remain in tune with changing patterns
of racial thought: "In pedagogy, as in physics," he observed,
"a body will not remain in stable equilibrium so long as the
center of gravity falls outside the basis of support."[38]

Beyond this necessary adjustment to changing times, and
perhaps of greatest importance in explaining Miller's belief
that it was time for blacks to take control of their colleges,
was his recognition that the "painfully self-conscious" black
students of the 1920s had become so suspicious of Caucasians that they "will not complacently learn lessons of social
import from white instructors." In the early years of black

[37] Dyson, *Howard University*, pp. 413–418; Locke, "Negro Education Bids," pp. 569–570; Houston, "Weaknesses of the Negro College,"
p. 122.

[38] Kelly Miller, "The Past, Present and Future of the Negro College," *Journal of Negro Education* 2 (July 1933): 411–422; "Kelly
Miller Says," 14 November 1925, 3 July 1926; Miller, "Higher Education of the Negro," pp. 276–277; Alain Locke, "The Negro Speaks for
Himself," *Survey* 52 (15 April 1924): 71–72.

higher education, Miller wrote, "The Southern whites withheld all social intercourse with Northerners who so far demeaned themselves as to put themselves on a plane of easy social touch and familiarity with the erstwhile slaves."[39] Consequently, the black students and white teachers on the Negro campuses mixed easily and relations of trust were established between fellow groups of pariahs. With the passage of time, however, the South accorded the white teachers a degree of social acceptance, and when the teachers were allowed to partake in activities prohibited to blacks racial tension inevitably appeared. By the turn of the twentieth century, the Jim Crow laws were rigorously enforced, and whites were not allowed to participate in the life of the blacks; they could not ride in the same coach or stay at the same hotel or send their children to the same school.

Knowing that the colleges depended on the sufferance of the surrounding white communities, the white teachers, in the interest of institutional survival, were forced to make ignoble compromises with white supremacy—never wearing a hat for fear one might have to lift it when meeting a Negro woman, for example, or shifting entertainments from one's home to the students' dining room. Under these circumstances, grave suspicions—and sometimes even a deep social gulf—developed between the white instructors and the black students, for, as Miller noted, "whenever the teacher, justly or unjustly, incurs the suspicion of insincerity, his influence and usefulness . . . are gone. . . . The teacher must break down and not build up barriers. The moment he gives the student to understand that where I go you cannot follow, he weakens the *cordiale entente* which is essential to the true relationship of disciple to master."[40]

Although Negroes at Howard in the 1920s affirmed the value of their heritage and demanded black control of the university as a necessary prerequisite for cultural reassess-

[39] "Kelly Miller Says," 20 December 1924, 12 November 1927.
[40] Woodson, *Mis-Education of the Negro*, pp. 27, 128; Miller, "Higher Education of the Negro," p. 275.

ment, the main thrust of their argument was integrationist. Miller urged that blacks "preserve a just balance between the white world and the black world." It would be just as wrong for the Negro "to think altogether black" as it would be to continue with a curriculum so weighted "in the direction of whiteness . . . that [the] Negro has come to despise himself." Locke also denounced separatism and insisted that "the racialism of the Negro is no limitation or reservation with respect to American life." According to Locke, "The Negro mind reaches out as yet to nothing but American wants, American ideas," and hence the choice was "not between one way for the Negro and another way for the rest, but between American institutions frustrated on the one hand and American ideals progressively fulfilled and realized on the other." Emphasizing racialism as a way "to repair a damaged group psychology" by showing that blacks had contributed to civilization and were entitled to the rights and privileges of full citizenship, Locke hailed group pride and collective effort not as ends in themselves but as a means of converting "a defensive into an offensive position, a handicap into an incentive."[41]

Locke and his colleagues were laying the foundation for ethnic pluralism, not separatism. Like the young black tenor Roland Hayes, who declared that he would "never sing spirituals without classics or classics without spirituals,"[42] the Howard intellectuals were proud of their ethnic heritage and also demanded the right to participate fully in the larger American society.

IV

By refusing to interfere in the domain of the black deans, President Newman withstood the rising tide of racial consciousness from 1912 to 1918. Newman was more interested

---

[41] "Kelly Miller Says," 12 March 1923; Alain Locke, "Enter the New Negro," *Survey* 53 (1 March 1925): 632–633.

[42] Roland Hayes, quoted in Locke, "Roland Hayes," pp. 356–358.

in poetry than administration and was inclined to retire to his study in times of stress. He arranged unusual compromises with audacious professors. When the faculty of one professional school employed the unique method of smoking to keep the emphysematous president away from discussions of controversial issues, Newman was delighted to have an excuse for returning to his books. Yet some trustees believed that the resulting decentralization—with deans virtually autonomous within their spheres—led to "miserable mismanagement" and underscored the lesson that "there can be but one general to command an army." Consequently, when Newman resigned in 1918, "The hope grew that a real educator in the prime of life might take hold of the situation and work out a solution."[43]

In James Stanley Durkee the trustees discovered an energetic executive who believed that centralization of authority was the necessary prerequisite for expansion and improvement. As a first step in this direction, Durkee persuaded the trustees to create a new university office, that of the secretary-treasurer-business manager, who would report to the president and have responsibility for overseeing the finances of the previously independent professional schools as well as the regular academic departments. The new president then persuaded Emmett Scott to accept this position —an astute choice, for Scott had been Booker T. Washington's confidential secretary for eighteen years and as the *de facto* director of the Tuskegee Machine he had wielded enormous power in the black community.[44]

After asserting control over the university's finances,

[43] Dyson, *Howard University*, pp. 63–65; Logan, *Howard University*, pp. 146, 165; Alumnus, "Durkeeism," 1 August, 9 May 1925; Charles B. Purvis to Francis J. Grimke, 10 September 1920, in Woodson, *Francis J. Grimke*, IV: 285–288.

[44] Dyson, *Howard University*, pp. 65–66, 397; Minutes of the Meeting of the Howard Board of Trustees, 3 June 1919, Howard Archives; James Stanley Durkee, "Development at Howard," p. 5 (pamphlet, n.d.), Howard Archives.

Durkee proceeded with an ambitious plan to reorganize Howard's academic structure. Claiming that there was no longer a need for preparatory work on the campus, the president recommended that the academy (high school) and the Commercial Department be terminated. In addition, he proposed that the College of Liberal Arts be divided into a junior college for freshmen and sophomores and senior schools—each with its own dean—for upperclassmen specializing in fields such as education, applied science, music, public health, or liberal arts. At the same time, Durkee suggested that the faculties of all the undergraduate schools be combined into one "general faculty," with Durkee as presiding officer, that the trustee committees be restructured so as to permit more presidential influence, and that the president be given a special assistant to take responsibility for alumni relations. The trustees endorsed each of these suggestions, and thus Durkee quickly established the fact "that he intended to mold the University according to his desires."[45]

Durkee doubtless knew that his program of centralization would anger many blacks, especially those who sympathized with the two most prominent deans, Miller of the College of Liberal Arts and Cook of the Commercial Department. Miller had taught mathematics and sociology at Howard for more than thirty years and could count on widespread support when he protested against the subdivision of his large college into several relatively weak segments. And the attempt to abolish the Commercial Department was certain to arouse widespread sympathy for its dean, Cook, who had been at Howard for fifty-seven years

[45] Logan, *Howard University*, pp. 192–203; Durkee, "Annual Report, 1921," pp. 4–5; Durkee, "President's Annual Report, 1923," pp. 1–2, 11 (typescript), Howard Archives; Durkee, "President's Annual Report, 1925," pp. 7, 13 (typescript), Howard Archives; *Howard University Catalogue, 1924–1925*, p. 42; *Howard University Catalogue, 1925–1926*, p. 43; Minutes of the Meetings of the Howard Board of Trustees, 3 June, 7 February 1919, Howard Archives.

as a student, tutor, professor, dean, acting president, athletic organizer, and alumni secretary. Nevertheless, Durkee evidently counted on unqualified support from the trustees and, to make an impression on potential critics, he let it be known that his annual compensation had been set at $10,000 —triple that of the highest paid academic deans and an amount that, as the president himself boasted, "would make it unnecessary to count nickles and dimes."[46]

The Negro press subjected Durkee's centralizing program to withering scrutiny, and Miller led a delegation of ten faculty members who formally protested against the decision to divide the College of Liberal Arts. The president stood his ground and refused to make any concessions. Acknowledging that "there are those who yet fail to see the untold advantages of . . . our internal reorganization," he insisted that the senior schools made it possible for Howard's undergraduates to focus on studies that would be relevant to their future occupations. The senior schools had reduced "the number of those who graduate without knowing what their life's work shall be from about 75 percent for the whole country to less than one percent at Howard." Of course some devotees of the liberal arts recoiled from such rhetoric, and the chairman of the English department resigned with a parting shot at what he considered another incident in a long-standing racist campaign to limit the opportunities of blacks by extracting classics from the curriculum and substituting vocational training.[47]

Yet Durkee dismissed critics as people whose "eyes . . . cannot see and [whose] minds are closed" and warned students not to "let the months drag by in a careless and unfocused way. As soon as possible, determine your goal, and

[46] J. Stanley Durkee, quoted in Alumnus, "Durkeeism," 11 July, 1 August 1925.

[47] Alumnus, "Durkeeism," 11 July, 1 August, 18 July 1925; Durkee, "Annual Report, 1923," pp. 1–2; G. David Houston to Durkee, 23 October 1919, quoted in *Baltimore Afro-American*, 16 January 1926.

then walk straight toward it. You will gain many years, per-chance, by knowing early in your course what profession you mean to follow."[48]

It is clear that Durkee underestimated the tenacity of his opponents, perhaps because his previous experience as a pastor in the white suburbs of Boston afforded little oppor-tunity for familiarity with the racial consciousness that pre-vailed at Howard during the 1920s. Given the prevailing black mood, the centralization of power in the hands of a white president inevitably aroused opposition. The decision to demote the most powerful black deans stimulated indig-nation and provided a personal focus for the abstract demands for black autonomy. Moreover, far from being in-timidated by Durkee's $10,000 compensation, most profes-sors—who knew that "it takes years and years to train a col-ored educator to the stage where his efforts will bring him a yearly salary of $2,000"—were incensed at the thought that the trustees would give such a large sum to a white man who had no previous experience in education.[49]

Durkee himself belatedly recognized some of his initial blunders, and he assured one group of students that "if I were fool enough to try to dismiss Dean Miller, I would be too big a fool to be president of Howard University." But black people could not down the suspicion that Durkee was plotting to oust Deans Cook and Miller, for, as one alumnus explained, "Banquo's ghost was never more unnerving than the presence of these two deans."[50]

During the course of his eight years at Howard Durkee also engaged in angry confrontations with some of the most prominent black professors. Some Negroes believed there was "a sinister influence . . . to keep the youth of the race from being exposed to men of strong character who teach

[48] J. Stanley Durkee, "Opening Address at Chapel," *Howard Uni-versity Record* 17 (November 1922): 9–12.

[49] Alumnus, "Durkeeism," 25 July, 18 July 1925.

[50] J. Stanley Durkee, quoted in Alumnus, "Durkeeism," 16 May 1925; ibid., 18 July 1925.

them that they are men and women despite the many things that are thrown in their paths which teach them to the contrary."[51]

In 1919 there was a collision with Dean Woodson who, without consulting the president and after the trustees had rejected his request for a course in black history, sent out circulars inviting public school teachers to attend history seminars on the Howard campus. Hot words were exchanged and the trustees demanded that Woodson "apologize in writing to the President." Instead, Woodson resigned with a ringing declaration that because Durkee could not distinguish "between personal service and educational administration, it will be necessary for me to sever my connections with Howard University." Similarly, Houston relinquished his position in the English department and charged that conflict with the "strongest colored professors" was inevitable when the trustees chose "poorly equipped white men [for] positions which ought to be filled by well-equipped colored men."[52]

In a ludicrous incident, the 200-pound Durkee lost his temper and actually assailed Prof. Thomas W. Turner, a 150-pound botanist who refused to leave the president's office when Durkee denied his request for about five hundred dollars worth of laboratory equipment: " 'Well,' said the President, 'then I'll put you out,' and with that he pounced on Turner, who had on his overcoat and glasses, grabbed him around the shoulders, pushed him over chairs and around the room like a madman; and finally when it was found the door was too small to push Turner through he gave up."[53]

Of the president's many imbroglios with black professors,

[51] *St. Louis Argus*, 12 June 1925.

[52] Logan, *Howard University*, p. 208; Carter G. Woodson to J. Stanley Durkee, quoted in *Baltimore Afro-American*, 20 June 1925; Houston, "Weaknesses of the Negro College," p. 123.

[53] W. E. B. Du Bois, "The Durkee-Turner Incident," *Crisis* 32 (May 1926): 37-38.

the disputes with Miller and Locke deserve special attention as examples of the controversy that plagued Howard
during the years of Durkee's presidency. As noted above,
Miller first crossed swords with the president in 1919 when
the dean vigorously opposed the division of the College of
Liberal Arts. Hard feelings evidently persisted, for Durkee
later called Miller from his classroom and berated the dean
for drawing criticism down on the university by participating in a controversy over the superintendency of Washington's Negro schools. Miller replied that he would not allow
anyone to restrict his right to speak on public issues. And
when Miller testily added that only his respect for the presidency of the university prevented him from slapping
Durkee in the face the president became irate and called
the dean a "contemptible puppy."[54]

Relations between the two men became strained again in
1924 when one of Miller's letters almost cost Howard a special $500,000 congressional appropriation for the univer-
sity's medical school. The Republican leaders of the Senate
had assured the university that they would do their best to
have this special appropriation enacted as a supplement to
the usual funds for the general support of the university,
but Senate Democrats had threatened a filibuster that endangered the entire package. In these circumstances Dean
Miller, who often acted as a lobbyist for the university, left
a note with one of the Republican leaders, Sen. Reed Smoot
of Utah, suggesting that "if the $500,000 appropriation jeop-
ardized the regular appropriation . . . , then it would be
wise not to insist upon it." Of course this note was to be released only in the event that the Democratic filibuster
seemed likely to succeed. Amid the confusion that often ac-
companies the legislative process, however, Smoot released
the note just as there was a good chance to pass the entire

[54] Kelly Miller to W. E. B. Du Bois, 11 August 1925, WEBD
Papers; Du Bois, "Contemptible Puppy!" *Crisis* 30 (October 1925):
270; testimony of Miller and J. Stanley Durkee, "Stenographic Record
of the Durkee Trial" (1925 typescript), Howard Archives.

package. Fortunately for Miller and for the university, the matter was explained satisfactorily to the Republican leadership and eventually the Senate authorized both the regular and the special appropriations. Yet President Durkee was understandably miffed at the dean's indiscretion, and the next year Durkee devised an ingenious plan to remove his *bête noir* from the Howard campus.[55]

The trustees had commissioned a certain Dr. Robert J. Leonard of Columbia Teachers College to make recommendations concerning the future programs and operations of the university. In 1925 Leonard suggested that in order to broaden Howard's appeal the university should "enter upon an intensive, well-directed program of educational publicity." Knowing that the person responsible for this work would have to spend most of his time on the road speaking to alumni and potential friends of the university and recognizing that Miller's literary and oratorical skills and his long association with Howard made the dean well qualified for this work in public relations, Durkee persuaded the trustees to give this assignment to Miller.[56]

When blacks learned of this arrangement there was a nationwide protest that disrupted Durkee's plans for sending his rival away from the campus. Du Bois wrote that "the dismissal of Kelly Miller from Howard University after a lifetime spent unselfishly in the service is a disgrace so deep and hateful that J. Stanley Durkee must answer to an indignant public opinion for its perpetration." The editors of the *Messenger*, were equally angry: "To summarily drop Kelly Miller from Howard is just the same as summarily dropping Charles W. Eliot from Harvard. We are unreservedly opposed to the high-handed, indefensible, despotic policy which is responsible for this blow at Kelly Miller below his

[55] *Baltimore Afro-American*, 29 February 1924; *Washington Tribune*, 1 March 1924; *Norfolk Journal and Guide*, 15 March 1924.

[56] Leonard's report was published in the *Chicago Defender*, 27 June 1925. J. Stanley Durkee to New York alumni, 30 September 1925, quoted in *New York Age*, 10 October 1925.

belt." Arthur W. Mitchell, the president of the alumni's
Howard Welfare League, spoke for most graduates when
he declared that it was a disgrace to send Miller away and
thus divorce "the inspiration and enthusiasm of his brilliant
leadership . . . from the student life of the university." Bowing to this wave of protest, the trustees reversed themselves
and allowed Miller to stay at the university, where he
would play an important part in the campaign to force the
resignation of President Durkee.[57]

Unlike the powerful deans, philosophy professor Locke
was not a rival to the president. With a Ph.D. from Harvard, recognition as the first American Negro Rhodes Scholar, and impressive publications in aesthetics and art history,
Locke was generally recognized as one of the foremost
scholars of the race. But this diminutive and impeccably
dressed bachelor was not a hail-fellow-well-met and he enjoyed little influence beyond academic circles. Yet Locke's
fellow professors at Howard recognized that in addition to
his mastery of abstruse academic specialties, the dapper
professor also possessed the exact combination of stern will,
independence, and concern with bread-and-butter issues
that make an ideal shop steward. Consequently, in 1921
Locke's colleagues prevailed upon him to become secretary
and chief spokesman for the faculty's Salaries Committee.
It was in this capacity that Locke confronted President
Durkee and the trustees.

The years immediately after the First World War were
especially difficult for the traditionally hard-pressed professoriate, for the general cost of living soared by about 50
percent from 1915 to 1920 while academic salaries increased
by only 5 percent. To support themselves and their families,
many professors in technical and scientific fields took more
remunerative positions in business and industry. A growing
number of academic men devoted their sabbatical leaves

[57] W. E. B. Du Bois, "Kelly Miller," *Crisis* 30 (August 1925): 164;
"Kelly Miller and Howard University," *Messenger* 7 (July 1925): 260;
Arthur W. Mitchell, quoted in *Philadelphia Tribune*, 22 August 1925.

and summer vacations not to scholarly research but to preparing profitable "pot boilers."[58]

This commercialization of scholarship elicited expressions of alarm from leading academicians. Economist Thorstein Veblen feared that the ideal of scholarship—a community of scholars laboriously inching the world toward truth—was being perverted because only the well-to-do could afford the luxury of academic research. Philosopher Arthur O. Lovejoy concluded that this conversion of "men who should be engaged in serious intellectual enterprises into compilers of superfluous elementary textbooks" was "a grave menace" to the life of the mind.[59]

Along with these assertions that Sunday supplement features were no substitute for serious works of scholarship, the nation's press carried many articles stressing that the faculty was the essential ingredient in higher education and recommending that universities postpone the expansion of physical plant and the development of new programs in order to give top priority to increasing faculty salaries.

With the aid of an unprecedented fifty-million-dollar gift that John D. Rockefeller earmarked specifically for the purpose of easing the economic plight of the professors, many colleges in the early 1920s were able to increase faculty salaries by 25 percent or more.[60] Howard University received

[58] Many articles were written on the economic condition of the professoriate. See "Academic Salaries," *School and Society* 13 (1 January 1921): 16–17; "The Poor Professor and His Wife," *School and Society* 11 (24 January 1920): 115–117; Aubrey J. Kempner, "How Professors Live," *School and Society* 12 (6 November 1920): 436–441; and Robert J. Aley, "College Salaries," *Educational Review* 59 (March 1920): 244–249.

[59] Thorstein Veblen, *The Higher Learning in America* (New York: B. W. Huebsch, 1918); Arthur O. Lovejoy, "The Economic Condition of the Profession," *School and Society* 10 (27 December 1919): 749–753.

[60] "Mr. Rockefeller's Gift," *School and Society* 11 (14 February 1920): 191–192; General Education Board, *Annual Report*, 1919–1920,

none of this money, however, not because the Rockefeller
people lacked sympathy for Negro education but because
salaries were higher at federally subsidized Howard than
at other black colleges and were very close to the median
for all private colleges. Yet this statistical parity came peril-
ously close to the equality of the breadline and offered little
comfort to impoverished Howard professors who had seen
their purchasing power diminish to the point where, as William V. Tunnell noted, " 'twas all that men like [Kelly] Miller and myself with our large families could do to make
ends meet on account of prices."[61] Under these circumstances, and knowing that federal support militated against
the likelihood of assistance from private philanthropy, the
Howard professors organized to reverse their deteriorating
economic situation.

As secretary of the faculty's Salaries Committee, Locke
prepared a memorial that was signed by sixty members of
the academic faculty and presented to the trustees in June
of 1921. Asserting that most professors were "discontented
and restless" because meager salaries allowed "no adequate
opportunity for the pursuit of scholarship," this petition
called on the trustees to subordinate "all expansion involving financial outlay to the task of giving substantial financial
relief" to the faculty. The professors specifically requested
"a definite salary scale . . . making the compensation of the
full professor $4,000 a year with the other salaries related
to this figure." Rather than endorse this proposal, the trustees replied with a statement that, according to the Salaries
Committee, abounded "in expressions of cordial goodwill
and hopes of harmonious relationship . . . but . . . does not
furnish any adequate answer to our memorial."[62]

pp. 3-6; Raymond B. Fosdick, *Adventure in Giving: The Story of
the General Education Board* (New York: Harper and Row, 1962),
chap. 11.

[61] William V. Tunnell to Francis J. Grimke, 21 June 1937, in
Woodson, *Francis J. Grimke*, IV: 574-575.

[62] The original memorial of June 1921 is not available, but several

Although rebuffed by the trustees, the faculty did not abandon its efforts. Similar petitions were presented in 1922 and 1924, with additional rhetoric alluding to "startling inequalities in salaries" and requesting "a copy of the complete salary list of all [administrative] officers." The trustees initially refused to provide such a list, but when the professors threatened to focus public attention on the impropriety of "a secret and inaccessible payroll involving the expenditure of public funds" several conferences were arranged between the faculty's Salaries Committee and the trustees' Budget Committee. These conferences encouraged the faculty to hope "that substantial relief would be . . . forthcoming." In the end the trustees saw their way clear to add only $15,100 to the total salary bill of the university—an amount that left the Salaries Committee "disappointed . . . to express the situation mildly" and led to an angry charge that "there was not the slightest attempt to respond to our memorial either in substance or in the terms in which it was presented."[63]

Locke then prepared an extraordinary statement that fifty-three professors signed and released to the press. Noting that "on opening our pay envelopes we found that the allotments were so small that we hardly knew whether to frown or laugh," the professors characterized their raises as "aggravating pittances" and dourly observed that once again the trustees had neglected faculty salaries and emphasized the need for new buildings and equipment. The professors acknowledged that it was easier "to persuade Congress to grant a building or material equipment than to vote for an increase in salaries," but they nevertheless as-

portions of that memorial were quoted in subsequent "Petitions" and "Memorials" to the president and board of trustees. The petitions of 1 June 1922 and 15 November 1924 are available in the Howard Archives.

[63] "Petition to the President," 1 June 1922; *Washington Daily American*, 10 December, 22 December 1924; "Memorial of the Teachers," 15 November 1924.

serted that "the faculty is the center of gravity as well as the seat of loyalty and devotion of any institution of learning." They sarcastically noted that "the action of the Budget Committee in doling out pittances in answer to our request for the adoption of a reasonable salary scale is not calculated to add to 'the happiness of our experiences.' "[64]

The professors' disappointment turned to indignation when they learned that most of the dissident faculty members had received small raises of from $60 to $120 per year, while supporters of the administration received as much as $720. Such glaring discrepancies naturally intensified dissatisfaction. The professors noted, "It humiliates the just dignity and . . . pride of any body of professional workers to have the administration piece out their pay by doling out a few dollars here and there according to its goodwill and pleasure." Inevitably there were professors who suspected that Durkee was bent on converting Howard "into a veritable plantation, where slaves must get the goodwill of the master or suffer the consequences." Some believed that the faculty was divided more sharply between "men and henchmen" than between blacks and whites.[65]

Most members of the academic faculty saw no justification "for the glaring disparity existing among instructors and officers of the same grade." Thus Locke and the other members of the Salaries Committee demanded a salary scale "not merely because of the higher compensation it carries, but also that a teacher may know beforehand his salary from his grade." Everyone acknowledged that proper credit should be given for publication and other evidence of scholarship, but the members of the Salaries Committee believed that scholarly attainments should be rewarded when promoting a teacher from one rank to the next. ("If a teacher is

[64] "Correspondence of the Salaries Committee," in *Washington Daily American*, 22 December 1924; "Memorial of the Teachers," 15 November 1924.

[65] "Correspondence of the Salaries Committee," 22 December 1924; Alumnus, "Durkeeism," 25 July 1925, 20 February 1926.

not worthy of the compensation, he should not be promoted to the grade.") In their view, the main problem at Howard was arbitrary administration and the sycophancy it spawned, and they insisted that "within a given grade, advancement from minimum to maximum should be automatic."[66]

Writing privately to Du Bois, Locke confided that this was the key to the controversy:

In the salary campaign . . . we have stressed not merely the raising of salaries but the standardizing of grade by a definite salary schedule. The real reason for refusing this has been that it would take political patronage and favoritism out of the hands of the administrative officers —their best club in breaking faculty morale and prestige. All sorts of anomalies exist—many associate professors receiving more than full professors, and assistants more then associates, etc., not so much because of limited funds as because of favoritism and pay for political service and espionage. . . . Dr. Durkee has repeatedly insisted on "personal loyalty and cooperation," and favored, promoted, and made close counsellors of men who would give it, and persecuted, embarrassed and demoted men who would not.[67]

In addition to complaining about arbitrariness with regard to salaries and promotions, several professors charged that President Durkee ignored proper administrative channels and usurped the prerogatives of the faculty. The deans of the schools of liberal arts, education, and medicine all complained of instances where Durkee had forced the appointment of professors in spite of opposition from the deans and faculties.[68]

[66] "Petition to the President," 1 June 1922; "Correspondence of the Salaries Committee," 22 December 1924.
[67] Alain Locke to W. E. B. Du Bois, summer 1925, WEBD Papers.
[68] Ibid.: *Washington Post*, 7 June 1925.

These accusations disturbed even those who initially were disposed to stand by the president. Writing to a fellow black trustee in 1920, Charles B. Purvis had expressed little sympathy for the dissident members of the faculty. He thought there had been "entirely too much freedom of criticism of the presidents of the University," and he recommended that the trustees "grant to every dissatisfied professor the right to resign." As a doctor and former professor of medicine at Howard, however, Purvis believed that "only medical men are competent to decide who is fit to be a medical teacher." He was thus outraged by Durkee's 1921 decision to disregard the written protest of Dean Edward Balloch and the medical faculty and offer a professorship to a certain Dr. A. B. Jackson. Thereafter, instead of condemning "the spirit of disloyalty pervading the serveral departments," as he had in 1920, Purvis was "pleased to see the Faculty show their self-respect." Privately he confessed that Durkee was "a conceited and overbearing man [who] coveted absolute authority," and he predicted that there would be "trouble ahead if we . . . do not consider the rights of fully grown men who make up our professional departments."[69]

The most glaring example of administrative arbitrariness occurred in the spring of 1925 when, in addition to assigning Kelly Miller to public relations work, Durkee recommended the retirement of the sixty-seven-year-old George William Cook and the dismissal of Locke and three other professors (mathematician Alonzo Brown and French teacher Metz T. P. Lochard, both of whom were thought to sympathize with the student opposition to compulsory ROTC, and Orlando C. Thornton, an instructor in accounting). As was the case with Dean Miller's new assignment, these decisions allegedly were made in accordance with the

[69] Charles B. Purvis to Francis J. Grimke, 10 September 1920, 8 June, 13 July 1921, in Woodson, *Francis J. Grimke*, IV: 285–288, 314–315, 318–319; Purvis to Andrew F. Hilyer, 29 June 1921, in ibid., pp. 315–317.

recommendations of Leonard's report on the future operations of the university. Leonard had recommended retirement for those over sixty-five years of age and consolidation of courses in the Commercial Department—advice that accounts for the decisions with regard to Cook and Thornton. Yet the report's advocacy of thrift was so general that members of the Howard community immediately challenged Durkee's claim that the dismissals were made solely "for the good of economy and efficiency."[70]

The Howard Alumni Club of New York said the administration's official explanation was "but a pretext of the President to discipline those who have dared to differ with him on any issue." Roscoe Conkling Bruce, the assistant superintendent of Washington's Negro schools, averred, "These professors were simply too manly and intelligent for Durkee to dominate. The President's mind is of such low grade that it simply cannot grasp the concept of academic freedom."[71]

The belief that Durkee was punishing independent scholars—"humiliat[ing] them until he is satisfied that servility has displaced scholarship and manhood"—aroused Negroes throughout the country. "There is a widespread tendency to intimidate and crush real manhood displayed by Negroes," one alumnus declared. "This slap [at the professors] is not merely academic. It is a racial matter." The president of the Howard Welfare League pointed out, "In a well-regulated institution of learning no administration would think of summarily dismissing a full professor unless on specified charges sustained by his accusers." To others, discharging Locke and Brown—full professors with thirteen and sixteen years' service at Howard—without a hearing and with only

[70] *Chicago Defender*, 27 June 1925; *Baltimore Afro-American*, 27 June, 8 August 1925; J. Stanley Durkee to Hubert Work, 18 June 1925, National Archives, Record Group 48, File 20–14.

[71] *New York Age*, 10 October 1925; Roscoe Conkling Bruce to "Jessie," 27 June 1925, WEBD Papers.

two weeks' notice violated generally accepted standards of academic procedure and made it clear "that a professor's career at Howard University is held in the hollow of Dr. Durkee's hand." Spokesmen for the Student Council believed that Locke, Brown, and Lochard had been dismissed "not because of the reorganization, but because they had refused to go along with the administration . . . [and] as a warning to other members of the faculty that unless they think less of academic freedom and more of the administration's program, they, too, will be dismissed." A committee of the faculty belatedly insisted that no professor should be dismissed without written charges that won the concurrence of two-thirds of the members of the faculty's Personnel Committee.[72]

To supplement these charges of arbitrary administration, Durkee's critics searched for evidence indicating that the president himself shared the prevailing white insensitivity in racial matters. These critics knew that if there was one conviction that united the men and women of Howard it was the belief that, as trustee Francis J. Grimke phrased it, "any white man who aspires to be president of Howard University or of any colored institution must be absolutely square on what is popularly known as 'The Negro Question.' . . . A white man who isn't openly and above-board straight on the race question is entirely out of place at a colored institution."[73] Fortunately for the critics, just as the controversy with Miller and Locke was building to its climax in the spring of 1925 it was learned that Durkee clearly had compromised himself.

[72] Alumnus, "Durkeeism," 21 November, 1 August, 27 June 1925; Arthur W. Mitchell, quoted in *Philadelphia Tribune*, 22 August 1925; unidentified student, quoted in *Washington Tribune*, 20 June 1925; *Baltimore Afro-American*, 26 December 1925; "Policy Governing Suspensions and Dismissals" (typescript, n.d.), Howard Archives.

[73] Francis J. Grimke to Carl Holliday, 3 March 1916, in Woodson, *Francis J. Grimke*, IV: 161.

For forty years the Curry School of Expression in Boston had barred blacks from its lessons in elocution. After the death of its Tennessee-born founder, the school declined to the point where there were only thirty-seven students and the directors asked Durkee, one of the school's prominent graduates, "to direct it from Washington until we might get it on its feet, reconstructed." Of course Durkee recognized the paradox of simultaneously serving as president of a Negro university and of a school that refused to admit blacks, but evidently he felt that he could help the Curry School slowly surmount its discriminatory policies. Accordingly, Howard's trustees approved Durkee's request to assume direction of the school, and Durkee let it be known that "if we can make it live, there will be little difficulty, within a couple of years, of having it overcome its prejudices of all these years. If it will not do so, then frankly I shall have nothing further to do with it."[74]

Yet Durkee's two-year timetable suggested a lack of urgent commitment, and many Negroes were furious when the school insisted that it must defer to the wishes of "the large percent of Southern people who come here" and continued to reject black applicants. Blacks were quick to note that this was a hackneyed excuse. Many concluded that Howard could not afford to have at its head a leader who lacked strength of conviction. Graduates of the university characterized the Curry policy as "back-door practices," an "unpardonable insult to the self-respecting colored people of America." They demanded "flat-footed and unyielding resistance where matters of principle are at stake." Students at Howard placarded the campus with posters portraying Durkee as a two-faced hypocrite. In one scene he is sitting on a throne with fat salary bags at his side, telling his black charges that "there is nothing in this world that is too good for you." In a second picture he is standing in the door of

[74] J. Stanley Durkee, quoted in *Baltimore Afro-American*, 4 April 1925; Minutes of the Meeting of the Howard Board of Trustees, February 1925, Howard Archives.

the Curry School declaiming, "You cannot matriculate here.
. . . No Negroes allowed."[75]

The *Washington Daily American* summed up a widespread resentment when it noted, "Every case of discrimination and segregation finds its excuse in the time-worn expression, 'Of course, personally we like colored people, but
our patrons would not stand for justice to them.' These are
cowardly leaders. These leaders deserve more censure than
the individuals of the mob, for they are in positions to demand that right be done and fail to avail themselves of the
opportunity."[76]

To placate critics, Durkee resigned from the Curry
School after only a few months' service, and the university
trustees eventually modified two of his recommendations:
They granted a reprieve to Cook, delaying his retirement
until he reached the age of seventy, and voted a full year's
severance pay for Locke, Brown, Lochard, and Thornton.[77]
Yet these concessions were not enough to mollify the
aroused alumni who organized a campaign to force the resignation of President Durkee and the reconstitution of the
board.

The strategy of the dissident alumni focused on publicity
and was remarkably similar to that employed by Du Bois
at Fisk and by Sinclair and Archibald H. Grimke in their
1906 campaign to oust Howard's President John Gordon.
They collected documents, letters, sworn statements, resolutions, and personal narratives that G. David Houston, writing under the *nom de plume* "Alumnus," published in fifty

[75] E. V. McQuarris (Registrar, Curry School) to unidentified Negro
girl, quoted in *Washington Daily American*, 2 June 1925; Alumnus,
"Durkeeism," 15 August 1925; Charles B. Washington to editor of un-
identified newspaper (clipping), Dwight O. W. Holmes Scrapbook,
Morgan State College Library (hereafter cited as Holmes Scrapbook);
Baltimore Afro-American, 17 October 1925.

[76] *Washington Daily American*, 2 June 1925.

[77] *Washington Post*, 8 May 1925; Minutes of the Meetings of the
Howard Board of Trustees, June, December 1925, Howard Archives;
Official Statement of Trustees, 1925, Howard Archives.

remarkable installments in the *Baltimore Afro-American*. The paper was then edited by Carl Murphy, another former Howard instructor who had left the university with a grudge against Durkee.[78] To supplement this lengthy and often intemperate recital of grievances, the hostile alumni laid careful plans to elect their candidate for the presidency of the General Alumni Association, George Frazier Miller, a socialist clergyman from Brooklyn. But before the alumni could put their plan into effect, the students at Howard staged a well-publicized strike against compulsory ROTC, a strike that virtually closed the university for eight days in May 1925.

V

The background of faculty and alumni protest doubtless called the authority of the Durkee administration into question and in this sense prepared the way for student unrest. Yet only a minority of the students wanted to link their struggle against compulsory ROTC with the faculty's fight. According to student leaders Edward Lovett and Arthur Brady the strike was not directed at Durkee but at an intolerable faculty requirement that all male students had to take four years of physical education courses and two years of military training. Durkee tried to reconcile the students and teachers, and though some students hissed when the president appealed, "Let the 'old man' handle this thing," the student newspaper noted, "There are so many student opinions regarding our prexy that it is difficult to formulate a representative one. Some students severely criticize him, but there is a very appreciable number who are very fond of him."[79]

[78] The series appeared almost every week, beginning in April 1925 and continuing until July 1926.

[79] *Washington Post*, 8 May 1925; J. Stanley Durkee, quoted in *Herald Times*, 11 May 1925 (clipping), Holmes Scrapbook; *Howard Hilltop*, 18 February 1926.

Given this division in student opinion, it cannot be said that student opposition was a crucial ingredient in the storm gathering around President Durkee. But the student strike of May 1925 merits discussion as a catalytic agent that dramatically underscored the chaotic state of affairs on campus and further persuaded many friends of the university that Durkee's resignation was a necessary prerequisite for lifting Howard "out of this chronic and devastating confusion."[80]

The strike at Howard was at once part of a widespread surge of student opposition to compulsory ROTC on campuses throughout the country and also a protest against the way military requirements were enforced on the hilltop. As early as March 1924 the Student Council had expressed its opposition to compulsory ROTC, declaring that it was "a crime to see Howard students always on dress parade preparing for war . . . , sell[ing] their birthright because a few are receiving money from the government." Prior to the spring of 1925, however, opposition to ROTC was muted, largely because the ROTC department was short of personnel and was willing to disregard the absence of students who refused to attend the required drills and classes. Yet this failure to enforce attendance led to grumbling among the loyal ROTC cadets. The faculty finally acceded to the request of the ROTC department and voted that "when a student has accumulated a total of ten unexcused absences in physical education and ROTC combined, he shall be called before his Dean for warning, and when a student has accumulated a total of twenty unexcused absences in physical education and ROTC combined, he shall be dropped from the college."[81]

[80] "Negro Students," *Messenger* 8 (February 1926): 46.

[81] The background of widespread student protest against ROTC is discussed in James A. Wechsler, *Revolt on the Campus* (New York: Covici, Friede, 1935); Seymour Martin Lipset, *Rebellion in the University* (Boston: Little, Brown and Company, 1971), pp. 158–178, and in numerous articles appearing from time to time in that lead-

On May 5 the university suspended five young men who had incurred twenty cuts. The Student Council thereupon called a mass meeting which voted for a strike unless the rule governing attendance was abrogated and the five students "unconditionally reinstated in the university." Seeking to avoid a walkout, most members of the faculty were relieved to learn that the ROTC attendance records had been kept erratically—a condition that was brought to their attention "by fellow students who were willing to expose the laxity of the system by owning to having not attended regularly, some of them not at all." Consequently the faculty voted on May 6 to reinstate the five suspended students "because of inaccuracy of records," and President Durkee privately agreed "to let the rule lapse without official abrogation." The students, who knew of the reinstatement but were not informed about the president's arrangement to return to the policy of beneficent neglect, declared that "reinstatement of the students does not abrogate the obnoxious rule," and on May 7 they voted in favor of a strike.[82]

The Howard campus was placarded with posters proclaiming, "Don't Be an Uncle Tom," and asking, "What Is This Going To Be—An Army or a University?" Picket lines were established, and meetings were continuously in progress —with 602 students signing the strike roster on the first day, the senior class circulating a petition urging the strikers to "stick to their guns," and coeds in Miner Hall voting "to accept suspension when it comes and go home." The great majority of Howard's students supported the strike, and Kelly Miller commended "the solidarity of these young folk, the

---

ing student journal of the 1920s, *New Student*. For the situation at Howard, see *Howard Hilltop*, 29 March 1924, 8 May 1925; and Alain Locke to W. E. B. Du Bois, 9 August 1925, WEBD Papers.

[82] F. D. Wilkinson, "Chronology of Events Leading up to the Strike" (typescript), Holmes Scrapbook; Locke to Du Bois, 9 August 1925; *Washington Daily American*, 6 May 1925; *Washington Post*, 8 May 1925.

future leaders of the Negro race," who had learned "that the race must hang together or hang separately." Of course a certain amount of tension inevitably accompanied the strike, but one reporter claimed that "a jocular spirit" prevailed on the campus. Another observed, "The ROTC band seems to be an inexhaustible source of music, with the students that are not engaged in one of the demonstrations . . . dancing the latest in fox trots, etc." There were reports that "human barricades were formed at the entrances of the classroom buildings, and . . . the strikers succeeded in preventing 'lukewarm' students from entering the classrooms." But to most observers the strikers were conscientious and nonviolent. Miller insisted that "these Howard students waged an orderly campaign. They did not create excitement, damage property or injure persons. There was never any real need of the police, though the blue coats paid the campus a visit, only to return for the lack of business."[83]

Despite the general orderliness of the protest, most professors resented having "demands" made upon them and believed it would be irresponsible to compromise with students who were acting in "direct defiance of our constituted authority." Yet the faculty was far from united behind a positive program. Some professors exhorted their colleagues "to stand firm and issue . . . an ultimatum." Others voiced appeals to "be human and grant the students' demands." For four long days the professors debated the issues, and at a marathon meeting on May 12 they finally decided to issue an ultimatum "that the students who continue to obstruct other students from attending classes . . . will be suspended." Students who absented themselves from classes for fourteen days were warned that they would be "flunked." Along with these stipulations, however, a faculty mediating

[83] *Opportunity* 3 (June 1925): 164; *Baltimore Afro-American*, 16 May 1925; *Washington Post*, 8 May, 13 May 1925; "Kelly Miller Says," 23 May 1925; *Washington Daily American*, 9 May 1925; *Herald Times*, 11 May 1925 (clipping), Holmes Scrapbook.

committee informed the students that the professors were "willing to consider any complaint or grievance after they [students] return to normal relations with the University." Members of the committee were authorized to throw out the hint that if the students "would only return and recognize the authority of the faculty, their demands would be granted."[84]

The students naturally objected to the faculty's refusal to negotiate while the strike was in progress, and at first they chose to ignore warnings of impending suspensions and failures. When the faculty's decisions were posted in various buildings, one newspaperman reported that students could be heard all over the campus shouting: " 'Are we scared?' followed by an explosive 'No!' " When the deans prepared typewritten excuse slips for the protection of students who wished to indicate that the blockade had prevented their attendance at classes, the leaders of the Student Council advised all students to sign the excuse slips and thus subvert the faculty's efforts to keep attendance records.[85]

Publicity naturally increased as the strike ended its first week. Miller was only one of several professors who believed "it is a safe bet that this strike will be carried to the floors of Congress . . . when the appropriations are discussed." As if to fulfill Miller's ominous prediction, Cong. Henry B. Stegall of Alabama lost little time in declaring, "We've got plenty of good plow land down in my country that isn't being cultivated and that's where these strikers ought to be. . . . The proper place for these niggers is in the cotton fields or out on the railroad tracks, where they'd have to bend their backs and learn the value of a dollar." Echoing this view, another Alabama congressman, Miles C. Al-

[84] Locke to Du Bois, 9 August 1925; Wilkinson, "Chronology of Events"; *Chicago Defender*, 16 May 1925; *Washington Post*, 13 May 1925.

[85] *Washington Post*, 13 May 1925.

good, claimed, "This whole university is simply a Republican vote-catching machine."[86]

Fearing that the students might be characterized as "ungrateful and unpatriotic" and that this would reinforce traditional southern opposition to the university, one black newspaper criticized the students for playing into the hands of enemies of the race:

> Institutions of higher learning for Negroes are scarce— too scarce to be thus needlessly endangered. In every case they have owed their existence and continuance to the philanthropy of those who have contended, against large odds on the part of the southerners, that higher education for the Negro was the desirable thing. . . . Negroes are not in a position to finance and support such schools. . . . In the light of such consideration as this and taking into consideration the crying need for more institutions of higher learning . . . it is hard to understand or to sympathize with such outbreaks as the Howard students have been guilty of.[87]

Beyond fearing that the continuation of the strike would give Howard unfavorable publicity and jeopardize the annual congressional appropriation, many alumni believed that both the faculty and the rebellious students had worked themselves into positions from which neither group could easily extricate itself. Consequently, members of the local alumni association established a reconciliation committee which, after two days of practically around-the-clock negotiation, managed to convince the students of the legitimacy of the faculty's prerogative and the faculty of the justice of the students' complaints. Accordingly, on May 14 the students agreed to return to classes, and the faculty rein-

[86] "Kelly Miller Says," 23 May 1925; Henry B. Stegall and Miles C. Algood, quoted in *Chicago Defender*, 23 May 1925; "Two Congressmen from Alabama," *Chicago Defender*, 30 May 1925.
[87] *Dallas Express*, 30 May 1925.

stated the five students whose initial suspension had touched off the strike, granted amnesty to all who had boycotted classes, and agreed not to require attendance at ROTC until after a special committee completed its study of the twenty-cut rule and the general status of military training and physical education.[88]

This committee postponed filing its report until after the summer vacation, and then it was decided to revise the regulations so as to reduce the physical education requirement from four years to two, with ROTC as one of several options available. This solution seemed to please everyone, from students who demanded freedom of choice to professors who insisted that the new regulations make it clear "that the students did not have the remotest intention of deserting the ROTC but merely fought conditions incidental thereto." Thus the furor over compulsory ROTC receded, and the student newspaper noted that while military training was "daily becoming more and more unpopular" at some other colleges, the removal of the stigma of compulsion had actually made ROTC more attractive at Howard, where the army unit recorded "a marked increase in size. . . . And most important of all, the spirit of the men is much improved."[89]

VI

Despite the resolution of the strike, many blacks feared that unless Durkee resigned there would be "ceaseless conflict between the president and the student body as well as hesitant and grudging loyalty and devotion on the part of the members of the faculty." One alumnus recalled that the seven years of Durkee's presidency had been "consumed with bickerings and clashes." Another concluded that "Durkee

[88] Wilkinson, "Chronology of Events"; *Baltimore Afro-American*, 23 May, 6 June, 23 June 1925.

[89] *Howard Hilltop*, 7 October, 4 November 1925; "Kelly Miller Says," 23 May 1925.

must go if Howard University is to be saved—there is no alternative." Roscoe Conkling Bruce believed that if Durkee had enjoyed "the wholehearted confidence of the Negro people, . . . the specific student grievances would never have developed into outright rebellion against constituted authority." The *New York Age* noted, "The root of the trouble at Howard appears to be a lack of teamwork between the president and the faculty," and concluded, "The board of trustees must recognize the fact that harmony and cooperation are necessary elements in maintaining a great university."[90]

Far from expressing concern over the mounting controversy and disorder at Howard, the trustees reaffirmed their "confidence in the devotion and efficiency of President Durkee." They made it clear that "no official actions are taken except at the will and command [of the trustees]." To make certain that everyone understood their meaning, Charles R. Brown, the dean of the Yale Divinity School and president of Howard's board of trustees, publicly declared that "the trustees of Howard university and not a group of disaffected people are in control of the university." Brown later added that "strikes are so common in educational institutions that they are virtually a part of college education [and] surely no reflection on Dr. Durkee." These statements naturally delighted Durkee, who confided that "things are absolutely in hand, are going in a fine way, and will eventually come thru allright."[91]

Critics such as George Frazier Miller, by way of contrast, declared, "This is a challenge . . . to the alumni. . . . If it does

[90] *Messenger* 8 (February 1926): 46; Alumnus, "Durkeeism," 25 July 1925; George Frazier Miller, quoted in unidentified press clipping, Holmes Scrapbook; Roscoe Conkling Bruce to Hubert Work, 15 May 1925, WEBD Papers, *New York Age*, 19 September, 24 October 1925.

[91] "Statement of Trustees," quoted in *Chicago Defender*, 22 August 1925; "Statement of Charles R. Brown," ibid.; Brown, quoted in Alumnus, "Durkeeism," 5 September 1925; Durkee to Work, 18 June 1925.

not arouse them to do something to liberate their alma mater from the hands of its exploiters, they stand before the world adjudged contemptible cowards." Repeating Miller's contention that the trustees had thrown down the gauntlet, the *Washington Daily American* editorialized sarcastically that the statements of the board amounted to this: "We trustees, the majority of whom are white and not alumni of the university, are your lords and masters. What we say is law, no matter what you colored people and alumni think. As a matter of fact, we do not even care to hear your complaints against the administration, for anyone who dares to disagree with our policy of running your school belongs to a disaffected and disloyal group. We have spoken."[92]

Of course the intransigence of the trustees played into the hands of the Washington-based graduates who had begun to organize the opposition even before the student strike brought the Howard controversy to the boiling point. When the General Alumni Association held its annual meeting on the campus only three weeks after the strike had been settled, the graduates responded enthusiastically to Neval Thomas's thunderous anti-Durkee speech, "Loyalty to the University Means Hostility to the Administration." George Frazier Miller, the candidate of the opposition, was elected president of the association. The alumni then resolved that "Dr. J. Stanley Durkee has outlived his usefulness as president," and several prominent graduates spoke against Durkee in no uncertain terms. Attorney Thomas B. Dyett declared it would be unconscionable for the alumni to remain silent "while Dean Kelly Miller is being kicked about, Alain Locke . . . thrown out on the pretext of economy, and other savants as Dr. Woodson, Professors Houston and Brown, Dr. Turner and many others forced out of the school, for no other reason than personal differences with the president." Making a similar point, Arthur Mitchell

[92] George Frazier Miller to General Alumni Association (n.d.), Holmes Scrapbook; *Washington Daily American* (clipping, n.d.), Holmes Scrapbook.

urged his fellow graduates to "rise to the occasion [and] acquit themselves like men."[93]

Yet this rising tide of alumni protest failed to shake the trustees' confidence in Durkee. The trustees knew that Howard's undergraduate academic programs had received their initial Class-A accreditation in 1921. They were aware, too, that the university enjoyed unprecedented financial success under Durkee, with the annual congressional appropriation increasing from $118,000 in 1918 to $591,000 in 1925. Most of the trustees thought that this academic and economic recognition was a clear indication of administrative efficiency, and they tended to accept Durkee's characterization of the critics as "a disgruntled element . . . in Washington with nothing else to do, except find fault with the university."[94]

To reduce the influence of the Washington alumni, Durkee appointed Emory B. Smith to a $3,600-a-year position as alumni secretary. Smith immediately set himself to the task of discrediting the Washington-based General Alumni Association. He wrote that "the alumni situation at Howard has fallen into . . . disrepute" and that the opportunity to attend the annual meeting of the General Alumni Association was "necessarily restricted to those of our graduates who reside in the City of Washington or in nearby cities." Claiming that less than one hundred of Howard's six thou-

[93] *Washington Tribune*, 13 June 1925; *Washington Star*, 6 June 1925; *Washington Post*, 7 June 1925; *Baltimore Afro-American*, 13 June 1925; Neval Thomas to editor of *Washington Daily American*, 18 June 1925; Thomas B. Dyett to editor of *New York Age*, 26 September 1925; Arthur W. Mitchell to *Washington Daily American*, 24 September 1925; Mitchell to Charles R. Brown, 18 August 1925, WEBD Papers; Mitchell, 15 August 1925 (press statement), WEBD Papers.

[94] Resolution of the Howard Board of Trustees, June 1922, quoted in Durkee, "Annual Report, 1923," p. 6; Walter Dyson, "A History of the Federal Appropriation for Howard University, 1867–1926" (1927 pamphlet), Howard Archives; Logan, *Howard University*, p. 590; Durkee to Work, 18 June 1925.

sand alumni belonged to the "group now in control of the Association," Smith visited many of Howard's thirty-six alumni clubs and urged the creation of a new alumni council with each club electing representatives in proportion to its dues-paying members—a plan that Smith insisted would "break up the diabolical domination of the Washington faction."[95]

The established alumni leaders naturally dismissed Smith's plan as a scheme to place the alumni under university control, and nothing seems to have come of it except more hard feelings. Noting that the salary of the alumni secretary was larger than that of any professor on the faculty and that "the only thing which is nonrepresentative about the General Alumni Association is the fact that there is a handpicked Secretary," the critics condemned Smith as a toady and challenged him "to stand for election as alumni secretary."[96]

To combat charges that they were out of touch with the rank-and-file graduates, the leaders of the General Alumni Association sent William Sinclair on the road to visit several alumni clubs in the East and Middle West. To the delight of the dissident alumni, Sinclair returned with resolutions from fifteen different alumni clubs demanding Durkee's resignation. He also said that he had persuaded a few wealthy graduates to withdraw their pledges for thousand-dollar contributions to the university.[97]

The leaders of the General Alumni Association knew they would have to reinforce their appeals with the threat of continued disruption. They warned that they would picket when classes resumed in the fall. They sponsored "monster mass meetings" in several cities. And they escalated their

[95] J. Stanley Durkee, "President's Annual Report, 1925" (typescript), Howard Archives, p. 7; "Editorial," *Howard Alumnus* 2 (May 1924): 70; Statement of Emory B. Smith, 8 June 1925, Holmes Scrapbook.

[96] *Washington Eagle*, 13 June 1925.

[97] Alumnus, "Durkeeism," 9 January 1926.

122

rhetoric—with Thomas referring to Durkee as a "Negro-hating white man . . . who has . . . fired professors for teaching Negro students manly ideals," and Woodson refusing to appear "on the platform with any man who has insulted and exploited the Negro race to the extent that Durkee has." All of this tended, as one black editor wrote, "to place a chip on the shoulders of the students, and when they return to school they will be looking for trouble and upon the slightest provocation there will be friction."[98]

When classes resumed in September, however, the alumni shifted their attention away from the campus and toward Capitol Hill, where Southerners and strict constructionists were raising their annual challenge to Howard's congressional appropriation. Rejecting the traditional justification for this appropriation ("forty-five years of Congressional action . . . [and] the national importance of the Negro problem"), the opponents of the university saw "no legal ground on which the support of a private institution by Government funds can be justified; and there is no constitutional ground on which the federalizing of an institution for the benefit of a class of persons . . . can be defended." At least one southern congressman could be counted on to raise a point of order each year that would force the House to delete the Howard line-item from the general appropriations of the Department of the Interior. Defenders of the university would then restore the item in the Senate, and with the approval of the members of the House conference committee the money for Howard would finally be included in the general appropriations.[99]

[98] *Washington Eagle,* 13 June 1925; *Washington Sentinel,* 25 July 1925; *Baltimore Afro-American,* 29 August, 5 September 1925; Neval Thomas, quoted in unidentified clipping, Holmes Scrapbook; Carter G. Woodson to L. S. James, quoted in *Washington Tribune,* 14 November 1925; *Atlanta Independent,* 13 August 1925.

[99] Committee Report No. 163, to accompany H. R. 8466, 29 January 1926, 69th Congress, 1st Session, House Reports 1–362, serial no. 8531; Dyson, *Howard University,* pp. 301–314; Logan, *Howard University,* pp. 203–204, 258–265.

123

To obviate the necessity of these nerve-wracking negotiations, the trustees had thrown their support behind Rep. Louis C. Cramton's bill to authorize annual appropriations for Howard. The dissident alumni quickly recognized that protests jeopardizing the delicate congressional balance on Cramton's bill would make a greater impression on the trustees than a continuation of the turmoil on the campus. Accordingly, the critics played their trump card: They asked Congress to investigate charges of maladministration at Howard and to withhold action on Cramton's bill until Durkee was removed and a new method arranged for selecting trustees. Of course there was the danger, as Houston acknowledged, "that once the appropriations are withheld on the petition of colored people themselves, they may never be restored." But the critics had exhausted other alternatives and agreed with Houston that "no Howard University at all would be better than the present Durkeeised Howard." One reporter for the *Chicago Defender* summed up the prevailing mood: "We don't want to hold up Howard's money, but we're going to secure a federal investigation by asking Congress to consider the advisability of further appropriations for the university as it is now being conducted."[100]

The resulting spectacle must have perplexed even the most sympathetic legislators. Howard's black alumni were asking Congress to democratize the university's self-perpetuating board of trustees and to suspend appropriations while investigating charges of maladministration. The infuriated trustees had enough influence to head off a congressional investigation and to defeat Rep. Royal M. Weller's alumni-inspired bill to amend the university's charter to provide for a new board of not less than eighteen trustees, of whom one-third would be appointed by the United States commissioner of education, one-third elected by a mail ballot of the alumni, and one-third chosen by these two

[100] *Washington Tribune*, 19 December 1925; Alumnus, "Durkeeism," 4 July 1925; *Chicago Defender*, 19 December 1925.

groups. But the dissident alumni created enough confusion to prevent passage of Cramton's bill.[101]

The perennial southern opponents of the university naturally used the alumni charges as ammunition in their battle against federal expenditures for Howard. Rep. B. G. Lowery of Mississippi relished the opportunity to repeat alumni charges that it was irresponsible for Congress to give money to trustees who were not accountable "to the government or anybody else." And Rep. Butler B. Hare of South Carolina repeated the alumni's detailed charges concerning the use of government funds to reward sycophants at the expense of independent scholars. It is impossible to know the precise influence of such testimony, but evidently it was not without effect. Howard's 1926 appropriation was only $218,000, less than half the $591,000 appropriated in 1925 and the sharpest cutback ever inflicted on the university.[102]

Recognizing that critics of the administration had begun to exploit the university's most vulnerable weakness, the trustees at last agreed to consider the "extensive and persistent . . . criticism of, and charges against, the present administration of Howard University."[103]

A hearing was scheduled, and the General Alumni Association preferred eight charges against President Durkee:

1. His educational policies have been erratic, ill-advised and productive of sudden, arbitrary and disrupting changes in the organization and management of the university.

2. He has ignored the regular channels and customs of the university, especially in the appointment and dismis-

[101] *Washington Tribune*, 19 December 1925, 12 March 1926; Logan, *Howard University*, p. 204; Alumnus, "Durkeeism," 15 August, 5 September 1925.

[102] B. G. Lowery and Butler B. Hare, quoted in *Chicago Defender*, 8 May 1926; Dyson, "Federal Appropriation."

[103] Statement of Trustees, quoted in Logan, *Howard University*, pp. 233–234.

sal of faculty members without the advice, recommendation and knowledge of the deans and heads of the departments.

3. By reason of personal disagreement with Dr. Durkee, the university has lost a number of the most scholarly members of the teaching force, some of whom had national and international reputations.

4. He has pursued an arbitrary and dictatorial policy, supported by a system of espionage and intimidation and has established a reputation of personal suspicion, unreliability, reliance upon rumor without investigation, and personal animus and bias.

5. He has disregarded and antagonized the officials of the alumni association . . . by imposing upon this body an alumni secretary of his personal choice. . . .

6. He has insulted and violently handled faculty members, particularly Dr. Thomas W. Turner, whom he forcibly ejected from his office, and Dean Kelly Miller, whom he called a "contemptible cur."

7. He diverted approximately 50 percent of the sum of $15,000 provided by the trustees for increases of salaries of academic teachers to the employment of new teachers, all of whom he preferentially retained in June 1925 when his so-called retrenchment program went into effect. He has been arbitrary and vindictive in his recommendations of promotions, increases of salary and other executive action with reference to the teaching force.

8. His influence has been irreparably impaired by his open affront and insult to the Race in his acceptance of the presidency of the Curry School of Expression. . . .[104]

When the trustees met to consider these charges on December 10, 1925, the board room in Library Hall was a veritable court of law, with a presiding judge, Dean Benton

[104] Thomas B. Dyett, George Frazier Miller, and Isaac Nutter, "Statement of Charges Against Durkee" (typescript), Holmes Scrapbook.

Booth of the law school, attorneys representing both sides, stenographers, and more than fifty witnesses. Though the trustees agreed at the outset to grant "absolute immunity" to all witnesses, several professors were understandably reluctant to give a direct answer to the question: "Are you at the present time opposed to Dr. Durkee?" Charles Wesley, the chairman of the history department, objected "to being asked to testify with reference to the qualifications of a superior." He expressed the fear that the trustees might be conducting an inquiry "to find out the attitude of the faculty, possibly for other than mere purposes of information. . . . I am very much afraid that men who spoke their minds here, that ultimately it would get to the ears of those in power and do some damage, as in the past." Similarly, Dean Dwight O. W. Holmes of the School of Education suggested that if the trustees wanted honest answers they should "let everybody give his answer in a sealed envelope . . . without any signatures. It is very difficult, facing people who hire you, to say Yes or No."[105]

Despite misgivings, most of the forty-seven professors who testified expressed their firm opposition to Durkee. Kelly Miller was on the stand for nearly an hour and accused Durkee of being "vindictive" and of knowing "nothing about education." Wesley, putting aside his apprehensions for the moment, emphatically declared that Durkee was "more qualified for the pulpit" than for the presidency of Howard University. And Tunnell, while acknowledging that Durkee had done "very substantial work" in "increasing the financial and physical resources of the university," testified that Durkee was temperamentally unsuited for his office and attributed many of the university's difficulties to the president's "autocratic manners" and unsocial disregard for "the great rank and file of the people." Attorneys Thomas Dyett, James Lightfoot, A. S. Pinkett, and George Parker

[105] *Washington Daily American*, 10 December 1925; Logan, *Howard University*, pp. 232–237; "Stenographic Record of the Durkee Trial."

spoke on behalf of the specific charges preferred by the Alumni Association.[106]

Unfortunately, the incomplete stenographic record of the hearing does not contain the testimony of two of the university's most distinguished scholars, biologist Ernest E. Just and the recently fired philosopher Locke, but reports in the press make it clear that they were also outspoken in their criticism of the administration. Only a few professors spoke in support of President Durkee, most notably classicist Edward P. Davis and liberal arts Dean Dudley Woodard.[107]

After considering this testimony in a nine-hour executive session, the board voted unanimously "to exonerate Dr. J. Stanley Durkee . . . of all charges preferred against him by the General Alumni Association." Most of the accusations, according to the trustees, pertained to incidents in which Durkee was merely implementing the policies of the board itself, and the charges directed at Durkee's personal idiosyncrasies were not "sustained by adequate or convincing evidence." Beyond this, the trustees reiterated their view that Durkee was largely responsible for raising Howard "from a college of moderate size and influence to the most important institution for the education of the Colored Race in the United States."[108]

Yet no expression of trustee confidence could obscure the fact that this hostile testimony, in conjunction with the alumni's threat to Howard's congressional appropriation, placed Durkee in an untenable position and made his resignation inevitable. Even before the hearing, Arthur Mitchell had predicted that it would be impossible for Durkee to continue "in the face of a disaffected faculty, antagonistic student body, indignant parents, and a militant alumni." On

[106] "Stenographic Record of the Durkee Trial."

[107] Alumnus, "Durkeeism," 26 December 1925; *Washington Daily American*, 10 December, 11 December 1925; *Baltimore Afro-American*, 19 December 1925.

[108] Official Statement of the Howard University Board of Trustees, 10 December 1925, WEBD Papers.

the day after the trustees announced their exoneration of
Durkee, the *Washington Daily American* perceptively observed that "there must linger in the minds of the majority
of the Trustees themselves a fast-forming conviction that
when men like Kelly Miller, George W. Cook, Alain Leroy
Locke, Ernest Just, Dwight O. Holmes, William V. Tunnell,
and Charles Wesley speak so boldly and unanimously
against some if not all features of the present administration something is wrong. . . . The combined testimony of important members of the faculty is tantamount to a vote of
lack of confidence and . . . under the circumstances we fully
expect that the good sense of Dr. Durkee will cause him to
resign his presidency . . . while he may still do so with a
semblance of dignity."[109]

Durkee could see the handwriting on the wall. He knew
his usefulness at Howard was at an end, and he had come
to sympathize heartily with one of the black trustees who
had once suggested, "If a colored man is ambitious to be in
hell, let him be elected to the presidency of Howard University."[110] Thus in March 1926, only three months after his
exoneration by the board, Durkee accepted an invitation to
become pastor of the Plymouth Congregational Church of
Brooklyn, a pastorate made famous by Henry Ward Beech-
er and Lyman Abbott. In his letter of resignation, Durkee
made no reference to the stormy controversies that had accompanied his presidency, but to a friend he confided his
view of the situation:

> I did give everything I possessed of time and talent and
> consecration and prayer to Howard University. . . .'I did
> the things that had to be done, which no one else would
> do.' I knew great opposition would develop, I knew that
> those who could not see would fight. I did hope that I
> might be spared to put Howard University into the class

[109] Mitchell to Brown, 18 August 1925; *Washington Daily American*, 11 December 1925.
[110] Charles B. Purvis to Francis J. Grimke, 9 May 1921, in Woodson,
Francis J. Grimke, IV: 309–311.

of one of the greatest American universities. Our colored people would not permit that, so I turned away to a greater task—which is the task here at old Plymouth Church.[111]

VII

As soon as Durkee's resignation was announced, the underlying Negro desire to control Howard was voiced in explicit demands that the next president of the university be a Negro educator. Bruce insisted that "all other things being equal, distinct preference should [be] given an educational administrator of color. The appropriate president for a Jewish university is a Jew, for a Catholic university a Catholic, for a Negro university a Negro." The editors of the *Messenger*, while "not disposed to raise any special objection to having a capable white president," were "definitely and unqualifiedly opposed to the selection of such a president on the grounds that no Negro is available." Writing in the *Crisis*, Du Bois recommended that Howard "elect a colored man as president and this not because there are no white men fitted for the job but because no one of the white men best fitted will feel like stepping into Dr. Durkee's shoes."[112]

Expanding on this theme, Houston noted that it was difficult for white presidents to develop "a wholesome social intercourse" with their black constituents. He further argued that since the major white universities would not hire anyone who had been associated with a Negro college the whites who went to black schools tended to be either missionaries without scholarly ambitions or elderly men look-

[111] J. Stanley Durkee to B. F. Seldon, 20 June 1927, in Dyson, *Howard University*, p. 397.

[112] Bruce to Work, 15 May 1926; "The Passing of Durkee," *Messenger* 8 (April 1926): 110–111; Du Bois, "Howard and Lincoln," pp. 7–8.

ing for an easy 'retirement job.' " For these reasons, then, most alumni and friends of the university concluded that blacks were more likely than whites to possess the combination of academic and social attributes required for success as president of Howard.[113]

Recognizing the strength of this sentiment, the trustees met on March 25, 1926, and unanimously agreed that "the next President should be a Colored man." Harvard historian Albert Bushnell Hart stated that "the time had come to recognize that there were a good many colored men capable of serving as President." Retired YMCA secretary Jesse Moorland noted that blacks had developed a strong racial consciousness and doubted that "any white man can get at all the interests and difficulties that the colored people are dealing with." Col. Theodore Roosevelt, Jr., was sure a suitable colored president could persuade Congress to continue its appropriations for the university. Dr. M. O. Dumas of the National Medical Association was "for the fittest man whether he be black or white," but he was certain that among the large group of colored people "we ought to find a good man for the purpose." John R. Hawkins, the financial secretary of the African Methodist Episcopal Church, summed up the feelings of many trustees when he stated that " 'all his life' he had hoped that he would never have to consider any question on the basis of race, creed, or color. . . . 'But under the circumstances, the most inspirational act on the part of this Trustee board, . . . should be to find a colored man who would fit into this place.' "[114]

Alumni leaders feared that the trustees' definition of a "suitable" black candidate would differ from that of the critics who led the opposition to Durkee. One group of trustees campaigned energetically for their fellow board mem-

---

[113] Houston, "Weaknesses of the Negro College," p. 123.

[114] George Foster Peabody to Robert Russa Moton, April 1926, Peabody Papers; Minutes of the Meeting of the Board of Trustees, 25 March 1926, Howard Archives.

ber, Jesse Moorland. Moorland had been a trustee since 1907 and, according to George Foster Peabody, possessed "remarkable qualifications" for the presidency, not the least of which was his thorough familiarity with "all the personalities and problems that have been disturbing the peace." According to critics such as Houston, however, Moorland had consistently "been one of Durkee's most influential supporters," had "exercised some control (on the side of loyalty to the president) over other colored members of the board," and consequently was "in a very bad position to bring peace to the divided Howard community." Beyond this, the sixty-eight-year-old Moorland was not a college graduate, and Houston warned that "when the president's training has been a joke, the faculty can hardly do otherwise than to hold their self-styled leader in disgust."[115]

Houston was not alone in suspecting that "when the trustees learned that Dr. Durkee could not survive they set about laying plans for continuing their own policies through a nominal president." Several graduates pointed out that Moorland was singularly ill-equipped for the first important job that would face any new president, that of reconciling antagonistic factions. Others urged that "the next president of Howard University be an educator thoroughly qualified for his job"—a euphemistic code phrase for opposition to Moorland. Responding to this pressure (and also influenced by the contemporaneous success of the dissident alumni of Lincoln University [Pa.], who forced three successive presidents-elect to decline the nomination of their board), the trustees of Howard arranged a special conference with alumni leaders. Although there was an agreement not to divulge the results of this conference, one informed source revealed, "It is no secret that the alumni are bitterly opposed to the proposition to make Dr. Moorland president. . . . They are opposed to any candidate with such vulnerable qualifications. They want a live wire, and

115 Peabody to Moton, April 1926; Alumnus, "Durkeeism," 8 May, 15 May 1926.

not a person already certified as having reached the age of diminishing productivity."[116]

At this meeting with the trustees, the alumni stressed the desirability of appointing a professor or graduate of the university as the first black president of Howard. The past failure to make such an appointment allegedly amounted to an admission that the university had "failed dismally to produce an educator competent enough to be its president." Now, however, the trustees had "the opportunity to reverse such an unfortunate opinion," and many alumni favored the nomination of a Howard man. Most members of the faculty signed a round robin promising their full support for any professor selected by the trustees, and Kelly Miller and Dwight Holmes, both graduates of the university, and Charles Wesley, a graduate of Fisk, Yale, and Harvard, were frequently mentioned as candidates enjoying the support of the alumni.[117]

The trustees recognized the necessity of naming an experienced Negro educator as president of Howard, but they believed that candidates from within the university had been involved in the factionalism of the Durkee years and would be at a disadvantage in restoring peace to the campus. Consequently, the trustees offered the presidency to Bishop John A. Gregg of the African Methodist Episcopal Church, a black graduate of the University of Nebraska and a former president of Wilberforce University. The Negro press hailed this appointment as "a momentous decision" that marked "a significant advance in the policy governing Howard University." However, Gregg had commitments to return to missionary work in South Africa and declined the offer.[118]

[116] Alumnus, "Durkeeism," 20 February, 10 April, 8 May, 15 May, 22 May 1926. For the events at Lincoln see below, chapter 7.

[117] Alumnus, "Durkeeism," 29 May 1926; *Baltimore Afro-American,* 3 July 1926.

[118] Minutes of the Meeting of the Howard Board of Trustees, 8 June 1926, Howard Archives; *New York Age,* 12 June, 19 June 1926.

The trustees then decided by a vote of twelve to two to offer the presidency to Mordecai W. Johnson, a thirty-six-year-old black Baptist pastor who had received academic degrees from Morehouse, Chicago, and Harvard. Colonel Roosevelt, Jr., the chairman of the trustees' Committee on the Nomination of a President, acknowledged that the trustees had also considered the candidacy of Wesley, but explained that "on account of the internal troubles that have been rife in Howard University it was the belief of the trustees that it would be in the interest of all to select some outside man."[119]

Although a few leaders of the alumni association had reservations about the trustees' decision to bypass Howard men, all friends of the university recognized the necessity of joining together in support of Johnson's new administration. Du Bois stressed the importance of overcoming "clannish feeling," and the *Chicago Defender* encouraged blacks "to cooperate . . . in every possible way. We cannot afford to arouse factional feeling at this school." The editors of the *Messenger* developed this theme, "The white world will watch this experiment with great interest: our friends, hoping that nothing will go awry; our enemies, ever waiting and expectant that the slave psychology will reassert itself and precipitate a state of hopeless confusion because of distrust in Negro leadership."[120]

Fortunately for Howard, the goodwill induced by the appointment of a black president facilitated the necessary cooperation. Even Neval Thomas, perhaps the most vituperative critic of the trustees during the years of Durkee's administration, was carried away by the prevailing euphoria. "I am glad to have lived to see this day," he acknowledged.

[119] Minutes of the Meeting of the Howard Board of Trustees, 30 June 1926, Howard Archives; *Washington Post*, 1 July 1926; Theodore Roosevelt, Jr., quoted in *Baltimore Afro-American*, 10 July 1926.

[120] W. E. B. Du Bois, "Howard," *Crisis* 32 (August 1926): 167–168; *Chicago Defender*, 19 June 1926; *Messenger* 8 (August 1926): 167–168.

"Since my first entrance within her classic walls to sit at the feet of white and black alike, I have longed to see a Negro man or woman vested with leadership and living in the beautiful vine-clad mansion of the president. That day is here and we must appreciate it. We must get behind the new president with unanimous support. . . ."[121]

Johnson knew that honeymoons are ephemeral and that the erstwhile critics of the administration would scrutinize his policies. Consequently, within a year of his election the new president persuaded the trustees to endorse alumni petitions requesting the right to elect their own alumni secretary and restoring the eligibility for reinstatement of the four professors who had been dismissed in 1925. When the alumni then elected George Cook as their secretary, Johnson found other work for the ousted Durkee appointee, Emory Smith. And when Alain Locke returned to his position as professor of philosophy in 1927, the press reported that Johnson had established relations of "complete harmony" with the alumni. "Most significant of all," according to historian Walter Dyson, Johnson showed a genuine respect for teachers and department chairmen, who were given "a real budget over which they had control, and . . . a real voice in the appointment of teachers." Moreover, in perhaps the most important achievement of his early years as president, Johnson in 1928 finally succeeded in shepherding the Cramton bill through Congress, thereby removing any doubt about the legality of the Howard appropriation and thus ensuring financial support for the university. In these ways Johnson took advantage of the initial atmosphere of cordial friendship and laid the foundation for an enormously successful, although not always placid, thirty-four years as president of Howard University.[122]

[121] Neval Thomas, quoted in *Howard Alumnus* 5 (October 1926): 9-10.

[122] Emmett Scott to General Alumni Association, October 1926, Papers of Emmett Scott, Morgan State College Library; Dyson, *Howard University*, pp. 96, 370; Logan, *Howard University*, pp.

In assessing the controversy at Howard, the *Christian Century and Christian Work* hailed Johnson's election as "the passing of a new milepost in the long pilgrimage of a race."[123] This, indeed, was the greatest significance of the turmoil at Howard. Going beyond their brothers and sisters at Fisk, who demanded only that they be given a larger role in the management of their university, Negroes at Howard insisted on control of their school.

258–265; *Baltimore Afro-American*, 16 October 1926, 18 June, 9 July 1927.

[123] "Christian Century and Christian Work," quoted in *Howard's New President* (1926 pamphlet), Howard Archives.

Major Moton Defeats the Klan:
The Case of the Tuskegee
Veterans Hospital

I

While Fisk and Howard were preeminent among Negro colleges and universities of the 1920s, Tuskegee Institute was the most widely known black institution of higher learning. Established in 1881 in the midst of Alabama's black belt and renowned throughout the world, Tuskegee was a living monument to its founder, Booker T. Washington. To Washington, the keys to Negro progress were job training and interracial harmony. At Tuskegee students were instructed in more than forty trades, and Washington was famous for his skill in placating southern whites. He believed that no movement for the elevation of the southern Negro could succeed without the cooperation of southern whites, and thus he focused public attention on examples of white beneficence while slighting oppression and its consequences. He knew that "it is a hard matter to convert an individual by abusing him, and that this is more often accomplished by giving credit for all the praiseworthy actions performed than by calling attention alone to all the evil done."[1]

One of Washington's books, *The Man Farthest Down* (1912), developed the thesis that black Americans were better off than the peasants of Europe, and Washington consistently deprecated protest and agitation and empha-

---

[1] Booker T. Washington, *Up From Slavery* (New York: Bantam Pathfinder Edition, 1963), pp. 141, 165; Washington, "Chapters from My Experience," *World's Work* 21 (November 1910 to April 1911): 13783-13794.

sized the hopeful aspects of black life in the South. "The only time I ever become gloomy or despondent regarding the conditions of the Negro in the South is when I am in the North," he wrote. "When I am in the North I hear for the most part only of the most discouraging and disheartening things that take place in the South, but when I leave the North and get right in the South in the midst of the work and see for myself what is being done and how it is being done . . . then it is that I become encouraged."[2]

Along with flattering the white South, Washington stressed the importance of getting a job. His ultimate goal was equality of opportunity for blacks, but he believed that this would be achieved only after Negroes had acquired the skills and property that are prerequisites for respectability. He also believed that southern whites would not tolerate education for black equality, and consequently he let it be thought that Tuskegee was training Negroes for subordinate places in the American economy. As Henry Allen Bullock has noted, Washington struck a compromise and settled "for a special kind of education that would prepare Negroes for the caste position prescribed for them by white Southerners. . . . He left little doubt in the minds of large numbers of educators and philanthropists that Negroes required a particular kind of education for their particular condition." Of course Washington did not explicitly endorse the white program for training blacks only as hewers of wood and drawers of water, but through carefully selected ambiguities in language and by deemphasizing civil and political rights he managed to convey the impression that he accepted the southern orthodoxy. On rare occasions he unequivocally voiced the conventional wisdom of the white South; in 1915, for example, he assured fellow Alabamians that Tuskegee was "trying to instill into the Negro mind that if education does not make the Negro humble, simple,

[2] Washington, quoted in Basil Matthews, *Booker T. Washington: Educator and Interracial Interpreter* (Cambridge: Harvard University Press, 1948), p. 290.

138

and of service to the community, then it will not be encouraged."[3]

Many blacks were infuriated by Washington's synthesis of truckling and vocational education. Several black editors recognized that the Tuskegeean's emphasis on interracial reconciliation ran counter to the agitation that was their *raison d'être*. Negroes in all walks of life resented the implication that vocational training should operate within the constraints of white supremacy. While granting that industrial schools had some value, these blacks opposed the Tuskegee program because, as Monroe Trotter of the *Boston Guardian* explained, "the idea lying back of it is the relegating of a race to serfdom." Washington himself acknowledged that "serious injury will be done to the cause of hand training . . . if the idea once becomes fixed in the minds of people that industrial education means class education; that it should be offered the Negro because he is a Negro; and that the Negro should be confined to this sort of education."[4] But this is exactly the impression that came to prevail as the white South insisted on a second-class, demeaning training that prepared blacks for the subordinate roles accorded to the race.

Given the strength of the southern conviction that blacks must be kept down, it is difficult to see how Washington could have preached or his people practiced a radically different philosophy. Indeed, it may be that by reconciling southern whites to the idea of some training for blacks the Tuskegeean saved Negro education from total eradication. Nevertheless, it is not surprising that many blacks sympa-

[3] Henry Allen Bullock, *A History of Negro Education in the South* (Cambridge: Harvard University Press, 1967), pp. 89, 85; Booker T. Washington, quoted in Louis R. Harlan, "The Southern Education Board and the Race Issue in Public Education," *Journal of Southern History* 23 (May 1957): 200.

[4] Monroe Trotter, quoted in Stephen R. Fox, *The Guardian of Boston* (New York: Atheneum, 1970), p. 76; Booker T. Washington to Trustees of Tuskegee Institute, 31 May 1904, Papers of Booker T. Washington, Library of Congress.

thized with the delegates to the 1906 meeting of the Niagara Movement, who declared their unequivocal opposition to any system designed "to educate black boys and girls simply as servants or underlings, or simply for the use of other people."[5]

Black critics of Tuskegee particularly resented the fact that secular white philanthropy threw the weight of its influence behind vocational training and neglected the Negro colleges. Noting that the combined endowment of the two leading black industrial institutes of the 1920s, Tuskegee and Hampton, was seven times that of Fisk and Howard, W. E. B. Du Bois reiterated one of his most frequent complaints: that the philanthropists had "surrendered entirely to the white South on the matter of Negro education" and "undertook especially to restrain and starve Negro higher education and to concentrate upon what they regarded as the Hampton-Tuskegee industrial plan." "The South still wants these schools to train servants and docile cheap labor," Du Bois wrote in 1924. He also charged that in an effort "to divert . . . the already painfully meager revenues of the colored colleges" the leaders of the vocational institutes had lent themselves to "a long campaign of ridicule, abuse and argument [and] tried to tell colored people that the higher training of youth is unnecessary and wasteful." Explicitly rejecting the thesis "that education based on the Hampton-Tuskegee idea has been the real cause of the success of Negro education," Du Bois feared that "the slow strangulation of the Negro college" would be the inevitable "result of limiting the education of Negroes under the mask of fitting them for work."[6]

[5] "Niagara Address of 1906," in Herbert Aptheker, ed., *A Documentary History of the Negro People in the United States* (New York: Citadel Press, 1964), II: 909.

[6] W. E. B. Du Bois, "The General Education Board," *Crisis* 37 (July 1930): 229–230; Du Bois, "The Dilemma of the Negro," *American Mercury* 3 (October 1924): 184; Du Bois, "Hampton," *Crisis* 15 (November 1917): 10–12; Du Bois, "Colleges and Their Graduates

The bitterness of the controversy between Booker T. Washington and his critics subsided after the death of the Tuskegeean in 1915, and something of a *rapprochement* occurred in the 1920s when Tuskegee developed a separate collegiate curriculum that enrolled almost three hundred of the institute's fifteen hundred students. Partisans of the Negro colleges continued to resent Tuskegee's favored position with the white philanthropists and gloated over declining enrollments in the Institute's vocational courses. They hailed the development of Tuskegee's College Department as tacit admission that the original Tuskegee program had "not been successful and has been given up, while the essential soundness of the Atlanta, Fisk, and Howard program of general and higher education and teacher training has with all its omissions proved the salvation of the Negro race." Washington's successor as principal of the institute, Robert Russa Moton, had to make peace with the same forces that constrained the founder, but he also maintained excellent personal relations with the leading critic of vocational education for blacks, Du Bois. This friendship doubtless softened the enmity of the feud between blacks advocating collegiate education and those urging vocational training.[7]

Yet some tensions inevitably persisted. Several of Tuskegee's trustees feared that the institute was unwisely entering "into competition with other institutions in the college field," and Moton found it necessary to give repeated assurances that the institute had not departed "one iota from the principles or policies of its Founder. . . . The time

in 1914," *Crisis* 8 (July 1914): 129; Du Bois, "If I had a Million Dollars," *Crisis* 39 (November 1932): 347; Du Bois, "Education," *Crisis* 10 (July 1915): 133. As of 1928, the combined endowment of Hampton and Tuskegee amounted to $15,381,838; that of Fisk and Howard was only $2,098,543.

[7] Robert R. Moton, *Principal's Annual Reports 1923–1930* (pamphlets), Tuskegee Archives; Du Bois, "If I Had a Million Dollars," p. 347.

TUSKEGEE VETERANS HOSPITAL

is not yet in sight when Tuskegee Institute will not be needed as a training school for tradesmen such as it has been through all the years of its history." "In introducing vocational work on the college level," Moton explained, Tuskegee was not departing from its traditions but was simply making it possible for its graduates to acquire teaching certificates from accreditation boards that required college work. He also noted that Tuskegee gave no degrees in liberal arts, but merely supplemented vocational instruction with courses that familiarized students with "the liberal culture which every educated man should have."[8]

To reduce the possibility of hostile confrontations with the white community, the students at Tuskegee were subjected to as strict a disciplinary regime as that in force at any college of the 1920s. Male students were organized in quasi-military cadet regiments that drilled, performed guard duty, and policed the campus under the direction of the commandant of cadets, Col. William H. Walcott. Though the institute was not affiliated with any church, all students were required to have a Bible and to attend daily religious exercises. Other regulations required students to bathe regularly and to abstain from the use of tobacco, intoxicating drinks, and profane language, and there was a rigorous system of demerits and punishments. Students were not permitted to leave the campus without written permission from the principal, and when visiting the town of Tuskegee the boys were required to wear their regulation uniforms and the girls had to be accompanied by a female teacher. The institute openly proclaimed its right to open and censor students' mail, and no dances were allowed until the 1930s; even then the preceptresses were given strict instructions to enforce a rule requiring that couples be separated by at least one inch of open space.[9]

[8] Moton, *Annual Report, 1929–1930*, pp. 3–4, 27–32; Moton, *Annual Report, 1923–1924*, n.p.; Moton, *Annual Report, 1928–1929*, pp. 5–6.

[9] *Tuskegee Catalogue, 1924–1925*, pp. 18–20, 26; Horace R. Cayton, *Long Old Road* (New York: Trident Press, 1965), p. 195.

Under the circumstances, it is hardly surprising that there were continual rumors of student unrest at Tuskegee. Many students evidently shared the reaction of the young Claude McKay, who enrolled at Tuskegee to study agriculture but left within a year with complaints about "the semimilitary, machinelike existence there." Principal Moton himself acknowledged, "Too large a percentage of our students, for one reason or another, discontinue their studies before completing their courses." One member of the faculty claimed that most of the students "were well past high school age, and they were linked together against . . . the rigid, puritanical college rules. The student attitude [was] not dissimilar to the resistance many southern Negroes employed against whites. Maintaining outward servility and lip service to these New England moral principles, the students secretly rebelled and sometimes in most unusual ways."[10]

Nor was unrest confined to the student body. Many professors objected to the institute's efforts to ingratiate itself with the white South. There were complaints about the practice of segregating audiences on the campus and the maintenance of Dorothy Hall as a segregated residence for white guests. Almost everyone acknowledged the necessity of observing southern traditions when away from the campus, but many professors considered it obsequious for the institute to enforce the Jim Crow system on its own grounds. Segregation was insulting enough; it was doubly unfair to demand that Negroes themselves draw the color line.[11]

Yet the institute's administration would tolerate no dis-

[10] Kelly Miller, "Unrest in Negro Schools and Colleges," *Baltimore Afro-American*, 12 November 1927; "Claude McKay Describes His Own Life," *Pearson's Magazine* 39 (September 1918): 275-276; Moton, *Annual Report, 1926-1927*, pp. 7-8; Cayton, *Long Old Road*, p. 194.

[11] Jessie Daniel Ames, "The New Negro," in William Hardin Hughes and Frederick D. Patterson, eds., *Robert Russa Moton of Hampton and Tuskegee* (Chapel Hill: University of North Carolina Press, 1956), pp. 158-159.

sent, and G. David Houston, who taught at Tuskegee before moving to Howard, claimed that dismissal was the certain fate of anyone who dared to protest. He confided to friends, "I must leave here as soon as possible. I positively cannot remain here under such tyranny." Similarly, E. Franklin Frazier, who also began his teaching career at Tuskegee, recalled that he was once called in by the dean and admonished for carrying too many books on the campus. The dean feared that whites "would get the impression that Tuskegee was training the Negro's intellect rather than his heart and hands." To add injury to insult, when Frazier on another occasion refused to pay a voting tax to the city of Tuskegee, on the grounds that he was not permitted to vote, the institute paid the tax for him and then deducted the amount from his salary.[12]

Many professors doubtless agreed with Horace R. Cayton, a sociologist from the University of Chicago, who complained, "The administration was anxious to keep the goodwill of the southern white community, and all the old Booker T. traditions were carefully abided by." When Cayton explained to Moton that he felt uncomfortable at Tuskegee and asked permission to leave his position at the institute, the principal readily agreed. "I can understand your position," Moton replied. "Most of the teachers from the North don't fit in. We have a peculiar situation down here, and I imagine you have to be born in it to really understand it. Our race needs all sorts of people; probably you could contribute more in the North. You have my permission to leave."[13]

Given the administration's unwillingness to tolerate deviations from the southern orthodoxy and its close super-

[12] G. David Houston, quoted in Samuel R. Spencer, Jr., *Booker T. Washington and the Negro's Place in American Life* (Boston: Little, Brown & Company, 1955), p. 182; Louis Lomax, *The Negro Revolt* (New York: Signet Books, 1963), pp. 46–47.

[13] Cayton, *Long Old Road*, pp. 198–199; Robert R. Moton, quoted in ibid., pp. 204–205.

vision of blacks both on and off the campus, nonconformists generally removed themselves from Tuskegee. Thus the institute was free from the student and faculty protests that brought turmoil to other black colleges in the 1920s. This relative tranquillity no doubt confirmed many philanthropists in their view that vocational training was particularly suitable for blacks. In 1924 the Rockefeller General Education Board gave Tuskegee and Hampton half a million dollars each, on condition that the institutes raise a similar sum from other sources. Shortly after the terms of this offer were announced, George Eastman of the Eastman Kodak Company gave each institution an outright gift of one million dollars, and within two years the schools had raised five million dollars for their endowments.[14]

Commenting on the reason for the remarkable success of this endowment campaign, the *Chattanooga Times* praised Tuskegee's emphasis on "trades, agriculture, business, home economics, teaching [and] nursing," and said this concern for "essential practical training, rather than predominantly 'professional' and 'cultural' instruction, doubtless largely explains the rapid growth of Tuskegee as well as its popularity among the informed of both races." The *New York Times* made a similar point, "The institutions most effectively leading the way to the real emancipation of the race are of the type of . . . Hampton and Tuskegee." "There is a serious need of Fisk and Howard and their like," the *Times* acknowledged. "But there is a wider need of such schools as Hampton and Tuskegee to help the race to get on its feet economically and to go forward successfully in the walks of life which most of these millions will follow."[15]

Much of the credit for the success of the endowment campaign must be given to Tuskegee's principal, Robert Russa Moton, a man who, as the NAACP's Mary White Ov-

[14] Moton, *Annual Report, 1924–1925,* pp. 18–19; Moton, *Annual Report, 1925–1926,* pp. 3–5.
[15] *Chattanooga Times,* quoted in *Tuskegee Messenger,* 24 April 1926; *New York Times,* 1 October 1924.

ington asserted in 1927, would easily have won "if a vote were to be taken . . . among the white people to determine the best-loved Negro in the United States." Prior to his appointment as principal of Tuskegee in 1915, Moton had served for twenty-five years as commandant of cadets at his alma mater, Hampton Institute. In this capacity Major Moton (this was his rank as commandant and friends generally addressed him by this title) had demonstrated infinite patience and diplomacy in dealing with the difficult disciplinary cases that inevitably arose at a black school in the white South. Moreover, in speeches throughout the country Moton urged blacks to make peace with segregation and emphasized not the rights but the duties of the Negro. Blacks, he believed, should stay in the South and develop their own institutions, and he particularly stressed the importance of learning a trade.[16]

Like Washington before him, Moton also expressed an indomitable optimism concerning the future of race relations in the United States. The masses of people in most foreign countries were "far behind the Negro in such things as clothing, food, housing, education and the prospects of life in general," and he cheerfully concluded, "Relations between black and white in America are more cordial than the relations between the white race and the darker races in any other part of the world." "The world hears much of the occasional clashes between the races in the South," he acknowledged, but "little of the hundreds of cases of useful and helpful cooperation between blacks and whites that take place daily." This optimism was Moton's most endearing trait, and it was not unusual for southern newspapers to praise the principal of Tuskegee as "an ambassador from his people bearing the sincerest professions of goodwill for the white people, and recognizing the friendliness and helpfulness of the latter." Reflecting a widespread viewpoint, the

[16] Mary White Ovington, *Portraits in Color* (Freeport, N. Y.: Books for Libraries Press, 1971), p. 64; for Moton's career, see Hughes and Patterson, *Robert Russa Moton*.

Charlotte [North Carolina] *Observer* congratulated the trustees of the institute for appointing a principal whose regard for southern traditions guaranteed the "respect of the Southern people" and ensured the safety of "the fortunes of Tuskegee."[17]

Moton's popularity with whites inevitably aroused suspicions among blacks, especially those who believed that the Negro's cause was best served by demanding full citizenship rights. Some blacks acknowledged, "If certain exigencies demand that R. R. Moton . . . make certain statements for the benefit of the institution he serves, we need no assurances where R. R. Moton, the man, stands on the same propositions." But others wondered if Moton's conciliation did not exceed the requirements of expediency. The black editors of the *Cincinnati Union* believed that Moton was rising "to fame and fortune, as did his illustrious predecessor, . . . by bowing, cringing and nauseating servility." They reminded the major that while "fawning brings wealth from the great masses of white people all right, it also brings a vast amount of contempt." Most blacks recognized the need for a certain amount of conciliation, but nevertheless asked themselves "How far shall it go?" They sympathized with Du Bois who, in an open letter to Moton, expressed the "deepest solicitude in your case."[18]

Anxiety over Moton's leadership was elicited by a number of specific instances in which the major, in the interest of maintaining good relations with whites, was thought to concede basic rights. When Moton's wife was rudely ejected from a Pullman coach in 1916, for example, the trustees of Tuskegee Institute handled the publicity and released a statement announcing that Moton did not believe

---

[17] Moton, *Annual Report, 1926–1927*, pp. 21–23; *Albany Herald*, quoted in Moton, *Annual Report, 1922–1923*, pp. 27–28; *Charlotte Observer*, quoted in *Crisis* 12 (August 1916): 185–187.

[18] *Baltimore Afro-American* and *Cincinnati Union*, quoted in *Crisis* 12 (August 1916): 185–187; W. E. B. Du Bois, "An Open Letter to Robert Russa Moton," *Crisis* 12 (July 1916): 136–137.

in social equality, did not encourage Negroes to ride in Pullman cars, and bore no resentment against anyone for the treatment accorded to his wife. The implications of this statement were certainly deceptive, for Moton himself traveled by Pullman, as had Washington before him. Yet Moton, who was then beginning his career at Tuskegee, could hardly rush into print and contradict the trustees, and so he remained silent and suffered the bitter criticism of the Negro press.[19]

During the First World War the administration of President Woodrow Wilson depended on Moton to help dampen radical agitation among Negroes. The major sent Emmett Scott, the secretary of Tuskegee Institute, to serve as a special assistant to the secretary of war, but despite Scott's work for racial justice, many blacks were subjected to extraordinarily vicious discrimination in the United States army, while others received relatively fair treatment from the white people of France and England. This contrast made blacks all the more dissatisfied with conditions in the United States, and the Wilson administration feared there would be trouble after the war when the aspirations of the returning black soldiers collided with the prevailing white commitment to keep blacks in a subordinate position. Accordingly, President Wilson persuaded Moton to go to France, not to investigate charges of discrimination but to talk to the black troops and encourage them not to be arrogant upon their return. The plan did not work out happily for Moton, as the major received a great deal of criticism for allegedly whitewashing and excusing a very bad situation. When blacks refused to accept their subordinate "place" after the war, and instead competed with whites for jobs, political power, housing, and general *lebensraum*, the bloodiest race riots of the nation's history erupted in the summer of 1919. Yet except for an enigmatic statement rep-

[19] *Crisis* 12 (August 1916): 185–187; W. E. B. Du Bois, "Moton of Hampton and Tuskegee," *Phylon* 1 (Fourth Quarter, 1940): 348.

rimanding blacks for their "intense feeling toward the white people," Moton remained silent during this Red Summer, and again the condemnation of the Negro press rained down upon him.[20]

Criticism continued during the mid-1920s, when Moton devoted most of his time to fund raising, "traveling from city to city . . . addressing public meetings and holding private interviews in the interests of the [Tuskegee endowment] campaign." The editors of Harlem's *New York Amsterdam News* confessed, "Somehow we can't get up much enthusiasm over Robert R. Moton's 'goodwill tour.'" The *Baltimore Afro-American* protested vigorously against the old-time, hat-in-hand image projected by musical groups from Hampton and Tuskegee: "Anything to get money seems to be the idea," the *Afro* complained. "How far this has been carried can be seen from the fact that quartets from both schools have been broadcasting Negro spirituals nearly every Sunday to millions of radio listeners. . . . In the face of the constant efforts of thinking colored people to teach white people not to refer to them as 'darkies,' it is something of a shock to listen to . . . songs in which the word 'Darkey' occurs. . . . Five million dollars is a lot of money, [but] we believe the soul of Hampton and Tuskegee is worth more."[21]

Incidents such as these led many blacks to suspect that Moton was a weak-willed compromiser who sacrificed self-respect for a mess of pottage. Thus Du Bois, although he continued to count Moton as one of his closest personal friends, later confessed that the major's "almost childish faith in the goodwill of most white people made me at times angry. . . . I began to criticize him openly and bitterly. He became to me a symbol of 'Uncle Tom' and a 'white folks'

[20] W. E. B. Du Bois, "Robert R. Moton," *Crisis* 18 (May 1919): 9–10; *Crisis* 19 (November 1919): 345.

[21] Moton, *Annual Report, 1925–1926*, pp. 3–5; *New York Amsterdam News*, 6 December 1922; *Baltimore Afro-American*, 7 March 1925.

nigger.' I thought he was surrendering our rights and compromising with our enemies to even a greater degree than Booker T. Washington. The editorial pages of the *Crisis* attacked him without mercy."²² Given this persistent criticism, there was the danger that the reputation of Tuskegee Institute would be tarnished, not by a rebellion of students or faculty—an event that was almost inconceivable in the Alabama Black Belt of the 1920s and one that probably would have been doomed to failure—but by an erosion of sympathy for Tuskegee in the very black community to which the institute primarily belonged.

Yet this deterioration of Tuskegee's reputation was averted, partly because even the most severe black critics acknowledged that the institute, with its all-Negro administration, faculty, and student body, was as black as any institution in the land. Although many of the trustees were white, the issue of outside control was never as urgent at Tuskegee as it had been at Howard and other Negro colleges. Moreover, by 1923 Moton had seen the futility of always compromising with whites, and in the case of the Tuskegee Veterans Hospital he stood his ground and, amidst tremendous controversy and publicity, refused to yield to demands that whites be placed in exclusive control of the hospital. Though he was ever the wily diplomat who devised crafty stratagems that confused even his closest friends, Moton in this instance defied the threats of the Ku Klux Klan and at last lived up to the implications of his military title.

In choosing to battle for the principle of black autonomy, in this instance the right of sympathetic black physicians to minister to the wounded of their race, Moton demonstrated that he endorsed one of the cardinal demands of the New Negro militancy—that blacks themselves should control the major institutions that shaped their lives. In so doing, he formed new bonds of friendship with erstwhile black critics

²² Du Bois, "Moton of Hampton," p. 351.

who praised Major Moton for leading a rebellion that saved the soul of Tuskegee.

II

After the First World War the nearly 400,000 Negroes who served in the American armed forces were barred from all but a few wards in the government hospitals erected for disabled veterans. Black organizations naturally called attention to this discrimination, and a government survey substantiated allegations concerning "the inadequate provisions hitherto made for Negro veterans, many of whom were being 'farmed out' to private hospitals of inferior rank or, too frequently, not hospitalized at all even though seriously disabled."[23] Under these conditions, the Harding administration decided in 1921 to build a large federal hospital for black veterans. Yet this venture, initially conceived as a humanitarian undertaking, eventually became a storm center of interracial controversy.

At the outset, both blacks and whites protested against proposals to locate the Negro veterans hospital in the South. The board of directors of the NAACP and a national committee of black veterans both recommended that the hospital be constructed somewhere in the North. Explaining the rationale of the association, Du Bois pointed out that black soldiers should have been "cared for without discrimination in the same hospitals and under the same circumstances as white soldiers. But even if this were impossible because of race hatred, certainly the last place on God's green earth to put a segregated Negro hospital was in the lynching-belt of mob-ridden Alabama . . . [where] there is no protection . . . for a decent Negro pig-pen, much less for an institution to restore . . . life and health." Similarly, the NAACP's assistant secretary, Walter White, was "certain that the gathering to-

[23] Albon Holsey, "A Man of Courage," in Hughes and Patterson, *Robert Russa Moton*, p. 127.

151

gether of any considerable number of colored ex-soldiers, even though they be invalids, would cause opposition in the South. The South does not want any [black] men who have learned how to fight."[24]

This seemed to be the case, for white organizations in several southern communities refused to grant permission for the construction of a Negro veterans hospital in their midst. As one correspondent to the *Montgomery Advertiser* explained, "When the Government agents were trying to find a place suitable for the Negro veterans hospital, they came to Montgomery. Our people did not want it. . . . The Northern Negro wouldn't have good health in the Southern climate; nothing here would make him happy; and certainly he doesn't suit our people. . . . Our people will not stand for it."[25]

When it appeared that no southern city would permit the hospital within its confines, the government turned to Major Moton for advice on how to meet the problem. Moton sensed that the reputation of Tuskegee Institute would be enhanced if the hospital were constructed adjacent to the campus, and he proceeded to make inquiries to determine if the hospital could be located in Tuskegee. In this regard he quickly discovered that the white citizens of Tuskegee shared most of the fears and anxieties of their fellow white Southerners. The local state senator, R. H. Powell, later recalled, "When the negro hospital was suggested for Tuskegee, its white citizens objected strenuously, as did white citizens in other towns." They feared that "a bunch of negro officers, with uniforms and big salaries and the protection of Uncle Sam—negroes who are not responsible to our local

[24] *Baltimore Afro-American*, 18 November, 16 December 1921; W. E. B. Du Bois, "The Tuskegee Hospital," *Crisis* 26 (July 1923): 106–107; Walter White to Marianna G. Brubaker, 16 July 1923, NAACP Files, Library of Congress.

[25] Letter to *Montgomery Advertiser*, quoted in Holsey, "A Man of Courage," p. 128.

laws and not regardful of local prejudice—will quickly turn this little town into a place of riot."[26]

Of course all whites were not opposed to the hospital; some felt a paternalistic concern for blacks, and others believed that the hospital would stimulate the local economy. Yet most whites believed that safety required that the hospital be under the control of whites who understood and sympathized with the southern point of view on race relations. As one citizen explained, "We who know the negroes know that you cannot put them in charge or give them too much authority without their abuse of same. We have not forgotten the Brownsville or the Houston trouble. A negro when given authority and backed by the government will always abuse it. When negro soldiers were sent to Montgomery during the war they gave trouble and had to be removed."[27]

Major Moton recognized the depth of this sentiment and was willing to go out of his way to maintain the cordial relations so necessary to the life of Tuskegee Institute. Thus he did not object when Maj. W. N. Kenzie, a representative of the Treasury Department who had been sent to Tuskegee in 1921 to determine the sentiment of local whites, promised that the hospital would be directed by whites who understood the southern point of view on race relations. Nor did Moton protest when Kenzie produced a telegram from Dr. William Charles White, the chairman of a committee then supervising the veterans hospital program, pledging that the "hospital will be controlled and operated by whites." After receiving this assurance both blacks and whites en-

[26] R. H. Powell, "How U. S. Government Broke Faith with Whites and Blacks of Tuskegee," clipping from *Birmingham Daily News*, n.d., NAACP Files.

[27] William Watson Thompson to Frank T. Hines, 24 July 1928, National Archives, Record Group 15, Entry 2a, Director's File, Bureau of War Risk Insurance, Suitland, Maryland (hereafter cited as Director's Correspondence).

couraged the government to build the hospital in Tuskegee. Moton donated 316 acres of land adjacent to the campus of Tuskegee Institute. An additional 140 acres were purchased from a white woman for $7,000, and land for access roads was given at no charge by local white people.[28]

It should be emphasized, however, that all these arrangements were made on the assumption that whites would control the hospital. As Moton acknowledged in a confidential letter to his friend George Foster Peabody: "There was a definite promise . . . that the hospital would be under the management of white physicians. . . . I do not believe the hospital would have been [built] at Tuskegee had it not been for this promise specifically that it would be under white management. We would not have given the land or encouraged its coming if it had had the opposition of the leading citizens in the town of Tuskegee, and they would have undoubtedly opposed it had that promise not been made."[29]

Even without knowing that Moton had accepted the demands for white control, many blacks had grave reservations about locating the veterans hospital in Tuskegee. In addition to stating that black veterans would feel uncomfortable in rigidly segregated Alabama and that they would receive inferior treatment from unsympathetic whites, Negro "radicals" objected to the government's implicit recognition of Tuskegee as the capital of black America. Of course the Harding administration was merely following

[28] *Montgomery Advertiser*, 23 June 1923; *New York World*, 28 June 1923; Pete Daniel, "Black Power in the 1920s: The Case of the Tuskegee Veterans Hospital," *Journal of Southern History* (August 1970): 369–370n; Allan W. Ryff, "The Tuskegee Hospital Controversy, 1921–1924," (master's thesis, University of Delaware, 1970), pp. 3–5; "Official Resolution of the Alabama Legislature, 13 July 1923," Director's Correspondence; S. L. Brewer telegram to Frank T. Hines, 2 July 1923, Director's Correspondence; Robert R. Moton to Andrew Mellon, 17 November 1921, Moton Papers; Elliott Wadsworth to Moton, 26 November 1921, Moton Papers.
[29] Moton to George Foster Peabody, 11 July 1923, Moton Papers.

the precedent of previous administrations when it recognized the principal of Tuskegee Institute as the preeminent spokesman for the Negro race. But, as Herbert M. Morais has noted, "Times had changed, and the Tuskegee of 1921 was not that of 1895 or 1905, when Booker T. Washington was at the height of his popularity. More than a quarter century of unabashed Jim Crow and a war to make the world safe for democracy had brought into being a more militant Negro movement."[30]

By the 1920s many rank-and-file Negroes had come to look upon the primacy of Tuskegee with something of the skepticism long felt by radicals such as Du Bois and Monroe Trotter. Thus one veteran said that Moton's efforts to locate the hospital in Tuskegee were prompted by concern for the grandeur of the institute rather than by solicitude for the race. Another asserted, "We have been stultified . . . for many years by the assumption that the head of Tuskegee Institute was and is the accepted leader of the race." A spokesman for the National Medical Association, the black counterpart of the American Medical Association, warned that if the hospital were built in Tuskegee the "powers that be" would have taken another step in elevating the reputation of the institute. Claiming that "the dominance of Tuskegee . . . has reacted very unfavorably against our other institutions, like Howard, Lincoln and Fisk," this spokesman argued that "the dominating passion of Tuskegee is to centralize all Negro activities at that place, and to make it appear that the source of everything that is good for the Negro originates there."[31]

Most black physicians were graduates of either the Howard University Medical School or the Meharry Medical Col-

[30] Herbert M. Morais, *The History of the Negro in Medicine* (New York: Publishers Company, 1967), p. 113.

[31] George E. Taylor to *New York World*, 6 August 1923; anonymous veteran to *New York Amsterdam News*, 15 August 1923; unidentified spokesman, quoted in *Pittsburgh Courier*, 4 July, 1 August 1925.

lege (located adjacent to the campus of Fisk University), and many feared that the construction of a veterans hospital at Tuskegee would be the prelude to establishing a rival medical school at the institute. One Howard alumnus ominously predicted that "with its new Collegiate courses, with its large Preparatory classes, agriculture classes, and then a Medical School and a very large hospital, Tuskegee will be in a position to completely dominate Negro education; and it is easy to foresee that if a Medical School is ever established you can say goodbye to Howard University, because no appropriation will ever be gotten through Congress for a Medical School in the North as long as there is one at a favored spot like Tuskegee."[32]

Having at last discovered a community that would extricate the government from its predicament by accepting a hospital for black veterans, the Harding administration ignored black criticism and hastened to conclude negotiations. In May 1922 a $1,010,000 contract was awarded to Algernon Blair of Montgomery, Alabama, who completed the construction work in only twelve months. With facilities for six hundred patients in twenty-seven buildings spread over 464 acres, the Tuskegee Veterans Hospital was the third largest of the veterans hospitals and was the most significant federal project erected for Negroes prior to the New Deal. There were some complaints about the cost of the project—the final bill came to more than $2,500,000[33]— but allegations concerning cost overruns were almost obscured by a rising crescendo of controversy over control of the hospital. By 1922 Moton had come to recognize that a mood of greater militancy permeated the black community. To avoid estranging Tuskegee Institute from a people that had passed beyond the accommodationism of Booker T. Washington, Moton had no choice but to demand that the government appoint Negroes to the professional staff. But

---

[32] Unidentified graduate, quoted in *Pittsburgh Courier*, 1 August 1925.
[33] Ryff, "Hospital Controversy," pp. 5, 41n.

this, in turn, alienated whites who said that Moton's insistence that black professionals be employed at the Negro veterans hospital was inconsistent with his earlier promise that "the hospital would be under the management of white physicians."[34] Col. Charles F. Forbes, the director of the Veterans Bureau, sympathized with Moton's demand that blacks should not be barred from professional work at the Tuskegee Veterans Hospital. After conferring with Moton in June 1922 Forbes instructed one of his assistants to begin preparations for "building a personnel of colored professionals to man said hospital." Little was accomplished in this regard, however, and six months later, when the buildings at the hospital were approaching completion, Moton asked Melvin J. Chisum, the field secretary of the National Negro Press Association and a long-time Washington liaison for Tuskegee Institute, to inquire into the situation and "stir up" the government. Several officials in the Veterans Bureau assured Chisum that all was going well, but during a trip to St. Paul, Minnesota, Chisum quite by accident came upon a disconcerting "field letter" that was tacked on the bulletin board in the main lobby of Veterans Hospital No. 65. This letter, announcing the availability of positions at "The new U. S. Veterans' Hospital for colored veterans at Tuskegee," declared that "the medical personnel will be composed of white persons," and that "the medical coordinator selected to take charge of the post will be from the Reserve Corps of the Public Health Service, of Southern birth, and one who thoroughly understands the Negro." This letter shocked Chisum, since it flatly contradicted what he had been told, and led him to suspect duplicity on the part of "crackers holding key positions in the Veterans Bureau." He immediately wired Moton that "trouble was brewing" and urged the major to come to Washington and meet with the President.[35]

[34] Moton to Peabody, 11 July 1923.
[35] Melvin J. Chisum, "The Whole Truth About Tuskegee Hos-

This warning was hardly necessary, for the hospital had opened with a skeleton, all-white staff in January 1923, and Moton discovered that a white Alabamian, Col. Robert H. Stanley, was the chief medical officer in charge of the institution. This appointment was deeply disturbing, for when Moton donated the land for the hospital he had been assured that he would be consulted before anyone was appointed as director of the hospital. Moreover, it soon became apparent that Stanley was a confirmed white supremacist who unequivocally rejected Moton's suggestions that at least a few blacks should be appointed as physicians and nurses at the hospital. Such proposals, according to Stanley, were not to be taken seriously and must have been made "for diplomatic reasons," since a man of Moton's "mental ability and . . . knowledge of the situation would no more approve such a mixture than I would."[36]

Moton then suggested that Dr. John A. Kenney, the resident physician at Tuskegee Institute and the director of the John A. Andrew Memorial Hospital on the campus, be employed at the Veterans Hospital "as a consultant, to be called on when Col. Stanley desired for surgical work." To make this proposal as attractive as possible, Moton even suggested that "the surgical work might be done in our hospital, about a mile away, or that Dr. Kenney would take over his own nurse for surgical operations if it seemed best in order to avoid trouble." Yet Stanley considered even this sort of token black participation a violation of the Jim Crow system of racial separation; all he would permit was

pital: Inside Story of Developments, Together with Correspondence between the Principal Parties," *Pittsburgh Courier*, 30 June 1923; Pete Daniel, "Black Power in the 1920s," p. 370; Ryff, "Hospital Controversy," pp. 7–8; U. S. Veterans Bureau, Field Letter No. 78, 3 February 1923, NAACP Files.

[36] Du Bois, "Tuskegee Hospital," p. 106; Du Bois, "The Tuskegee Hospital Muddle," *Crisis* 26 (September 1923): 216; "Notes on the Tuskegee Hospital Situation," 11 April 1923, NAACP Files; Robert H. Stanley, quoted in Albon Holsey to Benjamin J. Davis, 30 May 1923, NAACP Files.

the use of black nurse-maids, whose employment was necessitated by an Alabama law which made it illegal for white nurses to touch black patients.[37]

Concluding that further conferences with Stanley would be futile, Moton wrote to President Harding on February 14, 1923, urging that blacks be given a chance to qualify for positions on the medical staff. The "leading white people of Tuskegee, including the probate judge and other prominent citizens," were ready to accept a mixed staff, Moton wrote, adding "that in this Hospital where there will be probably thirty or forty physicians, and perhaps sixty or seventy nurses, there should be at least one-half dozen colored physicians on the regular staff, and at least fifty colored nurses." The major admitted that the problem of staffing the hospital was "embarrassing me very much and will embarrass me and Tuskegee Institute more as time goes on." He warned that "if Negro physicians and nurses are debarred from service in this Hospital, without at least being given the chance to qualify under the civil service . . . it will bring down on my head, and on Tuskegee Institute, an avalanche of criticism which I think would be entirely justified." Making a similar point, and writing at Moton's specific request, James Weldon Johnson, the secretary of the NAACP, urged President Harding to issue orders "instructing the hospital authorities to employ qualified colored physicians and nurses, at least in part, for the personnel of this hospital devoted to colored soldiers."[38]

Harding knew very little about the racial situation in the South. Prior to his election to the presidency he was not familiar with Tuskegee Institute; he had only the sketchiest knowledge of the work of Booker T. Washington, and on first meeting Moton mistook the major for a job-seeking pol-

[37] Robert R. Moton to Bishop James Cannon, Jr., 31 July 1923, Moton Papers.

[38] Robert R. Moton to Warren G. Harding, 14 February 1923, NAACP Files; James Weldon Johnson to Harding, 31 March 1923, NAACP Files.

itician. Under the circumstances, most blacks doubtless agreed with James Weldon Johnson that "Mr. Harding will need to be educated on the race question . . . he knows absolutely nothing." To this end and assuming that the President was essentially a political man, blacks stressed the crucial importance of the Negro vote in certain states. Moton warned that the hospital controversy might "bring down upon your administration throughout the country, a storm of protest on the part of the Negro press and from Negroes, North and South, which I think would be most unfortunate."[39]

To avoid alienating blacks, and also because Harding was "uncompromisingly against every suggestion of social equality" and thought blacks should "develop their own leaders" capable of leading a separate Negro society, the President endorsed Moton's plea. Harding instructed the Veterans Bureau on February 23 that "there should be no designation of officials and nurses for the care of the colored soldiers at the United States Veterans Hospital at Tuskegee until there has been a thorough and determined effort to secure a civil service eligible list of colored citizens."[40]

After meeting with Moton and learning that it was difficult for blacks to qualify for professional positions because the Civil Service Commission "did not make distinction as to race, and thus had no way of knowing who were white and who were colored," the President also issued an executive order authorizing the commission to hold special examinations for Negro applicants. At the request of the President, Moton persuaded the Negro press to advertise these examinations, and the National Medical Association cooperated in

[39] Richard B. Sherman, "The Harding Administration and the Negro," *Journal of Negro History* 49 (July 1964): 156; James Weldon Johnson, memorandum on interview with Warren G. Harding, 15 January 1921, NAACP Files; Moton to Harding, 14 February 1923.

[40] Warren G. Harding, quoted in *New York Times*, 27 October 1921; George B. Christian to George E. Ijams, 23 February 1923, NAACP Files; "Notes on Hospital Situation."

the effort to find a sufficiently large number of qualified black professionals. To make certain that everyone understood the administration's intention, George B. Christian, the President's personal secretary, let it be known, "It is the plan of the Director of the Veterans Bureau, with the approval of the President, to man this institution completely with a colored personnel. . . . The Tuskegee experiment is going to afford the trained representatives of the colored race the opportunity to give proof of their capacity and efficiency in a highly important public service."[41]

This promise to install an entirely black staff at the Negro veterans hospital was quite consistent with the conventional Jim Crow separation of the races, but far from objecting to this form of segregation most Negroes were elated by Harding's policy. Several black ministers from Birmingham, Alabama, expressed their "respect [for] the white man's traditions, customs, laws, in the South in regards to separation of the races, and for this very reason we deem it wise to support the Government's policy in appointing Negro personnel in maintaining the Negro Veterans Hospital." Expressing the views of most partisans of Tuskegee Institute, Melvin Chisum gave the administration his "sincere personal word of thanks" for having saved Tuskegee "from deep humiliation." Had the President sided with those who demanded white control, Chisum explained, "we would have been engulfed in endless trouble for years to come [and] the colored people thruout the country would have blamed Dr. Moton and Tuskegee." Speaking for the NAACP, publicity director Herbert J. Seligmann enthusiastically endorsed the plan to man the hospital " 'complete-

[41] Holsey to Davis, 30 May 1923; Robert R. Moton to James Weldon Johnson, 21 March 1923, NAACP Files; *Norfolk Journal and Guide*, 10 March 1923; *New York Age*, 19 May, 9 June 1923; Frank T. Hines to Warren G. Harding, 18 June 1923, Director's Correspondence; John A. Kenney to Emmett J. Scott, 4 May 1923, Scott Papers, Morgan State College; Christian to Herbert J. Seligmann, 28 April 1923, NAACP Files.

ly' with a colored personnel." James Weldon Johnson admitted that "originally the NAACP protested against a segregated hospital," but he explained that "since . . . we are confronted with the situation that it will be manned either by unsympathetic whites or by Negroes, we insist upon the demand for an all-colored personnel."[42]

Among major black spokesmen, only the editors of the *Messenger* expressed reservations about *de facto* segregation: "For the Negroes it is a dangerous precedent to demand a jim-crow government institution. The hospital should be mixed with white and black porters, black and white physicians, nurses and maids. We are not impressed by the arguments that it can't be done. A yearly budget of $1,250,000 will make strange bedfellows." The *Messenger* thought it unconscionable "that an organization like the NAACP (whose very foundation stone is antisegregation) has demanded most vigorously that the Tuskegee Hospital be segregated!"[43]

The gentle chiding of the *Messenger* paled before the storm of protest that arose from white Alabamians. The state's junior United States senator, Thomas Heflin, assured President Harding that "ordinarily, I would say that it is all right for a negro hospital to be operated in every way by negroes." But in the case of the Tuskegee Veterans Hospital Heflin was "convinced that there was a distinct understanding between the government at Washington and the white people of Tuskegee that if they would consent for the negro hospital to be located there that it should be under control of white officials." Echoing this point of view, State Senator Powell accused the federal government of "a breach of faith

[42] Colored ministers of Birmingham to Frank T. Hines, 13 July 1923, Director's Correspondence; Melvin Chisum to George B. Christian, 28 February 1923, NAACP Files; Herbert J. Seligmann to Christian, 12 May 1923, NAACP Files; James Weldon Johnson to R. B. Lemus, 11 August 1923, NAACP Files.

[43] *Messenger* 5 (August 1923): 783; *Messenger* 5 (September 1923): 807–808.

and confidence" and declared, "We do not want any Government institution in Alabama with niggers in charge. White supremacy in this state must be maintained at any cost, and we are not going to have any niggers in the state whom we cannot control."[44]

In early May 1923 Powell and two other local whites traveled to Washington to present the views of white Tuskegee. Despite Negro fears that the President would succumb to this pressure from the white South, there was no change in the administration's official policy. On the contrary, shortly after Harding's conference with the white Tuskegeeans the President instructed his secretary to reassure the NAACP that "there is no possibility of the President receding from his policy of a colored personnel at Tuskegee." Assuming that the controversy had been settled, the NAACP's Walter White heaved a temporary sigh of relief and confided to a friend that he was "tremendously happy that the situation has cleared up. . . . It was a close shave but I am thankful that it came out as it did."[45]

The white citizens' committee was not willing to admit defeat, however, and their lack of success in persuading government officials in Washington strengthened their resolve to force Major Moton to accept white control of the hospital. Several anonymous threats were made against Moton's life, and to avoid trouble guards were stationed on the Tuskegee campus, a double watch was placed around the principal's home, and Mrs. Moton and the children were sent to the family's summer retreat at Cappahosic, Virginia. Nevertheless, a group of fifteen self-styled "leading citizens of the community" visited Moton in broad daylight and demanded that he sign a statement endorsing ex-

[44] Thomas Heflin telegram to Warren G. Harding, quoted in *Montgomery Journal*, 28 June 1923; R. H. Powell, quoted in Holsey, "Man of Courage," pp. 131-132.

[45] George B. Christian to Herbert J. Seligmann, 14 May 1923, NAACP Files; Walter White to Albon Holsey, 24 May 1923, NAACP Files.

clusive white management of the hospital. According to Moton, one member of the group told him, "Booker Washington gave thirty-five years of his life to build up this school. You, unless you are too stubborn to sign a little paper here, are going to have it all blown up in twenty-four hours." Another reminded the major that "we have the legislature, we make the laws, we have the judges, the sheriffs, the jails. We have the hardware stores and the arms." A third claimed, "A thousand men . . . will be over on an hour's notice and wipe out the whole ——— institution if things are not going the way [we] want them to go."[46]

At this point, Moton, who had compromised so often in the past, saw the futility of always yielding to white racism and took a resolute stand that surprised even his closest friends. Answering that "all my life . . . I have believed that white and colored Southerners could work together," Moton faced the whites and declared that if he was mistaken in this view then "the best thing that can happen to me is to die."[47] "You say my life is in your hands," he continued, "I do not doubt it. You have in your hands all the things you have mentioned—the laws, the judges, the jails, and even the guns. . . . I haven't a gun in my pocket or anywhere else. . . . You can wipe me out; you can take my life, gentlemen; but you can't take my character. If Negroes who are thoroughly educated and trained for such service can't serve their own people, can't serve in that hospital, on land given by a Negro school, for Negro veterans, provided by the Federal Government; if they can't practice in that hospital, then you may as well wipe out Tuskegee Institute and every other Negro institution in the world. The sooner you do it the better. . . . So far as I am concerned, gentlemen, I have only one life to give; but I would gladly give a dozen for this cause. . . . If I were to sign that paper, I

[46] Albon Holsey to James Weldon Johnson, 2 April 1923, NAACP Files; *Baltimore Afro-American*, 18 May 1923; Holsey, "Man of Courage," p. 132.

[47] Robert R. Moton, quoted in Ovington, *Portraits in Color*, p. 76.

would be deceiving my people and my country. . . . It's a Negro hospital, built for Negroes; and, gentlemen, if Negroes trained for the job can't run it, you can wipe out the hospital and the school and Moton."[48] This confrontation no doubt stunned the white committeemen and served as a catharsis that enabled Moton to discharge pent-up bitterness. But the major, who was more in character as an interracial diplomat than as a combative man-at-arms, knew that no black man in the South could defy the white powers consistently. Accordingly, at the very beginning of the controversy Moton had admitted to James Weldon Johnson that he might need "the help of the NAACP." After Johnson promised "the fullest cooperation," Moton's secretary, Albon L. Holsey, spelled out exactly what the major had in mind. "In view of the circumstances, it is necessary for Dr. Moton's friends to take up the fight through the press, and by telegrams to important Government officials with Dr. Moton left out, so that he can truthfully say that the colored people, themselves, are making the fight for the Hospital, and that . . . he is leaving the matter alone." Concluding with a reminder that "all of our correspondence concerning the situation [must] be confidential because it would be disastrous if it was known that we at Tuskegee Institute had any part, no matter how small, in organizing the colored people away from here to protest against this despicable situation," Holsey promised to keep the NAACP "advised from time to time of the situation as it develops."[49]

Having thus laid the foundation for continued agitation, if that should prove necessary, Moton evidently decided that discretion was the better part of valor. In June the major left Tuskegee for three months, a move ostensibly prompted by the need to cultivate northern philanthropists

[48] Robert R. Moton, quoted in Holsey "Man of Courage," p. 133.
[49] Robert R. Moton to James Weldon Johnson, 19 February 1923, NAACP Files; Johnson to Moton, 24 February 1923, NAACP Files; Holsey to Johnson, 2 April 1923.

but one that also removed Moton from a threat-filled and increasingly dangerous Tuskegee and enabled him to work behind the scenes with government officials in Washington. Joining the major in temporary exile from Alabama were Dr. Kenney, the most prominent black physician in Tuskegee and a potential candidate to head the new hospital, and Mrs. Booker T. Washington, the widow of the institute's founder.[50]

With Moton working *sub rosa*, the NAACP took the lead in the fight. Focusing on the hypocrisy and inconsistency of white supremacists and segregationists, the association's press service planted editorials ridiculing whites who wanted jobs so badly that they were willing to serve and wait upon black patients. Walter White wrote letters to the editors of several newspapers, suggesting that whites were interested only in the hospital's payroll and that race prejudice had fallen "with a bang before the almighty dollar." Making a similar point, Du Bois insisted that "the only interest of white people in Alabama in this hospital is economic and racial. They want to draw the government salaries and they do not want any Negro officials in Alabama whom the State cannot dominate."[51]

Most of the major black newspapers commented in this vein, and so did many whites. R. F. Darrah, the president of a Mississippi lumber company, admitted, "For the life of me I cannot see why my good fellow Southerners aren't willing and glad for the institution to be entirely manned by negroes. We are always talking about negro development along segregated lines and here is as fine an opportunity to help the negro and at the same time allow him to help himself as I ever saw." The *Greensboro* (North

[50] R. R. Taylor to Walter White, 7 July 1923, NAACP Files; Holsey, "Man of Courage," p. 132; Holsey to Robert R. Moton, 6 July 1923, Moton Papers; *Baltimore Afro-American*, 13 July 1923; *New York Age*, 14 July 1923.

[51] Walter White to editors, 14 May 1923, NAACP Files: Du Bois, "Tuskegee Hospital," p. 107.

Carolina) *Daily News* predicted that if the government accepted the "fantastic" demands of white Tuskegee, "within a year this very town of Tuskegee would be on its ear again, accusing the government of putting white women at work that no white woman should be expected to perform."[52]

III

At the beginning of the summer, 1923, it seemed that black doctors and nurses would be permitted to minister to wounded veterans of their race. Government officials had repeatedly declared that the hospital would be manned by an all-Negro staff; Major Moton had refused to endorse the demands for exclusive white management; and many white Southerners believed that black doctors and nurses should play a role in caring for disabled colored veterans. Nevertheless, when the Tuskegee Veterans Hospital officially opened on May 20, 1923, the professional staff was entirely white, and the white nurses, who received regular civil service salaries of from $1,680 to $2,500 a year, were assisted by $50-a-month black nurse-maids. Spokesmen for the Veterans Bureau insisted, however, that this arrangement was only temporary, that the bureau still planned "to man the hospital at Tuskegee with a complete colored staff" and was using whites only "until such a time as the Civil Service Commission can furnish lists of eligible colored personnel in sufficient numbers to provide for the present requirements of the hospital and to make replacements in case of resignations."[53]

[52] R. F. Darrah to Frank T. Hines, 19 July 1923, Director's Correspondence; undated clipping from *Greensboro Daily News*, NAACP Files.

[53] Albon Holsey to Walter White, 21 May 1923, NAACP Files; Melvin Chisum to Herbert J. Seligmann, 15 May 1923, NAACP Files; Frank T. Hines to E. D. W. Jones, 23 June 1923, Director's Correspondence; L. B. Rogers to M. O. Dumas, quoted in *New York Age*, 23 June 1923; statement of W. M. Cobb, quoted in *Baltimore*

Many Negroes naturally feared that the Harding administration had yielded to the forces demanding white control of the hospital. The *Norfolk Journal and Guide*, a leading black newspaper, declared that "the statements emanating from the Veterans Bureau are too indefinite and give evidence of pussyfooting." Du Bois charged in the *Crisis*, "The Civil Service Commission is delaying unnecessarily and unreasonably in arranging for examinations and qualifying colored physicians and without doubt [is] going to cheat in every possible way." Walter White confessed, "The situation looks exceedingly dark. It seems as though we have acted nice long enough and have got to go to the mat in opposing the wishy-washy attitude of President Harding in his attempts to pacify southern sentiment."[54]

Meanwhile, Melvin Chisum learned from dissident government employees that most departments within the Veterans Bureau were headed by Southerners appointed during the Wilson administration. Led by Major George E. Ijams, a white Southerner and one of the top men in the bureau, these minor officials, according to Chisum, were scheming "to defeat President Harding's and Dr. Moton's plan of staffing the Tuskegee Hospital with colored professionals." Ijams himself had prepared a report contending that there were no Negroes capable of holding staff positions at the hospital. He had also organized what Chisum called "a widespread propaganda through Alabama which has for its purpose the manufacturing of a surface display of feeling on the part of the whites." The Veterans Bureau had rejected more than fifty applications from black physicians and nurses, and Chisum concluded that "there has not been one jot of sincerity [in the government's program] to qualify our own men and women for this work, but on the con-

---

Afro-American, 13 April 1923; George E. Ijams to Robert R. Moton, 1 March 1923, Moton Papers.

[54] *Norfolk Journal and Guide*, 23 June 1923; Du Bois, "Tuskegee Hospital," pp. 106–107; Walter White to William R. Valentine, 14 May 1923, NAACP Files.

trary every subterfuge, scheme and trick known to the highly developed bureau of discrimination has been employed to prevent colored persons from qualifying."[55] Chisum believed that President Harding and Brig. Gen. Frank T. Hines, who had replaced Col. Forbes as director of the Veterans Bureau, were men of goodwill who had been deceived by "crackers left over from the Wilson Scourge." He reported to Moton "that instead of any effort being made on the part of officials in the Veterans Bureau to prepare the way for the obtaining of colored professionals for the Tuskegee Hospital, the minor officials are improving every moment to prepare the way to make it appear that it is an impractical thing to do." To his friend Robert L. Vann of the *Pittsburgh Courier*, Chisum exclaimed, "It is astonishing what fools the crackers make of Yankees."[56]

General Hines was nobody's fool, however, and he soon came to recognize that Major Ijams and others were working to thwart the plan for an all-black personnel. Consequently, Hines scrutinized his colleagues' reports very carefully, and when W. M. Cobb, the chief of personnel in the Veterans Bureau, concluded in mid-March that there was not "a sufficient number of colored professional and technical workers with which to staff the hospital," Hines assumed personal responsibility for finding qualified black professionals. By the end of June he was able to report to the President that "we have been able to obtain practically sufficient colored personnel to man Tuskegee." He insisted throughout the controversy that the whites employed at Tuskegee had been "temporarily transferred from other institutions" and that blacks would be substituted for whites as soon as a full colored staff could be assembled.[57]

---

[55] Chisum, "Truth About Tuskegee Hospital"; Daniel, "Black Power in the 1920s," p. 372.

[56] Chisum, "Truth About Tuskegee Hospital."

[57] W. M. Cobb to John R. Francis, 13 March 1923, NAACP Files; Frank T. Hines to L. B. Rogers, 24 July 1923, Director's Corre-

Yet Hines thought it was necessary to proceed cautiously with the substitution of blacks. Though he firmly believed that "any fair-minded person must agree with [the blacks] in their desire to have something to do with the care of colored disabled soldiers," Hines insisted that "the colored veteran is entitled to the same high standard of care and treatment as his white 'Buddy.' " He feared that some black politicians were using the demand for black professionals as a cloak to cover their own designs to use the hospital for patronage appointments. This was particularly true of Perry Howard and Henry Lincoln "Linc" Johnson, two prominent black Republican politicos who operated from a law office in Washington.[58]

In February President Harding had asked Howard and Johnson to get together with the National Medical Association and other black groups and prepare lists of black professionals who could qualify under the civil service. Instead of doing as the President requested, "Johnson and Howard attempted to . . . install their own men at Tuskegee, undoubtedly expecting to make the most of the payroll and the supplies that went to the hospital." Hines learned of this plot from Moton and the NAACP, who warned that the black politicians wanted "to get the hospital in their control as a sort of 'pie counter' " and create a "political checkerboard rather than an Institution of service to the sick and disabled Veterans of the race." The director of the Veterans Bureau then "read the riot act" to Linc Johnson and released a public letter reaffirming the administration's commitment to a Negro staff. Hines claimed that "a certain element, prompted by a desire to obtain positions for certain individuals that are not entirely qualified, are attempting

spondence; Hines to Harding, 18 June 1923; Hines to E. D. W. Jones, 23 June 1923, Director's Correspondence; Hines to *Argus* subscriber [draft], 19 July 1923, Director's Correspondence.

[58] Frank T. Hines to L. W. Johnston, 16 July 1923, Director's Correspondence; Hines to C. Bascom Slemp, 10 November 1923, Director's Correspondence.

to becloud the issue by the publication of statements that it is not the intention of the bureau to man the hospital by a complete colored personnel."[59]

Hines was also aware of the government's initial promise that whites would manage the institution, and he feared that the sudden intrusion of large numbers of black professionals would exacerbate tensions in Tuskegee. White Alabamians had repeatedly warned "that a complete colored personnel would result in racial trouble," and Hines acknowledged that it would be difficult to provide proper medical service if the local atmosphere were permeated with bitterness. Accordingly, he reassured whites on several occasions that the government would not be a "party to anything that would bring about trouble between the white people and the Negroes." He announced on June 26 that the bureau would temporarily stop recruiting black personnel and that he would visit Tuskegee in July to discuss the situation with local citizens.[60]

After consulting with Moton, Hines learned that the principal of Tuskegee, in the interest of maintaining the interracial cooperation that had been essential to the development of the institute, was willing to accept white management of the hospital. Throughout the controversy, Moton insisted that blacks should be represented on the professional staff, but he believed that biracial participation was the ideal, and he was willing to concede the top administrative posts to whites. Though Moton reportedly believed that if a mixed staff were impossible, "then there was only one other alternative, *and that was to have a full Negro staff*," he insisted that it was unfair to claim that the leaders

[59] Daniel, "Black Power in the 1920s," p. 374; Memorandum of conference between John Nail, Albon Holsey, and Walter White, 7 May 1923, NAACP Files; Holsey to George E. Cannon, 4 May 1923, NAACP Files; Hines to Harding, 18 June 1923.

[60] Frank T. Hines, quoted in James Weldon Johnson, "Views and Reviews," *New York Age*, 14 July 1923; Hines to C. E. Sawyer, 12 July 1923, Director's Correspondence; *New York Times*, 26 June 1923.

of the institute were demanding an all-black staff. With the principal of Tuskegee taking this position, Hines was all the more inclined to proceed cautiously with the introduction of black professionals, though he never abandoned his segregationist faith in the desirability of a separate black staff.[61]

Despite the decision to proceed slowly with the introduction of black professionals, the atmosphere in Tuskegee was filled with tension, and Hines feared "that while the white population . . . would not take part in anything that would result in trouble to the Hospital, they might take such steps that would affect the administration of Tuskegee Institute." "I do not see how the situation could be worse," Holsey reported from Tuskegee, "as we are really on top of a volcano and can almost literally hear the lava sputtering down below." The initial explosion occurred on July 3, 1923, when the first of the hospital's black professionals, John H. Calhoun, a young graduate of Hampton Institute, arrived at Tuskegee to begin work as an accountant. When Calhoun entered the hospital, Colonel Stanley, the medical officer in charge, delivered a letter in an envelope bearing no postmark and gave orders that Calhoun be escorted away from the hospital by three armed white guards.[62]

Calhoun retained his composure and, according to Holsey, "did one of the cleverest things I have ever seen done in a situation as trying as the one he had to face." He took the letter and put it into his pocket unopened "while . . . Stanley looked on with astonishment." Of course Calhoun left the hospital, but he kept the letter sealed in his pocket until two days later when he met with General Hines, who was then making his long-awaited visit to confer with the white citizens of Tuskegee. "WE UNDERSTAND YOU ARE RE-

[61] Hines to Sawyer, 12 July 1923; Holsey to Davis, 30 May 1923, (italics in original); Robert R. Moton to Holsey, 29 June 1923, Moton Papers.
[62] Hines to Sawyer, 12 July 1923; Albon Holsey to Emmett J. Scott, 2 July 1923, Moton Papers; *New York Age*, 14 July 1923; *Norfolk Journal and Guide*, 14 July 1923.

PORTING TO HOSPITAL TO ACCEPT DISBURSING OFFICERS' JOB," the message began. "IF YOU VALUE YOUR WELFARE DO NOT TAKE THIS JOB BUT LEAVE AT ONCE FOR PARTS FROM WHENCE YOU CAME OR SUFFER THE CONSEQUENCES*** 'K' 'K' 'K'."[63] Hines was astonished when he learned that Colonel Stanley had cooperated with the delivery of this threat and immediately reprimanded the chief medical officer and ordered Calhoun to return to the hospital and begin work. In a formal accusation of dereliction of duty, Hines later informed Stanley, "Your action in calling Mr. John H. Calhoun, Jr., to fill a position as bookkeeper . . . and then not taking the necessary steps to avoid any friction . . . is not in accordance with the wishes of the Bureau and does not clearly indicate that you were in full accord in carrying out the Bureau's policies with reference to the Tuskegee Hospital."[64]

Meanwhile, many whites urged the necessity of a decisive confrontation. A full-page advertisement in the *Montgomery Advertiser* asserted that the South belonged to the white man, and the *Birmingham News* said that black doctors and soldiers, many of whom had lived in the North and traveled abroad, would challenge the southern system of white supremacy and black subordination. Believing that many of the black veterans were "already shell-shocked and many of them mentally unbalanced," some whites also feared that "it would be impossible to prevent bootleggers and dope vendors from selling their wares to them and that when these disabled veterans became charged with bad liquor and dope a colored staff would be unable to control them." State Senator Powell insisted, "We of the South . . . know the Negro far better than the Northerner does. We know that the Negro cannot control even himself. . . . The white race is the controlling race. . . . Here in Tuskegee, our

[63] Holsey to Moton, 6 July 1923; KKK to John H. Calhoun [3 July 1923], Director's Correspondence.
[64] Frank T. Hines to R. H. Stanley, 17 July 1923, Director's Correspondence.

ratio is about one [white] to four and a half [blacks]. Here the white man has controlled and will continue to control."[65] Responding to this sentiment, the Ku Klux Klan prepared a mass demonstration for the evening of July 3, Independence Eve. An initial rally was held at the state capitol in Montgomery, and then an automobile caravan transported the leading Klansmen to Tuskegee. Rendezvousing with approximately one thousand whites at the local railroad depot and led by a large car sporting a massive American flag, the hooded knights marched through the streets of Tuskegee in a single file that extended over two miles. As darkness fell, the soldiers of white supremacy lit a forty-foot cross on the outskirts of the town and then continued their procession down the road that led through Tuskegee Institute to the hospital. Confident that their message was unmistakable, the Klansmen maintained silence throughout most of the demonstration, and there were no overt threats against either the institute or the hospital. After the group disbanded, some twenty of the hooded demonstrators, who evidently were employees of the hospital, returned to their quarters for a meal prepared by the chief dietician.[66]

Blacks had no way of knowing that there would be no reprisals against Tuskegee Institute, and many Negroes evidently were prepared to use force to defend Booker T. Washington's school. There are no surviving documents on this point, other than one cryptic note from a certain John G. Porter, "If I can be of any service I am only forty-four miles from Tuskegee. I am ready. You can trust me." But blacks who lived through the confrontation say that earlier

[65] *Montgomery Advertiser*, 1 July 1923; *Birmingham News*, 28 June 1923; "Physician" to *New York World*, quoted in *New York Age*, 21 July 1923; R. H. Powell, quoted in Holsey, "Man of Courage," p. 135.

[66] *Montgomery Advertiser*, 4 July 1923; *Savannah Tribune*, 12 July 1923; *New York Age*, 14 July 1923; *Pittsburgh Courier*, 4 August 1923; Daniel, "Black Power in the 1920s," pp. 378–379; Ryff, "Hospital Controversy," pp. 26–27.

in the afternoon, before the arrival of the Klansmen, several carloads of blacks arrived at the institute, prepared to use firearms if the Klansmen made any move against Tuskegee Institute or assaulted the dormitory where John H. Calhoun was staying. According to these recollections, Colonel Walcott, the commandant of cadets at Tuskegee, "stationed these black militants about the buildings, along the highway, and across the access routes, allowing his reserves to remain nearby in the countryside ready to speed in if trouble broke out." Fortunately for all concerned, the Klansmen never strayed from the serpentine road that led through the campus to the hospital.[67]

General Hines arrived in Tuskegee two days after the Klan's demonstration and discussed the situation with local whites. He admitted that the Harding administration planned "to place colored physicians in charge of the hospital" and claimed that the officials who had earlier promised that the hospital would be "controlled and operated by whites" had no authority to bind the government. Nevertheless, Hines recognized the obstinate mood of the white citizens and concluded that it would not be feasible to install a completely black staff at that time. "In order that the ex-servicemen may receive the proper treatment," he explained, "it will be necessary to have the cooperation of the local white people and, hence, we will give due consideration to their views." He assured whites that the government would do nothing that might "bring disorder to this community." He promised that he would work with a committee of local whites to arrange a compromise settlement.[68]

Far from being reconciled to the inevitability of a compromise, the leaders of the NAACP thought Hines had been

[67] John G. Porter to James Weldon Johnson, 28 June 1923, NAACP Files; Daniel, "Black Power in the 1920s," p. 378; Ryff, "Hospital Controversy," pp. 26–27.

[68] Frank T. Hines, quoted in *Pittsburgh Courier*, 14 July 1923, *Norfolk Journal and Guide*, 14 July 1923, *New York Sun and Globe*, 6 July 1923, and *New York World*, 7 July 1923.

intimidated. The association's board of directors urged President Harding to stick to his promise of a "complete colored staff" and recommended that federal troops be dispatched to Alabama to protect life and property at Tuskegee Institute. James Weldon Johnson claimed the white people of Alabama had "put forth arguments that could not be matched in a convention of lunatics." "This whole situation," he declared, "is one which again tests the Administration's attitude towards colored people, as well as the government's integrity in the face of the Ku Klux Klan mob. . . The government could settle this whole matter in an hour by taking a firm stand. The Ku Kluxers around Tuskegee are bluffing, and will carry that bluff as far as they can. If President Harding has a backbone the size of a toothpick, he will call that bluff, and that will be the end of the present disgraceful situation." James A. Cobb, an attorney who often represented the NAACP, warned Hines that "if the Government, thru you, yields to the threats and intimidation of a few alleged citizens . . . it will amount to setting in motion a poisonous stream that in the long run may be the Government's undoing."[69]

For his part, Walter White explained that the NAACP was "making a fight on the situation because I for one feel that all [the Veterans Bureau] plans to do is to quiet the storm of criticism, and particularly that of colored people. Then, when the matter has blown over, Negroes for some time to come will have a very tough time of getting into the institution." Maintaining close contact with Shelby Davidson, the secretary of the NAACP's Washington branch, White devoted much of his time during the summer of 1923 to the Tuskegee controversy. The NAACP was doing every-

[69] Minutes of the meeting of the Board of Directors, July 1923, NAACP Files; James Weldon Johnson telegram to Warren G. Harding, 5 July 1923, NAACP Files; Johnson, "Views and Reviews," 14 July 1923; James A. Cobb to Frank T. Hines, quoted in *Norfolk Journal and Guide*, 14 July 1923.

thing it could to help Tuskegee Institute in its hour of difficulty, and White noted, "Our fight in the Tuskegee Hospital matter is one of the best—and I am sure it is one of the most popular—that we have ever made. I believe that it has created a feeling of support among a great number of people who hitherto have been somewhat antagonistic toward the Association. If we can win this fight completely—and I believe that we shall—it will be one of our most important victories."[70]

Yet at this juncture Major Moton broke ranks with the NAACP and acknowledged the need for some sort of a compromise settlement. Certainly Moton was not lacking in physical courage, for, as noted above, in mid-May the major had ignored threats to his life and had emphatically rejected demands that he endorse a statement calling for the exclusion of black professionals from the veterans hospital. By July Moton and his family were safely settled at their summer home in Virginia, but the events of July 3—the expulsion of Calhoun, the Klan's parade, and the narrow avoidance of what would have been a pitched battle—shocked the major and made him recognize the need for peace.

Thus Moton was disposed to comply when W. W. Campbell, a leading white citizen who was both a trustee of the institute and a member of the committee that had threatened Moton in May, promised the major that "no steps [will] be taken that would disturb [the] Institute" if Moton would wire Hines "that it is your desire [that] he cooperate in [the] fullest possible way with [the] white citizens of Tuskegee." Perhaps because his own personal safety had not been threatened on this occasion, Moton could assess the situation objectively and appreciate what the whites meant when they warned, "This agitation has given rise to

[70] White to Valentine, 14 May 1923; White memorandum to James Weldon Johnson, 7 July 1923, NAACP Files; White to Shelby Davidson, 27 July 1923, NAACP Files.

a situation that . . . seriously threatens the successful operation, both of the Hospital and the Institute." Accordingly,
Moton immediately urged Hines to "cooperate in every possible way to effect [a] satisfactory adjustment of [the] hospital situation." He even arranged a special meeting between the leaders of the black National Medical Association
and prominent whites of Tuskegee, where, according to the
black doctors, Moton "took the floor and for twenty minutes
talked about the harmony and goodwill of the whites and
blacks of that section, and felt that the only way this could
be maintained was by agreeing to the attitude of the white
representatives."[71]

It should be emphasized, however, that while Moton was
willing to compromise in the interest of restoring interracial
harmony, he did not sacrifice his basic principles. He never
ceased insisting that black doctors and nurses had "a right
above all other people to serve their own." But after the
crisis of early July Moton was acutely conscious of "the necessity of preserving intact those relations of goodwill and
mutual helpfulness between white people and black people
at Tuskegee . . . which was the outstanding achievement of
the career of Booker T. Washington." Consequently, when
local whites ceased demanding that black professionals be
excluded from the hospital, Moton was willing to agree that
whites should be appointed to the supervisory positions at
the institution. Although it required a good deal of haggling
to determine the exact number of supervisory offices—with
local whites claiming that seventy-five jobs fell in this category and Moton insisting that the definition should be applied only to the commanding officer, the executive officer,
and the clinical director—Moton was willing to accept
white management of the hospital and informed Hines "that

[71] W. W. Campbell telegram to Robert R. Moton, 4 July 1923,
Moton Papers; Moton telegram to Frank T. Hines, 5 July 1923, Moton
Papers; statement of the National Medical Association, quoted in
Baltimore Afro-American, 26 March 1932.

for the present, at least, it would be desirable to have a white Commanding officer and white executive staff."[72] Hines was in basic agreement with Moton. Thus the director of the Veterans Bureau emphatically rejected the local whites' initial suggestion that all professional officers be white, pointing out that this proposal "would take away the opportunity of any of the professional colored element's taking part in the administration of [the hospital]" and was "so at variance with the policy adopted by the administration . . . that it would wholly defeat the main purposes of the Tuskegee Hospital." Instead, Hines decided that it would be necessary to replace Colonel Stanley with another white commanding officer who could work more effectively with Negroes and then begin the substitution of blacks in all positions except that of the commanding officer and his two chief assistants. "As vacancies occur at other stations, the white personnel on duty . . . will be given an opportunity of transfer," Hines explained to one congressman. "Vacancies created in this way will be filled by colored personnel." Hines also told Moton in the strictest confidence that if this transition of personnel went smoothly it would be possible at some future date, perhaps in one or two years, to name a black commanding officer and thus fulfill President Harding's promise of an all-black staff.[73]

Many blacks, unaware of these detailed negotiations and confidential understandings, believed that Moton had sacrificed honor for expediency. Once again, it seemed, the principal of Tuskegee Institute had endorsed the system of

[72] Speech of Robert R. Moton, quoted in *Norfolk Journal and Guide*, 25 August 1923; Moton, quoted in Hines to Sawyer, 12 July 1923.

[73] Hines to Johnstone, 16 July 1923; Hines to Sawyer, 12 July 1923; Hines to Ruth Burke Webb, 30 August 1923, Director's Correspondence; Hines to George W. Lee, 28 September 1923, Director's Correspondence; Hines to Clark Burdick, 22 August 1923, Director's Correspondence; Albon Holsey to James Weldon Johnson, 7 July 1923, NAACP Files.

white supremacy and black subordination. "The attempt to compromise at Tuskegee by appointing three white men at the head of the hospital is a disgrace to all persons concerned," Du Bois declared in the *Crisis*. "There is no reason in the world why white persons should not be appointed to the Tuskegee Hospital but the head of the hospital and the chief men in charge should, by every dictate of justice, be black men."[74]

In a personal letter to Moton, J. R. Coffey, an attorney from Oklahoma, acknowledged that "you can possibly make life easier for yourself and for the race in Alabama for the next few months . . . by yielding to the uncivilized white contention," but Coffey nevertheless urged the major to "go down [to defeat], if go down you must, with your boots on, fighting for Negro management of that one hospital." Writing to Hines, editor Benjamin Jefferson Davis of the *Atlanta Independent* warned that if Moton "tells you, as he told me, that a fifty-fifty personnel would satisfy our people, he is misrepresenting the facts." And said Chisum, after conferring with Hines, "Those of us who have stood four square for a Negro personnel at the Tuskegee hospital represent the warp and woof of the true sentiment of the Race, and if, as I understand from your remarks yesterday, there be any black men of either high or low estate who are compromising in this situation and advising a part white staff at this hospital, then those persons do not represent the wishes and better judgment of their race."[75]

Even Fred Moore of the *New York Age*, Moton's closest friend among the black editors, doubted that the tenure of the white executive staff would be temporary and admitted

[74] W. E. B. Du Bois, "No Compromise," *Crisis* 27 (November 1923): 7–8.

[75] J. R. Coffey to Robert R. Moton, 5 July 1923, Moton Papers; Benjamin J. Davis to Frank T. Hines, 7 July 1923, Director's Correspondence; Melvin Chisum to Hines, 7 July 1923, Director's Correspondence.

that the compromise settlement was "not entirely satisfactory." Moore believed, however, that the mere presence of blacks on the professional staff was testimony "to the firm insistence and unremitting efforts of Dr. Robert R. Moton."[76] Going beyond criticism of a compromise that seemed to ensure the continuation of white supremacy, several black editors denounced Moton's dissembling methods. The *New York Amsterdam News* repeatedly censured Moton's failure to "speak out in clear and unmistakable tones" and urged him "to give the facts to the public." When the principal of Tuskegee continued to work quietly behind the scenes, the editors openly wondered where the major won his rank and concluded that Moton "has been found wanting in everything except physical weight. He seems to be lacking in the necessary courage to face issues of vital concern to the Negro today." Similarly, when it was discovered that Moton had urged the white citizens' committee of Tuskegee to come to Washington "with all secrecy to see General Hines, with whom I have just concluded [a] confidential interview," the editors of the *Washington Tribune* concluded that Moton was engaged in some sort "of underhand, double-faced work."[77]

By then many blacks must have agreed with Ben Davis of the *Atlanta Independent*, who advised Moton to stop working behind closed doors and return to Tuskegee and "defy the cowardice of the mob and the Ku Klux Klan." "Come home, Major," Davis declaimed. "Good soldiers never desert their post. . . . If anything should happen to Tuskegee and your life was saved by being absent, you would go down in history as a slacker who deserted his post when the institution needed you. . . . The world despises a man who runs away from the conflict to save his life, and leaves others to die at the post at which he should have

[76] *New York Age*, 8 September 1923.
[77] *New York Amsterdam News*, 13 June, 27 June 1923; *Washington Tribune*, quoted in *New York Amsterdam News*, 8 August 1923.

stood the supreme test. The fellow who seeks to save his life, loses it."[78]

The leaders of the NAACP were even more disillusioned with Moton, for they had reason to believe that the major had concealed the real nature of his plan from the association as well as from the white citizens of Tuskegee. As early as May 12, 1923, Shelby Davidson warned that "friend (?) Moton does not allow himself to be heard in any wise—in other words it seems an attempt to let us believe he favors the colored staff and at the same time he tries to lead the southern whites to believe he is with them." Three months later Davidson reported that Moton had told government officials that opposition to white management of the hospital was limited to northern blacks who did not understand the intricacies of the racial situation in the deep South.[79] Thus it was, Davidson believed, that Moton managed to grasp defeat from the jaws of victory: "It now develops that some double-crossing has been done," he reported, "and the work which we thought we were doing was being undone from quarters least suspected." Moreover, Dr. J. R. A. Crossland, a not altogether credible black physician then employed by the Veterans Bureau, simultaneously reported that Moton had encouraged the NAACP to demand an entirely black staff so that he could present himself to government officials as an advocate of a moderate compromise that avoided the extremism of irresponsible blacks and whites.[80]

After receiving these reports from Washington, the NAACP withdrew from the hospital controversy, claiming that "the final victory . . . was lost when the authorities at Washington became convinced that the heads of Tuskegee would be content with a mixed staff." In a special memoran-

[78] Benjamin J. Davis, quoted in *Baltimore Afro-American*, 20 July 1923.

[79] Shelby Davidson to Walter White, 12 May, 14 August, 1923, NAACP Files.

[80] Davidson to White, 5 January 1924; J. R. A. Crossland to Frank T. Hines, quoted in *Norfolk Journal and Guide*, 1 September 1923.

182

dum for the files, Walter White noted that through the joint efforts of the NAACP, the black newspapers, and the National Medical Association "the right for a complete colored personnel was definitely won. At this juncture, a disappointing experience largely nullified the success of the whole campaign when, according to authoritative information in possession of the NAACP, Major Moton . . . said to the President and to General Hines . . . that the heads of Tuskegee Institute were satisfied with a mixed staff and were willing for the hospital to be directed by white men just so long as there were colored doctors and nurses on the staff; that the officials at Washington should disregard the 'agitation of northern radicals who were merely trying to make propaganda out of the situation at Tuskegee.' With this attitude of double dealing, the Association withdrew from the case."[81]

IV

With the NAACP out of the case and Major Moton reconciled to the inevitability of white executives, the remaining pressure on the government came from the white citizens of Alabama. Shortly after the Klan's demonstration, the state legislature unanimously demanded that the hospital "be absolutely controlled, managed, and operated by white men, trained and experienced in the control of shell-shocked and mentally weak ex-servicemen, and fully capable of handling them in such way as to prevent them from being a menace to the people of the community." Throughout the summer of 1923 various citizens wrote to the Veterans Bureau, reminding General Hines of the government's promises that whites would control the hospital and urging that, as one correspondent put it, "the assurance so given be observed. To do otherwise would endanger racial

[81] *Fourteenth Annual Report of the NAACP* (1923), p. 29, NAACP Files; "The Negro Veterans Hospital at Tuskegee Institute," memorandum for the files, 31 December 1923, NAACP Files.

harmony which would be exceedingly unfortunate from every viewpoint and especially for Tuskegee Institute."[82]

Yet opinion in the white South was far from unanimous on this point. The *Jackson* (Mississippi) *Daily News* editorialized, "All this fuss and feathers at Tuskegee over the placing of Negro officers in a government hospital for the rehabilitation of Negro ex-servicemen strikes us as being downright silly. If the Negro soldiers are satisfied with Negro physicians, . . . the white folks ought to have nothing to say about it." The *Norfolk Virginia-Pilot* claimed that "if there is a sound objection to staffing with competent colored personnel a hospital set aside exclusively for Negro patients . . . , nobody outside of Ku Klux circles in Alabama seems to be aware of it." The *Charlotte* (North Carolina) *Observer* thought that "the demonstrations by the Ku Klux Klan . . . were ill-advised and should meet with the protests of all good American citizens." The *Mobile* (Alabama) *Register* acknowledged that "The Ku Klux Klan demonstration in Tuskegee will probably make it harder for the government to recede from its purpose to place a wholly Negro staff in charge of the new hospital for Negro soldiers. While intended to show the strength of the opposition to the government's plan, it has also the aspect of a threat."[83]

Even Oscar W. Underwood, the senior United States senator from Alabama, who had been out of the country during the early months of the controversy, sympathized with the blacks and thought the Klan's demonstration was foolish and needlessly provocative. He told the white citizens of Tuskegee quite frankly that they were "wrong in this hospital matter. You have no case. This man Moton has got you

[82] Resolution of the Alabama State Legislature, 13 July 1923, Director's Correspondence; S. L. Brewer telegram to Frank T. Hines, 2 July 1923, Director's Correspondence.

[83] *Jackson Daily News*, quoted in *New York Age*, 21 July 1923; *Norfolk Virginia-Pilot*, quoted in *Norfolk Journal and Guide*, 21 July 1923; *Charlotte Observer*, 6 July 1923; *Mobile Register*, 5 July 1923.

184

in a hole and you're bound to lose. Furthermore, the best white people in the South are with him."[84]

This division within the white South made it possible for Hines to ignore the anguished cries of white Tuskegee and to proceed with his plan to give blacks all but the three top executive positions. Thus in mid-August it was announced that six black physicians had been assigned to Tuskegee. Later in the month the Negrophobic commanding officer, Colonel Stanley, was transferred to New Mexico and replaced by the more cooperative Maj. Charles M. Griffith, a Georgia-born white physician who had been serving at the veterans hospital in Alexandria, Iowa. Many blacks protested against this arrangement, on the ground that it contemplated "white management with colored subordinates." Linc Johnson claimed that no "self-respecting colored man in this country [would] accept a place in that hospital so long as any white man was acting officially there." The six hundred delegates to the annual conference of the National Medical Association adopted a resolution calling on black physicians to refuse positions at the Tuskegee Veterans Hospital "unless assured they are to serve under Negro officials."[85]

Surprisingly, however, the whites of Tuskegee were chastened by the ridicule heaped upon them by fellow Southerners and accepted the inevitability of black professionals. In stark contrast to the furor touched off by the arrival of John H. Calhoun in July, white Tuskegee quietly acquiesced in the arrival of the six black physicians; less than a score of loyal Klansmen braved a rainstorm to attend a "protest

[84] Oscar W. Underwood, quoted in *Pittsburgh Courier*, 15 September 1923.

[85] *New York Times*, 16 August 1923; Frank T. Hines to R. H. Stanley, 22 August 1923, Director's Correspondence; "Kelly Miller Says," *Baltimore Afro-American*, 31 August 1923; H. L. Johnson to Frank T. Hines, quoted in *Baltimore Afro-American*, 31 August 1923; *Baltimore Afro-American*, 7 September 1923.

barbecue," and the *Montgomery Advertiser* relegated its account of the coming of the new doctors to three paragraphs on the second page. By September Dr. Kenney, who in June had fled Tuskegee in fear for his life, reported to a friend that tranquillity prevailed at both the institute and the hospital, "and from that standpoint no one would suspect that there is or has been any abnormal condition during recent months."[86]

Hines continued to replace whites and by the end of 1923 it was generally acknowledged that all professional positions—including those of the three ranking administrative officers—eventually would be occupied by Negroes. Yet the recognition that a black doctor eventually would take command at the hospital precipitated a new division among Negro leaders. On the one hand, the black politicians, hoping to make the most of the payroll, supplies, and contracts, continued their struggle to control the hospital. Meanwhile, the ambitious and enigmatic Dr. Crossland, the black director of a special Veterans Bureau program in vocational training for colored men, had concocted an involved plan to have himself named as the ranking black official. As early as July 4, Chisum had warned Hines that Crossland was working "to discredit any person other than himself whom you might decide to send" to Tuskegee. Chisum reported that the physician had informed Alabama's Senator Heflin that the Veterans Bureau was planning to appoint "a bunch of firebrands . . . to head up the hospital staff." One of Chisum's informants within the bureau also reported that Crossland was allied with "that arch scoundrel Ijams" and other southern officials who, though now reconciled to the necessity of black leadership, wanted to appoint accommodating Negro executives who would be in sympathy with the attitudes prevailing in white Tuskegee. At the time, however, Hines evidently considered these reports too far-

[86] *Baltimore Afro-American*, 10 August 1923; *Montgomery Advertiser*, 16 August 1923; John A. Kenney to M. O. Dumas, 24 September 1923, NAACP Files.

fetched to be credible and approved Ijams's proposal to have Crossland sent to veterans hospitals in Philadelphia, New York, and Boston for three months of intensive training in hospital administration.[87]

Despite explicit objections from Moton and the National Medical Association, which had already excommunicated Crossland for alleged "duplicity . . . in a mad effort to have Tuskegee Hospital run by himself and a white man," Crossland was assigned to Tuskegee in November 1923. Though he had no more authority than the other black physicians on the staff, Crossland immediately began lobbying for a promotion to an executive position and reported that because of his "longer years of experience" the other black doctors regarded him as "the Dean" and had elected him to the presidency of the local Medical and Surgical Association. Writing to Hines, Crossland also claimed that the white people of Tuskegee were "most cordial and . . . ready and expect daily that the hospital will be turned over to the colored people 'to whom it belongs.' " Yet Crossland also let it be known that he was willing to serve as second in command to a white executive if Hines felt that the time was not yet right for the appointment of a black commanding officer.[88]

Moton was willing to accept biracial management of the hospital, but he had somehow managed to obtain copies of Crossland's correspondence and was determined to rid Tuskegee of a man whom he regarded as a troublemaking schemer. "It [is] imperative that this man be ordered from

[87] Daniel, "Black Power in the 1920s," pp. 385n., 387; Melvin Chisum to Frank T. Hines, 4 July 1923, Director's Correspondence; "G. B." to Chisum, 20 November 1923, NAACP Files.

[88] Robert R. Moton to Melvin Chisum, 24 November 1923, Moton Papers; Moton to Frank T. Hines, 28 November 1923, Moton Papers; Resolution of the National Medical Association, paraphrased in *Norfolk Journal and Guide*, 8 September 1923; J. R. A. Crossland to Hines, 29 December 1923, Director's Correspondence; Crossland to Seldon P. Spencer, 2 January 1924, Moton Papers.

here at once," Moton wired Hines, "otherwise there will be more serious trouble than anything yet had."[89]

For his part, Crossland did his best to discredit Moton, whom he characterized as "a powerful, local, ambitious individual of my race whose influence is great and who seeks to bring about a change in my official career." The black doctor also charged that the hospital was in desperate need of administrative reorganization. The "men in the N[euro]-P[sychiatric] wards have dirks, guns, and rocks," he warned, and "there is likely to be happenings among the ex-servicemen (N-P) that would be a blot against the hospital and from which the whole race would recoil." He described the commanding officer, Major Griffith, as an incompetent administrator and "the most tricky, scheming southern man you ever saw in your life." Griffith not surprisingly reciprocated this antipathy and later reported that Crossland "tried in every way possible to create as much dissatisfaction among the personnel and patients . . . as he possibly could. Under no circumstances do I need, or could I use this man's service in the future."[90]

This controversy undoubtedly embarrassed Hines, who was forced to look elsewhere for a suitable black executive. In the meantime, Crossland was left in an embarrassing medical limbo—"standing around here waiting for more than a month to be given my position, with no place to even hang my hat or coat as an office." Screwing up his courage in late December, the embattled physician appealed to Hines: "I wish to exercise patience," he began, but he nevertheless expressed the hope that his "embarrassment to linger and wait will be of as short duration as possible. . . . I turn to ask that I sit on the anxious seat no longer than you can most speedily arrange matters." In final cries of desperation, he even appealed to senators, congressmen, and

[89] Robert R. Moton to Frank T. Hines, quoted in *New York Age*, 26 January 1924.

[90] Crossland to Hines, 29 December 1923; Charles M. Griffith to Hines, 23 January 1924, Director's Correspondence.

the discredited Linc Johnson: "Write me and tell me for God's sake what to do." All this was to no avail, however, and in February General Hines announced that Crossland had been relieved of his duties at the Tuskegee hospital.[91]

With Crossland removed from the scene, the way was prepared for Hines to appoint the highly respected black physician Joseph H. Ward as assistant to Major Griffith. Ward, a graduate of the Indiana Medical College who had practiced medicine in Indianpolis for twenty years, served with distinction at the Mayo Clinic, and risen to the rank of major in the American Expeditionary Force, quickly won the confidence of Griffith, who considered Ward "superior in every respect." After a few months' apprenticeship, Hines decided that the time had come to complete the conversion to an entirely black staff, and in July 1924, he announced that Ward had been promoted to chief medical officer and head of the hospital.[92] Although this announcement was made almost exactly one year after the whites had driven John H. Calhoun from the hospital and confidently boasted that no more Negroes would be assigned to duty there, Ward's appointment occasioned very little controversy. Time and firm diplomacy had combined to pave the way for the inauguration of a completely black staff.

The successful resolution of the Tuskegee hospital controversy was a great victory for Moton and Hines, who in retrospect seem to have always been in control of the situation. Moreover, during the years since 1923 the development of the hospital under Negro management has undoubtedly justified the faith of Moton and Hines. The hospital, which many originally thought to be beyond the

[91] Crossland to Spencer, 2 January 1924; Crossland to Hines, 29 December 1923; Crossland to H. L. Johnson, 8 January 1924, Moton Papers; Crossland to Congressmen, 3 January 1924, Moton Papers; *Baltimore Afro-American*, 1 February 1924.

[92] Charles M. Griffith to Frank T. Hines, 11 March, 7 July 1924, Director's Correspondence; Daniel, "Black Power in the 1920s," pp. 387–388.

realm of Negro managerial ability, has grown steadily in services rendered and in modern buildings and other equipment. Originally planned as a large facility with 600 beds and a dozen doctors, the Tuskegee Veterans Hospital is now, fifty years later, a hospital of 1200 beds, 37 physicians and dentists, 136 nurses, and a total of 1200 full-time employees. Although located in a small community, it has entered into a variety of cooperative relationships with neighboring hospitals and medical schools, has played a major role in improving health service in Alabama, and has on several occasions been ranked "among the best 10 percent of all Federal hospitals in the United States." Equally important, the success of this enterprise laid to rest all doubt concerning the Negro's ability to manage such an institution. As Holsey noted, the dream of Robert Russa Moton, "once questioned even by the members of his own race, has been fully realized in the extraordinary development of an institution which now ranks high among all of the Veterans' Hospitals of the country."[93]

Even more important for the purposes of this study, the victory in the hospital controversy helped to keep Moton and Tuskegee Institute in the mainstream of black higher education. The institute had long been considered the outstanding example of the American Negro's managerial ability, and this carried a special appeal in the 1920s when many black students and educators demanded that Negroes control their own institutions. Yet many blacks of that era, and especially the college-educated elite, had passed beyond the accommodationism generally associated with the founder of Tuskegee Institute. Thus, by first introducing a collegiate curriculum and then resisting the Ku Klux Klan and fighting to make sure that Negroes themselves would play a leading role at the Tuskegee Veterans Hospital, Moton convinced many blacks that he had broken with

[93] Robert S. Wilson to author, 19 June 1972; Holsey, "Man of Courage," pp. 141–142.

the servile deference that many thought had characterized his leadership in the past.

Moton's struggle for black management of the Tuskegee hospital doubtless increased his popularity among Negroes and dissuaded potential rebels at the institute. Even if external circumstances in central Alabama had not been so inhibiting, it is doubtful that any considerable number of students and professors would have risen in rebellion against a militant principal who, at least in the mid-1920s, was seen as an embattled major leading a campaign for racial self-determination. In the past, Du Bois acknowledged, "the white Southerners regarded [Moton] as putty under their fine Italian hands—and the American Negro was disposed to agree with them." But in the case of the Tuskegee Veterans Hospital Moton "stood firmly and calmly with his back to the wall. He and the Negro world demanded that the Government Hospital at Tuskegee be under Negro control." "Our hats are in the air to Tuskegee and Moton," the editor of the *Crisis* exclaimed. "A New Black Man has risen—a Joseph who knew not Pharaoh."

As Joseph had used his influence with pharaoh to effect a rapprochement with his Hebrew brethren, Moton had used Booker T. Washington's Tuskegee Machine to establish harmonious relations with the advocates of black autonomy. In the past the power of Tuskegee had often been used to thwart the aspirations of the Negro colleges, but in the case of the veterans hospital Moton and Tuskegee joined the ranks of the New Negro militants.[94]

[94] Du Bois, "Dilemma of the Negro," pp. 181–182; Du Bois, "Moton of Hampton and Tuskegee," p. 348; Du Bois, "Tuskegee and Moton," *Crisis* 28 (September 1924): 200–202.

CHAPTER V

The Travail of Nathan B. Young

RACIAL self-determination was a major issue in the black college rebellions of the 1920s. This included the insistence that black people should determine the nature of their educational curriculum. Nowhere was this more evident than in the controversies that engulfed Nathan B. Young at two of the most prominent state supported, land-grant colleges for Negroes, Florida A. & M. College and Lincoln University (Mo.). Here the battle lines were drawn sharply between egalitarian advocates of full-manhood education and vocationally oriented partisans of special education for blacks.

I

Established in Tallahassee in 1887, Florida's State Normal College for Colored Students offered a two-year course for prospective teachers, and its first president, Thomas de Saille Tucker, was a graduate of Oberlin College. Tucker taught classical subjects and believed that a teacher training program should focus on the traditional liberal arts. His emphasis on academic subjects clashed with the prevailing view in the Florida panhandle—where many whites feared that liberal training would ruin good field hands—and the college inevitably came in for criticism. Yet Tucker dominated the situation until well into the 1890s, when the college was designated as a land-grant institution entitled to federal appropriations under the second Morrill Act (1890). This new income enabled Tucker to relocate the college in spacious accommodations at "Highwood," a hilltop mansion overlooking the state capital, but it also increased the leverage of government officials who wanted to transform Tucker's academically oriented normal college into a conformist vocational institute.[1]

In 1896 Florida's state superintendent of public instruction charged that there was "an obvious inattention to agricultural and industrial training" at the college. Other officials later called for Tucker's resignation on the grounds that he was "not in healthy sympathy with industrial education" and that he was "too exclusive; not in touch and sympathy with the masses of his race." Tucker tried to appease these advocates of special education for blacks by changing the name of the school so as to reflect an emphasis that would justify the receipt of government funds—first to the State Normal and Industrial College for Negroes and later to Florida Agricultural and Mechanical College. Yet Tucker never disguised his belief that black teachers should have a sound foundation in literary subjects, and political pressures continued to mount against him. He finally resigned his position in 1901, and state officials began the search for a new president who, they hoped, would "remedy many of the defects complained of and surround the institution with a different spirit from that which seems to have taken possession of it."[2]

Prior to accepting the presidency of Florida A. & M. Nathan B. Young had taught for six years at Tuskegee Institute and for six years at the Georgia State Industrial School. The ruling powers in Florida evidently assumed that these labors in the vineyards of vocationalism ensured that the new president was an apostle of trade training for Negroes. Yet Young, who had also received a baccalaureate in liberal arts from Talladega College and a graduate degree in Greek and Latin from Oberlin College, believed that the vocational and

[1] Leedel W. Neyland and John W. Riley, *The History of Florida Agricultural and Mechanical University* (Gainesville: University of Florida Press, 1963), pp. 11–47.

[2] Ibid., pp. 37, 41–42, 47.

classical emphases should be synthesized. He regarded himself as an "educational frontiersman" pioneering the development of multifaceted institutions that would emphasize both trade training and academic education. He saw Florida A. & M. as the state's only tax-supported college for Negroes and determined that it should offer "the same type of educational opportunities to its constituents as other institutions offered to their constituents."[3]

With a lifetime of experience in the South, Young was well aware of white hostility to the higher education of blacks and knew that he would have to proceed cautiously with his plan to develop Florida A. & M. During the first nine years of his presidency, the institution was generally referred to as a "school," and Young took care to reassure Floridians that he planned simply to send "properly trained teachers" to the state's Negro schools, "well-equipped artisans" to its shops and farms, and "intelligent, law-abiding and thrifty citizens" to the state at large. Along with this soothing rhetoric, however, Young improved the academic programs significantly: the two-year normal course was well regarded throughout the black South, and baccalaureate programs were gradually introduced in the arts and sciences. While singing the praises of vocationalism, Young quietly developed A. & M.'s academic programs to the verge of accreditation and to the point where, according to the United States Bureau of Education, the institution would soon become "an excellent State College for Negroes. . . . [It] is just at the beginning of a period of great development and usefulness."[4]

Throughout the first twenty years of his presidency,

[3] Nathan B. Young, "The Quest and Use of an Education: An Autobiographical Sketch" (unpaginated typescript), Archives of the University of Missouri, St. Louis.

[4] Nathan B. Young, quoted in Neyland and Riley, *Florida A. &M.*, pp. 50, 52; Arthur J. Klein, *Survey of Negro Colleges and Universities* (U. S. Department of the Interior, Bureau of Education Bulletin 7, 1928), p. 223.

Young worked quietly to ensure the appointment of sympathetic trustees who shielded the college and enabled its president, faculty, and students to be as inconspicuous as possible. In this way, Young later recalled, Florida was "unwittingly led . . . into making a real effort at the *higher* education of the Negro." Yet a reaction inevitably set in as A. & M. approached accreditation and became highly regarded among blacks throughout the South. Frantic efforts were made to put the college "into reverse gear, to 'softpedal' *cultural* education as being undesirable for Negroes" and instead make the Negro an economic asset to the white South by training him "narrowly as a Negro, not broadly as a man and a citizen." Friends who had sympathized with what they thought was Young's program expressed reservations about exposing Negroes to the liberal arts. It might lead to "social equality," one trustee explained. "To be educated like a white man begets a desire to be like a white man."[5]

Yet the controversy over the status of liberal arts at Florida A. & M. might never have attracted public attention had it not been for A. A. Turner, a Tuskegee-trained black bureaucrat who had been sent to Florida to supervise the Smith-Hughes program in vocational education. Turner discovered that A. & M.'s emphasis on trades was confined pretty much to an hour or two of daily instruction for students enrolled in the high school division, while most of the college students focused on academic subjects and received no trade training. This, Turner believed, violated the terms under which land-grant funds had been appropriated to A. & M. When the matter was brought to Young's attention, however, the president of Florida A. & M. rejected Turner's demands that the college place more emphasis on agriculture and industry. Young pointed out that this "would practically scrap the program

[5] Young, "Quest and Use of an Education"; Young, "These 'Colored' United States," *Messenger* 5 (November 1923): 866, 896 (italics in original).

in progress, by changing the objective of the school, making it purely a vocational enterprise."[6]

Turner then carried his demands to the board of education and to the Democratic nominee for governor, Cary Hardee. Hardee made effective use of this issue in his 1922 campaign. There was a near-panic among landlords who feared ruin if black field hands continued the emigration from rural Florida that had reached unprecedented proportions. Seizing on the fear, Hardee portrayed academic education as a symbol of all the forces that threatened the rural South and demanded that A. & M. be reorganized around vocationalism. This appeal was enormously popular, and Nathan B. Young's resignation was one inevitable consequence of Hardee's victory at the polls in 1922.[7]

During the course of his two decades at the helm of Florida A. & M., Young repeatedly demonstrated an extraordinary tact that enabled him to adjust to the demands of life in the deep South. In the controversy with Turner and Hardee, however, Young rejected compromise and instead focused public attention on the manner in which federal vocational agents were working to thwart the higher education of Negroes. Writing in the *Messenger*, he warned that there was "a well-defined movement, quickened by federal vocational agents throughout the South, to *substandardize* the few state-supported Colleges for Negroes by devoting them solely or mainly to vocational training." He urged blacks "to look into this phase of the federal educational activities and see to it that the federal vocational agents do not work *overtime* in industrializing the state institutions for Negroes."[8]

In a public letter that was widely circulated in the black

[6] Young, "These 'Colored' United States," pp. 866, 896; interview with Judge Nathan B. Young, Jr., April 1971; *Savannah Tribune*, 26 April 1923.

[7] Interview with Young, Jr., April 1971.

[8] Young, "These 'Colored' United States," pp. 866, 896 (italics in original).

community, Young further explained that he was "retiring from the presidency of Florida A. and M. College after twenty-two golden years of service, and that too for an appreciative people. I am leaving them not on their nor my own initiative, but upon the initiative of the 'powers that rule' to whom I have become a *persona non grata* because, forsooth, I refused to sneeze when the Federal Vocational Agents took snuff."[9]

Beyond challenging the agricultural bureaucracy, Young wanted at all costs to avoid being forced into the mold of black leadership then promoted by Turner and other representatives of Tuskegee Institute. The Tuskegeeans, according to Young, endorsed a system under which absolute power over Negroes was given to reliable blacks who could be trusted to suppress Negroes who challenged the status quo. Such an arrangement encouraged the emergence of black power brokers who could transform themselves from sycophantic Uncle Toms—when in the presence of whites— to dictatorial Emperor Joneses—when dealing with blacks.

Young had seen this pathology take hold of more than one black college president, and he was determined to resist it. He admitted that his difficulties might have been avoided if he had "met the situations out of which they grew more diplomatically, with a certain political finesse." But this would have required "compromises that are not always ethical," and so Young adopted what he acknowledged to be "an undiplomatic attitude." He had "the *courage*, rather than the caution of his educational convictions," Young later recalled, and consequently he "faced the issue without bending the flexible knee, and took the results on the chin standing up." Only two years before his very close friend Richard R. Wright had been forced to resign from the presidency of the Georgia State Industrial School in the wake of Tuskegee-inspired demands that he "cut this Latin out and teach these boys to farm." Like his friend, Young chose

9 W. E. B. Du Bois, "Nathan B. Young," *Crisis* 26 (September 1923): 226–227.

to draw attention to the operation of the Tuskegee Machine even though such defiance required that he dissociate himself from an institution that had been the center of his life's work for twenty-two years.[10]

Fortunately for Young, the controversy in Florida gave him a nationwide reputation as an advocate of higher education for Negroes. Thus he was thought to be well qualified to preside over the expenditure of the $500,000 that the Missouri state legislature appropriated in 1921 for the purpose of converting Lincoln Institute into a real university for Negroes. Young promptly accepted the offer of the presidency of this new Lincoln University, and several professors from Florida A. & M. moved to Missouri with him. It seemed that they were to have a second chance to develop the type of school for which they had been working in the lower South, the opportunity "to help make Lincoln University what its new name prophesies, a first-class institution of *higher learning*, a standard College for Negroes in the Middle West."[11]

II

Young's departure did not end the controversy in Florida. Many students and alumni were upset by the deemphasis on academic work at their school and particularly by the choice of W. H. A. Howard as Young's successor. Howard had been one of Young's students at the Georgia State Industrial School and had come to A. & M. at Young's invitation. Over the course of twenty years' service, he had risen through the ranks to become Smith-Hughes Professor of

[10] Young, "Quest and Use of an Education" (italics in original); Elizabeth Ross Haynes, *The Black Boy of Atlanta; Richard R. Wright* (Boston: House of Edinboro, 1952), pp. 90–95; interview with Prof. Cecil Blue, April 1971.

[11] Nathan B. Young to W. E. B. Du Bois, 3 August 1923, WEBD Papers (italics in original).

mechanical arts and dean of vocational studies. Although Howard had been an able aide to President Young, he had never earned an academic degree, and most blacks insisted that he was not qualified to be a college president. To complicate the situation further, there were persistent rumors that Howard had encouraged Turner's plan to vocationalize the college. Howard, it was said, lacked formal education, but he was not stupid. He knew he would be in line for the presidency if A. & M. were reorganized according to the gospel of vocationalism.[12]

The board of trustees no doubt thought that Howard's vocational background would be an asset in adjusting to the political demands of the time, but students and alumni denounced the new president. Thus the students circulated petitions claiming that Howard was "inferior educationally to the man he succeeded" and "not qualified to be head of a college since he . . . held no degree." Leaders of the Alumni Association declared that Howard's nomination for the presidency represented "an attempt on the part of those who rule to put into operation their plans as to what constitutes the best kind of education suited for Negroes." "The big lesson" to be learned from the imbroglio, according to the alumni, was that "those that rule in this section of the country are as determined today as ever to disregard the Negroes' wishes where and when they please and to thrust upon the Negroes that which they desire."[13]

Confident that they had the situation under control, the trustees refused to consider student and alumni petitions demanding Howard's resignation. Instead they instructed the new president "to permit no insubordination or 'striking' among the student body at the A. and M. College even if [you] have to expel the entire student body." In October

[12] Neyland and Riley, *Florida A. & M.*, pp. 77–79.
[13] Student petitions, paraphrased in *Norfolk Journal and Guide*, 3 November 1923; A. J. Kershaw to *Florida Sentinel*, quoted in *Savannah Tribune*, 15 November 1923.

NATHAN B. YOUNG

1923 stories were planted in the white press to the effect that Howard was "a well-balanced, practical and zealous worker . . . [who] has taught the negro boys how to make good citizens by teaching them how to make good carpenters, blacksmiths, painters, and other practical trades."[14]

Thus the students, alumni, and friends of Florida A. & M. faced a desperate situation. Their popular, academically oriented President Young had resigned under pressure, and several professors had also left Florida for better opportunities in Missouri. The vocationally oriented President Howard was suspected of complicity in deposing his predecessor and, in any case, was thought to be wholly unqualified to preside over a college. The trustees had evidently relinquished the role they had played during most of the preceding two decades, that of beneficent guardians who protected the college from the assaults of racist state officials. They had acceded to demands that A. & M. train Negroes for the jobs that were generally accorded to the race in the South. Whites had made it perfectly clear that they intended to control A. & M.

Under the circumstances, the students and alumni had only two choices: They could acquiesce or they could rebel. On October 8 the students at A. & M. announced that they were boycotting classes in protest against Howard's alleged incompetence and the lowering of goals at the college. For the next three days classes were generally deserted, and approximately 100 of the 325 students who had enrolled for the fall semester actually withdrew from the college and returned to their homes. Then, as if this were not enough to indicate the spirit of rebellion that permeated the campus, a flaming sky in the predawn hours of October 11 heralded the black belief that Negroes would be better off with no college than one perverted to serve racist purposes. Duval Hall, a major classroom building, was in flames, and within the next three months fires also destroyed the hated

[14] Neyland and Riley, *Florida A. & M.*, p. 79; *Tallahassee Daily Democrat*, 15 October 1923.

Mechanical Arts Building, and Gibbs Hall, the girls' dormitory, and damaged three other buildings.[15]

No one was ever apprehended and there was not enough evidence to sustain charges of arson in the courts. President Howard nonetheless expelled eleven young men, and it was common knowledge on the campus that rebellious students had been responsible for most, if not all, of the fires. In making his official report on these matters, the state supervisor of Negro education noted that "a condition of rebellion bordering on anarchy" existed on the campus during the first months of Howard's administration. He found solace only in the knowledge that the destroyed buildings had been covered by insurance.[16]

To compound President Howard's problems, the college's efforts to restore order seemed to increase the alienation of the black community. Thus the white guards who were assigned to the campus to enforce an after-dark curfew and to patrol Men's Union, the main men's dormitory, soon found themselves trading insults with indignant black students who claimed that there was "a reign of terror on the campus with white men standing over us with guns at their sides." Others resented Howard's claim that there were no substantial issues in the dispute and that the protest had been inspired by "a disgruntled teacher" who preyed upon the students' vain displeasure at the college's refusal to hire servants to clean their rooms. Statements such as this pandered to white racist stereotypes and Howard was thought to be responsible when Dean Homer Thomas received a written threat signed by "one hundred whites and fifty niggers" and immediately left the campus "walking thru the

[15] *Savannah Tribune*, 1 November 1923; *Norfolk Journal and Guide*, 3 November 1923; *Tallahassee Daily Democrat*, 13 October, 15 October 1923, 25 January 1924; Neyland and Riley, *Florida A. & M.*, pp. 79–81.

[16] Gareth Y. Marshall to author, 23 June 1972; H. Manning Efferson to author, 8 August 1972; interview with Young, Jr., April 1971; Neyland and Riley, *Florida A. & M.*, pp. 79–81.

bushes to catch the train out of the station in order to get
away." Well before the end of his first year as president of
Florida A. & M., Howard had become the subject of bitter
hatred and scorn in black Tallahassee.[17]

It was generally recognized that there could be no tranquillity on the campus as long as Howard continued as
president, and in May 1924 the trustees named a new chief
executive, J. R. E. Lee, a graduate of Bishop College who
had taught at Tuskegee and worked for the National Urban
League. Lee would remain at the helm of Florida A. & M.
for twenty years and was quite successful in steering the institution away from anarchy and onto the road of academic
progress.[18] In the meantime, however, the second battle in
Nathan B. Young's campaign for academic standards would
take place at Lincoln University in Missouri.

III

Initially financed by $6,000 collected around the Civil
War campfires of the Sixty-second and Sixty-fifth Colored
Infantry from Missouri, Lincoln Institute had prospered in
the years since it opened in 1867 with only two students enrolled in a small house in Jefferson City. When Nathan B.
Young became president in 1923, about four hundred students attended classes on a handsome hilltop campus on the
outskirts of the city. As a state normal school receiving regular appropriations from the Missouri legislature and a
land-grant college entitled to federal funds, the institution's
financial condition seemed secure.[19]

Prior to the 1920s, the great majority of Lincoln's stu-

[17] *Savannah Tribune*, 1 November 1923; *Norfolk Journal and Guide*, 3 November 1923; *Tallahassee Daily Democrat*, 15 October 1923; Nathan B. Young to *Tallahassee Daily Democrat*, 19 October 1923.

[18] Neyland and Riley, *Florida A. & M.*, pp. 81–174.

[19] W. Sherman Savage, *The History of Lincoln University* (Jefferson City, Mo.: Lincoln University, 1939).

dents were enrolled in either the high school division or in the two-year normal course for prospective teachers. But many black Missourians hoped that the institute would be upgraded and converted into a standard liberal arts college. Responding to this sentiment, Walthall M. Moore of St. Louis, the first Negro elected to serve in Missouri's state assembly, introducted legislation to appropriate $500,000 to convert the institute into a real university that would "afford to the Negro people of the state the opportunity for training up to the standard furnished at the State University of Missouri."[20] Gov. Arthur M. Hyde used his influence to ensure passage of this bill in 1921, and when Young was named to preside over the development of the institution it seemed that Missouri was serious about making Lincoln a real center of higher education. Yet in Missouri as in Florida, Young's work for academic excellence was eventually undermined by vocationally oriented blacks who had the ear of leading white politicians.

At the outset of his presidency Young candidly announced his major goal. He intended to make Lincoln University a standard, accredited undergraduate college for Negroes, and to achieve this purpose he insisted that it would be necessary to upgrade the quality of Lincoln's faculty. As a first step in this direction, Young made a sharp distinction between the high school teachers, who were organized in a separate department headed by a new principal, and the professors in the college, who for the first time were organized by ranks with the highest positions reserved for those with graduate degrees and scholarly publications. Beginning in 1925 Young required all new teachers in the high school to have baccalaureate degrees while new professors in the college were expected to have earned at least a master's degree. A system of sabbatical leaves at half pay was later inaugurated to encourage professors without the doc-

[20] Ibid.; *Vernon's Annotated Missouri Statutes* (Kansas City: Vernon Law Book Company, 1965), vol. 11A, chap. 175.050.

torate to return to graduate school in pursuit of the Ph.D.
Using the stick as well as the carrot, the new president persuaded the board of curators to rule "that teachers now employed in the College Department having less than the Master's Degree must complete at least eight semester hours
[of graduate work] per year until that degree is secured."[21]

As a result of these policies, the number of professors
with graduate degrees tripled within four years. The faculty was soon graced with scholars who gave Lincoln a reputation for excellence among the Negro land-grant colleges
—Harvard-trained Sterling Brown and Cecil Blue in literature and drama, William Dowdy of Cornell in biology, W.
Sherman Savage of Ohio State in history, and Langston
Fairchild Bate of Chicago in chemistry. These professors
were attracted to central Missouri by the opportunity to
work with Young in creating "the educational cynosure of
the Middle West for our race group." They also came because Young persuaded the legislature to invest funds in the
core academic facilities and to establish a salary schedule
well above the minimum needed to attract teachers of ordinary competence. Young knew that parsimony with regard
to teaching and research was false economy for an institution that aspired to high quality—that in academic life, as
elsewhere, an institution gets what it pays for.[22]

[21] *Lincoln University Record*, August 1924; interview with Prof.
William Dowdy, April 1971; Savage, *Lincoln University*, pp. 203,
234; Minutes of the Meeting of the Board of Curators, 19 June 1925,
Lincoln Archives.

[22] *Lincoln University Catalogue, 1924–1925*; *Lincoln University
Catalogue, 1927–1928*; *Lincoln University Record*, August 1925;
Savage, *Lincoln University*, pp. 182, 203. In his *Survey of Negro Colleges* (p. 480), Klein noted, "The annual stipends of the college
teaching staff at Lincoln University are above the average paid generally in negro institutions and in some cases compare favorably with
salaries in white colleges. Full professors receive from $2,250 to
$3,200; and assistant professors, including instructors, receive from
$1,800 to $2,250 annually. . . . In providing an equitable remunera-

By 1927 Young had managed to enhance Lincoln's reputation considerably. Impartial investigators from the United States Bureau of Education reported that "the training of the faculty of Lincoln University is of a high order" and characterized the scientific laboratories as "superior in quality" and the Inman Page Library as "a very good college library." Making a similar judgment, the state superintendent of schools declared, "Lincoln University has made more progress in the last three years under Young's leadership than it had in the thirty previous years. During the last three years, . . . the library and laboratories [have been] very materially improved, and the teaching personnel raised to a high standard." The United States commissioner of education agreed. "The University has made advancement," he reported. "The Library has been greatly strengthened and is now one of the best in the group of Negro land-grant colleges; the science department is excellent and up to date and meets the requirements for a standard undergraduate college; the teachers of the college are well trained and for the most part have done considerable graduate work in some of the best universities in the country."[23]

This substantial improvement in the quality of academic life was all the more remarkable in view of the fact that technical defects were found in the enabling legislation of 1921, and Lincoln was prohibited from spending the $500,000 initially appropriated to upgrade the institute. Thus Young found it necessary to lobby in the state legislature for a capital budget as well as for regular operating expenses. He scored a great victory when he persuaded the legislature to appropriate $400,000 for the biennial period beginning in 1925. This was almost double the amount al-

---

tion for the members of the faculty, it is apparent that Lincoln University has accomplished an achievement that few other negro colleges have been able to realize."

[23] Klein, *Survey of Negro Colleges*, pp. 479–481; Charles A. Lee, quoted in *Birmingham Reporter*, 23 April 1927; J. J. Tigert, quoted in *St. Louis Argus*, 24 June 1927.

lotted for the preceding two years, and a sum that kept alive the hopes of eventual collegiate status.[24] Yet Young knew it was by no means certain that appropriations of this size would be continued in the future. Consequently he spent a good deal of time organizing the black community in support of his campaign to make Lincoln a real university. He proposed to derive full advantage from the fact that the black people of Missouri, unlike those of Florida, were allowed to vote.

At the outset of his administration, Young organized the black community behind the campaign to upgrade Lincoln. It would be foolish, he maintained, "to keep our needs to ourselves and spring them on the legislature after it has met and depend on luck and lobbying for support." He prepared weekly news releases organized around a single theme: that "notwithstanding the wonderful work that our school has done in the past, . . . the fact remains that it is not an accredited institution of higher learning. It is not an institution in which persons may prepare to teach in the first-class high schools of the state. Neither is it an institution in which individuals may prepare for leadership in higher walks of professional life." To be sure, the state legislature had recently changed Lincoln's name from that of an institute to that of a university, but "the change to a real university is not so simple" and was, in fact, "the business . . . now before the people of the state." Everything would depend on the influence that the friends of Lincoln would bring to bear, "for just in proportion as the faculty, the students, and the patrons and friends hang together—hang together and pull hard—can we hope to realize our ambition to have Lincoln become a university in deed as well as in name." "The idea that President Young had in mind," historian Savage later recalled, "was to acquaint the people of the state with the needs of the school so that they could ask

[24] Lincoln University v. Hackmann, *Southwestern Reporter* 243: 320. *Vernon's Annotated Missouri Statutes*, vol. 11A, chap. 175.060; *St. Louis Argus*, 17 April 1925.

their own representatives in the legislature to give Lincoln University adequate support."[25]

Young's appeals were endorsed by the *St. Louis Argus* and the *Kansas City Call*, the state's two leading black newspapers. On the eve of the new president's formal inauguration in 1924, the *Argus* proclaimed, "It is now up to the citizens of this state, and especially the colored citizens, to make Lincoln University just what it ought to be." The *Argus* then arranged for a special train to carry well-wishers to Jefferson City to hear Young's inaugural address and to manifest their support for the new president. The *Kansas City Call* reminded its readers that until recently "our education had been left to men who felt that a Negro educated was a farmhand ruined." *Call* editor C. A. Franklin practically plagiarized Young's inaugural address when he declared that "man is more than food and raiment," and job training, even for the professions, was of less importance than "lifting the curtain which covers the finer things of life." "The treasures which a liberal education afford excel the gold. College, with its good fellowship, its books, its experiments and its philosophy, is a soul experience, an adventure greater than any other. Every young man and woman is the better for it."[26]

Throughout the state there were many "evidences of the mobilization of the citizens . . . behind the Lincoln University program." Testimonials were received from various Negro lodges and associations; Young was chosen as the honorary president of the Negro State Teachers Association; and in numerous small ways the black citizens of Missouri indicated that they appreciated the decision to "tone up" the university. Most significantly, some well-to-do

[25] Nathan B. Young to C. H. Kirshner, 29 February 1924, quoted in Savage, *Lincoln University*, p. 188; *Lincoln University Record*, August 1924, October 1924, December 1924; Savage, *Lincoln University*, p. 188.

[26] *St. Louis Argus*, 25 January 1924; *Kansas City Call*, 27 February 1926, 30 May 1924.

blacks, who in the past had sent their children out-of-state for college, changed their attitude and sent them to Lincoln. Indeed, in a dramatic reversal of the past practice that had seen aspiring black youths "attracted elsewhere for an education which their home state does not furnish them," some out-of-state students began to matriculate at Lincoln. Thus, according to the *Kansas City Call*, instead of "losing each year an appreciable number of high-type citizens," black Missouri was receiving fresh draughts of "ambitious, energetic Negro youth . . .—the kind who make the best citizens."[27]

While cultivating public sentiment in support of higher education for blacks, Young worked assiduously to have Lincoln recognized as a standard, accredited college. At the outset of his administration, he requested an inspection by the Association of Colleges for Negro Youth and used its strictures concerning the deficiencies of Lincoln's scientific work as the basis for successful requests for new laboratory facilities. Then in 1925 Young succeeded in having Lincoln's high school department accredited by the state Department of Education, and in 1926 the North Central Association of Secondary Schools and Colleges recognized the normal department as a standard teachers college.[28]

These accolades were interpreted by the *Kansas City Call* as evidence that Lincoln was "gradually forging toward the front rank." The *St. Louis Argus* rejoiced, "This puts the high school department in the same rank of . . . any other high school, and the college department in the rank of any other teachers college in the state." The university's baccalaureate programs in the higher arts and sciences still lacked accreditation, but the black newspapers were confident that "with more money for buildings and equipment, [Lincoln] will step into the class of accredited A–1 institu-

---

[27] *Lincoln University Record*, October 1924, March 1925; *St. Louis Argus*, 8 May, 23 November 1925; Savage, *Lincoln University*, p. 194; *Kansas City Call*, 17 April, 23 January 1925.

[28] Savage, *Lincoln University*, pp. 189–190, 221.

tions of higher learning before another freshman class will have graduated." They insisted that it was "now up to the alumni, patrons and friends of Lincoln University to induce the General Assembly to provide means for the completion of the work of making it a *bona fide* institution of higher learning."[29]

IV

Negroes throughout Missouri generally endorsed Young's program, but the new president encountered significant opposition on his own campus, especially from professors whose orientation, distant academic training, or marginal credentials made them either unwilling or unable to meet the demands of the new regime. These professors, according to the *St. Louis Argus*, "knew that if President Young carried out his program they could not hold their offices." Hence they complained that Young was "ten years ahead of his time" and was "trying to do too much."[30] Of course some criticism of this sort was to be expected, but it became a potent force when it was endorsed by two particularly well-known and well-connected members of the faculty, S. F. Collins and J. W. Damel.

Collins, the senior professor in Lincoln's normal department, was known throughout the state as one of the leaders of the Missouri Association of Negro Teachers. He feared that Young's emphasis on subject matter ran counter to his own department's stress on teaching technique. Damel had earned a master's degree at Hiram College in 1890 and had been teaching science at Lincoln for twenty-five years. He therefore resented his demotion to the high school faculty at a salary of $1,800 (as compared with the $3,000 paid to Ph.D.'s who had just finished graduate school). Young evidently felt Damel's thirty-five-year-old degree did not make

[29] *Kansas City Call*, 20 August 1926; *St. Louis Argus*, 29 October 1926.

[30] *St. Louis Argus*, 12 June 1925.

him an adequate teacher of physics in the 1920s. Damel was furious when he learned that on passing the physics classroom Young often quipped, "That's where Jack Damel teaches in the name of physics." Moreover, as a long-time resident of Jefferson City, a prominent activist in the Negro lodge movement, and a former acting president of Lincoln, Damel had political connections and was in a position to strike back at Young.[31]

Collins and Damel formed an alliance with two leading black politicians, C. G. Williams, who held a political appointment as a $200-a-month food inspector, and Duke Diggs, a Jefferson City mover. Williams and Diggs recognized that Young's academic standards threatened their own patronage. They feared that the president's use of the Negro press to organize the black community threatened their own lodge-based control of the black vote. For many years Williams and Diggs had enjoyed enormous influence at Lincoln. There were even knowledgeable insiders who thought that Williams, operating from a ramshackle desk in the grocery store of Jefferson City's Booker T. Washington Hotel, actually assigned more university contracts and made more appointments to the faculty than the previous presidents.

These politicians thought of the university's payroll, contracts, supplies, and faculty positions as choice rewards for deserving blacks who helped carry crucial wards and precincts. They were outraged when Young, at the beginning of his administration, filled vacancies with former colleagues from out of state. Young's idea of the university as an assemblage of scholars of the greatest possible distinction made no sense to Williams and Diggs. They had all too few rewards to parcel out among blacks who had been active in politics, and they did not propose to remain idle while Young stripped their control over the prestigious ap-

[31] *St. Louis Argus*, 24 April 1925; Nathan B. Young to W. E. B. Du Bois, 22 July 1925, WEBD Papers; interview with Prof. J. D. Parks, April 1971; Savage, *Lincoln University*, pp. 276–277.

pointments and lucrative contracts of Lincoln University.[32]

Young's situation was complicated further by legal provisions that prohibited the governor of Missouri from serving more than one four-year term and prescribed that the curators of Lincoln University, while eligible for reappointment, should serve staggered four-year terms. This meant that each new governor would have an opportunity to appoint curators. It also meant that there would be frequent changes in the board as the two political parties, or factions within the same party, exchanged control of the governorship. Thus when the Republican governor, Arthur M. Hyde, who had enthusiastically supported the efforts to upgrade Lincoln, was forced to leave office early in 1925, attention focused on his successor, Sam W. Baker.[33]

A Republican and a former state superintendent of schools, Baker had served on Lincoln's board of curators at the time Walthall Moore's $500,000 appropriation had been enacted. Governor Baker was thought to be in sympathy with Young's ambitious program. Moreover, Baker's margin of victory in the gubernatorial election of 1924 had been only six thousand votes—far less than the practically solid black vote that had been cast against the Democrats' Ku Klux Klan-endorsed nominee, Arthur W. Nelson. Negroes assumed that political considerations would keep Baker favorably disposed toward Lincoln University.[34] Still, given the political camaraderie that often crosses color lines, perhaps it was inevitable that in the scramble for influence with the new governor the earthy Williams would prevail over the idealistic and forthright Nathan B. Young.

As an astute politician, Williams made the most of white fears that higher education would "spoil" Negroes. Thus, according to the St. Louis Argus, he and his friend Diggs spread "propaganda of the sort which appeals to a certain

[32] Interviews with Professors Blue, Dowdy, and Parks, April 1971; Savage, Lincoln University, pp. 182, 194.
[33] Savage, Lincoln University, pp. 167–168.
[34] St. Louis Argus, 7 November 1924.

class of white people . . . who believe that Negro youth are only entitled to a certain kind of education." They endorsed the work of good, reliable professors who were satisfied with vocational education and teacher training—men like Collins and Damel—and claimed that Negroes would never be content with humble work so long as they were taught by "uppity" academicians. They also enlisted the support of other black politicians, such as the state inspector of Negro schools, N. C. Bruce, who traversed the state claiming that black youths should be trained for "the work they must do if they are to get any work at all." For instance, in the small town of Moberly Bruce explained to the board of education that this was "an industrial, economic and strictly business age" and therefore blacks should have courses in "scrubbing, cooking and nail driving instead of book learning." All would be well if state officials would squelch "book-learned folk [who] don't want practical and industrial training [because] they don't want to work" and instead support sensible blacks who realized that "the Negro must be taught his place and how to work like his old parents."[35]

This pandering to white prejudice naturally enraged many Negroes. The *St. Louis Argus* condemned Williams as a "traitor to his race"—a man who "put his own interest first" and was content to let "the welfare of the people go to h—— just so long as he, and his, are cared for." Editor Franklin of the *Kansas City Call* proclaimed, "No man, no city authorities can limit Negroes if we do not permit them to set boundaries to our ambitions." And in dozens of letters to the state's Negro newspapers, blacks made it clear that they were no longer content "to let whites think we . . . have a place above which we do not expect to rise." Summing up the prevailing Negro viewpoint, *Call* columnist Roy Wilkins, who would later become executive secretary of the NAACP,

[35] *St. Louis Argus*, 1 May 1925; N. C. Bruce to *Kansas City Call*, 18 June 1926; Bruce, quoted in *Chicago Defender*, 12 June 1926.

observed, "The harm is not in Mr. Bruce's belief that this
type of practical education, as he chooses to style it, is good
for Negroes, but his unqualified recommendation of it as a
general program for all Negroes. . . . We can't get along
without the higher book-learning, and the man who said so
is either playing to a cracker-hillbilly gallery for a mess of
pottage, or else he is woefully ignorant."[36]

But the machinations of the disgruntled black professors
and politicians were not without effect. Shortly after his
inauguration, Governor Baker noted that some Negroes did
not want "the kind of school President Young is attempting
to give them." He refused to reappoint Curators Edgar B.
Rombauer and Julia Childs Curtis—two trustees who had
played important roles in the campaign to upgrade Lincoln.
The failure to reappoint Rombauer and Curtis raised astonished eyebrows in the black community. Surprise turned
to anguish a few months later when the governor said
that "all the Negroes need there is a high school," and appointed Williams and Sam W. James, the Republican chairman of Pettis County, to fill the vacancies on the board of
curators.[37]

James was elected president of the reconstituted board,
and he quickly dispelled any lingering doubts as to what
was in the offing. He admitted to Young that "so far as I
know, your personal integrity has not been assailed [and]
your official ability may be first rate." But, the new president of the curators candidly explained, "the ideas of the
new board [were] entirely different from the old, and that
in selecting the head of Lincoln University they would look
for the man whom they felt would most nearly carry out
their ideas of what the University should be. . . . If we can

[36] *St. Louis Argus*, 8 May 1925; *Kansas City Call*, 18 June 1926; Roy
Wilkins, "Talking It Over," *Kansas City Call*, 11 June 1926.

[37] *St. Louis Argus*, 24 April, 23 January, 13 February 1925; Savage,
Lincoln University, pp. 191–192; Sam. W. Baker, quoted in *Kansas
City Call*, 19 June 1925; Minutes of the Meeting of the Board of Cura-
tors, 14 April 1925, Lincoln Archives.

secure the services of one whom we believe would do more for the Negro race in the state than you could do, then I feel it would be our duty to make a change, and I think a majority of the members of the board feel as I do about the matter." To remove any possible doubt, the new president of the board then let it be known that he thought Christopher Hubbard, the principal of Lincoln High School in Sedalia and an influential Republican politician in Pettis County, was "the leading educator among colored people in the United States."[38]

This threat to Young's presidency touched off an indignant furor in black Missouri. An unprecedented number of Negroes signed protest letters and telegrams, and special delegations traveled to Jefferson City to speak on Young's behalf. Accusing Hubbard of being "a half-educated lickspittle" who had never received a degree from an accredited college, blacks declared that "no worse blow could have been dealt us than to treat our education as a joke." They charged that "at the bottom of it all is a well-laid plan to place the school back in politics." Governor Baker was accused of using Lincoln "for the payment of political debts." It was said that he had "promised . . . James . . . and . . . Hubbard . . . whatever they wished if they could carry Pettis County for him." Of course this politicization of the university would undermine standards at Lincoln, but, as Roy Wilkins noted, "Baker by his actions proved he wasn't a bit concerned about Negro youth in the state getting an education." The opposition to Young, according to most blacks, was led by men with "an utter lack of appreciation of what Lincoln University should be," men who "didn't give a 'cuss' about the youth of the race . . . so long as the positions [at Lincoln] could be used to sell and bargain."[39]

[38] Sam W. James to Nathan B. Young, 25 April 1925, quoted in Savage, *Lincoln University*, p. 193; James, quoted in *St. Louis Argus*, 8 May 1925.

[39] *Kansas City Call*, 17 April, 19 June 1925; *St. Louis Argus*, 8 May, 24 April, 12 June 1925; Roy Wilkins, "Talking It Over," 5 March 1926.

The vehemence of this black reaction took Governor Baker by surprise, and his aides let it be known that Williams was thought to be responsible for having misled the administration about the state of black public opinion. Still, Baker had made commitments to Williams, James, and Hubbard, and the governor stiffened with irritation as letters, telegrams, petitions, and resolutions descended on his office. "The letters will do absolutely no good, and it is useless to attempt such propaganda," Baker informed the principal of the Crispus Attucks School in Kansas City, and he decided to force Young out of the presidency at the first opportunity. When the curators met on May 4, 1925, however, Baker discovered that he lacked the votes needed to oust Young. To be sure, Williams and James were opposed to Young, as was Clifford Scruggs, a reliable Democrat whom Baker appointed to give the board the appearance of bipartisanship. Yet C. H. Kirshner, a holdover from the Hyde administration, was committed to the plan to upgrade Lincoln, and the two remaining black members, Aaron Malone and Dr. J. E. Perry, knew they would forefeit the regard of their fellow blacks if they voted to remove Young.[40]

This left the decisive vote in the hands of the one ex-officio curator, Charles A. Lee, the white state superintendent of schools and a Democrat who was eager to lure black voters away from their traditional Republican affiliation. Lee abstained from voting at the May meeting, thus deadlocking the board, three votes to three, and leaving Young's fate uncertain for another month, during which blacks continued their fervid condemnation of the Baker administration. Then, when the board met again in June, Lee broke the tie with a vote in Young's favor. That vote renewed Young's lease on the presidency for two more years and also, as the St. Louis Argus noted, opened "the eyes of many

[40] Kansas City Call, 15 May 1925; St. Louis Argus, 10 July 1925; Sam. W. Baker to W. H. Harrison, quoted in Kansas City Call, 8 May 1925; Minutes of the Meeting of the Board of Curators, 4 May 1925, Lincoln Archives.

Negroes of the state and the nation to the fact that there are Democrats who are high-class men and who have as fine a sense of right and justice as our so-called friends, the Republicans."[41]

Although friends of the university were pleased that Young had been granted a reprieve, everyone knew that the terms of the pro-Young curators would expire in 1927 and that Young's tenure would be temporary unless Governor Baker changed his views. In this regard, there was some hope that Baker would mend his ways when he recognized the importance of the Negro vote. Hence the black newspapers and the Negro teachers' associations redoubled their efforts to organize blacks behind the campaign to upgrade the university. The *Kansas City Call* pointedly noted that few Republicans could win at the polls in Missouri without the Negro vote, and warned that "from this time on, a man to deserve Negro votes must have a record of service to Negroes."[42]

Along with this work to politicize the black community in support of Young's program, blacks vigorously criticized Williams and James. Williams was portrayed in the Negro press as an arch scoundrel, with his picture accompanied by stark captions identifying him as a "Race Traitor" and "Ebony Benedict Arnold." James was assailed on two counts. In the first place, critics noted that when it became clear that Baker's appointees constituted only a minority of the curators, James refused to call any further meetings of the board and instead assigned all work to an executive committee composed of himself, Williams, and Scruggs. Then, in a move that the *St. Louis Argus* characterized as "graft or its first cousin," James contacted several professors and suggested that their positions would be more secure if they stayed out of the controversy over Lincoln's presi-

[41] Minutes of the Meeting of the Board of Curators, 9 June 1925, Lincoln Archives; *St. Louis Argus*, 12 June 1925.
[42] *Kansas City Call*, 29 January 1926.

dency and instead bought stock he was selling in the Standard Savings and Loan Company of Kansas City.[43]

James's salesmanship was the subject of considerable discussion in the Negro press. Indeed, it precipitated so much discussion that one enterprising hosiery saleslady visited the Lincoln campus claiming that she was Mrs. James and that those who valued their jobs would be well-advised to purchase her line of stockings. Eventually the Missouri state assembly established an investigating committee to determine if James had used illegal duress in his sales work or had ignored a state law requiring that the curators meet at least twice a year. In the course of holding five hearings and examining seventeen witnesses, this committee discovered a number of irregularities: Pro-Young curators had not been appointed to any committees of the board and were not notified of scheduled board meetings until after the meetings had actually taken place. And nineteen professors were paying a total of about $350 a month to purchase James's stock. While stopping short of calling for James's resignation, the committee found that the curators' meetings "were not held in strict conformity with the statutes of the state of Missouri," and that "the sales of the aforesaid stock . . . [were] unethical and that the practice should cease."[44]

Negroes demanded that James be removed at once. A mass meeting at the St. Louis YMCA resolved that he was "unfit" to serve as president of the curators. The *Argus* declared, "The colored people of the state are disgusted, sick and tired of [James's] conduct. . . . So far as we are able to see, the only salvation of Lincoln University is the removal of one Sam W. James." Instead of removing James, how-

[43] *Kansas City Call*, 25 February, 4 March 1927; *St. Louis Argus*, 8 May 1925, 18 February, 11 April, 18 April 1927.

[44] *Kansas City Call*, 25 February, 4 March 1927; *St. Louis Argus*, 25 March, 11 April 1927; *Chicago Whip*, 2 April 1927; *Journal* of the House of the State of Missouri, 54th General Assembly 2 (1927): 1377–1378, 1616–1617.

217

ever, Governor Baker waited until the terms of the remaining pro-Young curators expired early in 1927, and then proceeded to appoint three new curators who had promised to depose Young.[45]

The black newspapers and teachers' associations again rallied to Young's defense, proclaiming that he was "doing a giant's work and doing it like a master." But with six of Baker's appointees among the seven curators, Young's fate was sealed. When the new board met on April 11, 1927, it promptly decided, by a vote of six to one, to appoint Duke Diggs as the university's business manager and to replace Young with Clement Richardson, a former member of the faculty at Tuskegee who was then serving as president of the small Western Baptist College in Kansas City. The dissenting ex-officio curator, Charles Lee, voiced the sentiment of most Negroes when he characterized Young's dismissal as "untimely, unwise, and a gross injustice both to President Young and to the cause of Negro education in the state."[46]

After deposing Young, Governor Baker and the curators lost no time in making it clear that the university would be reorganized with less ambitious academic goals. President Young's request for $625,000 for the biennial period commencing in 1927 was pared down to $278,000, a sum that was only slightly larger than the amount budgeted for the two years immediately prior to Young's arrival. The choice of Clement Richardson as president-elect was itself a significant indication of the curators' plans for the future: Richardson had served as president of Lincoln Institute from 1918 to 1922 and was known to believe that Negroes were particularly suited for vocational education. Thus blacks had good reason to believe that the development of Lincoln University had been thwarted "by meagre appro-

[45] St. Louis Argus, 4 March, 25 February, 25 March, 4 February, 15 April 1927; Kansas City Call, 25 February 1927.

[46] St. Louis Argus, 25 February 1927; Minutes of the Meeting of the Board of Curators, 11 April 1927, Lincoln Archives; Charles A. Lee, quoted in Birmingham Reporter, 23 April 1927.

priations, by changing the administration, and by ignoring attempts at grafting." "Governor Baker and the Lincoln University Board of Curators do not care a hoot about what kind of a school the Negro citizens of the state want," the *Kansas City Call* declared. "They mean to have the kind of school at Lincoln that they want."[47]

The curators wanted to use Lincoln to pay off political debts contracted with loyal blacks who had served the Baker administration. Young's dismissal was only the first of a series of at least fifteen terminations ordered by the curators during the spring of 1927. Eleven of these dismissed professors had testified against James at the hearings held by the state assembly's investigating committee. But even the anticipated charges of "political reprisal" were hardly sufficient to dissuade the curators from creating new jobs. As a disgusted curator Lee explained, there had been "a determined effort upon the part of some persons to secure positions at Lincoln" and "when President Clement Richardson was elected President of Lincoln University, he was elected upon the promise that he would choose some of these persons for positions." "As we think of this sort of stuff for the next two years," the *Argus* lamented, "the future for higher education for the Negro youths of this state is beyond our contemplation." Many blacks must have agreed with Roy Wilkins that it would be better to close the university than to allow it to go "limping along, making a sorry effort to educate the few pupils who go there not knowing what sort of institution they are attending."[48]

As black protests became increasingly bitter, Richardson declined the offer of the presidency and thus upset the smooth progression of the curators' plans. Richardson's de-

[47] St. Louis Argus, 25 February, 29 April 1927; Kansas City Call, 7 January, 21 January, 11 February, 4 March, 1 April, 15 April 1927.

[48] Chicago Whip, 14 March 1927; Kansas City Call, 6 May 1927; St. Louis Argus, 13 May, 20 May 1927; Charles A. Lee, quoted in St. Louis Argus, 13 May 1927; Roy Wilkins, "Talking It Over," 11 February 1927.

cision doubtless came as a surprise, for he had attended some meetings of the board and had made recommendations for filling some of the new vacancies on the faculty. Yet Richardson was annoyed when Williams demanded the right to approve all appointments. He knew too that many blacks felt that anyone who cooperated with the board would "cease to be a man devoted to education and become a tool of politics." Given the depth of black opposition to the Baker administration, Richardson knew that there was "nothing to expect up the road but trouble, trouble, trouble." Hence he decided to stay at Western College. He knew, as the *Argus* had explained, that "none of the leading and thoughtful colored people of the state have any confidence in the Board, and therefore anyone they select will be looked upon with suspicion. This suspicion would be so pronounced that two years would be as long as one could hope to stay, and troublous times would be before him during that brief period."[49]

As Clement Richardson had foreseen, trouble soon visited the campus. Informed observers reported in October 1927 that there was "a restlessness in both student body and instructing force" and claimed that "almost without exception the student body resents the ousting of former President N. B. Young." Asserting that the students knew "what everybody else in the state knows, that Governor Sam Baker, C. G. Williams, and S. W. James are not interested in the education of Negro students," one student explained, "We are not interested in our lessons any more. You see, everybody knows that the real gang that runs this university is downtown [in Jefferson City] and over in Sedalia. We know that they are not running it for our benefit, but

[49] Clement Richardson to Board of Curators, in Minutes of the Meeting of the Board of Curators, 2 June 1927, Lincoln Archives; Minutes of the Meeting of the Board of Curators, 23 May 1927, Lincoln Archives; *Kansas City Call*, 13 May 1927; *St. Louis Argus*, 3 June 1927.

for their own. . . . We want an administration that is for us and for the school, not for themselves."[50]

With the morale of the university thus "shot to pieces," strike talk was "in the air" and most blacks believed that "something has to happen soon." Finally, the tension was broken when the Student Council called for a boycott of classes, and roving bands of wildcatters roamed the campus breaking windows and doing minor damage to other property. An undetermined number of students left the university "in disgust, never to return again," and some parents ordered their children to withdraw and return to their homes.[51]

V

The students' boycott and disruption subsided rather quickly. This was in part because the governor promptly dispatched armed prison guards to police the campus and also because blacks knew that Lincoln's problems were essentially political in origin and could be solved only by seeking redress at the polls. Thus, immediately after Young had been deposed, editor Franklin urged blacks to prepare for the 1928 elections. "The Negroes of the state made known their wishes about Lincoln," his *Kansas City Call* declared. "Governor Baker had his way in 1927. It will be the people's turn again in 1928." Negro sentiment in favor of breaking loose from the traditional Republican affiliation increased perceptibly when their lone champion on the board of curators, State Superintendent Lee, announced his candidacy for the Democratic gubernatorial nomination and then named Nathan B. Young to replace N. C. Bruce as state inspector of colored schools. Lee was clearly "the one man who will command more Negro votes than any

[50] *Kansas City Call*, 28 October 1927.
[51] *Kansas City Call*, 28 October, 11 November 1927; *St. Louis Argus*, 14 October 1927, 10 February 1928.

other candidate the Democrats could put up." Although the party's nomination ultimately went to Francis M. Wilson, Lee's Democratic affiliation and his subsequent support for Wilson paved the way for many Missouri blacks to leave the party of Abraham Lincoln.[52]

Governor Baker was forbidden by law from succeeding himself, but many Negroes thought that the Republican gubernatorial nominee of 1928, Judge Henry S. Caulfield, was compromised by his Republican affiliation and especially by his association with members of the Baker administration. It was these Republicans who allegedly "were robbing the youths of the race of an education by using [Lincoln] to pay off political debts." The *Call* editorialized on the "Folly of the Straight Vote" and urged Negroes to vote for Herbert Hoover for President, "despite his fool friends," while rejecting Caulfield, "blighted already by the bad faith of the Baker administration and compromised by its support." Yet when the ballots were counted in November, Caulfield emerged victorious and it appeared that many blacks had remained loyal to the party of emancipation. The *Call* did find solace, however, in the knowledge that Democrat Wilson received 47 percent of the vote in the four overwhelmingly black wards in Kansas City. This was almost twice as much as the share of the vote that had gone to the Democratic gubernatorial candidate in 1924, and the *Call* claimed that there was a remarkable spirit of political independence in the black community. Thousands of blacks had split their tickets in the face of an overwhelming pro-Hoover tide. "Promise-breakers like Baker have made us know that we are wise to vote for our friends, no matter under what party label," the *Call* concluded. "Only the Hoover landslide defeated Wilson."[53]

If Baker disappointed those who had expected a former

[52] *Kansas City Call*, 15 April, 2 December 1927; *St. Louis Argus*, 13 January 1928.

[53] *St. Louis Argus*, 13 January 1928; *Kansas City Call*, 2 November, 26 October, 2 December, 9 November 1928.

curator and state superintendent of schools to be committed to higher education for Negroes, Judge Caulfield proved to be a pleasant surprise. In his inaugural address, the new governor endorsed the Hyde administration's plan to make Lincoln a real university, and one of his first official acts was to establish a State Survey Commission, composed of distinguished educators from throughout the nation, to prepare a report on the needs of Lincoln and all other state colleges. This commission eventually recommended that Lincoln raise its salary scale to $4,500 for outstanding professors and that the university continue its efforts "to secure well-prepared persons with the doctor's degree."[54]

Governor Caulfield endorsed these proposals enthusiastically, and then persuaded the legislature to appropriate $400,000 for Lincoln's operating expenses for the biennial period beginning in 1929, and an additional $250,000 for new buildings on the campus. This extraordinary financial support was necessary, the governor insisted, if Lincoln were to become a real university and thus enable the state to "make educational equality more than a mere phrase."[55]

Given his commitment to quality education for Negroes, Caulfield naturally refused to reappoint Governor Baker's curators. Thus Williams, James, and Scruggs were allowed to leave the board when their terms expired in 1929; and somehow Caulfield persuaded the three remaining Baker men on the board (E. H. Otto and Drs. E. O. Bunch and J. W. McCleland) to resign. Then the new governor proceeded to name an entirely new board of curators, headed by Charles Nagel, a trustee at Washington University in St. Louis and a former secretary of commerce in the Cabinet of William McKinley. The new board also included the ex-officio Charles A. Lee, J. D. Elliff, a professor at the University of Missouri, J. B. Coleman, a black launderer from Columbia, and three former curators whom Governor Baker

[54] Savage, *Lincoln University*, pp. 214–215.
[55] Henry S. Caulfield, paraphrased in Savage, *Lincoln University*, pp. 215, 221.

had refused to reappoint in order to make places for his own henchmen—Rombauer, Curtis, and Dr. Perry.[56]

Erstwhile critics of the Baker administration were delighted with Caulfield. The new governor "set a high standard for education in . . . his inaugural address," one black newspaper rejoiced, "and followed this up by appointing the present high-type Board of Curators." The curators, in turn, immediately forced Diggs to resign from his position as business manager and restored Acting President William Jason to his position as dean of the college and professor of mathematics. A search committee was then formed to screen potential candidates for the presidency. Although the board considered the credentials of several outstanding educators there was never any doubt that their first choice to head this new "forward-looking program for developing the institution to one of first rank" would be Nathan B. Young.[57]

Young had reservations about returning to Lincoln. After twenty-six years' service as a college president and two knockout fights in Florida and Missouri he knew that "uneasy lies the head that wears a crown wrought by the fortune of political change." Yet Young had been genuinely moved by earlier demonstrations of public confidence in his work. "Despite handicaps encountered," his years at Lincoln had been "a real delight" because he enjoyed "the support of the people of the state and because the service offered a challenge to one who desired to see a school developed." Though he was approaching seventy years of age and must have yearned for tranquillity, he could not refuse this new chance "to secure for the Negro youth of our state the same educational opportunities (both in extent

[56] Minutes of the Meeting of the Board of Curators, 30 May 1929, Lincoln Archives.

[57] St. Louis American, 14 September 1929; Minutes of the Meetings of the Board of Curators, 30 May, 13 June, 27 August, 10 September 1929, Lincoln Archives.

and in content) that are guaranteed by Missouri to her white youth."[58]

Thus in September 1929 Young returned to the task of making Lincoln a real university. Yet he had been back on the job for only nineteen months when the curators, without any warning or public explanation, suddenly released Young again and named a new president.[59] The reasons for this abrupt decision remain shrouded in mystery, for the curators feared a repetition of the sort of public controversy that accompanied Governor Baker's efforts of 1925 and 1927 and hence they made their plans of 1931 in absolute secrecy. Fortunately, however, there are a number of clues as to the source of the difficulties Young encountered during his second administration. Although the evidence is hardly incontrovertible it is possible to offer an admittedly incomplete explanation.

In the first place, it is clear that some members of the faculty were no more reconciled to Young's academic objectives in 1929 than they had been at the outset of his first administration. Damel and Collins were still disparaging the president's academic ambitions, and they found a new ally in the person of former Acting President Jason. Young recognized these three as a "cabal of malcontents" and tried to force their resignations, but the board could not bring itself to dismiss a powerful triumverate that included two former acting presidents and a senior professor. Thus the dissidents were able to organize and arrange meetings with Governor Caulfield and various curators.[60]

Among the curators, J. D. Elliff, a white professor of edu-

[58] Nathan B. Young to Friends of Lincoln, quoted in *St. Louis Argus*, 9 September 1927; Young to Dr. and Mrs. J. P. Wragg, 15 January 1927, paraphrased in Savage, *Lincoln University*, p. 202.

[59] Minutes of the Meetings of the Board of Curators, 6 April, 2 June, 16 June, 13 July 1931, Lincoln Archives.

[60] "Statement of N. B. Young," *St. Louis American*, 11 April 1931; interview with Professor Parks, April 1971.

cation and a widely respected author of several volumes on secondary education, was a principal adviser to Governor Caulfield and the most influential member of the board. Elliff worked hard to ensure fair appropriations for Lincoln and wanted to upgrade the institution to the point of accreditation as a standard college. Yet Elliff's own speciality was "progressive vocational education"—he was best known as the author of course outlines and suggestions of new techniques for high school teachers of agriculture. Nathan B. Young, Jr., a recent graduate of the Yale Law School who had then just begun to edit the *St. Louis American*, claimed that "Elliff's knowledge and vision of Negro education is decidedly limited."[61]

There are no surviving documents indicating that Damel, Collins, and Jason turned Elliff against Young, but Damel and Collins belonged to the same lodge as another curator, J. B. Coleman. Coleman was Elliff's closest black friend and also, according to the Negro press, a " 'Man Friday' and go-between who has worked with a clique of disgruntled teachers, . . . especially at night and behind closed doors."[62] It would seem likely, then, that Coleman kept Elliff fully informed concerning faculty opposition to Young, and that Elliff relayed this side of the story to Governor Caulfield.

This interpretation is admittedly speculative, and it may never be known whether Elliff's opposition to Young was prompted by a deep-seated vocationalist suspicion of the liberal arts, by a progressive methodologist's dislike of a traditional classicist, or by his dependence on Coleman for advice on matters relating to the black community. It should be noted, however, that it was the custom of the time for whites to place great faith in trusted black advisers who were then given enormous authority over other Negroes. Elliff relied on Coleman's advice relating to blacks

[61] J. D. Elliff, "A Concise Statement of the Needs of Lincoln University" (1929 typescript), Lincoln Archives; *St. Louis American*, 11 April 1931.
[62] *St. Louis American*, 11 April 1931.

as assuredly as Governor Caulfield depended on Elliff's suggestions with regard to Lincoln. Young had fallen twice before as a victim to this system of interracial relations—once to the Turner-Hardee *mésalliance* in Florida and again to Williams, James, and Baker in Missouri. It appears that he fell the third time before the combined influence of Coleman, Elliff, and Caulfield.

In any case, Elliff persuaded Governor Caulfield not to reappoint Rombauer and Curtis, Young's staunchest friends on the board of curators. A reconstituted board then met secretly in April 1931 and with no prior warning voted unanimously to release Young from the presidency. Of course the Negro press was astonished, and the outcry was not limited to Missouri. Robert S. Abbott of the *Chicago Defender* declared that Young was "perhaps our foremost educator" and that his treatment "would be scandalous elsewhere than in Missouri . . . that paradise state of machinations."[63] The *Pittsburgh Courier* noted that "no formal charges were made against Young, who is one of the outstanding educators of the country," and said that "politics is openly placed at the bottom of the move."[64] Writing in the *Baltimore Afro-American*, Carter G. Woodson sagely observed that too many black professors specialized "in curbstone politics to have their salaries raised and their friends and relatives appointed to positions. . . . These forces of antagonisn usually develop sufficient weight by the end of the fourth year of a president's administration to have him dismissed in the sixth."[65] The *St. Louis American* declared that the curators' decision was "both reprehensible and ridiculous. Their cold-blooded act of deposing the president without according him a chance to defend himself . . . and with a 'to-hell-with-the-colored-citizens-of-Missouri' attitude, stands as the biggest piece of educational

[63] Minutes of the Meeting of the Board of Curators, 6 April 1931; *Chicago Defender*, 2 May 1931.
[64] *Pittsburgh Courier*, 18 April 1931.
[65] *Baltimore Afro-American*, 18 April 1931.

hijacking . . . in the long history of disruption at Lincoln.
. . . Their vast secrecy and haste are clear indications that
they were afraid to allow the public to know what they
planned to do."[66]

For his part, Young was disgusted with the whole situation in Missouri and chose to avoid angry recriminations
and instead retired to live with a daughter in Tampa, Florida. He claimed that he could relate "a tale . . . as to activities against my administration that would be well-nigh startling in its details," but he refused to pitch the dispute "on
that low level."[67] Fortunately, he did leave notes, though
rather sketchy and enigmatic, that he hoped might later
serve as the basis for a complete autobiography. At the outset of his second administration at Lincoln, he noted, there
was general agreement among the curators that the university should be upgraded until it was universally recognized
as a standard, accredited college. Yet by 1931

> the opinion dominated the . . . Board that the President
> was actually retarding his own program by a certain ad-
> ministrative conservatism. . . . And so it was decided that
> a "new model" executive was necessary for the speedy
> completion of the program. To be sure, there was also
> that well-known mission brand of politics in the maneu-
> vering, but such is perhaps not worth the space to add
> here. Anyway, the experiment of putting new wine in old
> bottles produced a ferment that, while it did not destroy
> the bottle, shattered him who was making it. There arose
> an irreconcilable [difference of] opinion as to methods
> of management that led to his elimination from the serv-
> ice and that too just as the goal was in sight. In the words
> of popular college parlance, the ball was on the one yard
> line when the Coach put in a substitute to put it over.[68]

[66] St. Louis American, 11 April 1931.
[67] "Statement of N. B. Young," 11 April 1931.
[68] Young, "Quest and Use of an Education."

Politics would continue to confound Lincoln University for at least another decade after Young's departure, but the institution was fully accredited in 1934 and is today one of the best, and perhaps the most thoroughly integrated, of the original land-grant colleges for Negroes. The foundation for this later development was laid in the 1920s, when Young struggled against primitive traditions and prejudices so that later generations might carry on under more favorable conditions. Of course the old president regretted being deposed before the battle was won. He confessed that he appreciated "what Moses must have felt when he was . . . told that he could not enter . . . the land toward which he had been journeying for forty years." But just as Moses' disappointment was softened by the thought that he had been to the mountaintop and had seen the promised land, so Young was consoled by the knowledge that he had "played the major role in converting Lincoln Institute to Lincoln University—changing a secondary industrial school into a college of liberal arts with fair prospects of becoming what its new name promises—an institution of higher and professional learning."[69]

[69] Ibid.

CHAPTER VI

Rites of Passage: Hampton Institute Becomes a College

I

Established by the American Missionary Association in 1868, Hampton Institute went through two distinct phases of development in the years before the First World War. Under the leadership of its first principal, Samuel Chapman Armstrong, Hampton was for twenty-five years essentially a normal school preparing teachers for work in the black South. This emphasis on teacher training was supplemented with a work program that enabled some students to support themselves and made it possible for the school to raise and save money, but prior to the 1890s Hampton was primarily concerned with general education.[1]

In the years between 1893 and 1917, however, Armstrong's successor, Hollis Burke Frissell, raised the work-study program to the point where it became a gospel that disavowed higher education for blacks and stressed a new approach—the so-called Hampton Idea. This was the doctrine that Negro education should emphasize job training and inculcate moral values. Although Armstrong had insisted in 1872 that "the academic department (or normal school) is the leading department to which all others are subsidiary," Frissell proclaimed in 1897 that "Instead of making the industries the stepping stone to the academic

[1] For the history of Hampton Institute, see Edward K. Graham's forthcoming book, *A Tender Violence: The Biography of a College*, and William H. Robinson, "The History of Hampton Institute, 1868–1949" (Ph.D. diss., New York University, 1953).

department, the academic department is now made the stepping stone to the industrial and trade work."[2] Frissell's emphasis on vocational training was part of a larger effort to ingratiate the institute with those who believed that blacks should be trained for subordinate positions in American society. Thus the color line was drawn more and more within the school—with dining rooms and guesthouses segregated by race. Frissell inaugurated a system of interracial etiquette that, according to one observer, was "so intricate and baffling that it took more time and energy to avoid introducing Colonel Carter to George Jones than to teach carpentry and farming." While Armstrong had sought the tolerant acquiescence of the white South, Frissel actively solicited the friendship of Southerners and the assistance of the organized northern philanthropies that deferred to the white South on the proper education of Negroes. Hampton reaped handsome financial dividends as a result—boasting an endowment of $8,500,000 in 1925, a sum that placed the institute first among black schools and seventeenth among the 176 American colleges then possessing endowments valued at more than a million dollars.[3]

Yet it was hardly surprising that some blacks believed that Hampton's endowment had been purchased at too great a cost, and among black critics of Frissell's Institute none was more outspoken than W. E. B. Du Bois. The editor of the Crisis charged that Hampton not only emphasized technical training but decried the work of other black schools, "criticizing and belittling their ideals while her friends continually seek to divert to Hampton the already painfully meager revenues of the colored colleges." Du Bois further asserted that Hampton placated the white South to the point where whites "felt that Hampton belonged to

[2] Samuel Chapman Armstrong and Hollis Burke Frissell, quoted in Graham, A Tender Violence, chap. 7.

[3] W. E. B. Du Bois, "Hampton Institute," Crisis 26 (August 1929): 277–278; Baltimore Afro-American, 4 April 1925.

them and that the students were there to sing for them, wait on table, and guide them through the beautiful grounds." "We do not feel that Hampton is our school," Du Bois declared. "On the contrary, we feel that she belongs to the white South and to the reactionary North, and we fear that she is a center of that underground and silent intrigue which is determined to perpetuate the American Negro as a docile peasant and peon."[4]

When whites applauded Frissell's executive ability and success in gaining the support of both North and South, Du Bois insisted that the principal of Hampton should also possess "a knowledge of the present thought and aspirations of the American Negro" and an "ability to unite not only North and South, but white and black." The editor of the *Crisis* also noted that Hampton's academic faculty was almost entirely white, and he warned, "The time has gone when the colored people of the United States are going to have the world interpreted to them solely by white people."[5]

James Edgar Gregg, who became Hampton's third white principal in 1918, was an unlikely choice to placate black critics, for he had enjoyed only limited contacts with blacks during his student days at Harvard and Yale and during fifteen years of active ministry at various churches in Massachusetts. Yet Gregg recognized that blacks possessed "a new self-consciousness, a new impatience of their disadvantages and a new eagerness to get knowledge, skill, culture, wealth, and all else that is suggested by the word 'progress.'" Thus he worked to give blacks a larger and more active role at Hampton. During Gregg's eleven years at the institute more than a score of Negroes were appointed to teaching positions in the academic department. Others were appointed to teach in the applied fields and as directors of

[4] W. E. B. Du Bois, "Hampton," *Crisis* 15 (November 1917): 10–12; Du Bois, "Hampton Institute," pp. 277–278.

[5] W. E. B. Du Bois, "Advice," *Crisis* 15 (March 1918): 215; Du Bois, "Hampton College," *Crisis* 24 (July 1922): 104–105.

the Library School, the School of Home Economics, the School of Music, and the Extension Service. Moreover, Gregg enthusiastically devoted himself to developing cultural programs in black and African studies, organizing essay contests on topics such as "The Ideals of Negro Poetry" and "The Value of the Study of Negro History." He launched a West African Student Union, presided over the *Southern Workman's* publication of some sixty articles on Africa, and persuaded the trustees to fund programs for summer study and sabbatical leaves for faculty members.[6]

In terms of establishing harmonious relations with critics who feared that the higher aspirations of the race had been sacrificed in order to obtain financial support from wealthy philanthropists, Gregg's most important work focused on upgrading the institute to the collegiate level. Gregg noted that accrediting agencies in several southern states had begun to demand college training for all certified teachers. He then persuaded the trustees in 1920 to expand the two-year normal course into a standard four-year program and to have the institute's charter amended so as to provide for granting the degree of bachelor of arts in education. This was speedily accomplished; and within the next few years additional baccalaureate programs were inaugurated in home economics, business, music, and library science, as well as a master's program in school administration. In terms of student registration these new programs were extraordinarily popular, for while the total number of students enrolled at Hampton remained at about a thousand throughout the 1920s, the number of students in the college division grew steadily—from 21 in 1920–1921 to 417 in 1927–1928. By 1929 no new high school students were admitted, and only remedial work was offered at the secondary level. "In terms of the function and structure of the institution,

<hr>

[6] James E. Gregg, "Principal's Annual Report, 1928" (typescript), Hampton Archives; Graham, *Tender Violence*, chap. 8.

the most significant development of the Gregg years was Hampton's transition from school to college."[7]

Yet this transition could not be accomplished without growing pains. "Turning a secondary school into a college is never easy," the editor of the institute's *Southern Workman* acknowledged. In Hampton's case the task was complicated by the reluctance of some of the faculty, alumni, and benefactors to admit that their school was no longer the center of a special approach to Negro education but simply one of many standard black colleges. A few senior teachers spoke of "the glory of Hampton," its unique tradition, and the necessity of "not building too fast for our foundation . . . The danger lies in being called a college before doing collegiate work."[8]

Many trustees expressed similar reservations. Thus Francis Greenwood Peabody looked askance at what he called the "movement to transform Hampton Institute into a college with perhaps a vermiform appendix of trade school and industrial education." And Robert Russa Moton, the only black trustee, protested against the transformation of his alma mater and reminded his colleagues that Hampton had made its reputation because it "dared from the beginning to do things educationally that other people are ashamed to do." Still other trustees were alarmed when the editor of the local white newspaper warned that collegiate education might stimulate the students' racial pride to the point where they would resent the domination of whites and thus become a threat to the established order of race relations in the South."[9]

[7] Minutes of the Meeting of the Hampton Board of Trustees, 4 May 1922, Hampton Archives; Graham, *Tender Violence*, chap. 8.

[8] "Growing Pains," *Southern Workman* 56 (1927): 544–545; Graham, *Tender Violence*, chap. 8.

[9] Francis Greenwood Peabody and Robert R. Moton, quoted in Minutes of the Meeting of the Hampton Board of Trustees, 25 April 1929, Hampton Archives; *Newport News Daily Press*, 15 October 1927.

To allay fears that college-educated blacks would lose sight of their "place" in society, Hampton developed what Edward K. Graham has called "a pattern of thinking which looked toward keeping the student in his or her place."[10] In 1919 Gregg posted an order prescribing that

> students must be in bed when the lights are out, no talking or whispering is allowed. . . . Every student is expected to bathe at least twice a week. . . . No student is allowed north of the line passing through the center of the Principal's house except when on school business. . . . Students are forbidden to use tobacco or intoxicating liquors in any form. . . . Rowing, sailing and bicycle riding on Sundays, except on school duty or by special permission, is forbidden.[11]

The ringing of a bell told students when to get up, go to classes, go to meals, go to work, and go to bed. Compulsory chapel services were held every day, and matrons and janitors were authorized to inspect the students' rooms "at any hour of the day or night." Outside observers such as Prof. Paul Hanus of Harvard, whom the trustees employed to prepare a lengthy appraisal of the situation at the institute, were shocked by the general climate on the campus. "Hampton," Hanus observed at one point, "is a serious place" where students had required assignments that consumed between nine and a half and thirteen hours on weekdays, and might range up to ten and a half hours on Sundays.[12] Principal Gregg emphasized that the institute sought "above all to make the right kind of men and women."

[10] Graham, *Tender Violence*, chap. 8.

[11] "General Order No. 2, Rules and Regulations" (bulletin), Hampton Archives.

[12] "Student Room Inspection" (1922 bulletin), Hampton Archives; Paul Hanus, "Report of a Study of Hampton Institute," pp. 72–76 (typescript), Hampton Archives.

Hence its administrative officers had "not felt it wise or fair to leave spiritual discipline . . . to the voluntary and variable impulses of its students." Gregg and his chief lieutenants spent long hours in weekly deliberations over the appropriate punishments for students guilty of violating Hampton's regulations. Thus two young women were put on probation for playing cards, a young lady was suspended for a year in punishment for having been "seen on the grounds with some young man" whom she did not have permission to receive as a guest, and a girl who left the campus with a man and did not return until 11:30 p.m. was "severely disciplined by the Dean and sent off the next morning not to return."[13]

In a further attempt to appease white sentiment, the trustees continued to refer to the school as an institute rather than as a college. Even when Hampton was accredited as a college by Virginia's Department of Education, Principal Gregg insisted that the institute was "not a liberal arts college and should never seek to be." According to Gregg, Hampton's "distinctive place of highest usefulness . . . is without question . . . that of a technical and professional college." He assured all who would listen that Hampton would not forsake "any of the characteristics that made it famous in the years gone by—characteristics which included wholesome respect for hard work and hand skill, as well as for character, moral fitness, trustworthiness and dependability."[14]

However reassuring these statements may have been to apprehensive whites, many students and teachers came to believe that Gregg's soothing rhetoric was an outward manifestation of a basic vacillation with regard to Hampton's central purpose. Thus Harry J. Doermann, the white direc-

[13] James E. Gregg, "Principal's Annual Report, 1923" (typescript), Hampton Archives; Edward K. Graham, "The Hampton Institute Strike of 1927," *American Scholar* 38 (Autumn 1969): 672.

[14] James E. Gregg, quoted in *New York Age*, 12 November 1927; *Baltimore Afro-American*, 11 April 1925.

tor of the Academy and Normal School, complained that Hampton was "trying so hard to be loyal to her past that she is cherishing the letter and losing the spirit." According to Doermann, the institute had once evinced "a courageous pioneering spirit with its eye to the future when . . . there should be no barriers to the completest development of all talents." Hampton was drifting in the early 1920s because its leaders were afraid to explain "the presence of collegiate departments to our Northern friends." As a result of these misgivings concerning the higher education of Negroes, Doermann believed that "except in the Normal School no conscientious effort has been made to . . . abide by well-known minimum requirements" for college-level work. "Far better," he believed, "never to have established 'schools of normal or collegiate grade' than to fail to measure up to well-recognized standards."[15]

Thus Hampton's efforts to develop a collegiate program whetted the appetites of egalitarians while spreading apprehension among vocationalists. Neither group was wholly satisfied with the new Hampton compromise, and each prepared to assert itself: the advocates of special job training with a legislative campaign to force Jim Crowing on the campus and thereby demonstrate their control over the institute, and the black students with a strike against those who were thought to be thwarting the higher aspirations of the race.

II

White apprehensions mounted along with the steady growth of enrollments in Hampton's college programs. However much Gregg might attempt to disguise the egalitarian implications of college training, many Virginians feared that exposure to the higher curriculum would lead blacks to think that they should enjoy equal opportunities

[15] Harry J. Doermann memorandum to James E. Gregg, 26 June 1923, Hampton Archives.

and equal treatment before the law. Moreover, this fear was tinged with a certain amount of envy. After charging that Hampton taught "racial equality," one Virginia newspaper also complained that the institute was "richer than the University of Virginia, William and Mary College or any other state institution of learning. . . ."[16] Many whites undoubtedly believed that Hampton fostered egalitarian aspirations—that in the parlance of the day it was a school for "uppity" blacks who were dissatisfied with their subordinate "place." These whites thought the time had come to reassert white control over black education.

The white offensive centered on Hampton's right to hold integrated meetings in its own halls and auditoriums. Though officers of the institute provided a segregated residence for visitors, the Holly Tree Inn, they believed that whites who taught and worked with blacks had to treat Negroes as social equals if they were to maintain the necessary interracial rapport and cooperation. Hence meetings of the board of trustees were mixed, although Moton, the only black trustee, was housed elsewhere than at the Holly Tree Inn. Blacks also mingled with whites in the campus chapel, at various meetings, and at public entertainments held in Hampton's commodious Ogden Hall. This had been the practice for some years, and knowledgeable men and women recognized that whites who crossed the color line and entered Hampton's campus would be ostracized if they did not treat blacks as equals. Du Bois warned, "Either black folk are going to be treated as social equals or they are going to refuse to cooperate with the world."[17]

There had been occasional protests about "race mixing" on the campus, as when the Anglo-Saxon Club of the city of Hampton demanded that the governor of North Carolina

<hr>

[16] *Newport News Daily Press*, quoted in *Baltimore Afro-American*, 4 April 1925.
[17] Robert R. Moton to Allen Washington, 24 January 1929, Moton Papers; W. E. B. Du Bois, "The Battle of Washington," *Crisis* 30 (July 1925): 114-115.

prohibit his state university's glee club from performing for an integrated audience. But it was not until 1925, in the wake of a performance given by a dance troop headed by Ruth St. Denis and Ted Shawn, that the controversy was brought to a head. Despite Ogden Hall's ability to accommodate some two thousand spectators, tickets for the Denishawn dancers were hard to come by, perhaps because, as one trustee later explained, "The dancers were practically naked and therefore everybody went." Among those in attendance was the young wife of Col. W. S. Copeland, the aging editor of the *Newport News Daily Press*. Mrs. Copeland, who arrived late for the performance and was ushered to the only remaining seats next to some Negroes, returned home full of anger that there was no separation of the races in the auditorium. Soon thereafter Colonel Copeland escalated the controversy with a blistering editorial charging, "Here in this old Virginia community, rich in history and tradition, here where the first permanent white man's settlement was made, there is an institution which teaches and practices social equality between the white and Negro races."[18]

Principal Gregg was terribly alarmed by this criticism. He immediately released a lengthy public letter assuring whites that there had been no change in Hampton's policies and that the school certainly did not encourage "social mingling of the races under circumstances which would lead to embarrassment on either side." "It should hardly be necessary to add," Gregg continued, "that association of a romantic nature such as might conceivably lead to intermarriage is contrary to the wishes and judgment of the overwhelming majority of Negroes as of white persons."[19]

[18] *New York Age*, 21 November 1925; Graham, *Tender Violence*, chap. 8; George Foster Peabody to Newton D. Baker, 4 January 1926, Peabody Papers; *Newport News Daily Press*, 15 March 1925, 16 February 1926.

[19] James E. Gregg to *Newport News Daily Press*, 15 July, 16 July 1925.

This assurance failed to placate Colonel Copeland. Although it was admittedly "a very courteous reply and written in good temper," the editor of the *Daily Press* complained that it answered none of his major criticisms. Copeland, who for ten years had uncomplainingly attended integrated meetings of Hampton's board of overseers of landgrant funds, now claimed that racial egalitarians at the institute wanted to wean "whites of the Old Dominion . . . away from their traditions." Social equality in the theater was but a prelude to "amalgamation" and "the destruction of the Anglo-Saxon race in America and the substitution of a race of mulattoes." Far from attempting to stir up bad blood, Copeland insisted that he was "trying to stir up the best blood; to arouse the Anglo-Saxons to the danger which threatens."[20]

"If you wipe out the color line we are gone," Copeland warned. "There will be no power on earth to prevent the nigger from entering our homes and marrying your daughter. We are going to have serious trouble if you do not . . . protect our citizens and our womanhood against this horrible practice of social equality." Referring to the Denishawn concert, Copeland envisioned "beautiful white women in the nude with nigger youths gazing at them and there was the flower of our womanhood seated next to the black." There were "a certain amount of women who can not resist temptation," and he insisted that it was the duty of white men to protect these women "by maintaining the barrier that southern manhood has always stood for."[21]

Copeland was determined to agitate this question until it became a matter of concern in communities throughout Virginia. This was easily accomplished, for the public was

[20] W. S. Copeland, quoted in Lawrence T. Price to Members of the Advisory Committee of the Hampton-Tuskegee Endowment Fund, 10 July 1925, WEBD Papers.
[21] Ibid.; Copeland, quoted in J. A. Rogers, "Massenburg Hearing," *Baltimore Afro-American*, 27 February 1926; Graham, *Tender Violence*, chap. 8.

extraordinarily interested in the subject of miscegenation at that time. A controversial racial integrity bill had just been introduced in the state legislature, and the state's many Anglo-Saxon clubs were lobbying on behalf of this legislation and suggesting that a racial census would show that thousands of allegedly white Virginians, including members of some of the most prominent families of the Old Dominion, should be classified as "colored."

Thus Copeland had little difficulty enlisting the support of the chief spokesman for the Anglo-Saxon clubs, a concert pianist named John Powell. Copeland also persuaded Lawrence T. Price, the titular leader of the Anglo-Saxons, to warn southern newspapers and contributors to the Hampton-Tuskegee Endowment Fund that Hampton had "no moral right to teach and practice anything which is contrary to the Virginia spirit and our sense of propriety, nor to ignore in any degree time-honored customs." Price further suggested, "in all modesty," that contributors demand that Hampton practice segregation on its campus "before permitting the continued use of your name" for fund-raising purposes.[22]

Copeland, Powell, and Price did not lack brains, and they knew that Hampton was violating no law, although it certainly was deviating from the standard practice in the rest of Virginia. Hence they resolved to do something about the law, and in November 1925 Copeland arranged for John Powell to address a mass meeting of the citizens of Hampton on the dangers of "mongrelization of the races." A resolution was then adopted, condemning "indiscriminate seating of blacks and whites in public assemblages as fostered, fashioned, and founded at the Hampton Normal and Agricultural Institute." The assembled citizens then demanded

[22] J. A. Rogers, "Interview with John Powell and Ernest Sevier Cox," *Baltimore Afro-American*, 6 March 1926; Rogers, "Leading Virginia Families," *Baltimore Afro-American*, 13 March 1926; *Opportunity* 2 (June 1924): 163–164; *New York Age*, 27 February 1926; Price to Members of the Advisory Committee, 10 July 1925.

that their local representative to the state legislature, Capt. George Alvin Massenburg, "introduce a bill at the next General Assembly . . . prohibiting the mixing of audiences at the public assemblages." In what must have been an understatement, the reporter for the local newspaper observed that the discussion had bordered "on the lively"—a condition doubtless stimulated when Frank Foster, a teacher of Bible at the institute, noted that the Anglo-Saxons were themselves mongrels as their name clearly indicated.[23]

In due course Captain Massenburg drafted a bill and sent it on its way through the state legislature. There were a few moments of comic relief—as when a prominent local attorney explained, "The races were seated without reference to color while those almost nude [Denishawn] dancers performed," and a fascinated Senator Garrett inquired, "Did they do the Charleston?" But the officers of the institute knew this was no laughing matter. They recognized that "it would be disastrous to the work at Hampton if we changed our present policy. . . . If Hampton were to attempt such segregation it might as well go out of business."[24]

The leaders of the alumni association reported that a poll of prominent graduates and ex-students from all sections of the country indicated that any attempt to enforce segregation on the campus "would destroy the great usefulness of the institution to Negro people, [and] would lose the friendship and confidence and goodwill . . . which [it] has taken the school fifty years to win." Expressing a similar point of view, the *New York Age* proclaimed that Hampton "cannot take a backward step. It must help uphold . . . and maintain the principles of equality of manhood and womanhood upon which it was founded."[25]

[23] Graham, *Tender Violence*, chap. 8; *Newport News Daily Press*, 27 November 1925.

[24] Senator Garrett, quoted in *Newport News Daily Press*, 16 February 1926; Allen Washington to Robert R. Moton, 2 February 1926, Moton Papers.

[25] Minutes of the Meeting of the Hampton Board of Trustees, 3

Du Bois claimed that the officers of Hampton Institute should answer the charges of the *Daily Press* with a ringing declaration on behalf of Negro rights:

> Yes, we do practice social equality at Hampton. We always have practiced it and we always shall. How else can teacher and taught meet but as equals? Yes, we eat together at times. To be sure, we have some "Jim Crow" dining halls to appease our Southern friends but we are ashamed of this and try to conceal it. Yes, our white principal and some of our white teachers are entertained in the North and in the South now and then. . . . The results of the social equality practiced at Hampton have been fine friendships, real knowledge of human souls, high living and high thinking. . . . When white folk . . . come voluntarily as our guests we welcome them and treat them with every courtesy, although we cannot expect for our students reciprocal courtesy from them. But when they demand the right to cross this color line which they themselves have drawn, and then to have a second and internal drawing of race distinctions inside a Negro institution, we say, No. You are not compelled to enter this colored world and it is monstrous when you do come as guests to ask us to insult these already twice-insulted people. . . . No other civilized group in the world . . . is asked to accept such personal insult in their own homes and schools and in their own social life as you demand of these Hampton Negroes.[26]

Yet, given the prevalence of white supremacist views throughout Virginia, few legislators could afford to vote

March 1926, Hampton Archives; Hampton Alumni Visitation Committee to James E. Gregg, 19 April 1926, Hampton Archives; *New York Age*, 1 August 1926.

[26] W. E. B. Du Bois, "Social Equality at Hampton," *Crisis* 30 (June 1925): 59–60.

against Captain Massenburg's bill. Friends of the institute hoped that the legislators would be "so busy with other bills that they will not have time to pay attention to the Massenburg measure." They tried to delay consideration of the bill until the adjournment of the legislature in 1926, but Captain Massenburg steered his bill to the floor, where it passed in March 1926 by a vote of thirty to five in the Senate and sixty-four to two in the House. The new law required those in charge of "any place of public entertainment or public assemblage which is attended by both white and colored persons to separate the white race and the colored race, and to set apart and designate in each such public hall . . . certain seats therein to be occupied by white persons . . . [and] certain seats therein to be occupied by colored persons."[27]

The passage of the Massenburg law presented Hampton Institute with a dilemma: it could not disobey state law, and yet segregation on the campus would breed racial resentment and undermine black confidence in the officers of the institute. Most blacks believed that Hampton should protest forcefully against this Nordic nonsense and should go to court to test the constitutionality of the new law. Robert Moton advised Principal Gregg that if Hampton should "make a test case . . . [it] would thus become the champion of a cause much larger than itself with the moral advantage which such a cause would have." Blacks would rally to Hampton as they never had before. On the other hand, Moton warned that if Hampton should retire without a vigorous protest it would alienate many alumni and other blacks who expected Hampton to serve as a "chief advocate of Negro interests." Though generally a compromiser, Moton was prepared to fight on favorable terrain, and he believed that in a campaign against the Massenburg law

[27] Allen Washington to Robert R. Moton, 2 March 1926, Moton Papers; Minutes of the Meeting of the Hampton Board of Trustees, 22 April 1926, Hampton Archives; *Acts of the Virginia Assembly*, 1926, p. 945.

Hampton would enjoy many of the advantages that he had possessed in his own fight against an exclusively white staff at the Tuskegee Veterans Hospital.[28]

The board of trustees acknowledged that "for the Institute to take such a backward step and segregate its colored teachers and visiting alumni even at their own meetings would of course have a disastrous effect upon the morale of our colored constituency." Consequently a committee of five was appointed in January 1926 to draft "a dignified protest" against the Massenburg bill. Two months later, however, the trustees voted to withhold this protest. Trustee James Hardy Dillard, who was intimately associated with the Jeanes Fund, the Slater Fund, and the General Education Board, and was perhaps the most influential of all the white philanthropists working in the field of Negro education, had "advised strongly against testing the new law in the courts, and said he thought the Institute had come through the affair well by doing nothing and saying nothing." William Howard Taft, then the Chief Justice of the United States Supreme Court as well as a trustee of Hampton Institute, insisted that "the question is one to be settled by 'wise restraint' rather than by public protest. . . . An official protest would be unwise, though such action might be desired by our colored constituency."[29]

Rather than protest against the Massenburg law, the leaders of Hampton Institute searched for a *modus vivendi*. After consulting their attorney, they learned that the new law required only that "public assemblages" be segregated and that private meetings limited to invited guests would not come under the law. Consequently, the trustees decided to give up all assemblages that might be considered public and to admit people from outside the campus by invitation

[28] Robert R. Moton to James E. Gregg, 25 March 1926, Moton Papers.

[29] Minutes of the Meetings of the Hampton Board of Trustees, 30 January, 3 March, 22 April 1926, Hampton Archives; James E. Gregg to Robert R. Moton, 30 March 1926, Moton Papers.

only. Expressing the sentiment of the board, Trustee Peabody explained that Hampton could obey the new law if it made "one slight change in our practice here. The law is specifically enacted against public assemblages and the word 'public' is repeatedly emphasized. We must therefore conduct our gatherings . . . as private meetings which shall be open only to members of the school community or to those who are our invited guests." Adding that "any act of imprudence or misconduct among us here is sure to be seized upon and exaggerated," Peabody urged everybody connected with the school "to abstain from controversy, to conduct themselves with prudence, to avoid situations which might give ground for malicious reports: In a word, to hold the good name of Hampton in their keeping and to do our work both with courage and self-restraint."[30]

The trustees evidently thought that this was the best arrangement that could be made. Principal Gregg later reported that the institute had issued annual invitation guest cards to local friends and had thereby complied with the Massenburg law without enforcing segregation. Yet many blacks must have agreed with Moton that this policy amounted to "a retreat under fire . . . [and] sounds very much like Davy Crockett's, 'Don't shoot, I'll come down.' " Declaring Hampton's entertainments private functions, off-limits to all but invited guests, enabled the institute to avoid controversy; but failure to come out in forceful opposition to the Massenburg law was, as Edward K. Graham has noted, "anything but reassuring to the Alumni, to many of the staff, and to Hampton's supporters throughout the region. That the college could accept an additional Jim Crow law with what appeared to be no more than pro-forma resistance was a puzzlement to the black community. The fact that this particular Jim Crow law was to be imposed on Hampton's own people, in one of their own buildings, was

[30] John Weymouth to James E. Gregg, 22 April 1926, Moton Papers; Francis Greenwood Peabody, quoted in Minutes of Hampton Board of Trustees, 22 April 1926.

246

a particularly disturbing matter for generations brought up in the doctrine that Hampton's role was one of leadership—not accommodation—in elevating the status of the Negro. Now, it seemed, a relatively small segment of society just beyond the college gates was dictating social patterns within the college itself. The implications were hardly lost, either, on the student body."[31]

III

Even before the passage of the Massenburg Law, there were unmistakable signs that life at Hampton was anything but tranquil. One member of the class of 1926 recalled "the anonymous student publications that mysteriously appeared from time to time on the campus." Another complained, "As soon as one problem is solved, one hundred more pop up." In 1924, for example, the Student Council declared that eight-thirty chapel interfered with study time and demanded, "respectfully, but with firmness," that the evening services be scheduled for six-thirty. When the teachers complained that such an early hour would make for a hasty supper, the council continued to agitate the question for an entire year, "When so many objections can be raised against late chapel and so many benefits may be derived by a change in time . . . we can do no less than press our claim for six-thirty chapel."[32]

This dispute over evening chapel services was only one of many indications that students were dissatisfied with an administration that allegedly had failed to adjust its academic and disciplinary policies to make allowance for the

[31] Minutes of the Meeting of the Hampton Board of Trustees, 29 January 1926, Hampton Archives; Moton to Gregg, 25 March 1926; Graham, *Tender Violence*, chap. 8.

[32] Wesley D. Elam, "The Hampton Alumni and the Strike," *Hampton Alumni Journal* 4 (March 1928): 15–17; "Why Not More Democracy in our Schools?" *Hampton Student* 13 (15 February 1925): 18; "Why Not Chapel at 6:30?" *Hampton Student* 13 (15 October 1925): 13–14.

fact that Hampton was no longer a school for docile elementary students but for young men and women who could think for themselves. One student complained, "Dr. Gregg and all of his co-workers have spent more time trying to teach the Negroes their places . . . than they have spent trying to give them an education that would make them men and women capable of facing the world and its great problems." Others claimed that Hampton's officers had "failed to adapt themselves to the new conditions." "The present day youths cannot be treated in the same manner they were treated twenty-five years ago," one black newspaper warned. Another declared that Hampton was one of many black colleges that were "still run more like disciplinary barracks or reform schools . . . than like educational institutions attended by the sons of free men and women."[33]

Fearing that the officers of the institute would yield to the demands of those who opposed college education for blacks, Hampton's students of the early 1920s repeatedly insisted that academic standards should be raised. Thus in 1924 the Student Council charged that the director of the trade school had so little formal education and used such poor English that he was not qualified to teach. Similar accusations were lodged in 1925 against several teachers in the school of agriculture. There were additional complaints that some of the missionary teachers were less concerned with academic subjects than with inculcating "the morality that should be taught at home before the student enters college." The Alumni Visitation Committee reported in 1925 that many students feared that "the proposed advances in the curriculum of the several departments of the school might not be put into effect." These fears increased in the wake of the Massenburg controversy. Five white teachers were known to have participated in a Ku Klux Klan parade in support of the new law, while others established a segre-

[33] L. F. Coles to *Philadelphia Tribune*, 10 November 1927; alumni to *Norfolk Journal and Guide*, 22 October 1927; *Washington Eagle*, 21 October 1927; *Pittsburgh Courier*, 29 October 1927.

gated club and openly opposed the employment of qualified black teachers. This of course compounded dissatisfaction among the students, who questioned "whether the entire staff was in full sympathy with the ideals of the institution —or if there were not a few whose sympathies were not with the ideals of the proponents of the bill."[34]

Meanwhile, the editor of the *Hampton Student* charged, "Schools are monarchies; they should be democracies," and demanded a greater degree of student participation in the government of the institute. Yet while students demanded rights and freedom, the administration stressed duties and responsibility and allegedly held "fanatically to the old traditions and customs which have so long made ideal Uncle Tom graduates." It was inevitable under the circumstances that some students would come to believe that "at Hampton everything is dominated by members of the Caucasian group," and that the rigid disciplinary regulations were part of an elaborate plan to mold "hat-in-hand and me-too-boss Negroes." Most students agreed with their student newspaper's contention, "There is too much suspicion between officials and students."[35]

Among the many disputes that agitated the campus in the early 1920s, none was more protracted than the controversy over the use of Negro spirituals and plantation melodies. Hampton had discovered that many whites were pleased and reassured by the rendition of these traditional songs, and the chorus and glee club included this popular music in their repertoire, especially when performing in conjunc-

[34] L. F. Coles to *Baltimore Afro-American*, 5 November 1927; *Pittsburgh Courier*, 29 October 1927; *Norfolk Journal and Guide*, 22 October 1927; *Chicago Whip*, 29 October 1927; "Report of the Alumni Visitation Committee," in Minutes of the Meeting of the Hampton Board of Trustees, 23 April 1925, Hampton Archives; Visitation Committee to Gregg, 19 April 1926; L. F. Coles to *Norfolk Journal and Guide*, 29 October 1926.
[35] "Why Not More Democracy?" p. 18; alumni to *Norfolk Journal and Guide*, 22 October 1927; *Washington Eagle*, 21 October 1927; *Washington Tribune*, 21 October 1927.

tion with the institute's many fund-raising activities. The celebrated "singing of plantation songs" by the entire student body was a regular feature of the Sunday evening chapel services that were attended by whites from throughout the surrounding countryside. But while the trustees and officers of the institute considered these performances invaluable in winning the friendship of whites, many blacks associated the songs with unseemly submissiveness. On several occasions students indignantly protested against excessive emphasis on this music, and in the spring of 1925 the members of the Hampton Choir had walked off a Washington stage rather than sing spirituals for a segregated audience.[36]

Much of the controversy over plantation melodies swirled around Hampton's director of music, R. Nathaniel Dett. Prior to coming to Hampton in 1913, Dett had studied at the Oberlin Conservatory of Music. He was the first black American to receive an academic degree for original musical composition. Dett believed that the plantation melodies were not really Negro songs, but songs of a certain group of slaves—a group whose social status was alien to many twentieth-century American blacks and to all Negroes outside the United States. Moreover, Dett was essentially a composer and arranger, and he was primarily concerned with using the plantation melodies as the basis for more complex forms of orchestral music. He wanted Hampton's musical groups to develop a new music that reflected the sophisticated style of the New Negroes of the 1920s.

Dett's artistic theories placed him on a collision course with one of the institute's most influential trustees, George Foster Peabody. Going beyond other trustees and administrators, who valued the plantation songs as a means of placating the white South, Peabody thought these songs represented the most beautiful musical expression born in America. He feared that the intrinsic quality of the songs would

[36] Du Bois, "Battle of Washington," pp. 114–115; *Philadelphia Tribune*, 9 May 1925.

be lost if they were not presented simply and without elaboration. Peabody acknowledged that Dett enjoyed a "unique position as one of the first composers in the country, and as a leading musical genius of his race." Nevertheless he urged Principal Gregg "to make Mr. Dett understand that we wish him to keep what is best in the old Negro folk songs." At times Peabody insinuated that Hampton's director of music was not interested in preserving these black treasures because he was, perhaps unconsciously, ashamed of his race.[37]

Some modern soul brothers have celebrated the sensual, rhythmic character of the urban blues and have suggested that "emotion is as completely Negro as reason is Greek." Like them, Peabody believed that blacks had accumulated a precious quality that was in short supply in a prosaic, business-oriented civilization—humanity, soul. He thought that blacks were warm, responsive, emotional people who could make a special contribution to America's pluralist culture. He therefore urged Dett to emphasize the plantation songs as part of a campaign "to bring the Negroes up to a sense of pride in their race" and make them more "appreciative of themselves as factors in the building up of the great democratic commonwealth." He firmly believed that "a great effort should be made to conserve and develop this seventeen-tone expression which only Negro people have so far shown to the world." He assured Dett that "the Lord has called you to be in the place of a Moses or an Aaron."[38]

[37] George Foster Peabody to Robert R. Moton, 4 March 1931, Peabody Papers; Peabody to James E. Gregg, 13 September 1918, Peabody Papers; Gregg to Peabody, 14 September 1918, Peabody Papers.
[38] George Foster Peabody to R. Nathaniel Dett, 20 May 1929, Peabody Papers; Peabody to Paul Robeson, 4 January 1926, Peabody Papers; Peabody to Gregg, 13 September, 24 September 1918, Peabody Papers. For the soul brothers' emphasis on black emotionalism see William Braden, *The Age of Aquarius* (New York: Pocket Books, 1970), pp. 185–187, 204–205; and Charles Keil, *Urban Blues* (Chicago: University of Chicago Press, 1966).

The belief that rhythmic emotionalism was the essence of blackness also led Peabody to fear that academic education was not well suited to the Negro's temperament. He had long thought that the "so-called academic education was the true weakness of the Negro educational system," and he shared his fellow trustees' misgivings about the development of college-level studies at Hampton. Under the circumstances, Peabody thought it was essential that black students continue to render the plantation melodies. He believed that these songs had been a crucial part of the disciplinary program that had enabled Hampton to tame adolescent blacks. He explained in 1926 to his friend and fellow philanthropist, George Eastman, that "this musical emphasis" deserved much of the credit for "the remarkable moral standards which have been maintained from the beginning. . . . During the whole fifty-seven years of coeducational work with these adolescent students . . . there has always been noted a definite moral uplift and inspiration . . . [and] we have never had any trouble from sexual scandals."[39]

With Peabody attributing such enormous influence to the plantation melodies, the officers of Hampton Institute discouraged Dett's efforts to elaborate on the traditional themes. Dett naturally resented this lack of support, and on several occasions he let it be known that he would leave Hampton if he were not encouraged to develop his artistic talents. Peabody generally backed away from these confrontations, for he admired Dett's orchestral arrangements, acknowledged that the director rarely failed to include some traditional plantation works in his programs, and thought that this dispute, like so many in life, was essentially a controversy over proper emphasis. Peabody also admitted "that Dr. Dett's devotion of his time and energy to Hampton's Music Department is clearly at the sacrifice of a very considerable sum of royalties and concert and lec-

[39] George Foster Peabody to Henry A. Goetchins, 30 January 1911, Peabody Papers; Peabody to George Eastman, 24 February 1926, Peabody Papers.

ture appearances which he might otherwise avail himself of."[40]

Dett remained miffed by the argument that "when one takes a Negro theme as the basis for an anthem, a suite or a choral work, it robs the music of its original charm." He noted that "no one argues that the music of Tchaikovsky is not typically Russian, and Tchaikovsky's work forms one of the finest examples we have of the use of folk tunes in the more elaborate phases of art-form development." This controversy over spirituals continued for more than a decade, until Dett was finally forced out in 1931. In the meantime, Peabody explained, "Dr. Dett's temperament, which is usual to the musical genius, [was] rather on the nerves of the people at Hampton."[41] This protracted dispute—pitting the institute's most famous black teacher against one of its most influential trustees—doubtless served to exacerbate racial tensions on the campus.

IV

With so much evidence of unrest and dissatisfaction on their campus, and with the added knowledge that student strikes had already reached epidemic proportions at other black colleges, Hampton's trustees and administrators took steps to contain the spreading recalcitrance. In 1924 the board noted that students who were "seeking freedom from restraint, and demanding self-expression, present unaccustomed difficulties and cause real concern to those in charge of their development." Appeals were then sent to the alumni for assistance "in every way in selecting students who are earnest and who have fine standards of conduct . . . [and]

[40] Minutes of Hampton Board of Trustees, 22 April 1926; George Foster Peabody to George Ketcham, 21 February 1930, Peabody Papers.

[41] R. Nathaniel Dett, typescript of 1918 article for *Musical America*, Peabody Papers; George Foster Peabody to Robert R. Moton, 4 March 1931, Peabody Papers.

can be counted upon to cooperate with those in authority in maintaining Hampton's 'Good Name.' "[42]

Meanwhile, in a belated effort to adjust to a student body increasingly composed of college men and women rather than high school boys and girls, the faculty promised to consider the possibility of allowing Greek-letter fraternities and sororities on the campus and authorized certain minor changes in the social regulations. Thus in 1926, at a time when the average age of girls entering the school was a bit more than nineteen years, the faculty acceded to repeated requests that college men be permitted to escort female students to and from school functions. Liberalization of social rules did not put an end to controversy, however, for the faculty soon complained of "whispering, talking, and laughing both before and during entertainments in Ogden Hall."[43]

As the students gathered to view the Saturday evening movies on October 8, 1927, they learned that the lights were to be left on at the rear of the auditorium, above the seats assigned to college students with escort privileges. These students objected to the lighting and expressed their displeasure by calling "lights out" and scraping their feet. The lights remained on, and the students' discontent was compounded when members of the administration gave contradictory explanations. Some claimed that one teacher had twisted an ankle while stumbling in the dark the week before and the new lighting was designed to prevent mishaps. Others stated that Hampton was simply making "an experiment in improved theatre lighting." A few admitted their lack of confidence in the students and protested that there was "too much kissing over there in the dark."[44]

[42] Minutes of the Meetings of the Hampton Board of Trustees, 24 April 1924, 25 January 1927, Hampton Archives.

[43] Minutes of the Administrative Board, 23 November 1926, Hampton Archives.

[44] "Chronology of Hampton Strike" (typescript), Hampton Archives; "The Strike at Hampton," *Southern Workman* 56 (1927): 569–572; C. L. Spellman, *Rough Steps on My Stairway* (New York: Exposition Press, 1953), pp. 100–106; *Newport News Star*, 13 October 1927.

Whatever the reason, the students considered the lights "a direct insult to the student body and especially to the womanhood of the Negro race." They launched a protest that would shake the very foundations of Hampton Institute. In view of what was to transpire, there was a degree of irony in the choice of *Chang*, a powerful documentary film, for the evening's entertainment. "Filmed in the jungle country of northern Siam, *Chang* told the story of a Lao tribesman, who had moved from the security of his village to new surroundings, and of his struggle for survival."[45]

Many students considered the new theater policy the climax of a long series of insults, and as they returned to their dormitories their resentment flared into rebellion. The singing was spotty at church services on Sunday morning and at the noontime grace, and the men of James Hall locked their doors and refused to submit to inspection. By afternoon Principal Gregg was clearly worried, for Sir Gordon Guggisberg, the governor of the Gold Coast, and W. T. B. Williams, the field agent of the Jeanes Fund, were to be special guests at the celebrated Sunday evening "singing of plantation songs." Throughout the afternoon Gregg pleaded with the students, "asking them to cooperate in the chapel service especially on account of the presence of Sir Gordon." But when the song leader took his position that evening he found himself singing a solo. Although Gregg had the presence of mind to give a brief prayer on the theme, "Father, forgive them, for they know not what they do," nothing could disguise the fact that Hampton's refractory students had made a shambles of the usual Sunday evening showcase.[46]

By themselves, of course, the questions of theater lighting and plantation melodies were relatively minor, but the confluence of the two aroused the students' indignation. The

[45] W. E. B. Du Bois, "The Hampton Strike," *Nation* 125 (2 November 1927): 471–472; Graham, "Hampton Institute Strike," p. 668.

[46] "Chronology of Hampton Strike"; "Strike at Hampton," pp. 569–572; Graham, "Hampton Institute Strike," pp. 673–674.

young men and women of Hampton granted that "the matter of the lights was unusually small," no more than "the
accidental puff of wind that touched off an already smol-
dering fire." But the flame of rebellion spread across the
campus as hundreds of students extemporaneously promised not to attend classes when instruction resumed on
Monday. One senior girl summed up the prevailing view
when she declared, "This thing has been trying to happen
for the last ten years." Another observer noted, "He who
believes that the students struck because the lights were
turned on in Ogden Hall . . . is as radically mistaken as the
historian who tells us that the World War was 'caused' by
the assassination of an Archduke."[47]

Principal Gregg suspended classes on Monday morning
and summoned the male and female students to separate
meetings in Ogden Hall. Making pointed references to alleged student misbehavior during the Saturday evening
movies, Gregg gave his charges a wholesale dressing down
and made especially pointed references to their refusal to
sing on Sunday. The principal further emphasized "the importance of attendance at classes and other scheduled work
as an evidence of loyalty and cooperation." Many students
understood him to have said that "the root cause for all student dissatisfaction was simply the arrangements made for
the moving picture on the preceding Saturday night; that
not only would there be a continuation of past administrative practices and procedures, but also and more important-
ly, until students demonstrated 'right spirit' there would be
no exploration or discussion of student viewpoints."[48]

The students now recognized the seriousness of the situa-

[47] Hampton Student Protest Committee, quoted in *Newport
News Daily Press*, 16 October 1927; *Norfolk Ledger Dispatch*, 15
October 1927; J. Raymond Henderson, "Pros—Cons on the Hamp-
ton Strike," *Norfolk Journal and Guide*, 29 October 1927.

[48] Graham, "Hampton Institute Strike," p. 674; James E. Gregg
to Parents and Guardians, in Minutes of the Administrative Board,
14 October 1927, Hampton Archives.

tion. Twenty-one young men were chosen for service on a Student Protest Committee, and they represented a cross-section of Hampton's most promising scholars and leaders, including the president of the Student Council, the president of the senior class, the president of the YMCA, and officers of the drama club, the Society for the Study of Negro History, and a variety of other campus organizations. The committee members had already been enrolled at Hampton for an average of 3.8 years per man, and ten members had graduated from Hampton's Academy (high school). Clearly, these were not marginal youths seeking to find a status in protest that they had been unable to achieve by working through traditional channels. Most were superior students, and eight had been designated as "ranking scholars" at the institute. Three would later earn doctorates from Ivy League universities, and another would be appointed in 1966 by Queen Elizabeth to the Order of the British Empire.[49]

Instead of meeting with Principal Gregg early on Tuesday morning, October 11, as they had been ordered to do, the male students boycotted classes and sent the members of the Student Protest Committee as their representatives. Gregg insisted that "an official conference with the committee would be practicable only when obedience and order had been entirely restored," and he refused to discuss any grievances until the students manifested "a right spirit and a cooperative attitude" by calling off their strike and returning to classes. The students, who obviously wanted to be accommodating and also recognized that they would have to suspend their strike if their grievances were to be discussed, agreed to these terms and returned to classes at three-twenty that afternoon. Principal Gregg then agreed to discuss "The Petition of Hampton Students," and it appeared that the strike might be settled quickly. There was

[49] Minutes of the Administrative Board, 11 October 1927, Hampton Archives; Graham, "Hampton Institute Strike," p. 677.

257

one potential source of trouble, however, for the students had made it clear that their decision to resume normal activities was based on the expectation "that there be no ineligibility rules or punishment inflicted upon the participants of this protest."[50]

The Student Protest Committee returned to Gregg's office at 7 p.m. that Tuesday evening with a list of seventeen grievances. These could be grouped into two broad categories: objections to the existing disciplinary regime at Hampton, and demands that the educational program be upgraded and made more rigorous. With regard to discipline, the students' entreaties were quite specific: they wanted dancing at a few socials, ten days for Christmas holidays, better food in the dining hall, calling days for secondary students, and a more effective student council composed exclusively of students and without faculty participation. Admitting that some of these demands might appear to be "trivial in themselves," the students believed that the many complaints, in the aggregate, were "significant because they deal with wrongs which affect the daily life of the student and which have been allowed to go unremedied by departmental heads even in the face of past complaints."[51]

Addressing themselves as well to the fundamentals of education, the students demanded that Hampton live up to its collegiate pretensions. They insisted that "our educational system be so revised that we shall no longer be subjected to instructions from teachers whose apparent education is below that of the average student." To ensure this revision, the Protest Committee called for the resignation of a number of trade teachers who had not completed high school. They further recommended that in the selection of future teachers more emphasis should be placed on formal

[50] "Strike at Hampton," p. 570; "Chronology of Hampton Strike"; Student Protest Committee to Administrative Board, Minutes of the Administrative Board, 11 October 1927.

[51] "The Petition of the Hampton Students," October 1927, Hampton Archives.

academic preparation and less on religious spirit. Other demands called upon Hampton to offer all the courses listed in the institute's catalogue, to permit college students to enroll in more elective courses, and to allow high school students to study until 10:30 p.m. Some of these points had been mentioned by students in 1924 and 1925, but the administrators of 1927 feigned complete surprise: "The complaints with regard to education are possibly unique in the annals of student strikes, demanding as they did more and better education."[52]

After stating that some of the students' complaints were "distinctly noteworthy" while others were "not of great importance," Principal Gregg agreed to consider the petition carefully and to confer again with the Student Protest Committee. He also let it be known, however, that the administration would take disciplinary measures against those who had been insubordinate or had failed to report to classes on Monday afternoon and Tuesday morning. At the same time Gregg gave assurances "that membership on the Student Protest Committee would not as such be regarded as an offence or blot on the individual members of the committee" and that the administration would judge "each individual case on its merit." Nevertheless, most students were dismayed by the thought that punishments were in the offing. The members of the student committee noted that the protest had been orderly and honorable, and they believed there was no warrant for disciplinary reprisals.[53]

Yet Gregg had already decided that the administration would have to mete out some penalties in order "to guard against a recurrence of the strike." Consequently, he called his administrative advisers to still another meeting on Wednesday morning, October 12, after which the principal announced "that though [the students'] motives may be of

[52] Ibid.; "Strike at Hampton," pp. 569–572.
[53] Gregg to Parents, 14 October 1927; Minutes of the Administrative Board, 11 October 1927; Newport News Daily Press, 13 October 1927; Spellman, Rough Steps, pp. 100–106.

a high order, nevertheless, flagrant insubordination . . . should bring a penalty." The girls and new students were thought to be innocent and were exempted from punishment, but all others who had absented themselves from classes were put on probation. In a warning evidently aimed at the members of the Student Protest Committee, Gregg also announced that additional penalties would be levied against "those guilty of insubordination or of inciting others to insubordination."[54]

Far from preventing a renewal of the strike, the administration's refusal to grant an amnesty infuriated students. They rallied behind their threatened committeemen, called an open meeting, and voted by a healthy majority to resume their strike. The prevailing student view was that no punishment was in order. They had only boycotted classes, had destroyed no property, and had taken special care to maintain essential services—the milk delivered, the livestock attended to, the teachers' meals served. The students' meetings had been opened and closed with earnest prayers, and student leader G. James Fleming noted that most students felt "that theirs is a religious duty, and a sacred obligation to posterity, and to all the best that Hampton Institute stands for."[55]

C. L. Spellman, a member of the Student Protest Committee, pointed out that "not a single dollar's worth of institutional property was damaged during the time, although . . . there were irresponsible students among us. So complete was our control over the students that . . . they would have literally torn buildings down brick by brick if the word had been given." Yet the student leaders would not

[54] "Strike at Hampton," p. 571; Minutes of the Administrative Board, 10 a.m., 12 October 1927, Hampton Archives; Minutes of the Administrative Board, 7 p.m., 12 October 1927, Hampton Archives.

[55] *Newport News Daily Press*, 15 October 1927; Graham, "Hampton Institute Strike," p. 676; G. James Fleming, quoted in *Newport News Daily Press*, 13 October 1927.

condone "one mite of destruction," and hence they believed that "if ever an institution owed a debt of gratitude to a group of students, Hampton owed one to that student committee." The administration's official account of the strike acknowledged, "Throughout the trouble the student leaders had a larger degree of control of strikers than might have been expected, and as a result the Hampton campus remained remarkably free from disorderly conduct and rowdyism. The leaders attempted and in a measure succeeded in turning their effort into a seeming 'holy war' for the ultimate good of the Institute. . . . The strike was therefore, perhaps in the minds of many students, *for* Hampton, not *against* their school."[56]

On Thursday morning, October 13, this is how things stood. Students had taken exception to the lighting arrangements at the movies the previous Saturday, had refused to sing on Sunday, and had boycotted classes on Monday and Tuesday morning. They had also elected a Student Protest Committee that drew up a statement of grievances, conferred with the administration, and persuaded fellow students to maintain perfect order and to return to classes on Tuesday afternoon. The administration had acknowledged that some of the students' complaints were "distinctly noteworthy" and that the committee had acted "reasonably." Principal Gregg nevertheless announced on Wednesday that disciplinary measures were needed to prevent a recurrence of disorder. This announcement disappointed the great majority of students, who resumed their strike on Thursday. Du Bois aptly characterized the situation as "one of those silly games of stalemate which colleges are so fond of staging":

Students . . .: "Hear our complaints!"
Faculty . . . : "First go back to classes!"
Students . . . : "We'll go, but hear our complaints and

[56] Spellman, *Rough Steps*, pp. 105-106; "Strike at Hampton," pp. 569-572.

261

promise no punishment for this protest."
Faculty . . . : "We will hear the complaints but we promise no immunity. . . ."

Thereupon the principal . . . proceeded first to commend the order and discipline maintained by the students and then went on to [threaten] the ringleaders; and . . . the whole school, men and women, new and old, struck again.[57]

The administration responded to this renewed strike with a lockout. On Friday, October 14, Gregg announced that "Hampton Institute is closed until further notice" and students were "expected to leave for their homes promptly." Explaining that the work of the school could not be carried on "with students who are disorderly and lawless," the principal made it clear that Hampton wanted no students save those "who give evidence of their sincere purpose to cooperate with the officers and teachers in maintaining peace, order, and the mutual friendliness and confidence without which no school can be truly successful." He promised that Hampton would be reopened soon, but all returning students would be required to apply for readmission and to sign a written pledge "to do my part to carry on the work of the Institute in loyalty, obedience and cooperation."[58]

Gregg further announced that "four young men, quite evidently ringleaders, have been formally dismissed"; that all who were guilty of insubordination were to be put "on probation immediately"; and that "further discipline is still under consideration . . . [and] suspension of a number of others will probably be necessary." On October 17 nineteen additional students, all but two of whom were members of the Student Protest Committee, were suspended "for at least the balance of the present school year," and on the following day thirty-eight more students were found to be

[57] Du Bois, "Hampton Strike," pp. 471-472.
[58] Gregg to Parents, 14 October 1927.

262

"unacceptable." Altogether sixty-nine students were eventually suspended, and hundreds of others were placed on probation. With the exception of a single young man who evidently acted as an informer (and for his pains had his room wrecked and personal property destroyed), all members of the Student Protest Committee were suspended for the remainder of the 1927–1928 academic year. Hampton, in short, banished its most promising students. According to historian Graham, "With unerring accuracy the college singled out the backbone of its student leadership: young people whose subsequent careers in higher education, government service, business and public school teaching and administration would mark them as probably one of the most talented groups ever to leave a college or university campus."[59]

In addition to closing the institute and disciplining all students who were thought to have participated in the strike, Hampton took special pains to cultivate the press. The Hampton Institute Press Service disseminated an official account of the strike and kept black editors informed of the administration's side of the controversy. In this way the institute hoped to thwart "any effort that might have been employed by unscrupulous writers to play up misrepresentations."[60]

This policy soon paid handsome dividends, as major black newspapers endorsed Gregg's handling of the strike. The *Baltimore Afro-American* criticized strikers who allegedly "placed more emphasis on social relations with co-eds than upon a liberal education." The *Savannah Tribune* condemned what it called "a growing disposition among the young folks of nowadays to disrespect constituted authority." The *Atlanta Independent* warned, "College strikes in

[59] Ibid.; Minutes of the Administrative Board, 17 October, 18 October 1927, Hampton Archives; Graham, "Hampton Institute Strike," p. 677.

[60] "Strike at Hampton," pp. 569–572; *East Tennessee News*, 27 October 1927.

Negro schools are becoming a threatening menace to the life and efficiency of college and university education among our colored youth." The *Indianapolis Recorder* advised students to "never look a gift horse in the mouth." The *Norfolk Journal and Guide* insisted, "Those who are beneficiaries of philanthropy must well mark time before taking any steps the ultimate effect of which may be construed as evidence of their ingratitude."[61]

Principal Gregg was also pleased to note the "practically universal condemnation of the strike . . . by the alumni." The executive committee of the Alumni Association rushed to the campus for a meeting on October 21 and "unanimously voted to support the Administrative Board in their efforts to maintain discipline at Hampton during the recent strike." Several local alumni clubs also expressed their hearty support for the administration, and Moton wrote from Tuskegee that he thought Gregg had "handled the situation most wisely and I have no doubt but that things will work out satisfactorily."[62]

Most parents seem to have agreed. Many traveled to the campus for conferences with Gregg, and others sent their support through the mails. One distraught mother asked the principal

> to please read this note to my son and tell him not to send me any more telegrams unless signed by you. Mr. President, I am a hardworking woman with an invalid husband and I am not a young woman, but trying to work and give my boy an education. . . . I mean for him to be governed by you and you only. I feel that I should hear from you, for I do not know what my boy is raving about

[61] *Baltimore Afro-American*, 22 October 1927; *Savannah Tribune*, 27 October 1927; *Atlanta Independent*, 20 October 1927; *Indianapolis Recorder*, 29 October 1927; *Norfolk Journal and Guide*, 14 October, 22 October 1927.

[62] Gregg to Parents, 14 October 1927; "Strike at Hampton," pp. 569–572; Robert R. Moton to Gregg, 18 October 1927, Moton Papers.

and I do not want to know, but want you to keep him in school, the place and the only place I mean to send him.[63]

Contemporaries generally agreed that Hampton's incomplete transition from school to college was somehow responsible for the controversial strike and lockout. Even Gregg characterized the strike as "but one of many evidences . . . of the 'New Negro' that has arisen since the World War" and acknowledged that "the development of the collegiate life of the institute has brought new problems." Although the principal insisted that Hampton's disciplinary policies should remain "strict, thorough, positive," so that "the vital characteristics of the older Hampton training shall not be lost," many blacks believed that "the way the Negro student was handled thirty years ago is not the way to handle him now."[64]

Most black parents, alumni, and newspapers, it is true, had endorsed Gregg's firm handling of the October crisis, but many had done so with reservations. Thus the *Indianapolis Recorder* was favorably impressed by a well-documented student statement concerning the inadequate formal education of several of the instructors at Hampton. The *Washington Tribune* noted, "The student of today is not like the rough fellow from the pine woods of fifty years ago," and the *Chicago Whip* insisted that it was "high time that our educators awakened to the fact that . . . the abolition of unnecessary rigidity will bring out a better understanding." The *Hampton Alumni Journal* carried an article calling for "readjustment of the relations existing between faculty and students in order to keep up that mutual understanding and respect necessary for the smooth and efficient running of the educational machinery."[65]

[63] Unidentified mother to James E. Gregg, quoted in *Norfolk Journal and Guide*, 22 October 1927.
[64] Gregg, "Annual Report, 1928"; *New York Amsterdam News*, 19 October 1927.
[65] *Indianapolis Recorder*, 27 October 1927; *Washington Tribune*, 21 October 1927; *Chicago Whip*, 22 October 1927; Charles S. Isham,

The *Philadelphia Tribune* summed up a prevailing view when it noted,

Conditions have changed at Hampton. Among its students are men and women who are able to think and act for themselves. Conditions forced Hampton to raise its curriculum. It has been necessary to give a more liberal training. But Hampton is trying to do these things with the same kind of teachers and the same kind of rules and regulations that were used when it was no more than a grammar school. It simply cannot be done. It would save a whole lot of trouble and probably the disruption of the entire school if the present administration would undertake to make the changes necessary without being forced to do so.[66]

Beyond the belief that it was necessary to adjust to changing circumstances, there was no agreement concerning the meaning of the Hampton strike. Some whites, such as Colonel Copeland, saw the strike as the logical consequence of Hampton's alleged social equalitarianism. He thought that it was "folly to teach those students that the Negro race is the equal in all respects of the white race, and then tell them that men and women of their own race are not competent to administer the affairs of the institute."[67]

Agreeing with Copeland's contention that the strike was "a revolt against white rule," the *Norfolk Virginia-Pilot* attributed the dispute to "the new sensitiveness and self-consciousness that the present generation of colored students are acquiring by way of the *Opportunity-Crisis* influence." To the *Virginia-Pilot* it seemed clear "that all-Negro colleges will have to come under all-Negro administration and instruction before this field will know peace." The *Newport News Star* thought that Gregg's lockout gave evidence of

"The Strike at Hampton," *Hampton Alumni Journal* 4 (December 1927): 4–6.

[66] *Philadelphia Tribune*, 24 November 1927.

[67] *Newport News Daily Press*, 15 October 1927.

a certain estrangement from blacks. This white paper suggested that if the principal could not sympathize "with the viewpoint of Negroes because he is a white man then he ought to resign and leave the school to be run by someone who is in sympathy with their viewpoint."[68]

Most blacks, on the other hand, insisted that racial tensions were not at the bottom of the controversy. The *Baltimore Afro-American* characterized the contention of the *Virginia-Pilot* as "a good deal of rot," and the Hampton administration reported that "even in the tenser moments of the strike there was practically no suggestion of racial alignments." Most graduates endorsed the policies of the administration; even alumni critics, who recommended the employment of more black teachers and demanded an end to segregation at the Holly Tree Inn, were not opposed to white leadership but to insulting racial discrimination.[69]

As far as student spokesmen were concerned, the strike represented a forthright assertion of a new manhood. Thus Albert R. Senior lauded the students for sticking "solidly together . . . in defiance of threats which might formerly have driven Negroes into submission." W. Augustus Willie commended "the evolution of greater manhood and womanhood of the negro race." John F. E. Normil contrasted the valor of the strikers with the alleged timidity of earlier generations of "Uncle Tom Hamptonians." Robert A. Coles claimed that the students possessed "a Du Bois ambition" that would not mix with "a Booker Washington education." He insisted that the students at Hampton were New Negroes who "no longer want a practical education only, but a mental education as well."[70]

[68] *Norfolk Virginia-Pilot*, 17 October 1927; *Newport News Star*, 20 October 1927.

[69] *Baltimore Afro-American*, 29 October 1927; "Strike at Hampton"; Report of the Hampton Alumni Visitation Committee, 21 January 1928, Hampton Archives.

[70] Albert R. Senior to *Baltimore Afro-American*, 5 November 1927; W. Augustus Willie to *Newport News Daily Press*, 20

The editor of the *Crisis* of course endorsed the students' rebellion. He claimed that "it has long been known . . . that Hampton trustees and teachers did not all have feelings, opinions or ideals toward American Negroes which were acceptable to self-respecting black men." In the past blacks had no choice but to endure discriminatory paternalism, "just as beggars often endure the insult of impudent almsgiving." But Du Bois agreed with the students that "the time for an end to that endurance is surely at hand." While praising the students' "self-reliance, self-expression, honesty and decision," however, Du Bois feared that "the way in which graduates and parents repudiated their own children" might lead eventually to "the same attitude of subserviency and uncomplaining submission to caste which our fathers inherited from slavery." Comments such as these infuriated Hampton's administrators, and one trustee confided to another that "our friend Du Bois is at the bottom of this thing. . . . Scarcely any of the Hampton students fail to read the *Crisis* regularly and for ten years past it has been a real influence on the campus."[71]

Attributing the strike to the influence of Du Bois was in the best tradition of academic administration, for it was the custom of senescent trustees to believe that all would be well on their campuses if only the younger generation were not aroused by outside agitators. In this case, however, it was not altogether wrong to emphasize the influence of the editor of the *Crisis*. Du Bois played no active role in the events at Hampton, but he regarded the proper training of a black Talented Tenth as essential to the progress of the race. Thus he forthrightly chronicled and commented upon the many college rebellions of the 1920s, and black students

November 1927; John F. E. Normil to *Baltimore Afro-American*, 5 November 1927; Robert A. Coles, quoted in *Baltimore Afro-American*, 19 November 1927.

[71] W. E. B. Du Bois, "The Hampton Strike," *Crisis* 34 (December 1927): 347–348; George Foster Peabody to Francis Greenwood Peabody, 1 December 1927, Moton Papers.

at Hampton were well aware of his insistence that blacks should enjoy all the opportunities and freedoms available to whites.

There is, of course, no way to establish a cause-and-effect relationship between the editor's egalitarian ideology and the students' dramatic actions, but it appears that at Hampton, as well as at other black colleges, Du Boisian ideology and student protest reinforced one another. The editor had long believed that servility was a lethal state of mind, and he rejoiced in the 1920s when black students, at Hampton and elsewhere, demanded everything that white students demanded. "When four hundred students, well-trained, orderly, with excellent records, are willing to take their future in their hands and jeopardize their whole lives in an appeal to the world for justice . . . something must be absolutely wrong, and the business of parents and Alumni is to investigate before they condemn, to encourage and uphold their protesting children, instead of cowing and disgracing them. It is the Principal and Faculty of Hampton that are really at the bar of Justice and not the students who refused to sing for the entertainment of a white Englishman."[72]

V

Du Bois undoubtedly articulated the views of many students, but the editor could do little to help strikers who found themselves locked out of their school and abandoned by most parents and graduates. Under the circumstances the strike collapsed quickly, and the administration was able to reopen the institute on October 25, 1927. Gregg admitted that many of the foremost men on the campus were among the two hundred students who were either banished or refused to take the new loyalty oath, but this "wholesale slaughter that has come about of the school's best" was seen as a necessary evil that did not seriously detract from the administration's substantial victory. The *Birmingham Re-*

[72] Du Bois, "Hampton Strike," *Crisis* 34: 348.

porter exulted, "As the tendency toward this foolishness [student strikes] increases . . . administrative officials will turn to the method of Dr. Gregg as the best and, so far, the only successful method of combatting this resentment and insolence to authority."[73]

Although the strike was over, the student protest movement was far from dead. The returning students were more resentful than they were cowed, and they began a campaign of not always passive resistance. The commandant and chief disciplinarian reported in November that feeling was "running very high" after one black student thrashed a white teacher. The student newspaper later commented on a pervasive "discordant spirit" that manifested itself in repeated instances of "grumbling, . . . whispering and foot-shuffling." The Alumni Visitation Committee reported that there was a "general lack of respect for authority among the students." According to the alumni, "both boys and girls are in the habit of willfully breaking regulations in such ways as going from the grounds without excuse, attending movies without permission, staying away from church, failing to wear regulation uniforms, and neglecting drills." All of this indicated that student conduct was "beyond the control of authorities" who found it "increasingly difficult . . . to hold their regular meetings and to conduct public exercises without disturbances and disorder."[74]

Unrest on the campus was only one of several unwelcome conditions that troubled the leaders of the alumni association. When the alumni leaders returned to the campus in

[73] James E. Gregg, "Principal's Report," in Minutes of the Meeting of the Hampton Board of Trustees, 28 January 1928, Hampton Archives; Graham, "Hampton Institute Strike," p. 677; Du Bois, "Hampton Strike," *Crisis* 34: 345–346; *Birmingham Reporter*, 29 October 1927.

[74] Allen Washington to Robert R. Moton, 22 November 1927, Moton Papers; *Hampton Script*, 13 October 1928, 12 October 1929; "Report of the Alumni Visitation Committee," in Minutes of the Meeting of the Hampton Board of Trustees, 25 April 1929, Hampton Archives.

January 1928, they endorsed the students' recent charge that some instructors were "out of harmony with true Hampton ideals . . . [and] wholly unfit as teachers in an educational institution for Negroes." Perhaps the endorsement was an act of penance for their previous hasty endorsement of Principal Gregg's October purge. The alumni also sanctioned the students' plea for dancing at a few major social activities. They condemned segregation at the Holly Tree Inn as "a sore spot . . . to visiting Negroes" and "a disquieting influence among the students." They concluded with pointed criticism of the administration for paying too much attention to the opinions of neighboring whites while failing to listen to the requests of students on the campus. The alumni leaders attributed the strike "no less to ill-advised action on the part of students than to lack of consideration for their desires on the part of the Administrative Board."[75]

The Alumni Visitation Committee was particularly disturbed by the great amount of unrest among members of the faculty. Students had reported that several whites and most of the seven blacks on Hampton's fifty-member college faculty had sympathized with the October strike. Principal Gregg had denied these reports, but he had also refused to call any faculty meetings during the controversy and had consulted only with fellow administrators. Dialogue with the faculty was postponed until after the strike was over. Gregg then called a general meeting and, in the words of Louise A. Thompson, a young black English teacher, "issued an ultimatum. . . . He said that he had been made aware that there were those . . . who were student sympathizers and such persons as these were not wanted at Hampton. . . . Loyalty on the part of teachers to the present administration is just as necessary as the loyalty of students, and those who felt that they cannot back up the present policies were politely asked to get out." Thompson left the institute at the end of the year, "keenly aware of the state

[75] "Report of the Alumni Visitation Committee," 28 January 1928.

of hypocrisy, racial prejudice and backwardness into which Hampton has fallen."[76]

Louise Thompson was not the only teacher to leave Hampton in a disheartened state. Even before the strike the annual rate of faculty turnover was approximately 20 percent, and half of those teaching in 1927–1928 had been at the institute for less than three years. The alumni had long suggested that steps be taken to make Hampton's teaching positions more attractive, and outside observers reported, "The annual turnover in the faculty is altogether too large . . . for the best interests of the students."[77]

Although the teachers had several complaints that ranged beyond the sources of student discontent, their central grievance was remarkably similar to that of the students: They wanted Hampton to upgrade its programs to the point where the institute would become a real center of higher education. Unlike trustees who protested against "the transformation of this place into a second-rate Northern college, with the emphasis on book knowledge," many of Hampton's teachers wanted to emphasize the fundamentals of academic education. They looked askance at Hampton's attempts to reassure the white South that it had not departed too far from the gospel of vocationalism. They thought the time had come for the institute to be led by a president (not a principal), and for teachers to be given regular academic ranks (instructor, assistant professor, associate professor, professor). Although salaries at Hampton were better than those at many other black colleges, many faculty members also endorsed the call for "a definite publicly announced relationship between rank and salary."

[76] *New York Age*, 22 October, 29 October 1927; Louise Thompson to W. E. B. Du Bois, quoted in "Hampton Strike," *Crisis* 34: 345–346.

[77] Arthur J. Klein, *Survey of Negro Colleges and Universities* (U.S. Department of the Interior, Bureau of Education Bulletin 7, 1928), p. 896; "Report of the Alumni Visitation Committee," 28 January 1928.

They complained that "the principle of personal arrangement—always discouraging to teachers—is the basis of the
present salary scale, and that the secrecy which surrounds
salary matters is part of a strict paternalism toward faculty
and student body alike." Most of all, the faculty protested
that the administration was "not sufficiently rigid in maintaining high standards of scholarship for delinquent students."[78]

Student recalcitrance and contention between the faculty
and administration persisted for more than a year after the
end of the strike, and by the spring of 1929 Hampton was
on the verge of anarchy. The Alumni Visitation Committee
reported that "the administrative forces responsible for the
discipline of the school can only with difficulty command
the respect and obedience of the student body." The professional staff was "divided into factions whose contentions
have separated the school into opposing groups." It was "an
all too common practice for teachers and officers to discuss
their differences before and with students with the result
that students are allied with one or the other group of the
warring camps to the detriment of their own work and general morale." Confronted with this sort of disorder, Gregg
decided in May 1929 that it was "for the best interest of
Hampton Institute" that he resign his office as principal.
The board of trustees quickly concurred.[79]

Gregg's departure brought a temporary peace to the
campus, but he left office with two basic sets of issues unre-
solved. The first concerned the essential nature of the institution: Was Hampton to be a vocational institute or a stand-

[78] Francis Greenwood Peabody, quoted in Minutes of Hampton
Board of Trustees, 25 April 1929; Klein, *Survey of Negro Colleges*,
pp. 896–897; "Report of the Alumni Visitation Committee," 25 April
1929.

[79] "Report of the Alumni Visitation Committee," 28 January 1928,
25 April 1929; James E. Gregg to Board of Trustees, 14 May 1929,
Hampton Archives; Minutes of the Meeting of the Hampton Board
of Trustees, 15 May 1929, Hampton Archives.

ard college? Gregg had admittedly done a great deal to raise the level of academic operations, but always apologetically and with assurances that he was not departing from the older traditions. Though acknowledging that Hampton had become a college, he hastened to add that the school was "not like most other colleges." Its main objective was not the teaching of liberal arts as a broad, general preparation for later professional training in law, medicine, the ministry, or other professions. Of course such education was "altogether proper and highly desirable," but Gregg insisted that "this is not Hampton's particular business. . . . Hampton Institute is a vocational institute." He claimed that the school had developed advanced courses simply because "the Negro schools of the South are better than they used to be [and] demand and deserve more thoroughly trained teachers."[80]

By way of contrast, Gregg's successor, George P. Phenix, a white New Englander who had been at Hampton since 1904, forthrightly took pride in the development of advanced studies and thus legitimized the collegiate curriculum. Phenix admitted that "obviously Hampton has entered upon a new era," and he welcomed the chance to upgrade academic standards. He noted, "Some of our friends have been fearful lest Hampton were making a serious mistake in entering the college field." He insisted, however, that "instead of regret there should be rejoicing that the progress of the South in general and the needs of the Negro in particular should have been such as to render this step necessary." If the development of higher education contradicted Hampton's past philosophy of education, it was because this philosophy had "less validity than some of us had supposed." Phenix warned that educational institutions sometimes suffered from "an unwise excess of devotion to their founder. What to the founder has been a device to meet a temporary

[80] James E. Gregg, quoted in Robinson, "History of Hampton Institute," pp. 161–163.

situation his followers have too often allowed to congeal into a permanent policy. This we must avoid."[81]

The second set of problems that Gregg left to his successor, and to his successor's successors, concerned interracial relations on the campus: Should the institute continue to be governed by white administrators? This question had not been explicitly raised by the students during their strike of 1927, but some believed it was an unspoken issue. In his first report to the trustees Phenix confessed that there was "a good deal of uncertainty as to whether the Institute is to continue under white management and with a staff largely white or whether in a reasonably near future it is likely to pass under colored control."[82] This question would continue to agitate the campus for another twenty years and would play a part in the pressured resignations of three more white presidents of Hampton Institute.

[81] George P. Phenix, "Special Report of the Acting Principal," December 1929, Peabody Papers; Robinson, "History of Hampton Institute," pp. 163ff.
[82] Phenix, "Special Report," December 1929.

CHAPTER VII

Lincoln (Pa.), Wilberforce, and Points North

CONTEMPORANEOUS with the black college protests discussed in the preceding chapters, there were turbulent confrontations at a number of other southern Negro colleges. In the spring of 1914 students at Alabama's Talladega College went on strike "in protest against the paternalism of some of their white teachers and the indifference of others." In 1917 students at Morehouse College in Atlanta, Georgia, staged a four-day strike against required attendance at study hall and the prohibition of evening study in dormitory rooms. Students at Storer College in Harper's Ferry, West Virginia, went on strike in 1922 in protest against the expulsion of three young men who had been involved in a fight with local whites. In 1923 the president of Livingstone College in Raleigh, North Carolina, reported that his students had gone "on strike and remained out nearly all the month of May, most of them not returning at all."[1]

There were still more protests in the last half of the 1920s. Forty students at Kentucky's small Lincoln Institute withdrew from their school in 1925 with a demand for more social privileges. Later that year students at Knoxville College in Tennessee went on strike to protest the arbitrary suspension of three students. In 1926 the freshman class was sus-

---

[1] Sheldon Bernard Avery, "Up from Washington: William Pickens and the Negro Struggle for Equality, 1900–1954" (Ph.D. diss., University of Oregon, 1970), p. 32; Benjamin J. Davis, *Communist Councilman from Harlem* (New York: International Publishers, 1969), pp. 30–39; *Baltimore Afro-American*, 17 November 1922; J. H. Johnson to W. E. B. Du Bois, 27 June 1923, WEBD Papers.

pended at North Carolina's Johnson C. Smith University in the wake of protests against punishments meted out to those involved in a hazing incident. In 1927 practically the whole student body at St. Augustine Junior College in North Carolina went on strike to protest the punishment of football players who had violated training regulations. Seven hundred students at Mississippi's Alcorn A. & M. College staged a short strike in 1929 when their president suspended two students for "unbecoming conduct."[2]

The faculty was in the vanguard of the protest movement on many campuses. At the State Normal School at Bowie, Maryland, the entire faculty resigned in 1923 in protest against the low standards to which their school had fallen under the leadership of a black principal, Leonidas James. Similarly, during the mid-1920s North Carolina A. & T.'s black president, F. D. Bluford, was subjected to devastating criticism from those who believed he had lowered the quality of education at his school. At Shaw University in North Carolina the white president, Charles Francis Meserve, was forced to resign in 1919 in the wake of angry charges that he had betrayed the race by closing Shaw's schools of medicine, pharmacy, and law. Black protest continued at Shaw during the 1920s, and in 1931 Joseph Leishman Peacock, the last white president of the university, resigned after repeated complaints that he was not in sympathy with the Negro race and that the time had come for blacks to assume leadership at Shaw.[3]

Some of these protests were short-lived and grew out of complaints that, in retrospect and in comparison with the grievances of blacks at Fisk, Howard, Hampton, Lincoln

[2] *Chicago Defender*, 7 November 1925; *New York Age*, 6 November 1926; *Baltimore Afro-American*, 26 November, 3 December 1927; *Pittsburgh Courier*, 23 February 1929.

[3] *Baltimore Afro-American*, 10 February 1922, 6 April 1923, 27 June 1925, 23 July 1927; *Pittsburgh Courier*, 17 March 1928; Clara Barnes Jenkins, "An Historical Study of Shaw University, 1865–1963," (Ed. D. diss., University of Pittsburgh, 1965), pp. 63–68.

(Mo.), and Florida A. & M., seem to have been relatively insignificant. Nevertheless, the black students and alumni involved in the many protests insisted that more was at stake than their demands for social privileges, an end to arbitrary discipline, and for high-quality academic programs. In their view, the objectionable tutelary, punitive, and curricular policies were based on racist assumptions that blacks could not control themselves and would become too dangerous if they were allowed the exercise of liberty.

It was black opposition to racism that led many students to risk expulsion and jeopardize their chances for entrance into the black middle class. This gamble could not have been taken lightly, for many parents had worked and sacrificed so that their children would have the chance to attend college and rise above the masses who earned their living through daily labor. That so many black students nevertheless went on strike, many with the vocal support and encouragement of their parents, indicates the depth and pervasiveness of black discontent during the 1920s.

Rather than relate the interesting but needlessly repetitive details of these many controversies, however, this final chapter will look at the phenomenon of black college protest from another angle of vision, that of blacks associated with colleges in the North.

I

Located in the scenic countryside of rural Pennsylvania, Lincoln University was the first institution established in the United States "for the collegiate and theological education of Negro young men." Founded in 1854 by John Miller Dickey, a white Presbyterian minister from the nearby town of Oxford, and originally chartered as the Ashmun Institute, the school took the name of the Emancipator in 1866. In the late nineteenth and early twentieth centuries Lincoln steadfastly resisted the pressures toward industrial training. In the process the university lost one bequest of $200,000 and saw its annual gifts decline between 1890 and 1910 from $25,000 to $6,000 per year. Nevertheless, Lincoln survived precariously during the 1920s with income from the Presbyterian church and from tuition charges of $110 a year, the highest student fee then charged at a black college.[4]

Given the steep tuition, the necessity of paying still more for room and board at an isolated college, and the absence of "student jobs" in rural Chester County, only relatively well-to-do families could send their sons to Lincoln University. The students, in turn, were expected to master the standard preprofessional liberal arts, and during its first three-quarters of a century the great majority of Lincoln's graduates went into the learned professions—6 percent into law, 21 percent into medicine, 26 percent into teaching, and 32 percent into the clergy. The ethos of the campus was one of competitive middle-class striving; one disenchanted student later recalled that the young men of Lincoln "thought of education exclusively in terms of prestige value. They wanted to be doctors and lawyers—doctors mostly—professions to which they referred as 'rackets.' There was money in them, and they were motivated by the desire to possess, as indeed they put it, yellow money, yellow cars, and yellow women."[5]

Despite this *embourgeoisement*, Lincoln University was well regarded as a liberal arts college. Robert Russa Moton expressed a prevailing view when he declared, "No educational institution in America . . . is more highly honored in the character and achievements of its graduates than is Lin-

[4] "The Full Fruits of Freedom," p. 11 (1934 pamphlet), Lincoln University Archives; Marvin Wachman, "Lincoln University in Perspective," *Lincoln University Bulletin*, Winter 1968, pp. 4–5; Arthur J. Klein, *Survey of Negro Colleges and Universities* (U. S. Department of Interior, Department of Education Bulletin 7, 1928), p. 644; *Philadelphia Tribune*, 6 November 1926.

[5] "Full Fruits," p. 17; J. Saunders Redding, *No Day of Triumph* (New York: Harper & Brothers, 1942), pp. 34–35.

coln University. Their names stand out in the record of Negro progress with brilliant distinction. They stand at the front in every community."[6]

Except for occasional grumbling about punishments meted out to students involved in hazing incidents, there were no student protests at Lincoln during the 1920s. In part this was because little Lincoln, with only three hundred students, often dominated the Negro sports world, especially in football, and something of the camaraderie of the athletic teams seems to have permeated the campus. Equally important, Lincoln had neither the coeds nor the young high school students who were enrolled in the academy divisions of most other black colleges. Also, there were none of the unwholesome resorts that existed in the urban ghettoes that abutted many black colleges. Consequently, Lincoln's all-white faculty felt it was not necessary to supervise social life on the campus.

The black students and white professors lived in separate sectors, meeting a few hours a day for classes, and one student later recalled that "student-faculty relationships outside the classroom, while friendly, [were] not in any way free or intimate. . . . From chapel in the morning until classes were over in the afternoon, we saw our teachers only in the classrooms. After that until the next morning they disappeared into their houses bordering the campus, leaving the main yard and the dormitories entirely to the students —which gave student life a certain freedom not enjoyed by most Negro colleges. Indeed, dormitory life was entirely student-controlled—and sometimes highly hilarious."[7]

Hazing was a favorite pastime, with incoming freshmen "given the paddling of their lives practically every night. . . . They were called *dogs*, made to roll pencils with their noses, to clean the sophomores' rooms, to 'assume the angle' for paddling, and to write insulting letters to their girl

[6] Robert R. Moton, quoted in "Full Fruits," p. 17.

[7] Langston Hughes, *The Big Sea* (New York: Hill and Wang, 1963), pp. 278–284, 306–310.

friends. At Thanksgiving, just before the annual big game, in the dead of night, all freshmen were seized and their heads shaved bald." In winter there were snowball fights, a pond for skating, and a barn of a gymnasium for basketball. In spring there were elaborately planned water fights, with whole dormitories engaged in battles against one another.[8]

Most of Lincoln's students were satisfied with the quality of their education and so pleased by the pastimes of their bucolic retreat that they did not object to the fact that in the 1920s Lincoln University alone among Negro colleges prohibited blacks from serving on its faculty and board of trustees. Indeed, when Langston Hughes, a student at Lincoln in the 1920s, surveyed opinion on this matter he discovered that two-thirds of the 127 students enrolled in the junior and senior classes were opposed to having black professors. "The reasons given were various: that Lincoln was supported by 'white' philanthropy, therefore whites should run the college; that favoritism and unfairness would result on the part of Negro teachers toward the students; that there were not enough Negro teachers available; and that things were all right as they were, so why change? Three students even said they just didn't like Negroes. Two said they did not believe Negro teachers had the interest of students at heart. Another said members of his own race were not morally capable!" Only a handful of students objected to Lincoln's failure to offer special courses on the history and literature of people of African descent.[9]

Whatever the reasons for the students' attitudes, young Langston Hughes considered it "the height of absurdity for an institution designed for the training of Negro leaders to support and uphold, on its own grounds, the unfair and discriminatory practices of the American color line." He concluded that "the college itself has failed in instilling in these

[8] Ibid.
[9] Ibid., pp. 306–310; Hughes, "Cowards from the Colleges," *Crisis* 41 (August 1934): 226–228.

students the very quality of self-reliance and self-respect which any capable American leader should have."[10]

Writing in the *Crisis*, W. E. B. Du Bois predictably endorsed Hughes's viewpoint. Admitting that the professors at Lincoln had not deliberately inculcated disrespect for blackness, Du Bois nevertheless concluded that "they certainly have not actively and conscientiously instilled in their students a knowledge of what the Negro has done in the past, or what he is doing now, and of what he is capable of doing. . . . The failure of Lincoln to do this is bearing bitter fruit, and any persons, even graduates of Lincoln themselves, who have sons to send to college would do well to hesitate before putting them in an institution where they are liable to emerge with no faith in their own parents, or in themselves."[11]

Among graduates of Lincoln, none objected to the university's exclusionary policies more strenuously than Francis J. Grimke, a member of Lincoln's class of 1870. Grimke became a trustee of Howard University, and the influential pastor of the Fifteenth Street Presbyterian Church in Washington, D. C. As early as 1885 Grimke had publicly demanded the employment of "colored men as professors in colored institutions." Such employment would give individuals the opportunity to develop their academic talents, would stimulate the ambitions of young blacks who would know that they could aspire to professorships, and would "foster race pride and . . . engender a feeling of mutual respect." Conversely, Grimke warned, the exclusion of Negroes from these positions "strikes at what is most vital to the race: it tends directly to undermine, to destroy racial self-respect."[12]

[10] Hughes, *Big Sea*, pp. 306–307.

[11] W. E. B. Du Bois, "The Students of Lincoln," *Crisis* 36 (June 1929): 204.

[12] Francis J. Grimke, "Colored Men as Professors in Colored Institutions," *A. M. E. Church Review* 4 (July 1885): 142–149; Grimke, "Lincoln University," *Crisis* 32 (August 1926): 196–197.

Prior to the First World War Grimke's repeated protests against Lincoln's prohibition of black professors and trustees had fallen on deaf ears. He protested in vain, not only when he addressed a meeting of Lincoln's board of trustees, but also among fellow alumni who on one occasion refused to endorse his demands that the Presbyterian synod investigate the situation. In 1916, however, Grimke resumed his campaign against racial barriers at Lincoln. He published two pamphlets at his own expense and proclaimed, "The time has come when Lincoln ought to abandon the unworthy position which it has occupied during these fifty years, and take its place by the side of Howard, Atlanta, Fisk, Talladega and the other institutions that are laboring for the uplift of the race. An institution maintaining the attitude of Lincoln, whatever else may be said of it, is not helpful in developing in the race a manly self-respect." According to Grimke, "the wonder . . . is that the students have been content to submit all these years to the humiliating assumptions of inferiority which underlie this whole Lincoln regime. . . . It is a shame and every graduate of the University and all who may be thinking of going there should be made to feel it."[13]

Under Grimke's continued prodding and with evidence that Lincoln's exclusionary policy had in fact undermined the confidence and racial pride of some students, most alumni came to believe that blacks should play a larger role in the management of their *alma mater*. Yet there was no challenge to the established order in the early 1920s, for Lincoln was then under the tutelage of the revered John Ballard Rendall, a Presbyterian minister who, in tandem with his uncle, Isaac Norton Rendall, another Presbyterian

[13] Francis J. Grimke, "On Lincoln University," *Baltimore Afro-American*, 17 July 1926; "Dr. Grimke 15 Years Ahead of L. U. Alumni," *Baltimore Afro-American*, 17 July 1926; Grimke to George Johnson, 18 March, 25 March 1916, in Carter G. Woodson, ed., *The Works of Francis J. Grimke* (Washington: Associated Publishers, 1942), IV: 528–531.

minister, had headed the university ever since 1865. Upon the death of the second Rendall in 1924, however, the Lincoln Alumni Association came forward with emphatic demands that blacks be named to positions on the faculty and the board of trustees and that the alumni be consulted in the choice of Rendall's successor as president.

Although "not at all unmindful of the wholly natural desire of the alumni for a voice in the Government of their University," the board of trustees nevertheless decided to maintain its lily-white policy. Of course the trustees professed their appreciation for the past "loyalty of the alumni of Lincoln University." They "would be glad, 'they asserted,' if they could feel it for the best interest of the University to accede to the [alumni's] desire." Yet after giving the matter "most serious consideration," they refused to modify their traditional policy. Dr. John B. Laird, the president of the board of trustees, stated that any deviation from this policy would jeopardize the university's chances for receiving financial aid. He hoped that "in a very few years Lincoln University would be the possessor of an equipment both scholastic and material that would enable her to be administered altogether by the people for whom she was founded." But with Lincoln's "present poor material equipment" the trustees thought it was "for the best interests of all concerned" to continue the policy of exclusive white management."[14]

The trustees' decision naturally infuriated the alumni of Lincoln and blacks in general. The *New York Age* pointed out that "the principle of alumni representation on the board of trustees of institutions of higher education has been given general acceptance by educational authorities in all parts of the country, . . . [and] it is therefore exceptional to find an institution of the age and standing of Lincoln University without a single alumnus on the board."

[14] Minutes of the Meeting of the Lincoln Board of Trustees, 15 December 1925, quoted in *New York Age*, 3 April 1926; statement of John B. Laird, quoted in *New York Age*, 31 July 1926.

According to the *Age*, the trustees were victims "of the antiquated notion . . . that Negroes must be treated as children and not consulted on matters concerning their interests." The newspaper warned that "the failure to recognize the Negro as an interested factor in the work of the university will lead to disaster."[15]

Dr. E. P. Roberts, the president of the Lincoln University Alumni Association, insisted, "The time has long since passed when white men can successfully work or legislate for the Negro without his cooperation and help." Another alumnus, W. W. Walker, the pastor of the Madison Street Presbyterian Church in Baltimore, declared, "The time has come for every self-respecting alumnus of Lincoln University not only to resent manfully this insult on the part of the Board, but to accept its challenge and oppose it to the bitter end. . . . The time has arrived for war." Du Bois predicted that "no president is going to stay at Lincoln University without the consent of black folk."[16]

This prediction was fulfilled in the mid-1920s, when the alumni of Lincoln University organized a vigorous campaign to place blacks in positions on the faculty and on the board of trustees and also insisted that the trustees secure the advice and consent of the leaders of the Alumni Association before electing anyone to the presidency of Lincoln University. Until 1927 the trustees refused to yield to the demands of the alumni, and as a consequence the prerogatives of management at Lincoln were increasingly at issue and the university remained without a president for more than three years. On three separate occasions the trustees refused to consult with alumni leaders before electing white ministers to preside at the university. In each case, the presidents-elect then declined the position after learning in no uncertain terms that Lincoln's black graduates were pre-

[15] *New York Age*, 7 November, 5 December 1925, 1 May 1926.
[16] E. P. Roberts, quoted in *Baltimore Afro-American*, 31 July 1926; W. W. Walker, quoted in *Baltimore Afro-American*, 10 July 1926; W. E. B. Du Bois, "Howard and Lincoln," *Crisis* 32 (May 1926): 8.

pared to make life miserable for any president who was appointed without the concurrence of the Alumni Association.

The first test of strength between the trustees and the alumni occurred in the summer of 1925, when the trustees *unilaterally* offered Lincoln's presidency to the Reverend Dr. John M. Gaston, the secretary of the Colored Division of the National Board of Missions of the Presbyterian Church. The leaders of the Alumni Association regarded this appointment as an intentional slight, and they immediately set out to discredit the new president-elect. They pointed out that Dr. Gaston had no established reputation in scholarship, had never taught at the college level, and had served on the board of trustees of Biddle University during the years when that university closed its professional schools and reorganized with a less ambitious academic program and a new name, Johnson C. Smith University. It was noted, moreover, that Gaston was the nephew of E. P. Cowen, the chief proponent of the plan to convert Biddle into a trade school. Some blacks claimed that Gaston did not believe "in the education of colored boys upon the same basis and to the same degree as boys of other races" and that his appointment as president of Lincoln University was part of a Presbyterian cabal to "southernize the North." In addition, there were charges that Gaston had abused his position with the Presbyterian Church and forced black clergymen "to vote on ecclesiastical questions according to his dictation, without regard to their own opinions or convictions, penalizing those who defied him by reducing their salaries."[17]

Gaston was not without black defenders, and it is difficult to know if he was guilty as charged. The irate alumni were less concerned with the specific charges than irritated by a peremptory trustee appointment that they regarded as an open declaration of disrespect. They made it clear that, regardless of Gaston's personal qualities, he could expect

[17] *New York Age*, 8 August 1925; "Torch" to *New York Age*, 22 August 1925.

nothing but trouble at Lincoln. They insisted that "any man against whom the almost unanimous feeling of a great body of educated men array themselves is absolutely useless in doing acceptable work for that group." They pointed to "recent disturbances at Fisk and Howard . . . as an indication of eventual possibilities at Lincoln with a man of the type of Dr. Gaston occupying the presidential chair." Under the circumstances, Gaston declined the trustees' offer and decided to remain in his position as secretary of the Colored Division of the Presbyterian Church.[18]

The trustees were not chastened by this experience, for in the fall of 1925, and again without consulting the leaders of the Alumni Association, the board appointed the Reverend Joseph Lyons Ewing as president of Lincoln University. Ewing was the synodical superintendent of the Presbyterian Committee on National Missions. The trustees explained, "Lincoln must have money, large sums of money, . . . and since our legitimate field of appeal will be to the Presbyterian Church, . . . [we] feel that the new president should be a man known to the church."[19]

The alumni acknowledged that Presbyterian connections would be useful in raising funds, but they naturally resented the board's second refusal to consult with alumni before making a presidential appointment. The local alumni associations of Philadelphia, Baltimore, and Washington unanimously endorsed a round-robin resolution declaring that black colleges throughout the nation were "passing through critical days . . . because of the lack of proper contact, sympathy and understanding between president and trustees of the institution on the one hand and the student body and alumni on the other."[20]

The alumni then organized a successful campaign to dis-

[18] *New York Age*, 8 August, 5 September 1925; *Baltimore Afro-American*, 5 September 1925.

[19] *New York Age*, 14 November 1925; John B. Laird, quoted in *New York World*, 29 November 1925.

[20] Alumni statements, quoted in *New York Age*, 5 December 1925.

suade Ewing from accepting the presidency. Writing on behalf of the Alumni Association, Dr. Roberts dispatched a telegram urging Ewing "to decline the invitation to become president." Vague rumors were circulated to the effect that Ewing was "objectionable because of his . . . prejudicial attitude toward colored workers in the Presbyterian Church, which prejudice . . . has been shown on various occasions and in most pronounced manner." One alumnus complained that the trustees were "so used to treating Negro Presbyterians as wards [that] they are unable to treat colored men as men." Another observed that the controversy could "have been avoided if the trustee board had among its members one or two representatives of the alumni."[21]

The major black newspapers summed up the prevailing Negro opinion: The *New York Age* observed that it was "a startling reflection upon the outstanding qualities of the well-equipped professional men turned out by Lincoln . . . if none of them are deemed capable of advising in the conduct of the university that gave them their training." The *Baltimore Afro-American* declared, "If Lincoln University in sixty-five years has not turned out men capable of administration and instruction, it never will." Given the prevalence of this point of view, Joseph Lyons Ewing, like John M. Gaston before him, declined the trustees' offer and decided to remain in his position with the Presbyterian Church.[22]

The trustees met again on June 23, 1926, and, in a paroxysm of obstinacy, refused to consult with the alumni before naming another white minister as president-elect of Lincoln University. This time the unhappy choice was the Reverend Walter Greenway, the pastor of the Bethany Presbyterian Church in Philadelphia. Greenway's election

[21] E. P. Roberts telegram to Joseph Lyons Ewing, quoted in *New York Age*, 5 December 1925; statements of unidentified alumni, quoted in *New York Age*, 10 July 1926, 5 December 1925.

[22] *New York Age*, 5 December 1925; *Baltimore Afro-American*, 5 December, 26 December 1925.

288

had hardly been announced before he was engulfed in what the *Philadelphia Tribune* called "a deluge of protest that has inundated the country, from coast to coast, wherever members of the alumni hold forth." Alumni President Roberts warned that "unless the situation were wisely handled it would grow to such proportions as to no longer be an affair of the Alumni Association, but the concern of the entire Negro race and the public in general." The *Baltimore Afro-American* exhorted the alumni of Lincoln to "manifest the same unity and courage which characterized the alumni at Howard in their fight to oust President J. Stanley Durkee."[23]

The Lincoln alumni worked assiduously to discredit and intimidate Greenway. They noted that the new president-elect, like the two previous nominees, had no experience as an educator, and they concluded that this was *prima facie* evidence that the trustees were "not interested in the educational standing of Lincoln." The alumni also noted that Greenway hailed from the South, and that "his residence in the North has not removed his native antipathies." This judgment seemed to be confirmed when, during the very week of his election to the presidency of Lincoln, Greenway issued an extraordinarily impolitic statement criticizing the mayor of Philadelphia for refusing to allow the Ku Klux Klan to hold a parade in the City of Brotherly Love. However much Greenway might explain that he was not a member of the Klan but merely defending an unpopular minority's right to assemble publicly, most Negroes concluded that as a friend of the Negro the new president-elect left much to be desired. "There is no place at Lincoln University for a Ku Kluxer either in name or sympathy," the *Baltimore Afro-American* proclaimed.[24]

Unlike Gaston and Ewing, Rev. Greenway did not suc-

[23] *Philadelphia Tribune*, 10 July 1926; E. P. Roberts to John B. Laird, quoted in *New York Age*, 31 July 1926; *Baltimore Afro-American*, 10 July 1926.

[24] *New York Age*, 10 July 1926; *Philadelphia Evening Bulletin*, 28 June 1926; *Baltimore Afro-American*, 10 July 1926.

cumb immediately to pressure from aroused blacks. He made a special visit to the campus, although the situation was so tense that he had to travel incognito, and he assured the trustees that he could be "instrumental" in securing the appropriation of "a very nice sum . . . of money" for the university. Roberts nevertheless warned that Greenway would face "the hostile opposition of the Lincoln University Alumni Association [and] the violent attacks of the Negro Race." The criticism finally took its toll, and Greenway eventually decided to stay at the Bethany Church. He insisted that "the fact that the alumni didn't want me had nothing whatever to do with my declining the offer," but the Negro press reported that "belief everywhere is that Rev. Greenway would have accepted had it not been for the blunt opposition of the Alumni."[25]

Throughout the controversy at Lincoln the Alumni Association insisted that it was "not making an effort . . . to have the university administered by the people for whom it was founded; nor is it a question of black versus white; it is a sincere effort on our part to cooperate and share . . . the responsibility of wisely directing the institution." The alumni maintained that their only concern was to ensure the selection of "an educator of proven ability." On several occasions they endorsed the candidacies of two senior professors: mathematician Walter Livingstone Wright, a Princeton graduate who had been at Lincoln since 1893, and classicist William Hallock Johnson, another Princeton graduate who had served as professor of Greek and New Testament literature for twenty-five years.[26]

Most trustees were initially opposed to promoting anyone from the ranks of the faculty; they felt "that in the pres-

[25] Walter Greenway, quoted in *Philadelphia Tribune*, 10 July 1926; E. P. Roberts, quoted in *Baltimore Afro-American*, 17 July 1926; *Baltimore Afro-American*, 17 July 1926.

[26] Roberts to Laird, 31 July 1926; *New York Age*, 5 December 1925.

idency just now we need a man who in addition to being sympathetic to the work of Lincoln, . . . must be able to go out and by his personality and gifts of speech make the people see the greatness of this work and the claim it has on their benevolence." After three unsuccessful attempts to impose their unilateral choices, however, the trustees evidently recognized that no worthy candidate would accept the presidency of Lincoln in the face of overwhelming alumni opposition. Consequently, in December 1926 the trustees finally relented and named Johnson as president of the university and Wright as vice-president. These two scholars had served as acting presidents during the three-year interregnum and managed to keep perfect order on the campus, an achievement that undoubtedly helped some trustees overcome their initial reservations about the professors' administrative ability. The fact that Johnson was an ordained Presbyterian minister also must have sweetened the pill for the trustees. They could derive some solace from the knowledge that they were continuing Lincoln's tradition of ministerial leadership.[27]

The choice of Johnson and Wright was received enthusiastically by both alumni and students. Roberts exulted that "Lincoln's new president . . . meets all of the requirements. He is an educator and administrator and is steeped in Lincoln tradition." The rank and file alumni evidently felt the same way, for they "applauded for five minutes" when the new president made an unscheduled appearance at the alumni's annual Lincoln's birthday meeting. As the first year of Johnson's administration came to a close, the student newspaper observed that "instead of tiring of him, we have learned to cherish his amiable character, his earnest devotion to duty, and his hearty interest manifested in the welfare of the student body." Of Wright, who succeeded to the presidency when Johnson retired in 1936, it was said, "Even

[27] Laird to Roberts, 31 July 1926; *Philadelphia Tribune*, 11 December 1926.

if he does teach a subject that most of us do not grasp [mathematics], we are willing to undergo tortures simply because we like the man."[28]

Having taught almost every one of Lincoln's students for fully a generation, the new president and vice-president were in close sympathy with Negro aspirations. Johnson publicly acknowledged that he could not "succeed in making Lincoln the best university without the support of the Alumni." The new president informed the trustees that he would resign his position if the board were not "reorganized so that the alumni of the school would be given representation." The trustees evidently accepted this condition, for shortly after Johnson's inauguration Dr. Roberts was named as the first alumnus and the first black to sit on Lincoln's board.[29]

The problem of finding qualified black professors was more difficult. During their terms as acting president, Johnson and Wright had employed four black instructors, 25 percent of the faculty, but these blacks were recent graduates of the university and were restricted to work in the introductory freshman courses. It was not until 1931 that Johnson was able to announce the appointment of Lincoln's first black full professor, Joseph Newton Hill. Nevertheless, the alumni were generally pleased with the Johnson-Wright administration and launched an enormously successful endowment campaign that raised $500,000 within two years (half of which was put up by the General Education Board).[30]

[28] E. P. Roberts, quoted in *Philadelphia Tribune*, 11 December 1926; *Philadelphia Tribune*, 19 February 1927; *Lincoln News*, Thanksgiving, 1927, and January 1926.

[29] William Hallock Johnson, quoted in *Philadelphia Tribune*, 19 February 1927; *New York Age*, 27 November 1926, 26 November 1927; *Philadelphia Tribune*, 24 November 1927.

[30] George E. Cannon to W. E. B. Du Bois, 2 August 1924, WEBD Papers; Klein, *Survey of Negro Colleges*, p. 649; Du Bois, "Lincoln University, Pennsylvania," *Crisis* 38 (August 1931): 278–279; Johnson

At the end of the first year of Johnson's presidency, the *Philadelphia Tribune* rejoiced, "Those who control Lincoln University . . . understand that they can not expect to obtain the support of the colored public if they refuse to permit those whom they have trained to participate in the management of the institution."[31]

The inauguration of Johnson and Wright in 1927 brought an end to the controversy over the succession at Lincoln University. Once again blacks had made it clear that they had come of age and proposed to control their institutions of higher learning and to be represented by spokesmen of their own choice. A pleased W. E. B. Du Bois spoke for black America when he observed that it was "gratifying to know that the quiet persistent fight by the Lincoln alumni is bringing change and that the new president takes his chair with their approval and consent."[32]

II

In 1856 a group of white Methodists interested in the education of blacks established Wilberforce University in Ohio. Seven years later Bishop Daniel Alexander Payne purchased the institution for the African Methodist Episcopal Church. Since then blacks have managed the university, and to this day the official stationery of Wilberforce bears the legend, "America's First College Owned and Operated by Negroes." As an all-black institution, Wilberforce escaped many of the interracial problems that confounded other colleges for Negroes. Yet as a church school that avowedly endeavored "to build a solid moral character . . . on a firm foundation of the old-time religion," Wilberforce

---

to Robert R. Moton, 25 November 1927, Moton Papers; Moton to Johnson, 2 December, 16 December 1927, Moton Papers; J. Frederick Talcott to Moton, 29 January 1927, Moton Papers.

[31] *Philadelphia Tribune*, 24 November 1927.

[32] W. E. B. Du Bois, "Lincoln, Fisk, and Howard," *Crisis* 34 (March 1927): 33.

throughout the 1920s experienced difficulties with students who wanted more individual freedom. During the decade after the First World War, moreover, there were several perplexing religious and political controversies that kept Wilberforce in turmoil.[33]

The campus of Wilberforce University, like that of Lincoln University (Pa.), was located in the rural countryside near a small town (Xenia), but there were coeds on the campus, and the black clergymen who ruled the school insisted on "giving secular instruction to the children of the church in a well-charged religious atmosphere." Admission was denied to all save those "inclined to respect the Christian religion and its institutions." The university's official literature proclaimed that "a daily account is kept of each student in such a way as to afford a full exhibit of his habits." Du Bois, a young instructor at the university in the 1890s, was nearly fired when he refused to offer an impromptu prayer while observing a chapel service. Classes were frequently suspended in order to hold devotional services, and there were frequent revivals that prompted Du Bois to complain that he was "driven almost to distraction by the wild screams, groans, and shrieks that rise from the chapel."[34]

This religious ethos prompted extraordinarily strict regulation of social relations on the campus, and, according to a semiofficial history of Wilberforce, "In the early years of the [twentieth] century, there was a continuous struggle between the students and faculty for a modification of the old rules of the institution." The requirement that male and

[33] R. R. Wright, *Seventieth Annual Report of the President, 1933* (pamphlet), Wilberforce Archives; Frederick A. McGinnis, *A History and an Interpretation of Wilberforce University* (Wilberforce: Brown Publishing Company, 1941).

[34] McGinnis, *History and Interpretation*, p. 199; *General Information* (1910 pamphlet), Wilberforce Archives; W. E. B. Du Bois, *Dusk of Dawn* (New York; Harcourt, Brace & World, 1940), p. 56; Elliott M. Rudwick, *W. E. B. Du Bois: Propagandist of the Negro Protest* (Philadelphia: University of Pennsylvania Press, 1960), p. 28.

female students use different walks on their way to and from classes was particularly unpopular, and in 1912 the faculty, after bitter wrangling, granted the students the privilege of walking together to and from classes "if going in the same direction." At the same time the young men were given permission to "call formally upon the young ladies for one hour" on Monday afternoons. The students made the most of their new freedom and, according to critics, "took to long walks about the grounds . . . meandering up and down the walks, totally oblivious of the fact that there were other ways of using their time beside social intermingling." To stop this fraternization, the trustees demanded in 1919 that President William S. Scarborough restore "the old rules as to the association of the sexes." The president's order precipitated a minor rebellion as angry students organized picket brigades and barricaded all the entrances to classroom buildings with barbed wire entanglements.[35]

This student protest ended quickly when the beleaguered President Scarborough announced "that for the present the old rule would not be carried out." Yet Scarborough acknowledged that "the matter of discipline" continued to be "a serious problem with us at times." Statements to this effect became the refrain of Wilberforce's two other presidents of the 1920s. Thus in 1923 President John A. Gregg noted "considerable unrest among the students [who] would like to have certain privileges prohibited by the rules." In 1924, when a fire destroyed B. F. Lee dormitory, the press reported that authorities were "firm in their belief that the building was set on fire by . . . an organized band of students who have been creating much trouble in and around the university for the past two years." In 1928 President Gilbert H. Jones observed that "two or three threats of serious outbreaks" were nipped in the bud "by tact, vig-

[35] Frederick A. McGinnis, "A History of Wilberforce University," (D. Ed. thesis, University of Cincinnati, 1940), pp. 276–278.

orous and energetic handling of the situation, and rapid action at the crest of the crisis."[36]

Summing up the official view of the unrest prevailing on the campus, Jones explained that

> Youth is always restless, presumptuous as to its knowledge and ability, and rash to assume responsibility for its own future. . . . Youth is always trying to fight free from all forms of government and control, even though its freedom thus acquired involved it immediately in its own destruction. . . . Too much freedom and lack of supervision and direction is undoubtedly to invite destruction to all except the strongest of characters. There is no doubt . . . but that the intention of God, nature and society was that the old should care for the young, and train and direct them until they have formed habits that make them safe members of organized society.[37]

Even more disturbing than the matter of student unrest was a protracted controversy over the proper relation between Wilberforce University and the state of Ohio. As early as 1885 the university had fallen on hard financial times and approached the state with a request for assistance. The state replied two years later with an act providing for the establishment and support of a Combined Normal and Industrial Department that was to be located "at Wilberforce University" across a ravine from the main campus. The university insisted that "the clear purpose and intent" of this legislation was "to help a worthy institution carry out its objectives more effectively." Perplexing ques-

[36] Ibid.; W. S. Scarborough, *Fifty-fifth Annual Report of the President, 1918* (pamphlet), Wilberforce Archives; J. A. Gregg, *Sixtieth Annual Report of the President, 1923* (pamphlet), Wilberforce Archives; *Chicago Defender*, 9 February 1924; *Norfolk Journal and Guide*, 9 February 1924; *Baltimore Afro-American*, 8 February 1924; G. H. Jones, *Sixty-fifth Annual Report of the President, 1928* (pamphlet), Wilberforce Archives.

[37] Jones, *Sixty-fifth Annual Report*.

tions immediately arose concerning the constitutionality of state aid to a church school. Finally, in 1903, the state attorney general ruled that the C. N. & I. Department was "separate and distinct and independent of Wilberforce University. The statute makes it so, and indeed were it not for this provision of the statute the act providing for State aid to this department of Wilberforce University would be unconstitutional. The constitution of Ohio expressly prohibits any State aid to any sectarian institution."[38]

Notwithstanding this ruling, spokesmen for the university insisted that the C. N. & I. Department was merely one of the several departments *of* Wilberforce University and subject to the central authority of the university's trustees. President Scarborough emphatically rejected the contention that the phrase "*at* Wilberforce University" implied that the C. N. & I. Department was independent of the university. He insisted that all the departments were part of one community and that the university could not allow any encroachment upon its "organic unity." Moreover, although the state always said that the C. N. & I. Department was a separate institution, cooperating with Wilberforce University in certain ways that were mutually advantageous, the trustees of the university were allowed to appoint four of the nine C. N. & I. trustees. For many years these church-appointed trustees managed to prevent C. N. & I. from emerging as a rival college.[39]

During the second decade of the twentieth century this situation gradually changed, as C. N. & I. made great progress under the leadership of its state-appointed black superintendent, William A. Joiner. Joiner openly questioned the

[38] McGinnis, "History of Wilberforce," pp. 164–165; *State Relations at Wilberforce University* (pamphlet, n.d.), Wilberforce Archives; W. E. B. Du Bois, "Wilberforce," *Crisis* 20 (August 1920): 176–178.

[39] W. S. Scarborough, "Wilberforce University and the C. N. & I. Department" (typescript), Scarborough Papers, Wilberforce Archives.

propriety of establishing a Tuskegee-type industrial institute for northern blacks and instead emphasized teacher
training programs, which he upgraded and expanded to
four-year courses of study. As a consequence, enrollments
in the trades dwindled and the well-equipped industrial
plants were idle. Thus enrollment in the tuition-free normal
curriculum soared from 165 students in 1910 to 620 in 1920
—a student body 50 percent larger than that at Wilberforce
University (where annual tuition averaged about $50) and
a total enrollment that placed C. N. & I. second only to
Howard among black colleges.[40]

It was inevitable under these circumstances that a rivalry
would develop between Wilberforce and the C. N. & I. Department. President Scarborough believed that Superintendent Joiner was coaxing students away from the university, and officials at Wilberforce worked assiduously to
squelch press reports that were favorable to C. N. & I. A
state investigator reported in 1919 that "the two governing
bodies" manifested "a feeling of ill will toward each other."
A state auditor later reported that while the trustees of the
two schools were "very humanly and very naturally actuated by loyalty to their church," the superintendent of the
C. N. & I. Department was in "almost daily contact with the
state in a financial and business way" and consequently acquired "a growing loyalty to the state and to the state's
rights and expenditures."[41] Herein lay the seeds of future
controversy.

Most influential observers were favorably impressed by

[40] Frederick A. McGinnis, "History of Wilberforce," pp. 173–
179; Du Bois, "Wilberforce," pp. 176–178; Klein, *Survey of Negro
Colleges*, pp. 602–624.

[41] *Cleveland Gazette*, 12 July 1919; W. E. B. Du Bois, "The New
Wilberforce," *Crisis* 8 (August 1914): 191–194; Du Bois, "The New
Wilberforce," *Crisis* 9 (November 1914): 21; Du Bois to Joel E.
Spingarn, 17 October 1914, Spingarn Papers, Howard University;
L. F. Hopp to A. V. Donahey, 12 August 1919, S39, Item 4, Ohio
State House; E. Frank Brown, audit of Wilberforce University,
1919–1923, S39, Item 4, Ohio State House.

the growth of C. N. & I. Du Bois commended Joiner as "an honest and progressive servant," and the Ohio state auditor claimed that "the State has received from [C. N. & I.] more value for one hundred cents of investment than from any other institution in the State." The chairman of the legislature's appropriation committee agreed, observing that "no other institution of the state 'makes a dollar go as far.' " Another state legislator declared that "no other school can offer such advantages . . . at twice the expense." Thus state appropriations for C. N. & I. increased along with enrollments, and by 1920 the well-financed Department was clearly a rival to Wilberforce University.[42]

In the meantime, clouds of suspicion were gathering around Wilberforce University. In his 1916 survey of Negro colleges, Thomas Jesse Jones gave venerable old Wilberforce a substandard rating and claimed, "Owing to church politics the institution has been badly managed and its organization is not effective." That same year the general conference of the A. M. E. Church found Bishop Joshua H. Jones, the president of Wilberforce's board of trustees and until recently also the president of the university, guilty of "maladministration, stealing, lying, and conduct unbecoming a Christian gentleman." Jones had allegedly received kickbacks on university construction and had used student dining hall fees to purchase farms that then supplied the university with produce at inflated prices.[43]

By 1920, then, the efficient and relatively well-financed C. N. & I. Department was prospering while Wilberforce University was increasingly on the defensive. Indeed, the parent institution could not have survived had it not persuaded the state to enter into a complicated arrangement whereby the state paid Wilberforce to teach academic sub-

[42] Du Bois, "Wilberforce," pp. 176–178.
[43] Thomas Jesse Jones, *Negro Education* (U. S. Department of Interior, Bureau of Education Bulletin 38, 1916), p. 683; Du Bois, "Wilberforce," pp. 176–178; McGinnis, "History of Wilberforce," pp. 99–103.

jects to the normal students enrolled in the C. N. & I. Department. By the mid-1920s two-thirds of Wilberforce's expenses were charged to the state, and Du Bois declared that "had it not been for the generosity of the State, the church school would have either closed or been thoroughly reorganized." This situation naturally invited criticism from legislators who doubted the constitutionality of the arrangement and questioned the wisdom of exposing prospective black teachers to what one legislator called "disserviceable highly academic courses." There were, in addition, a number of vocal alumni who believed that "looseness of organization" had led to academic retrogression at their *alma mater*.[44]

Against this background, in 1919 a flurry of bills were introduced in the Ohio state legislature. The first, which failed of passage, proposed to cut off all state assistance to Wilberforce. Another, which was also defeated, called for the reorganization of the C. N. & I. Department as Wilberforce State Normal and Vocational College, with a separate seven-member board of trustees, all of whom would be appointed by the governor. The third, which passed by a large majority, proposed to weaken the union between church and state by reducing to two the university's contingent on the C. N. & I. board of trustees. Gov. James M. Cox vetoed this bill, however, stating that it "did not go far enough" and that "factional feeling within the place has assumed such a temper that it is really difficult to get at basic conditions." Cox then appointed a committee to look into the situation with an eye to making recommendations to ensure the efficient use of the state's money.[45]

[44] Du Bois, "Wilberforce," pp. 176–178; Klein, *Survey of Negro Colleges*, p. 604; G. H. Jones, *Sixty-seventh Annual Report of the President, 1930* (pamphlet), Wilberforce Archives; William H. Allen, "Report on the Combined Normal and Industrial Department at Wilberforce University," OLE 10, 9, Ohio State House; McGinnis, "History of Wilberforce," pp. 131–132.

[45] "State Relations at Wilberforce University"; Ohio House *Journal* 108: 1075; Du Bois, "Wilberforce," pp. 176–178.

Before this committee could make its investigation, Bishop Jones and his friends went to work persuading Republican politicians that the criticism of the university was inspired by C. N. & I. Superintendent Joiner and by disgruntled black Democrats. When Governor Cox, who in the meantime had received the Democratic nomination for the presidency of the United States, was defeated in 1920 by fellow Ohioan Warren G. Harding, the governorship passed to the GOP's Vic Donahey. Donahey was a close friend of the church school, and he vetoed proposals to alter the existing relation between Wilberforce and the state. He explained that "such splitting up and scattering of authority . . . would be not only unbusinesslike but an unwarranted insult to the colored race by reason of the general assembly's apparent distrust of the integrity of the board of trustees and its ability to manage its own affairs."[46]

With the churchmen thus confident of the governor's support, Bishop Jones persuaded the C. N. & I. trustees to appoint Richard C. Bundy, the son of an A. M. E. bishop, to replace Joiner as superintendent of C. N. & I. And then the Wilberforce trustees dismissed President Scarborough—a move evidently inspired by Bishop Jones's desire to turn the presidency over to his son, Gilbert H. Jones, who was then serving as dean of Wilberforce's College of Liberal Arts.[47]

At this point the student body rose in wrath and went on strike against, as their placards said, "Too Much Jones." One church officer reported from the campus, "Everything is chaos." To restore order Bishop Jones reconsidered his grand strategy, passed over his son, and persuaded a fellow bishop, John A. Gregg, to become the new president of Wilberforce University. Gregg's appointment was short-lived, however, for in 1924 he was transferred to missionary work in Africa and young Gilbert Haven Jones was finally inau-

[46] *Cleveland Gazette*, 24 April 1926; *Ohio Legislative History*, 1923–1924, 5: 62.

[47] McGinnis, "History of Wilberforce," pp. 106, 173–179; *Cleveland Gazette*, 10 July 1920.

gurated as president of the university.[48] Thus after 1924
the Joneses were dominant at Wilberforce. Frederick A.
McGinnis, an English instructor at the university, later
recalled,

> During the first four years of the incumbency of Presi-
> dent [Gilbert H.] Jones, his father, then a bishop in the
> A. M. E. Church, was president of the board of trustees
> and shared directly with his son the responsibilities of
> administration. During the other four years, his father
> was a vice-president of the board and a member of the
> executive committee. Moreover, both father and son re-
> sided at Wilberforce. Therefore, it is safe to say that the
> influence of the elder Jones was much in evidence in the
> policies of his son.[49]

The situation at Wilberforce naturally became the subject
of controversy in Ohio and throughout the nation. One state
representative characterized Jones's dismissal of Joiner as
"a shocking demonstration of contempt for the public." In
New York Du Bois wrote, "It is doubtful if one could imagine a situation fraught with more danger to the race: here
is a man, W. A. Joiner, who has made a splendid executive.
. . . He has been dismissed by a man whose reputation has
been blasted by his own church. If we let this pass unre-
buked what can we say if the State of Ohio puts white men
in charge at Wilberforce on the ground that 'Negroes cannot conduct a school'?"[50]

Even those who had previously supported the university
were shocked by the dismissal of President Scarborough.
Harry C. Smith, the editor of the *Cleveland Gazette* and a
trustee of the C. N. & I. Department, noted that he had
been "a consistent friend" of Wilberforce University for

[48] Du Bois, "Wilberforce," pp. 176–178; *Pittsburgh Courier*, 1
January 1927.

[49] McGinnis, "History of Wilberforce," p. 109.

[50] Allen, "Report on Combined Department"; Du Bois, "Wilberforce," pp. 176–178.

nearly four decades, and that "thousands upon thousands of our people . . . deeply regret the severing of [Scarborough's] relations with Wilberforce. . . . It seems hardly fair." The *Chicago Defender* portrayed Scarborough as a "gentleman, scholar, and educator," and decried the politics that allegedly prompted the A. M. E. bishops to drive him from the campus.[51]

At this juncture the alumni organized to protest against "the prevalence of church politics." To make certain that they could function "with the utmost freedom," the officers of the alumni association moved their headquarters away from Wilberforce. Then they began a determined campaign to publicize the misdeeds of the university's administration and to build "a strong alumni body which cannot be ignored." Alumni president Frank M. Reid declared that "the present unsatisfactory and unfortunate conditions at Wilberforce are [due] to the fact that the reins of administration have fallen absolutely into the hands of Bishop Joshua H. Jones . . . and his son, Dr. Gilbert H. Jones." Similar criticism was voiced by Gustavus A. Steward, the alumni treasurer, by Hallie Q. Brown, a former instructor at Wilberforce and the president of the powerful National Federation of Colored Women, and by Charles Gardner Reed of Chicago, who at one time had been the university's most brilliant football star. The refrain of this criticism was that "the present administration at Wilberforce University is not what it should be in morals and management; affairs of the school have been subordinated to church politics and ecclesiastical intrigue . . . [and] a steady decline in the affairs of the school has placed the university in the lowest scholastic rank." Under the leadership of the two Joneses, it was said, Wilberforce had retrogressed to the point where it had "a 'C' rating throughout the educational world."[52]

[51] *Cleveland Gazette*, 10 July 1920; *Chicago Defender*, 11 December, 21 August 1926.

[52] *Chicago Defender*, 11 July 1925, 3 January 1926; *Philadelphia Tribune*, 25 July, 8 August 1925; *Baltimore Afro-American*, 22

Alumni criticism persisted throughout the early 1920s and was reinforced when Profs. E. A. Clarke and E. H. Miller sued the university to collect back pay. Over the course of several years Wilberforce had achieved a dubious record with regard to honoring faculty contracts. Some professors were paid in full, but others were paid in notes that had to be sold at a discount to bankers and lawyers in nearby Xenia. This stood in marked contrast with the situation at the state-supported C. N. & I. Department, where salaries were paid on time and in cash. Under the circumstances, some professors at Wilberforce questioned the value of the university's vaunted autonomy and longed for the day when the state would assume control over the church school.

There is no evidence that either Clarke or Miller was in league with the alumni's efforts to discredit the administration of Wilberforce, but their successful suits to recover some $1,500 in back wages obviously damaged more than the university's treasury. The trials forced the university to reveal that some debts had been outstanding for years and gave Miller a forum for his contention that Wilberforce's administrators were guilty of "everything from mismanagement to general inefficiency." The university had good reason to "regret exceedingly that the institution was in such condition that it had to give notes to teachers in payment for their services."[53]

The sensational charges of Ira Bryant, editor of an A. M. E. publication called *The Young Allenite*, also damaged the reputation of Wilberforce University. According to Bryant the leaders of the church discovered in the mid-1920s that Bishop Jones was drawing money out of the university's building fund and had forced him to repay some $5,000 "under threat of exposure and indictment." In time

January 1926; Frank M. Reid, quoted in *Philadelphia Tribune*, 8 August 1925; McGinnis, "History of Wilberforce," pp. 131–132.
[53] *Chicago Defender*, 7 August, 21 August 1926; W. S. Scarborough, *Forty-seventh Annual Report of the President, 1910* (pamphlet), Wilberforce Archives.

the church leaders publicly repudiated Bryant's charges, and Jones's fellow bishops eventually denounced editor Bryant for "unwarranted and un-Christianlike attacks and slander." Nevertheless, there were many, including Fred Moore, the editor of the *New York Age*, who credited "the inside knowledge that Mr. Bryant has acquired of wrong-doing in high places" and praised his "courage in dragging these matters to the light and exposing the wrongdoers." Although Bryant never presented evidence that would sustain criminal charges in a court of law, his repeated allegations undoubtedly undermined confidence in Bishop Jones's administration at Wilberforce.[54]

Public criticism of Wilberforce increased with each passing year, and by the mid-1920s Negroes throughout the country recognized that something should be done to clear the air. Expressing one point of view, the *Chicago Defender* noted, "Something is radically wrong . . . when a school founded upon as firm a foundation as [Wilberforce] slides from a first- to a fourth-grade rating among schools." The *Defender* recommended, "For the good of the institution, the present administration should resign from the head down. . . . Housecleaning at Wilberforce is now in order." Striking a moderate note, the *Pittsburgh Courier* called for an investigation of the charges that were being bandied about.[55]

A. L. Foster of the Chicago Urban League voiced what must have been a widespread sentiment when he wrote to fellow Wilberforce alumni that "the time has come for action on our part. We must put aside any sentimental feeling which we may have in the matter and get to the bottom of the whole disgusting situation. It is our duty as loyal alumni to insist upon knowing the facts." Foster explained,

[54] *Pittsburgh Courier*, 10 December 1926, 2 January 1927; *Baltimore Afro-American*, 10 December 1927; *New York Age*, 15 January 1927.

[55] *Chicago Defender*, 1 January 1927; *Pittsburgh Courier*, 28 December 1926.

In view of the fact that the *Chicago Defender* and the *Pittsburgh Courier* and other newspapers have carried articles in their columns which reflect upon the good name of our Alma Mater, it is certainly fitting and proper that we demand explanations which will clear up the situation to our own satisfaction.

For several years there has been criticism of the management of the affairs of the institution and from time to time there have been hints that irregularities in the handling of funds have existed. It has also been charged that the school has been retrograding for the past ten years or more and that Wilberforce does not enjoy the scholastic standing now that she once enjoyed. . . .

[These] charges, if true, certainly should cause every alumnus to rise in wrath and demand the resignation of every official found guilty of participation in these acts of degradation. If, on the other hand, the charges are false . . . every alumnus should insist upon a retraction of every statement that has appeared in the newspapers and demand that justice is secured at Wilberforce.[56]

The leaders of the alumni association had anticipated demands for an investigation, but it was clear from the outset that the trustees of Wilberforce University would not cooperate with disgruntled graduates who were obviously looking for incriminating evidence. It was equally clear that there was no way to compel a private institution to open its books to investigators. The alumni leaders also believed that the A. M. E. Church possessed sufficient influence within the Republican Party to prevent the state from launching an investigation of the C. N. & I. Department. Consequently, in early 1926 the alumni struck out on their own and hired a special investigator who, it was hoped, would discover

[56] A. L. Foster to alumni, quoted in *Pittsburgh Courier*, 1 January 1927.

enough evidence to incriminate the leaders of the university and force the state to look into matters at C. N. & I. For this task the alumni selected one of the leading black sleuths of the day, Sheridan A. Brusseaux of the Keystone National Detective Agency in Chicago. Brusseaux had gained national recognition for his investigative work in connection with the celebrated Rhinelander divorce case and in the "Shuffle-Along Plantation Days" theatrical scandal.[57]

At the outset of his investigation Brusseaux focused on the old charges that had been leveled against Bishop Jones. He collected bills of lading indicating that the Bishop was still charging both the university and C. N. & I. for milk produced on his farm but never sipped by students in the dining halls. He uncovered documents indicating that Jones had engineered the sale of property left to Wilberforce as part of a permanent endowment. He persuaded former superintendent Joiner to submit an affidavit charging that Jones had once used the university's money to purchase a farm which Jones then registered in his own name; and he repeated Bryant's claim that the A. M. E. church had forced Bishop Jones to make restitution of $5,000 missing from Wilberforce's building fund. These revelations undoubtedly embarrassed the bishop; but Jones was in firm control of the board of trustees and was able to ride out the storm by dismissing Brusseaux's charges as the result of "jealousy and politics." Jones's son Gilbert claimed that although Brusseaux was "implying and insinuating everything, . . . Nothing is wrong at the institution."[58]

Having failed to discredit Bishop Jones in the eyes of his fellow A. M. E. trustees, Brusseaux attempted to force a

[57] *Philadelphia Tribune,* 1 January 1926; *Baltimore Afro-American,* 22 January 1926.

[58] *Chicago Defender,* 11 December, 18 December 1926, 22 January, 12 February 1927; *Baltimore Afro-American,* 22 January 1926, 1 January 1927; *Cleveland Gazette,* 15 January, 29 January 1927; *Pittsburgh Courier,* 11 December, 25 December 1926.

state investigation by impugning the probity and managerial ability of the superintendent of the C. N. & I. Department, Richard C. Bundy. The result, in the words of the *Pittsburgh Courier*, was "a tangled tale of loose and negligent business methods that bordered ridiculously close to the absurd." Brusseaux discovered that approximately $3,300 worth of merchandise allegedly purchased for the use of state-subsidized students had found its way into Bundy's home. The items included a baby grand piano, mahogany furniture, carpets, an expensive radio, plate glass mirrors, wallpaper, books, and magazines. The superintendent also had the use of "luxurious porch furniture, spinet tables, reed parlor sets, . . . library cases, shower baths, and other sundry things until his home looked like any other millionaire's." In addition, Brusseaux reported that Bundy received free food from Bishop Jones's plentiful larder and charged the state with the cost of purchasing and operating his chauffeur-driven Studebaker limousine.[59]

Brusseaux turned over his report and the supporting evidence to alumni officers who then relayed the information to black newspapers. The *Chicago Defender* concluded, "The Wilberforce account books will be listed hereafter in the library under 'current fiction.'" And then, as publicity mounted, Brusseaux and the alumni persuaded State Auditor Joseph Tracy to appoint one of his examiners, E. Frank Brown, to make a formal investigation to determine if the C. N. & I. Department was squandering state funds. The alumni leaders knew that "high officials at the State House are friendly to Wilberforce" and feared that Governor Donahey would engineer a whitewash. The press nonetheless reported on the eve of the investigation that the campus community was "pretty thoroly stirred up." When Brusseaux visited Wilberforce in the company of reporters from the *Chicago Defender*, chemistry professor Bruce Green

[59] *Pittsburgh Courier*, 12 February 1927; *Philadelphia Tribune*, 12 February 1927; *Chicago Defender*, 12 February 1927.

prompted a melee when he urged his students to "run the soundrels off the campus."[60]

Examiner Brown interrogated forty-three witnesses in the course of his investigation, and all the old charges of mismanagement and misappropriation were reiterated. The evidence relating to the presence of school property in Superintendent Bundy's home was so incontrovertible that Bundy entered a demurrer: He admitted that the items in question were used in his home but insisted that this use did not sustain charges of conversion because his home was an official residence used by the C. N. & I. Department for entertaining students, trustees, and visitors. The use of the chauffeur-driven Studebaker limousine on trips to Saratoga Springs and Atlantic City was more difficult to justify, but Bundy said that the trustees had instructed him to make "a trip down East . . . to hunt up likely applicants for certain teaching positions." The most embarrassing new evidence concerned kickbacks that Bundy allegedly received from C. N. & I.'s construction contracts. One affidavit by a plumber named Joseph Serra averred that Bundy had demanded a $600 rebate on a $2,500 bill: "What am I getting out of this?" the superintendent was said to have asked. "Do you think I am here for my health?" Other evidence indicated that money had been paid to a nonexistent "Columbus Plumbing Company" and that some bills had been paid twice, although the contractors insisted they had received only a single payment.[61]

Brown's investigation presented problems for the state's leading Republicans. In his formal report Brown pointed to "extravagance, bad management and business methods that are subject to great criticism." He concluded, "The duplication of payments for material, while perhaps not

[60] *Chicago Defender*, 11 December 1926; *Pittsburgh Courier*, 22 January 1927; *Cleveland Gazette*, 11 December, 18 December 1926.
[61] E. Frank Brown, "Auditor's Report," 3 February 1927, S39, Item 4, Ohio State House; Richard Bundy, "Answer and Explanation," S39, Item 4, Ohio State House.

criminal, was, to say the least, done in a way that looks like
an effort to deceive." Yet Governor Donahey was a friend
of Wilberforce and depended on A. M. E. church support
during his election campaigns, and State Auditor Tracy
noted that it would be "unfortunate to say that Negroes
cannot manage their own affairs." Consequently, the state
refused to prosecute Superintendent Bundy but released
Brown's report with the hope that the publicity would ensure the proper use of state funds in the future.[62]

The black community was divided over the meaning of
the investigation at Wilberforce. The *Chicago Defender*,
the *Pittsburgh Courier*, and the *Philadelphia Tribune* expressed one point of view when they denounced the diver-
sion of funds away from the education of students and
demanded the resignation of Superintendent Bundy,
President Jones, and Bishop Jones. The *Defender* asserted,
"Both sections of the institution have been run by men who
were disposed to take advantage of every opportunity
which presented itself to advance their own interests." On
the other hand, the *Cleveland Gazette* feared that criticism
would result in "lessening the financial and other support
given the State department by the Ohio assembly." And the
Baltimore Afro-American stated that Wilberforce was "in
the position of a useful citizen who has been set upon in the
dead of night by detectives, sand-bagged, thrown in jail,
accused of horrifying crimes and eventually released with
the excuse that the detectives thought him a highwayman."[63]

The trustees of the C. N. & I. Department emphasized
that the state had not required Superintendent Bundy to
make restitution of any funds, and they assured Bundy of

[62] Brown, "Auditor's Report"; Brown, quoted in *Chicago Defender*, 12 February 1927; *Pittsburgh Courier*, 12 February 1927; *Baltimore Afro-American*, 29 January 1927; Joseph Tracy, quoted in
Pittsburgh Courier, 22 January 1927.

[63] *Chicago Defender*, 12 February 1927; *Pittsburgh Courier*, 12
January 1927; *Philadelphia Tribune*, 12 February 1927; *Cleveland
Gazette*, 11 December 1926; *Baltimore Afro-American*, 19 February
1927.

their "continued support of your splendid management." Joseph L. Johnson, the president of the C. N. & I. trustees, denounced "all charges" against Bundy as "false and without foundation." He believed there was "a conspiracy" at Wilberforce—that certain anonymous informers had leaked "half-truths" to the state examiner—and in July 1927 the board dismissed eight professors who were thought to have given " 'inside' information anent alleged irregularities in the administration of state funds."[64]

Alumni leaders and some state officials were enraged by these reprisals. Hallie Brown said that "politics has been creeping into the institution as education was going out," and one trustee, Capt. Walter Thomas of Columbus, admitted that "politics had too large a play in the management of the school." R. D. Williamson, the chairman of the legislature's joint finance committee, warned that his committee would hold up all payroll appropriations for the C. N. & I. Department until the discharged professors were reinstated. Nothing came of this threat, however, for the state attorney general ruled that the legislature had no authority to interfere with hiring and firing at the C. N. & I. Department.[65]

Although the members of the joint finance committee could not effect the reinstatement of the renegade professors, they were in a position to demand that certain changes be made as a prerequisite for continued state aid to the C. N. & I. Department. Due to "certain irregularities at Wilberforce," chairman Williamson explained, the finance committee believed "that the present system of doing things at these institutions should be improved before any more of the state's money is alloted to them to expend." Consequent-

[64] *Cleveland Gazette*, 12 February 1927; Joseph L. Johnson to Joseph T. Tracy, 1 February 1927, S39, Item 4, Ohio State House; *Baltimore Afro-American*, 23 July 1927; *Pittsburgh Courier*, 23 July, 30 July 1927.

[65] Hallie Q. Brown and Walter Thomas, quoted in *Pittsburgh Courier*, 30 July 1927; *Baltimore Afro-American*, 23 July, 30 July, 13 August, 17 September 1927.

ly, the committee established a special board of control, chaired by a state-appointed financial officer, to pass on all expenditures of state money at Wilberforce. President Jones naturally objected "to the imputation . . . that our trustees are not capable of taking care of their own business." Jones believed it was unfair to "have it appear that we are a bunch of babies, unable to look after ourselves." The finance committee was adamant on this point, however, and chairman Williamson testily explained, "This arrangement is being made for your own protection. You have been accused of certain things and through this plan there will be no longer any opportunity for such accusations to be made. . . . When we appropriate money we want to know that it is going to be spent in the proper manner. By this system of having the executive clerk pass finally on all expenditures we will have reasonable assurance that everything is regular."[66]

With this arrangement in 1927, the controversy at Wilberforce subsided. The state had taken precautions to ensure the wise expenditure of its funds, and the church-dominated boards of trustees had reaffirmed their confidence in the executive officers of the university and of the C. N. & I. Department. President Jones remained in his office for another five years, and Superintendent Bundy stayed in his position until his death in the early 1930s.

The disaffected alumni were not entirely satisfied with this settlement, and criticism persisted throughout the 1920s. This criticism and the continued scrutiny of state auditors undoubtedly irritated the administrative officers at Wilberforce, and the general atmosphere of faultfinding must have called their authority into question and prepared the way for student unrest. The critics of Wilberforce hoped that their aspersions would arouse the campus community, and President Jones was not entirely wrong when he noted in 1928 that the "influence of outside forces" emboldened

[66] R. D. Williamson and Joshua H. Jones, quoted in *Pittsburgh Courier*, 19 March 1927.

"malcontents in the student body" and thus was partially responsible for "threats of serious student outbreaks." Jones noted, however, that "in a year of stress and stressful conditions . . . when many of our sister institutions have been torn to pieces by such conditions," the administrators at Wilberforce managed to calm the "brief stormy periods at the institution." Despite the students' persistent demands for more personal freedom, the undergraduates at Wilberforce, unlike those at some other black colleges, never allied themselves with the alumni against the administration.[67]

Although the authorities at Wilberforce managed to ride out the storm during the 1920s, their dominion was hardly secure. Beyond the alumni critics and the restive students lay the basic problem of church-state relations. Wilberforce could not survive as a major black university without subsidies from the state of Ohio, and it was inevitable that many legislators, as well as many secular blacks, would question the propriety of these subsidies. In retrospect it seems inevitable that the state eventually would make the C. N. & I. Department an autonomous institution; the surprise is that the church-state partnership lasted as long as it did. It was not until 1947 that the C. N. & I. Department severed all relations with Wilberforce University and became an independent, state-supported teachers college. Since 1951 this state school has been known as Central State University, and it now dwarfs the parent Wilberforce University, which continues to exist as a small church-supported liberal arts college "on the other side of the ravine."[68]

III

In addition to the 13,680 students enrolled in black colleges in 1927, there were at least 1,500 blacks enrolled in predominantly white colleges and universities outside the

[67] Jones, Sixty-fifth Annual Report.
[68] Frederick A. McGinnis, The Education of Negroes in Ohio (Wilberforce: Curliss Printing Co., 1962), p. 85.

South.[69] The black students at these integrated institutions were abused in many ways, and some blacks today say that these token Negroes were "whitewashed" intellectually. Exposure to a curriculum designed for whites and controlled by whites allegedly created a group of docile Negro graduates who made peace with the prevailing order and advanced their individual careers while ignoring the need to work for less privileged blacks. It is said that these "middle-class Negroes" were deracinated by their experiences at predominantly white colleges; they did well on the white man's examinations only because they internalized white values and became white men with black skins. It is alleged that, by way of contrast, "the real black man is proud of his identity and is committed to the advancement of black people. He is too steeped in his own culture to score well on white, culturally biased tests, but he has real abilities that he will use in service to his race."[70]

Although a good case could be made for the alternative proposition that most Negro collegians of the 1920s manifested an abiding concern for poor black people, a discussion of the social service and racial betterment work of the Negro college students and alumni would be beyond the scope of this study. It is clear, however, that the "integrated" black students of the 1920s, like their brothers and sisters on the predominantly black campuses, were not docile accommodationists. Although they did not demand a special curriculum for blacks and believed that many ghetto characteristics were the products of an unfortunate environment and not manifestations of authentic blackness, the integrated black students of the 1920s consistently

[69] "Enrollment in Negro Universities and Colleges," *School and Society* 28 (29 September 1928): 401–402; "The College Negro American, 1927," *Crisis* 34 (August 1927): 185.

[70] Thomas Sowell, "Radical Chic is Vicious," *Psychology Today* 6 (February 1973): 41. For examples of this point of view, see Harry Edwards, *Black Students* (New York: Free Press, 1970), and Nathan Hare, *Black Anglo-Saxons* (New York: Marzani & Munsell, 1965).

fought against racial discrimination on their campuses. Thomas W. Young, a black freshman at New York University, reflected the prevailing attitude when he insisted that it was "essential . . . to keep striking back at every injustice and mistreatment. . . . If New York University knows that for every offense there is a strong organization ready to 'strike back' she will not be so inconsiderate in her actions. She is fully capable of paying the price each time, it is true, but she will not be willing to pay if she knows that it will be exacted every time."[71]

Most white colleges refused to admit black students, and those that allowed Negroes to matriculate discriminated in one way or another. The president of Dartmouth College noted that blacks on his campus were usually treated as pariahs, and the registrar at Occidental College candidly explained that he did not encourage blacks "because . . . there are so few that they do not find it congenial and it usually means unhappiness to them." The president of Ohio State further explained to one prospective black engineer that although there was "no objection to your coming to the Ohio State University and entering any course for which you are qualified, . . . the sentiment north of the Ohio River seems to be so persistent against the Negro in skilled labor that I doubt very much whether an educated Negro has a fair show . . . in this part of the country."[72]

Despite the difficulties, small numbers of blacks continued to matriculate at northern colleges and universities. Only at Oberlin College, which had an historic association with the abolitionist movement, did blacks constitute as much as 4 percent of the student body. The University of Kansas, the state institution that probably led all others in terms of black students and alumni, counted only 175 blacks

[71] Thomas W. Young to Walter White, 21 January 1927, NAACP Files.
[72] W. E. B. Du Bois, "The Year in Negro Education, 1930," *Crisis* 37 (August 1930): 262–263; "Colleges and Their Graduates in 1914," *Crisis* 8 (July 1914): 129, 132.

in a student population of more than 5,000. Ohio State, Michigan, Pittsburgh, Temple, Indiana, Illinois, and New York University all enrolled a few score of black students, and several of the elite private colleges admitted talented black individuals.[73]

These blacks were denied practically every right except that of attending classes. At Kansas, for example, Athletic Director F. C. Allen insisted that blacks and whites should "not . . . play together in games of physical contact or combat." Even if Allen had felt differently, it is not likely that Kansas would have fielded black athletes, for the University of Missouri and the University of Oklahoma, sister members of the Missouri Valley Conference and schools that barred Negroes from their campuses, insisted on a "gentleman's agreement" that no Negro should play in any conference contest.[74]

These gentlemen's agreements were a thorn in the side of the few black athletes who represented northern colleges in the 1920s. Some schools, to be sure, loyally stood by their black student-athletes. Rutgers, for instance, informed the University of West Virginia that it would have to "play us with Paul Robeson or not at all." When Missouri objected to two blacks who were scheduled to play for Southern California in the 1924 Rose Bowl the Californians told the Missourians that if they did not like it they could return home with no expenses paid.[75]

[73] W. E. Bigglestone, "Oberlin College and the Negro Student, 1865–1940," *Journal of Negro History* 56 (July 1971): 198; Ernest H. Lindley to W. E. B. Du Bois, 11 December 1930, WEBD Papers; "College Negro American," pp. 85ff.

[74] F. C. Allen, quoted in Marcet Haldeman-Julius, "What the Negro Students Endure in Kansas," *Haldeman-Julius Monthly* 7 (January 1926): 150; Loren Miller, "The Unrest Among Negro Students: Kansas University," *Crisis* 34 (August 1927): 187–188; Haldeman-Julius, "What Negro Students Endure," p. 149.

[75] Cosmopolitan Club to Giles L. Courtney, 24 October 1929, NAACP Files; Haldeman-Julius, "What Negro Students Endure," pp. 149–150.

In other instances, however, integrated universities acceded to the demands of segregated schools. Thus coach Chick Meehan of New York University benched his best halfback, a black named Dave Myers, on the eve of a Yankee Stadium game against the University of Georgia. The Georgians exulted, "Even the most powerful binoculars could not discern the nigger in the grid pile" and congratulated coach Meehan for inventing "such a terrible injury—a damaged acromiclavicular ligament—to meet such a delicate emergency." Columnist Heywood Broun, on the other hand, characterized Meehan as "the gutless coach of a gutless college." The NAACP entered into protracted but ultimately unsuccessful negotiations to persuade New York University to renounce these shameful gentlemen's agreements.[76]

Another major problem, at Kansas and elsewhere, was the exclusion of blacks from the mainstream of social life on campus. Kansas and most other universities barred blacks from the dances, glee clubs, literary societies, dramatic associations, and ROTC—all of which partook of social life. Most schools also followed Kansas's example in refusing to permit blacks to live in the dormitories, although a few, including the University of Chicago, allowed men to live in university housing. The Pan-Hellenic leagues generally refused to recognize black sororities and fraternities (one of the first of which, Alpha Phi Alpha, was founded at Cornell in 1905). In one extraordinary instance, when a colored sorority achieved the highest scholastic average at Colorado Teachers College, the Greek council refused to award the customary cup and instead abolished the honor.[77]

At Kansas the greatest controversies resulted from the

[76] There is extensive correspondence on the Dave Meyers case in the NAACP Files, Autumn 1929; the quotations are from undated newspaper clippings in these files.

[77] Haldeman-Julius, "What Negro Students Endure," *passim*; Benjamin Mays, *Born to Rebel* (New York: Charles Scribner's Sons, 1971), p. 65; *Crisis* 37 (October 1930): 354.

segregation of semipublic facilities on the campus. University authorities promoted an informal arrangement that allowed blacks and whites to mingle in one-third of the cafeteria while reserving the remaining two-thirds for the exclusive use of whites. Chancellor Ernest H. Lindley explained that many whites would not patronize the cafeteria unless they were protected against black intrusions. "We have to make [the cafeteria] pay," and he urged blacks to adopt a policy of "voluntary segregation." Most black students evidently kept their distance, but Lindley complained that there was a "small minority" that demanded "the rapid and complete obliteration of any race distinction." These blacks "insisted on sitting uninvited at tables where there were white students." Lindley declared that "the result was the rapid diminution of white patronage."[78]

Similarly, Benjamin Mays reported that at the University of Chicago,

> Most Southern students, and some Northern students, would not eat at the same table with Negroes. Negro students therefore took great delight in increasing the physical activity of the prejudiced. In the university Commons . . . the service was cafeteria style, so that persons went through the line, selected food, and sat wherever they chose or where there was space. Those persons who would not eat at a table with Negroes were soon spotted. Many times I saw white men and white women, halfway through their meals, take up plates, silver, and glassware and move to a table where there were no Negroes. Some of us took pleasure in plaguing these people by deliberately seating ourselves at a table where some white person had fled to escape eating with Negroes.[79]

In addition to efforts to promote informal segregation, the authorities at Kansas enforced separation of the races in a number of facilities. Although no white student could

[78] Lindley to Du Bois, 11 December 1930.
[79] Mays, *Born to Rebel*, p. 65.

318

graduate from the university without knowing how to swim, the faculty of the physical education department voted in 1925 to prohibit black students from using the university's pool. Though blacks were permitted to sit wherever they wished at concerts for which no admission was charged, the faculty in dramatic arts segregated blacks on the extreme right of the balcony for all concerts for which tickets were sold. The university feared that "mutual discourtesies and even serious trouble might arise" if it did not maintain separate lounges in the Memorial Building. Women's rest rooms were segregated because, according to Chancellor Lindley, "Whenever colored girls use the rest rooms considerably the white girls make no protest but simply abandon these rooms to the colored girls." The fear of white boycotts also haunted merchants in the town of Lawrence, where blacks were generally refused service in first-class restaurants, hotels, and theaters.[80]

Given their small numbers and relative powerlessness, blacks could not change these discriminatory policies in the 1920s; but they did not acquiesce in silence. In the best tradition of agitators who protest against wrong and hold up a standard around which a later generation can rally, the blacks of the 1920s knew there would be no early end to discrimination—nevertheless they condemned racism and demanded equal opportunities.

In a number of ways blacks tested the legality of the prevailing color line. In Kansas they persuaded the legislature to establish a special committee to investigate the situation at the university. When university officials candidly admitted that they were discriminating on the basis of race, blacks demanded that the state's attorney general enforce the equal rights provision of the Kansas constitution. Kansas student groups, led by black Loren Miller in the 1920s and by white Wray Choate in the 1930s, then organized a pro-

[80] Haldeman-Julius, "What Negro Students Endure," *passim*; Miller, "Unrest Among Negro Students," pp. 187–188; Lindley to Du Bois, 11 December 1930.

tracted campaign "looking to the wiping out of the various discriminations in Kansas University." Yet Chancellor Lindley insisted that he was "not afraid of the courts or of publicity" and declared that "the University is a white school, built by white money for white students. If we want to get tough about it the Board of Regents could meet tomorrow and pass a ruling to exclude all out-of-state Negroes." As late as 1936, NAACP counsel Thurgood Marshall was urging Gov. Alfred M. Landon to "enforce the laws of your state."[81]

Meanwhile, students at New York University approached the NAACP with requests for legal aid in the fight against discrimination on their campus. The NAACP publicized the situation, threatened legal action, and got the university to promise to mend its ways. Yet discrimination persisted; the only change was in the official rhetoric. At about the same time, interracial clubs were organized at several colleges and universities, including Chicago, Ohio State, and Barnard. Students at the University of Illinois went to court to test the legality of segregation in the restaurants of Urbana. Coming at a time when white supremacy was the American orthodoxy and when the Supreme Court had endorsed the separate-but-equal doctrine, the suit was doomed to failure.[82]

Seeing no hope in legal redress, black and white members

[81] Roy Wilkins, memorandum to Charles Houston, 29 October 1935, NAACP Files; Report of the Kansas University Council of Race Relations, 17 May 1935, NAACP Files; Kansas Legislature, *Journal of the House*, 5 March 1935, pp. 2–4; C. A. Franklin to Walter White, 5 September 1935; Ernest H. Lindley, quoted in Report of the Kansas University Council of Race Relations, 17 May 1935, NAACP Files; Thurgood Marshall to Alfred M. Landon, 16 November 1936, NAACP Files.

[82] There is extensive correspondence on the situation at New York University in the NAACP Files, 1926–1929; Herbert Aptheker, "The Negro College Student in the 1920s," *Science and Society* 33 (Spring 1969): 165–166; *Pittsburgh Courier*, 4 July 1925; *Crisis* 37 (August 1930): 264; *St. Louis Argus*, 25 November 1927.

of the Negro-Caucasian Club at the University of Michigan took direct action against segregated restaurants in Ann Arbor. In what must have been some of the earliest sit-ins, "They simply strolled into a restaurant and . . . just sat at a table and waited." Of course they were not served. The remarkable thing is not that the protests were unsuccessful but that so many students protested against racial discrimination.[83]

Conditions at Oberlin College were not so oppressive as those at the major state universities. Oberlin had been an antislavery stronghold and was, in the words of Du Bois, "the great pioneer in the work of blotting out the color-line in colleges." Nevertheless, egalitarians of the early twentieth century were on the defensive even at Oberlin. Faculty members told Kelly Miller in 1913 that "it was impossible . . . to uphold old Oberlin's ideals because of student prejudice." President Henry Churchill King explained that "the attitude of the students toward the colored question as a whole is merely representative of the attitude of the whole North toward the question. Of course they are not zealous advocates of equal rights for Negroes as were the early students of the years when Oberlin first took her stand. . . . Our present students . . . are representative of the northern homes from which they come."[84]

The rising tide of color prejudice manifested itself at Oberlin in several minor but significant episodes. In the 1880s authorities had to counsel whites who refused to eat at the same tables with blacks. In the first decade of the twentieth century the Alpha Zeta and Phi Delta literary societies refused to admit blacks because, as one society man

[83] Oakley C. Johnson, "The Negro-Caucasian Club," *Negro History Bulletin* 33 (February 1970): 35–41.

[84] W. E. B. Du Bois and Augustus Granville Dill, eds., *The College-Bred Negro American* (Atlanta University Publication, No. 15, 1910), p. 41; Bigglestone, "Oberlin College and the Negro," p. 209; Henry Churchill King, quoted in *Cleveland Plain Dealer*, 20 September 1910.

explained, "the presence of a colored man in our ranks would for many of us spoil utterly the social side of society life. . . . Few of us would have been able to give him the glad hand of fellowship and social equality which would have been his due if admitted." Oberlin's integrated athletic teams frequently encountered difficulties with prejudiced innkeepers. At first the teams insisted on staying at inferior hotels when first-class accommodations could not be secured for black team members. In 1910, however, one coach declared that "the white members of athletic teams don't feel as if they should put up at second-rate hotels just to stick with the negroes." Thereafter black athletes occasionally had to make their own arrangements. "Of course it is humiliating for the negro to get out and shift for himself," the coach admitted, "but it is the only way out of a difficulty."[85]

The most dangerous manifestation of the rising tide of white racism at Oberlin occurred in 1919–1920, when the acting dean of women, Frances Hosford, gave her support to a few white students who were trying to discourage black girls from living in college dormitories. The college had never been able to provide sufficient dormitory space for all its students; almost all the men lived off-campus in private rooms, while the women were housed in seven dormitories and twenty-eight privately managed boardinghouses. Beginning in 1919 Oberlin introduced a "lot" system for awarding places in the dormitories and boardinghouses. Those who had the luck of the draw were given first choice for accommodations, and a few black girls received title to some of the most desirable rooms. Some whites objected to this and persuaded Dean Hosford to tell the blacks that they were pushing their way into social circles where they were not welcome and were showing a lack of confidence in their own race by refusing to room together in a separate

[85] Bigglestone, "Oberlin College and the Negro," pp. 200, 205–206; Du Bois and Dill, *College-Bred Negro*, p. 43.

boardinghouse. As often was the case in situations of this sort, Dean Hosford enjoyed the vocal support of a few local blacks who stood to profit by operating segregated boardinghouses that bore the college's seal of approval.[86]

Dean Hosford had not counted on the resourceful opposition of black Beulah Terrell, the daughter of Mary Church Terrell, one of Oberlin's most prominent alumnae. Although Terrell admitted that "some of us had really wavered a little and were inclined to be persuaded by Dean Hosford's argument," she rallied her fellow blacks to the point where they felt "very much more like sticking it out and insisting for our rights." Terrell also enlisted the support of the NAACP's William Pickens, who was determined that discrimination should "not be allowed to come to Oberlin without exhaustion of every effort to prevent it." "In the name of *democracy* what are we coming to if a reactionary sentiment like that should ever be allowed to have its way at Oberlin." The white girls who complained to Dean Hosford needed "broadening and democratizing. They need development of the sense of justice. They do not need to be pandered to."[87]

Oberlin's President King agreed with Pickens, and the black girls were admitted to the dormitories of their choice. Some fourteen white girls then moved out of the dormitories, and Dean Hosford explained that "The evolution of dormitory life has made the relation there social to an extent for which there is no precedent in our earlier history. . . . [Some whites] do not want social relations with the colored race, and they do not feel it to be a duty." Of all predominantly white American colleges, Oberlin came the closest to practicing racial equality, but discrimination per-

[86] Bigglestone, "Oberlin College and the Negro," pp. 207–211; Beulah Terrell to William Pickens, 29 April 1919, NAACP Files.

[87] Terrell to Pickens, 29 April 1919; Pickens to Frances J. Hosford, 1 May 1919, NAACP Files; Pickens to Harry E. Davis, 1 May 1919, NAACP Files.

sisted even there. As late as 1940 dormitory directors objected if they were asked to take more than two black girls per dormitory.[88]

Harvard's President A. Lawrence Lowell touched off the most publicized college discrimination controversy of the 1920s when he simultaneously barred Negroes from the freshman dormitories and inaugurated a quota system for Jewish students. Lowell's rationale was doubtless complex, but he appears to have been motivated essentially by a desire not to offend white racists and to maintain Harvard's aristocratic tradition. The exclusion of blacks was relatively easy to explain: Residence in the freshman dormitories had recently been made compulsory, Lowell noted, and "we have not thought it possible to compel men of different races to reside together. . . . We owe to the colored man the same opportunities for education that we do to the white man; but we do not owe it to him to force him and the white into social relations that are not, or may not be, mutually congenial."[89]

It was more difficult to explain the limitation of Jews. Lowell claimed that "anti-Semitic feeling is increasing, and it grows in proportion to the increase in the number of Jews." Behind this heightened ethnocentrism lay the fear that admission of large numbers of Jews somehow threatened the dominance of Harvard's established tradition. Many of the Jewish students of the early twentieth century were poor, of east-European extraction, and extraordinarily competitive in the classroom while withdrawing from social and athletic life. They were said to "live at home, eat a pocket lunch on the college campus, and leave the univer-

[88] Beulah Terrell to Mary White Ovington, 15 May 1919, NAACP Files; Bigglestone, "Oberlin College and the Negro," p. 211.

[89] A. Lawrence Lowell to Roscoe Conkling Bruce, quoted in *New York Age*, 20 January 1923; Lowell to Lewis Gannett, 19 June 1922, Papers of Moorfield Storey, Library of Congress (hereafter cited as Storey Papers); James Weldon Johnson to Lowell, 11 January 1923, NAACP Files.

sity grounds to earn the money for their tuition by night work. Many retain the gregariousness born of life in the Pale, and remain only half-assimilated." There were some Harvard men who believed that these new immigrants endangered the essential Harvard tradition—the flavor that stamped Harvard men as such, in no way to be confused with Yale men, Princeton men, or any other of the many academic breeds. Old Grads allegedly sent their sons to Harvard to attain this flavor, rather than any mere scholarly training, and there were those who claimed that the masters of the institution owed it "to themselves and to the alumni and to everyone else revering the name of Harvard, to maintain the conditions under which this flavor may be imparted."[90]

Summarizing this argument, the *New Republic* noted,

> The Harvard flavor can be imparted successfully to men of any race or religion. . . . But it is not to be denied that the flavor is most easily imparted to men of the old New England stock. Others take it effectively only when they are well immersed in social groupings of the original character. They must therefore be present in relatively small numbers. . . . Five Jews to the hundred will necessarily undergo prompt assimilation. Ten Jews to the hundred might assimilate. But twenty or thirty—no. They would form a state within a state. They would cease to take an active part in the general life of the college. . . . What they got out of Harvard might be worth their time and effort, but it would not be the priceless Harvard flavor. Thus it appears that, in the interest of the Jews as well as in the interest of the Gentiles, the number of Jews ought to be kept below the saturation point. Better one true Jewish Harvard man than ten mere Jewish scholars.[91]

[90] A. Lawrence Lowell, quoted in *Library Digest* 74 (8 July 1922): 28–29; *Nation* 114 (14 June 1922): 708; *New Republic* 31 (16 August 1922): 322–323.
[91] *New Republic* 31 (16 August 1922); 322–323.

President Lowell's racist policies were ultimately repudiated by Harvard's board of overseers. The overseers did not reach their decision without prompting, however, for thousands of students, professors, and alumni organized to protest against the intrusion of racism at Fair Harvard. James Weldon Johnson was undoubtedly correct when he noted that "President Lowell never for a moment imagined that he was going to raise such a hornet's nest around his ears." Du Bois was uplifted by the protest. "Deep as is the shame and humiliation of Harvard's recent surrender to the Bourbon South," he declared, "the spirited and whole-souled response that it has evinced is perhaps the most heartening sign of sanity on the race problem that has happened in fifty years. Not a single person of importance has yet dared to defend Lowell. . . ." Black and white liberals were convinced that Lowell had taken "an evil and indefensible position which, like a snake, must be scotched at once . . . or else it will, with its venomous bite, poison our entire educational system." Lowell's racist policy was thought to be "as bad for what it portends as for what it immediately inaugurates."[92]

Although it was generally acknowledged that Lowell's Jewish and Negro policies were fundamentally related, most blacks felt that their problem was more manageable than that of the Jews. Lewis Gannett, an editor of the *Nation* who circulated an alumni petition on behalf of the blacks, explained, "The question of discrimination against one class of students after their admission seems to have a much more certain answer than the question of limitation of enrollment."[93]

[92] *New York Times*, 10 April 1923; James Weldon Johnson to Butler R. Wilson, 27 January 1923, NAACP Files; W. E. B. Du Bois, "Harvard," *Crisis* 25 (March 1923): 199; *Messenger* 5 (March 1923): 621.

[93] Lewis Gannett to Moorfield Storey, 2 August 1922, Storey Papers; William B. Hixson, Jr., *Moorfield Storey and the Abolitionist Tradition* (New York: Oxford University Press, 1972), p. 120.

Blacks insisted that, as Raymond Pace Alexander put it, "no half-dozen men picked at random among the Harvard freshman class could present any better family history or training" than the six blacks who had been excluded from the dormitories. Bertrand C. Bland and William J. Knox, Jr., were from eminently respectable New England families; Cecil Blue was the son of a prominent Washington physician; Pritchett Klugh was the son of a distinguished Boston clergyman; Edward W. Wilson was a second generation Harvard man and the son of a noted Boston attorney; and Roscoe Conkling Bruce, Jr., was the son of a Harvard honors graduate and the grandson of a United States senator. Lowell's discrimination against these thoroughly acculturated blacks struck at the very foundation of the middle-class ethos, and this may explain the fervor with which Harvard's president was condemned by the black and white bourgeoisie.[94]

The *New York Amsterdam News* noted that Lowell's discrimination against young Bruce "should convince all of us that our success is not dependent upon individual attainment. The younger Bruce . . . is the grandson of Blanche K. Bruce, former Register of the United States Treasury and United States Senator from Mississippi from 1875 to 1881. His father is a distinguished educator. But to President Lowell and to thousands like him the younger Bruce's distinguished ancestry and preparation are as nothing when placed alongside of the fact that he is a Negro."[95]

The campaign against Harvard's exclusion of Negroes from the freshman dormitories began on the campus in the spring of 1922 when the black students, led by upperclassman Edwin B. Jordain, Jr., at that time the world's champion broad jumper, made a special appeal to President Lowell. This was to no avail, and editor Monroe Trotter of the *Boston Guardian*, a black alumnus who fondly recalled

[94] Raymond Pace Alexander, "Voices from Harvard's Own Negroes," *Opportunity* 1 (March 1923): 29.
[95] *New York Amsterdam News*, 17 January 1923.

"the democracy that I enjoyed at dear old Harvard," then publicized the matter. During the summer Moorfield Storey, Robert Benchley, Lewis Gannett, and four other white alumni circulated a petition among two hundred Harvard men. Altogether some 145 graduates endorsed a statement expressing dismay that "the long tradition of the College as regards Negroes has been broken." It was not sufficient, the graduates insisted, for President Lowell to say that southern men did not want to live in the same dormitories with blacks. Southern men who came to Cambridge could not rightfully expect the college to surrender its "Northern ideas of democracy" and its "Harvard ideals of justice." One graduate expressed the prevailing spirit when he added, "If any young man should decline to come because of his prejudice against some possible comrade I should say that the college was well rid of so narrow-minded a youth."[96]

In their private correspondence many Harvard men explained their reasons for opposing Lowell's racist policies. George R. Nutter noted that "the hope that individual merit will eventually receive its proper consideration lies at the very basis of what our institutions are trying to accomplish. . . . If a man is found worthy to enter Harvard College, he is worthy to stand on his merits without any of the artificial distinctions of race or color." Roscoe Conkling Bruce, Sr., admitted that "the wind just now is blowing in the direction of reaction," but he insisted that it did not behoove "a great center of enlightenment to be caught, like some paltry straw, in the gust." Moorfield Storey feared that "if Harvard College caters to this unchristian prejudice of some people against Negroes and other people against Jews . . . , it will be responsible for more mischief in this country and the policy will do more injury to the College than those who

[96] Alexander, "Voices from Harvard's," pp. 28–29; Stephen R. Fox, *The Guardian of Boston* (New York: Atheneum, 1970), pp. 261–263; Open Letter to the President and Fellows of Harvard College, attached to Lewis Gannett to Moorfield Storey, 2 June 1922, Storey Papers; *Nation* 116 (31 January 1923): 112.

favor it can possibly conceive." Congressman Hamilton Fish declared that racial discrimination was not consistent with "the spirit of democracy . . . the spirit of New England . . . the spirit of Harvard."[97]

John Jay Chapman pointed out that Southerners were quite accustomed to living in close proximity to blacks.

> If any white parent tells President Lowell that he cannot bear the thought of his son's sleeping in a room which abuts on the same quadrangle with a Negro's room, or eating in the same dining-hall with a Negro, that parent deceives Mr. Lowell. What the Southern parent demands is that some stigma be put upon the Negro. He wishes Harvard to hang out a flag discriminating against the black man.[98]

This was exactly the point. The *Nation* noted that "Harvard, so long as it follows President Lowell's lead in this matter, is accepting and preaching the Southern doctrine that every man with Negro blood in his veins is inferior to every all-white man." The *New York Evening Post* claimed that Lowell's policy negated the very reason for creating the freshman dormitories: "If the policy of compulsory residence in the freshman halls is to be justified at all, it is precisely because it applies to all freshmen. To say that all white freshmen or all Protestant freshmen or all native American freshmen shall live together, but that all other freshmen shall be barred from the freshmen dormitories, is to make the policy of compulsory residence ludicrous." The *Harvard Alumni Bulletin* observed that "for Harvard to deny to colored men a privilege it accords to whites ap-

[97] George R. Nutter, quoted in Lewis Gannett to Moorfield Storey, 26 July 1922, Storey Papers; Roscoe Conkling Bruce telegram to *Brooklyn Eagle*, 13 January 1923, NAACP Files; Storey to Julian W. Mack, 6 June 1922, quoted in Hixson, *Moorfield Storey*, p. 120; Hamilton Fish to A. Lawrence Lowell, quoted in *New York Age*, 20 January 1923.

[98] John Jay Chapman, quoted in *Nation* 116 (31 January 1923): 112.

pears inevitably as a reversal of policy, if not a positive disloyalty to a principle for which the university has hitherto taken an open and unshaken stand."[99]

With the press and the alumni outspoken in their criticism, President Lowell was placed in an untenable position, especially since he had unwisely neglected to discuss the situation with Harvard's board of overseers. "It seems to be a pity that the matter ever came up in this way," wrote overseer Franklin D. Roosevelt. "There were certainly many colored students in Cambridge when we were there and no question ever arose." In January 1923 the overseers held a special meeting to discuss Lowell's racial policies, and a faculty committee was appointed to study the matter. This committee later reported that the principle of "equal opportunity for all, regardless of race and religion," was an essential part of Harvard's tradition. The professors warned that any "covert device to eliminate those deemed racially or socially undesirable" would be interpreted as "a dangerous surrender of traditional ideals." The overseers thereupon unanimously overruled Lowell and banned discrimination for reasons of race or religion. Affirming the Negro's right to equal opportunity on the campus, the overseers declared that no man should be excluded from the dormitories "by reason of his color."[100]

Unfortunately the resolution of the dormitory controversy did not usher in an era of interracial brotherhood at Harvard. Members of the various ethnic groups still tended to congregate together in search of familiar company, and the exclusive private clubs barred blacks, Jews, and low-status Gentiles. There were, in addition, nagging problems

[99] *Nation* 116: 112; *New York Post*, quoted in *Literary Digest* 76 (3 February 1923): 32–33; *Harvard Alumni Bulletin* 25 (1922–1923): 830.

[100] Franklin D. Roosevelt to R. S. Wallace, 7 February 1923, quoted in Arthur M. Schlesinger, Jr., *The Age of Roosevelt: The Politics of Upheaval* (Boston: Houghton Mifflin Co., 1960), p. 696; *New York Times*, 10 April 1923.

that followed from the Harvard Medical School's relations with nearby obstetrical clinics. Harvard required its medical students to handle a certain number of obstetrical cases, but problems inevitably arose because many patients at the clinics refused to accept the services of black students. Consequently, it had been customary for blacks to arrange for referrals from the Negro physicians of Boston and Cambridge. This undoubtedly involved racial discrimination, in that black students were treated differently from whites. Black egalitarians inevitably challenged the propriety of this practice.

A case in point occurred in 1905, when a young black by the name of E. D. Brown refused, in the words of Harvard's medical dean, "to accommodate himself to these circumstances which are beyond the jurisdiction of the School, and which other colored students have heretofore cheerfully accepted." Brown acknowledged that Harvard could not force patients to accept an unwelcome student intern, but he demanded "the chance to get the cases if I could." He asked the dean "to put it up to the patients and leave me to face whatever difficulty might arise. . . ." He thought it was far better that he be snubbed by prejudiced patients than that these insults should be used by Harvard as a justification for racial discrimination.[101]

Harvard was not alone in this regard. The University of Vermont also discovered that "when it comes to the matter of clinical facilities, some white patients are not entirely willing that colored men have charge of their cases. This situation we are not responsible for and in fairness to colored students, we urge that they attend where they can avail themselves of clinical facilities supplied by their own race." Some schools went even further: The Marquette Medical School barred Negroes on the ground that "we

[101] W. L. Richardson to Moorfield Storey, 8 December 1905, Storey Papers; E. D. Brown to Storey, 31 October 1905, Storey Papers; William Pickens to Roscoe Conkling Bruce, 15 January 1923, NAACP Files

have found it exceedingly difficult to place colored students as internes."[102]

The University of Pennsylvania applied this rationale to teachers as well; it refused to allow black education majors to do their practice teaching in the integrated high schools of Philadelphia, although it did place a few students in the segregated schools of Wilmington, Delaware. At the University of Kansas blacks were segregated in both practice teaching and clinical work. Although Kansas law prohibited racial discrimination, the dean of the Medical School segregated the university's clinic "in order that the patients from Missouri and Oklahoma might not have the displeasure of the presence of physicians and nurses of color." An incensed Thurgood Marshall declared that he knew of no other case where "an officer of the state admits very glibly that he is violating the laws of the state and shows an attitude of defiance, rather than an attitude of willingness to obey the law. . . . It does seem a disgrace that this form of discrimination should persist in the state university of a state which prohibits discrimination by law."[103]

Given the prevalence of white racism on the integrated campuses, black students inevitably associated with one another in separate clubs and societies. Yet many did so with grave reservations. One student at Columbia declined to list his "race" on a form that requested this information "to assist in congenial groupings in the halls." He had never chosen his associates on the basis of their race, he said, and "it is indeed a sad commentary on American education when university students must be grouped or segregated according to race in order to be congenial."[104]

[102] Guy Bailey to George E. Whitney, 28 September 1926, NAACP Files; M. L. Melzer to F. L. Allen, 26 March 1930, NAACP Files.

[103] Sadie T. Mossell to W. E. B. Du Bois, 2 November 1919, NAACP Files; W. R. Wahl, quoted in Kansas Legislature, *Journal of the House*, 5 March 1925, pp. 2–4; Thurgood Marshall to Charles W. French, 16 November 1936, NAACP Files.

[104] *Philadelphia Tribune*, 5 September 1925.

In the most celebrated "voluntary segregation" controversy of the 1920s, the officers of the Cheyney Training School for Teachers were subjected to indignant criticism when they urged the Pennsylvania legislature to shore up their financially troubled black school. The leaders of the local NAACP feared that this would be a step toward legitimizing segregation in the Keystone State. They denounced the effort to make Cheyney "a perfect haven of refuge to unwanted and mistreated Negro pupils." "Our whole race might as well leave America because we are on the whole largely unwanted and mistreated!" the NAACP declaimed. "We are all American citizens, and we stand for and demand equal and identical school opportunities, both to learn and to teach, requiring no special training, demanding no special privileges, permitting no segregation or discrimination."[105]

The Cheyney School had been established in 1833 with a bequest from a Philadelphia Quaker named Richard Humphreys. In 1920 the school was accredited as a standard normal school for training Negro teachers, but its Quaker board of managers could not meet the school's growing financial responsibilities. Rather than close the school or restrict operations, the board "preferred to see the school continue on a solvent basis, guided by other hands." It therefore commenced negotiations looking toward "transferring this institution to the State, to be maintained as a regular part of our normal school system for the training of teachers."[106]

In 1922 these negotiations were brought to a successful conclusion, as the state board of education paid $75,000 for the purchase of the school plant and assumed responsibility for the management of the institution. Pennsylvania's Gov-

[105] G. Edward Dickerson and William Lloyd Imes, "The Cheyney Training School," *Crisis* 26 (May 1923): 18, 21.

[106] Carline F. Conyers, "A History of the Cheyney State Teachers College, 1837–1951," (Ed.D. diss., New York University, 1960), pp. 258–260, 265–267, and *passim*.

ernor Sproul, a Quaker and a personal confidant of some
of Cheyney's managers, then used his influence to secure
the appointment of Quakers to all but two places on the reconstituted board of trustees. The officers of the school
were pleased with this arrangement and concluded, "Under
State ownership and control, the school merely continues
the work it has always done, but on a stronger financial and
professional basis."[107]

Leslie Pinckney Hill, who served as principal and president of Cheyney from 1913 to 1951, was largely responsible
for forging the school's alliance with the Commonwealth of
Pennsylvania. A Phi Beta Kappa graduate of Harvard,
Pinckney Hill had published volumes of poetry and biography and had taught for nine years at Tuskegee and at the
Manassas Industrial Institute in Virginia. He also had definite ideas about Negro education. He avoided the controversy between the advocates of vocational training and the
partisans of academic education, but he insisted that, given
the persistence of racial discrimination, blacks had no
choice but to make their schools as efficient as possible. In
his judgment, it was "not . . . the part of wisdom to set up
. . . a general hue and cry about segregation." Negroes
should instead use segregation to make the finest possible
black institutions.[108]

Rather than subject sensitive black youths to inevitable
insults at integrated colleges, Hill encouraged them to
matriculate at black schools where they would be exposed
to "the development of our native Negro music, the teaching of Negro history and achievement, and the cultivation
of a wholesome race pride and race initiative." He was convinced that "Negroes can best develop themselves in their
own institutions. . . . It is only when Negroes can see their
people in their very best condition, and can have the stimu-
lus that comes from their own inspiring leaders, that they

[107] Ibid.

[108] Leslie Pinckney Hill, "The Cheyney Training School for Teachers," *Crisis* 25 (April 1923): 253.

334

can expect to develop self-reliance, skill and habits that will insure a lasting and worthy contribution by their group to American society." He viewed Cheyney as "a voluntarily segregated school, existing for the purpose of . . . training Negro teachers to minister to the special needs of Negro children." He expected Cheyney's students to "take themselves and their work seriously, to have an intelligent appreciation of the conditions of the Negro race in America, and to be earnestly desirous of returning to their people as effective missionaries."[109]

Although Cheyney probably could not have survived without state aid, many articulate black Pennsylvanians opposed the new arrangement for maintaining a tax-supported, segregated teachers college. The NAACP's Philadelphia branch joined with several prominent individuals in endorsing a statement that "Cheyney as a private school was all right; but . . . the moment [institutions] become *public* . . . they should have no special race, color, or creed in view." The NAACP noted that the state had created thirteen normal school districts, with "one state normal school in each district," and it claimed that state authorities would not have financed Cheyney as a rival to nearby West Chester State Teachers College if it had not been understood that Cheyney was to continue as a "school for Negroes."[110]

The state's major black newspapers joined in the attack: the *Philadelphia Tribune* charged that the new arrangement had been fostered "by those who think more of personal gain and glory than of the future of their children." And the *Pittsburgh Courier* characterized Pinckney Hill's appeal "not to kill a colored institution" as "the old tactics of the scuttle fish, who squirts out black juice in order to becloud the waters."[111]

[109] Conyers, "History of Cheyney," pp. 1–2, 235–236, 266–267, 271–272, 287.

[110] Dickerson and Imes, "Cheyney Training School," pp. 18–21.

[111] *Philadelphia Tribune*, 18 April 1925; *Pittsburgh Courier*, 28 March 1925.

G. Edward Dickerson and William Lloyd Imes voiced the general alarm:

> Cheyney, as constituted, is but the legal beginning of a complete segregated school system for the State of Pennsylvania. For, when the State has spent its money for the purpose of making segregated teachers, it will not hesitate to spend the necessary money to make the segregated schools, and will not hesitate to drive the colored children from the graded schools that are established, into dislocated and ill-equipped buildings where one colored teacher will be compelled to teach all of the primary and grammar school grades. When we have the bird we buy the cage and its appendages.[112]

No one abhorred racial segregation more than W. E. B. Du Bois. Du Bois acknowledged that Cheyney, as a public school, was required to admit qualified applicants of all races, and he noted that a few Negroes were enrolled in the state's other normal schools. Yet the editor of the *Crisis* was not inclined to dissemble on the question of racial separation. Rather than take cover "behind legal quibbles," he admitted that Cheyney was a *de facto* segregated school, and he condemned the white people of Pennsylvania for conspiring "to segregate all colored teacher training in the state at Cheyney, where . . . colored teachers will be educated and sent out for use in the growing system of segregated colored public schools." Pennsylvania law prohibited this segregation, to be sure, but the administrative authorities had devised a system of *de facto* separation, and black teachers were restricted to all-Negro schools. Du Bois claimed it was "the plain duty of all true Americans . . . to oppose this spread of segregation in the public schools," but he knew that "segregated schools are on the increase in the North and there is no doubt but what we shall see a larger

[112] Dickerson and Imes, "Cheyney Training School," pp. 20–21.

and larger number of them as the flood tide of Southern Negro migration increases."[113]

Du Bois believed that segregation would lead to calamity. "Education in the public schools by races or classes means the perpetuation of race and class feeling. . . . It means the establishment of group hostility in those tender years of development when prejudices tend to become 'natural' and 'instinctive.' "[114] Racial insult had prompted many Negroes to refuse all contact with whites, and Du Bois feared that this separation would eventually provoke racial chauvinism, hatred, and war. It was admittedly impossible for twelve million blacks to defeat a hundred million whites, but they could "hate the harder for their very impotence."

> Whether they migrate, die or live, can they not add the red flame of their bitter hurt to all that mounting bill of deviltry which the dark world holds against the white? No—there's no hurry; it will not happen in our day. No. But it will happen. "A day unto the Lord is as a thousand years," and even the blind can see in the segregation of the American Negro a rebirth of racial concentration, of group friction, of reciprocal hate and despising, of world war.[115]

Du Bois knew that "the demands of democracy" could not always be reconciled with "the demands of group advancement." Negroes were confronted by "a condition, not a theory." Racism was a fact of life, and, however much blacks might warn of dire impending consequences, segregation and discrimination would remain for the foreseeable

[113] W. E. B. Du Bois, "The Tragedy of 'Jim Crow,' " *Crisis* 26 (August 1923): 170–171.

[114] Ibid.

[115] W. E. B. Du Bois, "The Dilemma of the Negro," *American Mercury* 3 (October 1924): 185.

future. Thus Negroes had to do more than protest; if a Jim Crow school system were established despite their protest, there was "nothing to do but demand large appropriations, the very best teachers . . . and every effort to make the Negro school the best in the city." This was what Pinckney Hill was doing at Cheyney, and Du Bois saluted his effort. Du Bois supported the local NAACP's fight against segregation, but he refused to join the assault on Pinckney Hill. Instead he traveled to the Royal Theatre in Philadelphia and told a black audience that there was an important distinction "between what we as colored people often refer to as voluntary segregation, such as we have in our churches, and segregation enforced by custom or public opinion." Du Bois's black audience was disturbed. Some accused him of advocating segregation, and the editor of the *Crisis* presciently saw "in embryo signs of future cleavage within the Negro race as it faces this cruel paradox."[116]

Du Bois's own thought was still in flux, but he was working toward this conclusion:

> Theoretically, the Negro needs neither segregated schools nor mixed schools. What he needs is Education. What he must remember is that there is no magic either in mixed schools or in segregated schools. A mixed school with poor and unsympathetic teachers, with hostile public opinion, and no teaching of truth concerning black folk, is bad. A segregated school with ignorant placeholders, inadequate equipment, poor salaries, and wretched housing is equally bad. Other things being equal, the mixed school is the broader, more natural basis for the education of all youth. It gives wider contacts; it inspires greater self-confidence; and suppresses the inferiority com-

[116] Ibid., p. 181; Du Bois, "Tragedy of 'Jim Crow,'" p. 172; Du Bois memorandum to James Weldon Johnson, October 1924, NAACP Files; Johnson memorandum to Du Bois, 21 October 1924, NAACP Files; *Pittsburgh Courier*, 28 April 1923.

plex. But other things seldom are equal, and in that case Sympathy, Knowledge, and the Truth, outweigh all that the mixed school can offer.[117]

[117] W. E. B. Du Bois, "Does the Negro Need Separate Schools?" *Journal of Negro Education* 4 (July 1935): p. 335.

CHAPTER VIII

Conclusion

NEGROES of the 1920s were in revolt against both the paternalistic spirit and the industrial emphasis that characterized
black college education. Prompted by a growing racial consciousness and a larger ambition, black students and alumni
demanded a greater degree of control over their colleges
and a higher type of curriculum. They turned their backs
on the limited educational program of Booker T. Washington's Tuskegee Compromise and agitated for stiffer academic requirements. The *Christian Century* noted that
black students were "in full spiritual revolt against all discriminations and the invidious distinctions under which
they suffer severe limitations. . . . [The Negro student] is
standing with his eyes alight with a great race pride and
race hope, and he refuses to be any longer considered in
any category other than that of his fellow white man."[1]

Throughout the twentieth century many leaders in the
Negro rights movement have been graduates of the black
liberal arts colleges, including W. E. B. Du Bois (Fisk),
James Weldon Johnson and Walter White (Atlanta), Edward Brooke and Stokeley Carmichael (Howard), Thurgood Marshall, Archibald Grimke, and Francis Grimke
(Lincoln [Pa.]), James Farmer (Wiley), and Martin Luther
King (Morehouse). Some scholars, noting the paradox of
segregated schools having produced graduates who led the
fight against segregation, have maintained that this was an
"historical accident," that the founders of the separate black
colleges never envisioned that their students would challenge the Jim Crow system. Others have seen the civil rights

[1] *The Christian Century*, quoted in *Crisis* 30 (July 1925): 147.

movement as the culmination of the egalitarian work of northern missionaries and have maintained that the development of college-bred fighters for equal Negro rights should be seen as "a measure of the success of the educational adventure which the churches of the North launched at the close of the Civil War."[2]

This controversy over the motivation and legacy of the thousands of black and white missionaries and philanthropists can never be resolved definitively. It can be said with assurance, however, that many blacks of the 1920s believed that their colleges, in a mistaken effort to make black students acceptable to whites, were inculcating deferential habits and placing too much emphasis on vocational training for subordinate jobs. The black college rebels of the 1920s demanded self-determination so that they might develop "a class of thoroughly educated men according to modern standards."[3] Imbued with the belief that Negro colleges should develop a Talented Tenth that would lead the struggle for emancipation of the race, the black collegians demanded home rule and an elevated curriculum that would prepare them for full participation in American life. Whatever the intentions of the founders and patrons of the black colleges may have been, many black students and alumni of the 1920s were engaged in a deliberate effort to establish institutional bastions for the assault on segregation and white supremacy.

The thrust of the black college rebellions of the 1920s was chiefly integrationist. The dissident students and alumni of that time wanted to escape from the backwaters of American life and join the mainstream. No other group in America longed more eagerly for the day when the nation's racial practices would correspond with its professed ideals.

[2] Henry Allen Bullock, *A History of Negro Education in the South* (Cambridge: Harvard University Press, 1967), pp. xii–xv and *passim; Christian Century*, p. 147.

[3] W. E. B. Du Bois, "Negro Education," *Crisis* 15 (February 1918): 174.

While the black college protests of the 1920s undoubtedly elicited certain elements of racial chauvinism, Alain Locke was essentially correct when he noted in 1925, "The Negro mind reaches out as yet to nothing but American wants, American ideals. . . . The racialism of the Negro is no limitation or reservation with respect to American life. . . . The choice is not between one way for the Negro and another way for the rest, but between American institutions frustrated on the one hand and American ideals progressively fulfilled and realized on the other." Du Bois later acknowledged that during the 1920s he was "not questioning the world movement in itself. What the white world was doing, its goals and ideals, I had not doubted were quite right. What was wrong was that I and people like me and thousands of others who might have my ability and aspiration, were refused permission to be a part of this world. It was as though moving on a rushing express, my main thought was as to my relations with the other passengers on the express, not to its rate of speed and its destination."[4]

The black colleges of the 1920s promoted the mainstream middle-class culture. Black youths were taught that the patois of the lower-class ghettoes and fields was not proper English, and many folkways were deprecated as the unworthy legacy of an oppressive past. The colleges did not preserve folk culture but instead disseminated middle-class standards. Black students of the 1920s, like youths from other minority groups, were exposed to Anglo-Saxon norms and urged to become facsimile WASPS. Many students must have felt pangs of regret when they realized the extent of their estrangement from the folkways of the masses—an exaggerated version of what so many students of all races have felt when they returned from college and discovered that "you can't go home again." Whatever their reservations, however, most blacks of the 1920s saw no choice but

[4] Alain Locke, "Enter the New Negro," *Survey* 53 (1 March 1925): 632–633; W. E. B. Du Bois, *Autobiography* (New York: International Publishers, 1968), p. 156.

to surrender folkways in exchange for liberal education. James Weldon Johnson reflected the prevailing view when he recalled his classical education at Atlanta University: "I have at times thought that, in some degree, its training might have cramped and inhibited me. But generally I have felt that for me there was probably no better school in the United States."[5]

In their acculturation—their desire to be "in" not "out" with reference to American life—the rebellious black students of the 1920s resemble their counterparts of the late 1950s and early 1960s. The students participating in the early civil rights sit-ins were, it is generally acknowledged, "square and respectable . . . kids [who] only wanted their share of the middle-class American Dream." Their quarrel was with segregation and discrimination in the society at large, not with their own college curriculum, which, thanks in part to the work of the black college rebels of the 1920s, had become a standardized part of the American academic system. Until the late 1960s, most black students had "no quarrel with the learning that they were getting. . . . They understood it to be—as in fact it was—the same learning that their contemporaries in white colleges and universities were getting. And what was good enough for white folk was good enough for them."[6]

In the late 1960s and early 1970s black students at scores of colleges began to question the direction and ultimate destination of the American train. A growing number turned away from protests against discrimination in the larger society and instead demanded that their colleges be reorganized. Some of the recent black college protests have been against the modern equivalents of the tutelary discipline and second-rate education that blacks of the 1920s

[5] James Weldon Johnson, *Along This Way* (New York: Viking Compass Edition, 1968), pp. 83–84.
[6] Jack Newfield, *A Prophetic Minority* (New York: Signet Books, 1967), pp. 39–40; Saunders Redding, "The Black Youth Movement," *American Scholar* 38 (Autumn 1969): 584.

found so annoying. But most black college protests of the late 1960s and early 1970s had a decidedly separatist thrust and have been based on the belief that blacks could not make real progress until they renounced their cultural and psychological allegiance to middle-class Euro-American values and developed a unique national consciousness. According to contemporary separatists, racism is so deeply entrenched in white America that internalization of the mainstream values is tantamount to embracing racism.

It follows from this analysis that blacks must separate themselves mentally and develop autonomous standards and a distinct culture. Thus in 1968 black students at Berkeley declared, "We are not White. We do not wish to be White." Those at Howard engaged in what they called "a cultural revolution . . . a rechannelling of the student body's values toward changing Howard from a 'Negro college with white innards' to a black university relevant to the black community and its struggle." The nationwide demand for autonomous centers of black studies represented an attempt to institutionalize this separatist concern for self-definition and self-determination.[7]

As black students questioned the cultural values of the American mainstream, they became increasingly critical of college-bred middle-class Negroes who believe that equal opportunity and individual initiative are the keys to racial uplift. According to contemporary separatists, this middle-class "rise-by-merit" approach to Negro betterment "elevates individual members of the group but paradoxically, in plucking many of the strongest members of the group while failing to alter the lot of the group as a whole, weakens the collective thrust which the group might otherwise muster." All too often, it is said, the black college graduate

[7] Student statements, quoted by Andrew Billingsley, "The Black Presence in American Higher Education," in Nathan Wright, Jr., ed., *What Black Educators Are Saying* (New York: Hawthorn Books, 1970), p. 143, and Max Stanford, "Black Nationalism and the Afro-American Student," *Black Scholar* 2 (June 1971): 28.

is trying "to escape from the black community instead of returning to help build it." He has been characterized as a black Anglo-Saxon, "superpolite, particularly neat and clean, . . . affect[ing] 'white' accents" and removing himself "physically, socially, and psychologically as far away from the realities of the Black experience in America as he possibly could without doing the impossible and changing his racial heritage."[8]

Even white critics have complained that the black colleges have sifted out "the rebellious, the creative, and the alienated" and fashioned a Negro middle-class that is "extremely conservative on all issues other than racial equality, and sometimes even on that." Defining their responsibilities in terms of "a comparatively narrow, classical, campus-oriented view," complacent black educators have allegedly held themselves aloof from the impoverished black masses. More concerned with professional success than with racial uplift, these educators have failed to implement "what might loosely be called the 'land-grant' idea of public service and practical involvement in the affairs of the surrounding community."[9]

There are elements of truth in this criticism; some black graduates have immersed themselves in selfish materialism, and the colleges should have offered more technical services for Negro businessmen, more extension centers for aspiring white collar workers, and more refresher courses for middle-aged physicians. The resources of the black colleges have been extremely limited, however, and most of

[8] Nathan Hare, "What Should Be the Role of Afro-American Education in the Undergraduate Curriculum?" in John W. Blassingame, ed., *New Perspectives on Black Studies* (Urbana: University of Illinois Press, 1971), p. 12; Andrew Kopkind, "The Black Backlash," *New Statesman* 73 (26 May 1967): 708; Harry Edwards, *Black Students* (New York: Free Press, 1970), p. 13.

[9] Christopher Jencks and David Riesman, *The Academic Revolution* (Garden City, N.Y.: Doubleday & Co., 1968), p. 434. Also see Ann Jones, *Uncle Tom's Campus* (New York: Praeger, 1973).

their graduates have rendered valuable professional service
to their communities and have provided leadership during
a century of struggle for equal opportunity. Though un-
deniably middle class in their orientation, the black college
graduates have hardly been the cowering and selfish black
bourgeoisie portrayed in some radical parodies.

If today the middle-class Negro college graduates have
a bad press, it is largely because their cultural assimilation-
ism has led contemporary separatists to believe that black
collegians tamely accommodated to white supremacy. The
separatists have assumed that because the dress, manners,
diction, and goals of most black college graduates partake
of the middle-class mainstream, these blacks have been
docile Uncle Toms. Yet the disposition to think of black cultural separatists as "militants" while dismissing equal rights
integrationists as "moderates," "conservatives," or something worse has obscured the record of Negro resistance to
subordination.

The tension between cultural assimilation and alienation
has always rent the black community. The evidence of collegiate combativeness presented in this study probably will
not change the opinions of cultural nationalists who are
convinced that middle-class Negroes have been accommodating and docile, the victims of a schizoid socialization
that has left them in a state of cultural confusion and dis-
orientation. Indeed, nationalist criticism of the black middle
class may well increase, for the number of Negro college
students has grown from 15,000 largely middle-class youth
in 1927 to 814,000 in 1972. Many of these students come
straight from lower-class ghettoes and are alienated from
the style of the middle-class college.[10]

These lower-class black college students comprise an
estranged constituency that is predisposed to respond to the

[10] "Enrollment in Negro Universities and Colleges," *School and
Society* 28 (29 September 1928): 401–402; U.S. Bureau of the Census,
Statistical Abstract of the United States, 1972 (Washington, D.C.:
Government Printing Office, 1972), p. 109.

separatist gospel of alienation. Although many of these students retain aspirations for professional success, while at the same time hoping to help their people, most find it hard to compete academically with well-prepared white students and fear that they cannot survive on campus unless they create a sanctuary that is not subject to traditional academic standards. Even those who are able to make the grade recognize that successful college students must assimilate many of the Euro-American values that make them feel uncomfortable when returning to the lower-class neighborhoods whence they came. With intellectual achievement thus regarded "as elevating oneself to a higher plane and removing oneself from the black brotherhood," there has been a marked tendency for black students to withdraw from the academic mainstream and resegregate themselves culturally.[11]

The current vogue of black separatism on campus has touched off the most bitter and divisive intra-Negro debate since the controversy that pitted Booker T. Washington against W. E. B. Du Bois. While young blacks have scathingly characterized bourgeois college graduates as "the chief 'house pets' of whites for generations," middle-class spokesmen have described separatism as a rationalization for retreat. Thus Bayard Rustin, while sympathizing with poorly prepared black students who have been placed "in a difficult competitive situation," has criticized their tendency "to retreat into themselves and establish a black curriculum with separate—and lower—standards by which their performance shall be judged." Roy Wilkins has characterized separatists as escapists who "renounce 'white middle-class values' so they can refuse to be judged logically by the standards of the times in which they live. . . . [They are]

[11] William H. Grier and Price M. Cobbs, *Black Rage* (New York: Bantam Books, 1968), p. 120. Also see Henry Allen Bullock, *History of Negro Education*, chapter 11; and Martin Kilson, "The Black Experience at Harvard," *New York Times Magazine*, 2 September 1973, pp. 12–13+.

convinced of their inability to compete in the open market
with other Americans, and, accordingly, are seeking refuge
in a protective cocoon of racialism, fearful of facing the
harsh realities of the competitive society in which we
live."[12]

Cultural alienation is the trait that most distinguishes
contemporary cultural nationalists from the black college
rebels of the 1920s. While many black collegians of the
1920s had a racialist point of view and were interested in
developing racial pride, they steered clear of the separatist
nationalism of their day.[13] The black college rebels of the
1920s protested not against the prevailing culture, but
against their exclusion from it. They worked thoughtfully
and persistently to raise the academic standards of their
colleges to the level of their white counterparts. Given their
limited resources, the black collegians could not do everything that should have been done, and they wisely gave top
priority to establishing a few good colleges that would prepare a Talented Tenth to serve the Negro race and lead the
continuing struggle for equal opportunity. It was a paradox,
of course, that black professionals, trained to relieve whites
from the necessity of serving a race of pariahs, would lead
the fight for freedom. But it was no accident. Black students
and alumni had worked diligently to make their colleges
responsive to the highest aspirations of the Negro middle-
class.

[12] Edwards, *Black Students*, p. 49; Bayard Rustin, *Down the Line*
(Chicago: Quadrangle Books, 1971), p. 253; Roy Wilkins, "The Case
Against Separatism," *Common Sense Anyone?* (NAACP Pamphlet,
1969); Wilkins, "Whither Black Power?" *Crisis* 73 (August–September, 1966): 353–354.
[13] On this point see Martin Kilson, "Anatomy of the Black Studies
Movement," *Massachusetts Review* 10 (Autumn 1969): 718–725; and
Kilson, "The New Black Intellectuals," *Dissent* 16 (July–August
1969): 304–310.

BIBLIOGRAPHICAL NOTE ON
MANUSCRIPT COLLECTIONS

I have used traditional historical methods to investigate the conditions that prevailed at various black colleges. The footnotes indicate the full extent of my indebtedness to various sources. Instead of repeating this information in a lengthy bibliography I should like to conclude with a brief comment on "the state of the archives."

Among the many collections of private correspondence that proved useful for this study, none was more valuable than the Papers of W. E. B. Du Bois, formerly in custody of Herbert Aptheker and now at the University of Massachusetts, Amherst. I am indebted to Dr. Aptheker for first suggesting the feasibility of a study of the black college rebellions of the 1920s as well as for making the Du Bois papers available to me. Other collections that proved to be of great use were the extensive Papers of Robert Russa Moton at Tuskegee Institute, the Papers of Fayette Avery McKenzie at the Tennessee State Archives, the Papers of Julius Rosenwald at the University of Chicago, and the NAACP Files at the Library of Congress. Of more limited use were the Papers of Booker T. Washington, Carter G. Woodson, George Foster Peabody, and Moorfield Storey, all at the Library of Congress, the Papers of Dwight O. W. Holmes and Emmett J. Scott at Morgan State College, the Papers of Archibald H. Grimke and Joel E. Spingarn at Howard University, and the Papers of Nathan B. Young at the University of Missouri, St. Louis.

With the exception of Florida A. & M. University, which lost most of its official records to fires, the black colleges discussed in this book have kept very useful archives. All except Lincoln University (Pa.) permitted me to examine their files. I am indebted to officials at these institutions, and especially to Edward K. Graham for making available an extraordinarily complete set of administrative records for Hampton Institute.

In government archives there is useful information on the Tuskegee hospital controversy in the Director's File, Bureau of War Risk Insurance, Suitland, Maryland. Conditions at Howard University are discussed in the correspondence of the Secretary of the Interior, National Archives, Record Group 48. There is information on Wilberforce University in the documents organized under the heading S39, Item 4 at the Ohio State House.

Abbott, Robert S., 227
abolitionist tradition, 3, 8
African Methodist Episcopal
  Church, 293, 306, 307
Alcorn A. & M., 1929 student
  strike, 277
Alexander, Raymond Pace, 327
Algood, Miles C., 115-116
alienation and separatism among
  recent black college students,
  344-348
Allen, F. C., 316
Al Menah Temple, 38
Alpha Phi Alpha, 317
Alpha Zeta, 321-322
American Baptist Home Mission
  Society, 8
American Friends Service Com-
  mittee, 66
American Mercury, 40
American Missionary Association,
  8, 29, 70-71, 230
American Negro Academy, 86
Anderson, E. N., 59
Anglo-Saxon Clubs, protest ap-
  pearance of North Carolina
  glee club, 238-239; lobby for
  racial integrity bill, 241; call for
  Virginia law to prohibit inte-
  gration of public meetings, 242
Ann Arbor, Michigan, 321
Armstrong, Samuel Chapman,
  adjusts to conditions in post-
  Reconstruction South, 7; culti-
  vates well-to-do, 8; educational
  ideas, 230-231
Ashmun Institute, 278

Association of Colleges for
  Negro Youth, 208
Atkins, J. Alston, 48
Atlanta Independent, 263. See
  also Davis, Benjamin J.
Atlanta University, 4, 20, 21, 26,
  27, 141, 283, 340
Atlanta University Conferences,
  25

Baker, Sam W., governor of
  Missouri, 211; appoints new
  curators, 213; appoints additional curators and proceeds
  with plan to oust N. B. Young,
  215; condemned by blacks, 214,
  215, 219, 220, 221; reorganizes
  Lincoln along vocational lines,
  218, 222, 225, 227
Baldwin, William H., 11, 44
Balloch, Edward, 107
Baltimore Afro-American, publishes Howard "Alumnus" series, 111-112; censures ingra-
  tiating fund-raising tactics of
  Hampton and Tuskegee, 149;
  comments on forced resignation of N. B. Young, 227;
  criticizes striking students at
  Hampton, 263; discounts importance of racial consciousness
  at Hampton, 267; opposes lily
  white policies of Lincoln (Pa.)
  trustees, 288, 289; discounts
  criticism of Wilberforce, 310
Barnard College, 320
Bate, Langston Fairchild, 204

Benchley, Robert, 328
Biddle University, 286
Birmingham News, 173
Birmingham Reporter, 269-270
black studies, and educational
thought of W. E. B. Du Bois,
21, 22; at Fisk, 67-68; at
Howard, 84-87, 90; at Hamp-
ton, 233; at Lincoln (Pa.), 281;
and separatism, 344
Blair, Algernon, 156
Bland, Bertrand C., 327
Blue, Cecil, 204, 327
Bluford, F. D., 277
Booth, Benton, 126-127
Bowie, State Normal School at,
277
Brady, Arthur, 112
Brooke, Edward, 340
Broun, Heywood, 317
Brown, Alonzo, 107, 108, 120
Brown, Charles R., 119
Brown, E. D., 331
Brown, E. Frank, 308, 309-310
Brown, Hallie Q., 303, 311
Brown, Sterling, 204
Brownsville, Texas, 153
Bruce, Blanche K., 327
Bruce, N. C., 212, 213, 221
Bruce, Roscoe Conkling, 108,
119, 130, 328
Bruce, Roscoe Conkling, Jr., 327
Brusseaux, Sheridan A., 307, 308
Bryant, Ira, 304-305, 307
Bullock, Henry Allen, 16
Bunch, E. O., 223
Bundy, Richard C., appointed
superintendent of Combined
Normal and Industrial Depart-
ment, 301; investigated by
Sheridan Brusseaux and E.
Frank Brown, 308-310; sup-
ported by trustees, 310-311, 312
Buttrick, Wallace, 11

Calhoun, John H., threatened by
Ku Klux Klan, 172-173, 177,
185, 189
Campbell, W. W., 177
Capon Springs Conferences, 27
Carmichael, Stokeley, 340
Carnegie Corporation, 32, 62
Caulfield, Henry S., governor of
Missouri, 222; calls for upgrad-
ing Lincoln University and re-
constitutes board of curators,
223-224, 225, 226, 227
Cayton, Horace R., 144
Central State University, 313
"Chang," 255
Chapman, John Jay, 329
Charlotte Observer, 147, 184
Chattanooga Times, 145
Chester County, Pennsylvania,
279
Cheyney Training School for
Teachers, general background,
333-334; controversy over
voluntary *de facto* segregation,
335-339
Chicago Defender, condemns
Fayette McKenzie, 49; comments on opposition to Cramton bill, 124; urges an end to
factionalism at Howard, 134;
blames politics for resignation
of N. B. Young; demands resignation of leading administrators at Wilberforce, 305, 310;
comments on graft at Wilberforce, 306, 308
Chicago Fisk Club, 52
Chicago, University of, 317, 318,
320
Chicago Whip, 265
Childers, Lulu Vere, 75
Chisum, Melvin, confidential investigator for R. R. Moton,
157; commends Harding ad-

357

Howard, O. O., 70, 78
Howard Hilltop, 71
Howard Journal, 71
Howard, Perry, 170
Howard, Players, 71, 86-87, 87n
Howard University, 4, 38, 44; enrollment, 70; "capstone of Negro education," 70; accreditation, 121; general history, 70-71; congressional appropriations and financial support, 71, 99-100, 117, 121, 123-124, 125, 135; student discipline and social life, 71-73, 75; student protest against compulsory chapel, 73-75; student government reorganized, 76; student opposition to compulsory ROTC, 77, 112-118; student criticism of white domination of faculty, 77; rising tide of racial consciousness, 77, 82, 90-91, 93, 97; autonomy of black deans, 79, 82, 93; racial composition of faculty and board of trustees, 82, 90; black studies, 84-90; strife and contention on campus, 93-130; dispute over faculty salaries, 101-106; student strike, 112-118; final drive to oust J. S. Durkee, 118-130; trial of Durkee, 126-129; resignation of Durkee, 129-130, 137, 140, 141, 145, 150, 155, 277, 283, 287
Howard University alumni, oppose J. S. Durkee's plan to transfer Kelly Miller to field work, 100-101; oppose termination of Alain Locke and others, 108; organize campaign to oust Durkee, 111-112, 118-130; help to negotiate a settlement to student strike, 117; condemn

Durkee and Emory Smith, 120-122; oppose Jesse Moorland, 131-133; accept Mordecai W. Johnson, 134-135
Howard University Catalogue, 72
Howard University Medical School, 107, 155
Howard University Record, 75
Howard University trustees, on compulsory chapel, 74; offer presidency to succession of white ministers, 78; offer presidency to Wilbur Thirkield and Stephen Newman, 81; discourage black studies, 86, 90, 98; racial composition of board, 90; on need for centralization, 94; reorganize academic structure, 95; decisions on faculty salaries, 103-106; approve J. S. Durkee's request for permission to head Curry School of Expression, 110; grant reprieve to George William Cook and severance pay to Alain Locke and others, 111; reaffirm support for Durkee, 119-121, 128; consider charges against Durkee, 125-128; consider successor to Durkee, 131-134; elect Mordecai W. Johnson as president, 134
Howard, W. H. A., 198-202
Hubbard, Christopher, 214, 215
Hughes, Langston, 281-282
Humphreys, Richard, 333
Hyde, Arthur M., 203, 211, 223

Ijams, George E., 168, 169, 186, 187
Illinois, University of, 316, 320
Imes, William Lloyd, 336
Indianapolis Recorder, 264, 265

Meharry Medical College, 155-156
Men's Union, 201
Meserve, Charles Francis, 277
Messenger, The, condemns J. S. Durkee's effort to transfer Kelly Miller to field work, 100, 130; warns against danger of factionalism at Howard, 134; criticizes *de facto* segregation at Tuskegee Veterans Hospital, 162; publishes article on N. B. Young's difficulties in Florida, 196
Michigan, University of, 316, 321
Miller, E. H., 304
Miller, George Frazier, 112, 119-120
Miller, Herbert A., 63
Miller, Kelly, vies for presidency of Howard, 81; educational ideas, 83, 84, 85, 88, 89, 91, 92, 93; conflict with J. S. Durkee, 95-96, 97, 98, 99, 100, 101; salary, 103, 107, 109; on student strike at Howard, 114-116; testifies at trial of Durkee, 127, 129, 133, 321
Miller, Loren, 319
Miner Hall, 114
Missouri Association of Negro Teachers, 209
Missouri state assembly, 217
Missouri, University of, 316
Mitchell, Arthur W., condemns J. S. Durkee's effort to transfer Kelly Miller to field work, 100-101; urged Howard alumni to oppose Durkee, 120-121, 128
Mobile Register, 184
Montgomery Advertiser, 152, 173, 186
Montgomery, Alabama, 152, 153
Moore, Fred R., comments on

R. R. Moton's compromise during controversy over Tuskegee Veterans Hospital, 180-181; on scandal at Wilberforce, 305
Moore, Lewis B., 79, 81
Moore, T. Clay, 51
Moore, Walthall M., 203, 211
Moorland, Jesse, 131, 132
Morais, Herbert M., 155
Morehouse College, 276, 340
Morrill Acts, 10, 192
Moton, Robert Russa correspondence with Thomas Elsa Jones, 68; friendship with W. E. B. Du Bois, 141; educational and social ideas, 141-142, 146; comments on student unrest at Tuskegee, 143; popularity of, 145-147; as commandant at Hampton, 146; criticism of, 144, 147-150; Pullman coach incident, 147-148; and First World War, 148; and race riots, 1919, 148-149; fund raising activity, 145, 149; defies Ku Klux Klan, 150, 163-165; initial negotiations regarding construction of Tuskegee Veterans Hospital, 152-154, 158; deals with whites of Tuskegee, 157, 163-165, 177-179; demands that Negroes be appointed to professional staff, 156-159, 163-164, 178-179; confers with Warren G. Harding, 159-160; works behind scenes, 166, 181; urges compromise, 171-172, 177-179; breaks with NAACP, 177; criticized for compromise, 180-181, 182-183; opposes appointment of J. R. A. Crossland, 187-188; significance of his struggle for

363

New York Amsterdam News,
criticizes fund raising activities
of R. R. Moton, 149; comments
on exclusion of blacks from
freshman dormitories at Harvard, 327
New York Evening Post, 329
New York Fisk Club, 52, 57
New York Times, comments on
endowments of black colleges
and vocational institutes, 32-33,
145
New York University, 315, 316,
317, 320
Niagara Movement, 140
Norfolk Journal and Guide, 168,
264
Norfolk Virginia-Pilot, endorses
Negro demand for black
physicians at Tuskegee Veterans Hospital, 184; comments
on growing racial consciousness
at Hampton, 266, 267
Normil, John F. E., 267
North Central Association of
Secondary Schools and Col-
leges, 208
North Carolina A. & T. College,
277
nurses, at Tuskegee Veterans
Hospital, 159, 167
Nutter, George R., 328

Oberlin College, black enrollment
at, 315; rising tide of racial
discrimination in literary societies, athletics, and dormitories,
321-324; black protest against
racial discrimination, 323-324
Occidental College, 315
Ogden Hall, 238, 239, 254, 256
Ohio State University, 315, 316,
320

Oklahoma, University of, 316
Opportunity, comments on be-
quests of white philanthropists,
32; credited with responsibility
for Hampton student strike,
266
Order of the British Empire, 257
Otto, E. H., 223
Ovington, Mary White, 145-146

Pan-Hellenic Leagues, 317
Parker, George, 127
Patton, William W., 12
Payne, Daniel Alexander, 293
Peabody College, 37
Peabody, Francis Greenwood,
reservations about collegiate
curriculum at Hampton, 234;
advises compromise with Mas-
senburg law, 246
Peabody, George Foster, corre-
spondence with Thomas Elsa
Jones, 68; supports Jesse
Moorland for presidency of
Howard, 132, 154; reservations
about collegiate curriculum at
Hampton, 252; controversy
over spirituals and plantation
melodies, 250-253
Peacock, Joseph Leishman, 277
Pennsylvania, University of, 332
Perry, J. E., 215, 224
Petition of Hampton Students,
257-259
Phelps-Stokes Fund, 8, 14
Phenix, George P., 274-275
Phi Delta, 321-322
Philadelphia Tribune, calls for
liberalization of discipline at
Hampton, 266; comments on
Lincoln (Pa.) president-elect
W. Greenway, 289; welcomes
resolution of controversy at

Philadelphia Tribune (cont.)
Lincoln (Pa.), 293; demands
resignations at Wilberforce,
310; censures *de facto* voluntary segregation at Cheyney
Training School, 335
philanthropy, religious, 8-9, 12,
20-21, 29, 33. Also see Yankee
missionaries.
philanthropy, secular, educational
ideas, 8-10, 25-28; and universal
education, 14-15, 17, 33; censured by blacks, 63, 140. Also
see Du Bois, W. E. B.
Philippse, A. D., 37
Phillips, J. T., 51
Pickens, William, 49, 323
Pickett, A. S., 127
Pittsburgh Courier, blames politics for resignation of N. B.
Young, 227; calls for investigation of charges at Wilberforce,
305, 306; comments on graft at
Wilberforce, 308; demands
resignations at Wilberforce,
310; censures *de facto* volun-
tary segregation at Cheyney
Training School, 335
Pittsburgh, University of, 316
police, at Fisk and Howard, 48,
115
Porter, John G., 174
Powell, John, 241
Powell, R. H., 152-153, 162-163,
173-174
Presbyterian Board of Missions
for the Freedmen, 8
Price, Lawrence T., 241
Pullman coach incident, Mrs.
R. R. Moton, 147-148
Purvis, Charles B., 107

Red Summer, race riots of 1919,
17, 148-149

Reed, Charles Gardner, 303
Reid, Frank M., 303
Rendall, Isaac Norton, 283
Rendall, John Ballard, 283-284
Rhinelander divorce case, 307
Richardson, Clement, 218, 219-
220
Roberts, E. P., 285; urges J. L.
Ewing to decline presidency
of Lincoln (Pa.), 288; com-
ments on growing opposition
to lily white policies at Lin-
coln, 289; urges W. Greenway
to decline presidency of
Lincoln, 290; lauds choice of
W. H. Johnson as president of
Lincoln, 291; named as first
alumni member of Lincoln
board of trustees, 292
Roberts, Mr. and Mrs. Ernest
W., 56
Rockefeller, John D., 102
Rombauer, Edgar B., 213, 224, 227
Roosevelt, Franklin D., 330
Roosevelt, Theodore, Jr., 131,
134
Rose Bowl, 316
Rosenwald Foundation, 8, 9
ROTC, at Howard, 77, 112-118;
at Kansas, 317
Rustin, Bayard, 347
Rutgers University, 316

St. Augustine Junior College, 277
St. Denis, Ruth, 239
St. John's A. M. E. Church, 49
St. Louis American, 226, 227-228
St. Louis Argus, supports upgrading of Lincoln (Mo.), 207; on
Lincoln's progress toward accreditation, 208-209; on faculty
opposition to N. B. Young,
209; condemns pandering to
white prejudice, 211-212;

praises Charles Lee, 215-216;
censures Sam James, 216, 217;
laments demise of higher edu-
cation at Lincoln, 219; com-
ments on Clement Richardson's
declination of presidency, 220
St. Paul, Minnesota, 157
Sanhedran Conference, 91
Savage, W. Sherman, 204, 206
Savannah Tribune, 263
Scarborough, William S., com-
ments on discipline problems at
Wilberforce; on relations be-
tween Wilberforce and the
Combined Normal & Indus-
trial Department, 297, 298; dis-
missed from presidency of
Wilberforce, 301, 302
Scott, Emmett J., 94
Scott, Isaiah, 38
Scriber, Dora, 54-55
Scruggs, Clifford, 215, 216, 223
self-determination on black cam-
puses, viii; comments of W. E.
B. Du Bois, 18, 28; at Fisk, 69;
at Howard, 136; at Tuskegee,
150, 190-191; at Florida A. &
M. and Lincoln (Mo.), 192; at
Hampton, 232; at Lincoln
(Pa.), 293; at Wilberforce, 293,
340
Seligmann, Herbert, 161-162
Senior, Albert R., 267
separatism and alienation among
recent black college students,
344-348. Also see alienation
Serra, Joseph, 309
Shaw University, 277
Shawn, Ted, 239
Sinclair, William, 81, 111, 122
Sixty-second Colored Infantry
(Missouri), 202
Sixty-fifth Colored Infantry
(Missouri), 202

Slater Foundation, John F., 8,
9, 32
Smith, Emory B., 121-122, 135
Smith, Harry C., 302-303
Smith-Hughes Act and program,
10, 195
Smith University, Johnson C.,
277, 287
Smith-Lever Act, 10
Smoot, Reed, 99
social Darwinism, 5, 8
Southern California, University
of, 316
Southern Education Board, 8, 27
Southern Workman, 233, 234
special education, 15-16, 22
Spellman, C. L., 260-261
spirituals and plantation melodies,
at Fisk, 37-38; at Howard, 75;
at Hampton, 249-253, 255
Sproul, *Governor*, 334
Standard Savings and Loan Company, 217
Stanley, Robert H., appointed
chief medical officer at Tuskegee Veterans Hospital, 158;
refuses to employ black professionals, 158-159; embroiled
with John H. Calhoun and
Frank Hines, 172-173, 179; removed from Tuskegee Veterans Hospital, 185
State Survey Commission, Missouri, 223
Stegall, Henry B., 116
Steward, Gustavus, 303
Storer College, 276
Storey, Moorfield, 328
Streator, George, away from
campus on night of Fisk student demonstration at Livingstone Hall, 57; receives subsistence stipend from W.E.B.
Du Bois, 59; comments on ef-

165, 172; parade for white supremacy, 173-175; demand white control of Tuskegee Veterans Hospital, 183-184; chastened and acquiescent, 184-186, 189

Underwood, Oscar W., 184-185
United States Bureau of Education, 14, 194, 205
United States Congress, appropriations for Howard, 71, 99-100, 117, 121, 123-124, 125, 135
universal public education, 14, 27
University Rules and Regulations, Howard, 73
Urbana, Illinois, 320

Vanderbilt University *Hustler*, 45
Vann, Robert L., 169
Vardaman, James K., 5
Vass, S. N., 65
Veblen, Thorstein, 102
Vermont, University of, 331
Veterans Bureau, 167, 168, 186
Virginia, University of, 238
vocational training, a corollary of white supremacy, 3, 7, 10, 11, 15-16, 139-140, 341; for whites and blacks, 10n-11n; at Howard, 96; at Tuskegee, 137-139; at Florida A. & M., 193-197, 199-200; at Lincoln (Mo.), 218; at Hampton, 230-231, 272, 273-274

Walcott, William H., 142-175
Walker, W. W., 285
Ward, Joseph H., 189
Washington, Booker T., comments on missionary teachers and their curriculum, 4, 6; adjusts to conditions in the post-Reconstruction South, 7;

cultivates the well-to-do, 8; controversy with W. E. B. Du Bois, 20-21, 25-26; educational ideas, 20, 137-139, 141, 148, 155, 156, 159, 178, 267, 347
Washington, Mrs. Booker T., 166
Washington Daily News, 86
Washington Daily American, 111, 120, 129
Washington Tribune, 181, 265
Waters, W. F., 54
Weller, Royal F., 124
Wesley, Charles W., censures Fayette McKenzie for calling on the police, 48; comments at trial of J. S. Durkee, 127, 129; candidate for presidency of Howard, 133, 134
West Chester State Teachers College, 335
West Virginia, University of, 316
White, Walter F., opposes construction of Negro veterans hospital in South, 151-152; comments on white desire to control Tuskegee Veterans Hospital, 166, 168; supports R. R. Moton, 176-177; criticizes Moton, 183, 340
White, William Charles, 153
Wilberforce University, founded, 293; religious ethos, 293-294; discipline at, 294-295; student unrest, 295-296, 301-302, 312-313; church-state relations, 296-297, 299-301, 311-313; and Combined Normal & Industrial Department, 296-301; enrollment, 298; finances, 300, 304, 311-312; academic reputation, 299, 303, 305-306; church politics at, 299-303; disloyal pro-

369

Wilberforce Univ. (*cont.*)
fessors dismissed, 308; alumni
opposition to administration,
303-313
Wilberforce University, Combined Normal & Industrial
Department, enrollment, 298;
academic orientation, 298;
relations to and rivalry with
Wilberforce University, 296-
301; praised by W. E. B. Du
Bois and others, 299; finances,
300, 304; church-state relations,
296-297, 299-301, 311-313; investigation of graft at, 306-311;
312, 313
Wilberforce University trustees,
295; dismiss W. S. Scarborough, 297; support Gilbert and
Joshua Jones, 301, 307; C. N. &
I. trustees support Richard
Bundy, 310-311, 312
Wiley College, 340
Wilkins, Roy, accuses N. C.
Bruce of pandering to white
prejudice, 212-213; censures
Sam Baker, 214; disgusted with
political chicanery at Lincoln
(Mo.), 219; comments on
alienation and separatism
among black college students,
347-348
William and Mary College, 238
Williams, C. G., opposes N. B.
Young, 210-211, 212; appointed
to Lincoln (Mo.) board of
curators, 213, 215, 216, 220,
223, 227
Williams, W. T. B., 255
Williamson, R. D., 311-312
Willie, W. Augustus, 267
Wilson, Edward W., 327
Wilson, Francis M., 222
Wilson, Woodrow, 148

Wood, Hollingsworth, 44, 60-61
Woodard, Dudley, 128
Woodson, Carter G., educational
ideas, 83, 84-85, 86, 90; conflict
with J. S. Durkee, 98, 120, 123,
227
World War I, 148, 151
Wright, Richard R., 197
Wright, Walter Livingstone,
290-292

Xenia, Ohio, 294

Yankee missionaries, educational
ideas, 4, 5, 8, 12, 20-21. Also see
philanthropy, religious;
Houston, G. David; Miller,
Kelly; and Woodson, Carter G.
Young Allenite, The, 304
Young, Nathan B., 192; background and educational program at Florida A. & M., 193-
197; opposition to efforts to
vocationalize Florida A. & M.,
196-198; leaves Florida, 198,
202; goal at Lincoln (Mo.),
203; reorganizes and upgrades
Lincoln faculty, 203-204; lob-
bies for appropriations, 206;
organizes black community,
206-207, 216; works for accreditation, 208-209, 229; conflict with certain professors,
politicians, and curators, 209-
221; ousted from Lincoln, 218;
becomes state inspector of
colored schools, 221; returns
to Lincoln, 224-225; second administration at Lincoln, 225-229
Young, Nathan B., Jr., 226
Young, Thomas W., 315
YMCA and YWCA, at Howard,
72

LIBRARY OF CONGRESS CATALOGING IN PUBLICATION DATA
Wolters, Raymond, 1938-
  The new Negro on campus.

  Bibliography: p.
  Includes index.
  1. Negro universities and colleges—United States—
History. I. Title.
LC2801.W57   378.73   74-4662
ISBN 0-691-04628-X